CW01510440

FROM RYE TO
THE RHINE

FROM RYE TO THE RHINE

BY WAY OF

GUERNSEY, 'WIPERS' AND THE SOMME

The Great War Diaries
of
Driver Jack Hickman, RFA

*'A Sussex golfer among the Guernseymen and
'Jocks' of 9th Scottish 'Division'*

KEN WAYMAN

Reveille
PRESS

Reveille Press is an imprint of
Tommies Guides Military Booksellers & Publishers

Gemini House
136–140 Old Shoreham Road
Brighton
BN3 7BD

www.tommiesguides.co.uk

First published in Great Britain by
Reveille Press 2015

For more information please visit
www.reveillepress.com

© 2015 Ken Wayman

A catalogue record for this book is available
from the British Library

All rights reserved. Apart from any use under UK
copyright law no part of this publication may be reproduced,
stored in a retrieval system, or transmitted, in any form or
by any means, without prior written permission of the publisher,
nor be otherwise circulated in any form of binding or
cover other than that in which it is published and without
a similar condition being imposed on the subsequent publisher.

ISBN 978-1-908336-76-7

Cover design by Reveille Press
Typeset by Vivian@Bookscribe

Printed and bound in Great Britain

FROM RYE TO THE RHINE

'The war of 1914-18 was an artillery war: artillery was the battle-winner, artillery was what caused the greatest loss of life, the most dreadful wounds, and the deepest fear.'

John Terraine (1921-2003)

9th 'Scottish' Divisional Ammunition Column memorial stone, Point du Jour, Arras

Contents

LIST OF MAPS, DIAGRAMS & ILLUSTRATIONS

Dedication

For Maisie and in respectful memory of her father, Jack, who had
the foresight to record the terrible events he witnessed as
a young man.

And for the unsung lads of the Great War's divisional and brigade
ammunition columns without whose sterling efforts the vital
artillery of the Western Front and beyond could not have spoken
with such an authoritative and decisive voice.

And for George Wayman, born on 1st July 2013.
And for his great-gran Joan, 90 years young in July 2014!

PREFACE

As with many of the more satisfying history-writing projects, this one began entirely by chance. In a casual conversation as I accompanied one of my mother's friends to her car, Pam mentioned that her mother-in-law's father, Jack Hickman, had fought in and survived the Great War. What's more, he had kept hand-written diaries of his wartime experiences. Would I like to read them sometime? I think Pam knew the answer before I uttered it.

When the diaries arrived, accompanied by numerous, irreplaceable family photos and copious amounts of first-hand recollections written by Maisie Ballantyne, Jack's daughter who was born in 1920, all other reading matter was set aside. Turning the pages of Jack's spiral-bound reporter's notebook for 1915, it seemed that at first sight the story might be impossible to read. Pencil-scribed, faded by the passage of many years, the text required careful concentration; however, Jack's neat hand and lucid command of English made the task surprisingly straightforward. Once the 'knack' of reading his style of writing had been acquired, I became an addict, enjoying Jack's observations, being surprised by the 'everyday' shocks of war and feeling a sense of anticipation for what the next page might bring.

Sadly, most of Jack's entries for 1916 are currently, and maybe even permanently, missing. Perhaps they were lost in a rapid advance or in the early days of the German spring Offensive of 1918 (*'die Kaiserschlacht'* or 'Emperor's Battle'), the latter when Jack was seriously wounded and evacuated to 'Blighty'. Perhaps the diary was sometime discovered by whoever was temporarily performing the duties of censor – keeping such a record, detailed as it was and naming people and places, was wholly illicit as, in the hands of an enemy, the information might have proved useful. Once I was familiar with the diaries' content and transcription was complete, I considered how I might construct a viable book to give Jack Hickman's words a wider platform.

First I identified his military units, immediately being surprised by the early results. Holding the rank of 'Driver' in the Royal Field Artillery, I expected him to have responsibility for taking the 18-pounder field guns into and out of the gun-line. Never assume anything. It transpired that Jack was part of a Divisional Ammunition Column (DAC), about which I knew very little and was soon to discover that there was minimal dedicated material available. I was momentarily tempted to essay a book themed on the DAC but I'm no artillery expert even though my own father served as a Gunner on 25-pounders at El Alamein in 1942 and from Ver-sur-Mer in Normandy to Bochum in Western Germany between 1944 and 1946. Discovering Jack's Army Service Record for the Great War was a fortunate revelation as it opened two lines of research; unusually, for a Sussex lad, Jack had enlisted in Lord Kitchener's 'New Army' from the Guernsey Militia; the Guernsey 'Gunners' assumed the role of Divisional Ammunition Column as a single body of men and, moreover, the division to which they were posted was 9th 'Scottish' Division. Sussex, Guernsey, Scotland – the sequence intrigued me. Soon the place-names would include Flemish and French, near-unintelligible to the average 'Tommy', whose efforts would include *'Wipers'*, *'Whitesheet'*, *'Ocean Villas'* and *'Eat Apples'* (properly Ypres, Wijtschaete, Auchonvillers and Etaples respectively). Among the 9th Division infantry and pioneers were highlanders and lowlanders, men of the Black Watch, Royal Scots, Seaforths, Cameron Highlanders, Argyll & Sutherland Highlanders, Gordons and Scottish Borderers. The mix of accents must have been interesting, more so since, in 1916, one of the Scots brigades in the division would be replaced by the South African brigade!

Discovering the complex functions of the Ammunition Column and the associated changes throughout the war, was in itself an education – at present, I know of no other instance of a DAC man recording his personal war experiences. The role of the DAC was, like the Divisional supply train, essential to the success of any division's infantry and artillery. Whatever the conditions, whatever the amount of shelling, an Ammunition Column had a job to do and, certainly in the case of 9th Division, they did it consistently well.

Beyond the personal diaries of Jack Hickman, sources to shed light on the events witnessed by the lad from Sussex include the entire 9/DAC War Diary, the 9th 'Scottish' Divisional history, the Official History of Military Operations in France and Belgium (plus the Occupation of the Rhineland), soldiers' individual Army Service Records, Major Edwin Parks' work on Guernseymen in the Great War and research in respect of the 9/DAC Guernseymen kindly furnished by Mark Bougourd of the Channel Islands Great War Study Group.

As a tool, the Internet is difficult to beat for speed and for breadth of search; the excellent Great War Forum (created by Chris Baker), populated by the full spectrum of knowledge and experience from beginner to widely-published expert, has never failed to come up with ideas and answers whenever I have reached a mental 'road-block'. I've found the subscribers to the GWF both erudite and generous. However, I'm 'Old School' by education and inclination – I love handling and searching through books and documents on the trail of hidden gems of information – hence my own ever-expanding reference library! Several databases have provided valuable information that was more difficult to access when I was researching my first book on the Great War, now over a decade ago. War casualties, either killed or badly wounded are more easily traceable and in greater detail thanks to databases on CD-ROM such as *'Soldiers Died in the Great War'* and *'Silver War Badge'*[1]; understanding the topography of the battlefield and military dispositions thereupon no longer requires the un-folding and re-folding of delicate paper maps but the *'The National Archives British Trench Map Atlas'* on DVD-ROM offers quick and effective access to all sectors of the old Western Front.

Tracing the story of Jack Hickman took me from my desk in the North Midlands to Rye on the Sussex-Kent border, to Guernsey, to several sectors of the Western Front and to the National Golf Museum at St. Andrews in Fife. I hope the journey is deemed worthy of Jack's meticulous diary-keeping.

NOTE ON LAYOUT

I have tried to present Jack Hickman's words from his diaries in as close a form as possible to the way he wrote them, though on occasions I have added words of explanation in squared brackets. Jack's words always appear under the sub-heading, **Diary**. Broader, contextual information from a variety of sources appears under the sub-heading **Context**.

This is done merely to show Jack's diary entries within the overall picture of the units to which he belonged, of the war in general and of each offensive, attack or unit movement.

Sources of information are credited throughout – direct quotations appear within inverted commas.

---

1 These two CD-ROMs and the DVD-ROM are each published by the Naval & Military Press.

Thanks & Acknowledgements

First and foremost I would like to thank the descendants of Driver Jack Hickman, 9/DAC RFA. Prime among these must be Maisie Ballantyne, daughter of Jack Hickman, for kind permission to read Jack Hickman's surviving hand-written diaries and for answering many questions and providing many family photographs and documents for my perusal. It was however Pam Ballantyne, who is married to Jack Hickman's grandson, Chris Ballantyne, who initially brought to my attention the existence of Jack's diaries. What is more, Pam and Chris explained for me many facets of Jack's life and also assumed the role of 'go-betweens' with other members of the family, several of whom presently live in Norfolk.

It was soon apparent that a visit to Kent and East Sussex, the region of Jack's birth and of his family's roots, was a necessity, this coinciding neatly with another 'hijacked' family holiday. Seeing first-hand the broad agricultural acres of Romney Marsh, the 'island' of Rye Town, the churches at Iden and East Guldeford, the golf course at Camber, the Coast Guard cottages at Jury's Gap and the Royal Military Canal gave context to what I had learned early on about the Hickman family that had lived and worked there since the eighteenth century.

While staying in the Camber area of Rye we visited Salt's excellent Farm Shop in East Guldeford in order to replenish our stocks; we obtained much more than food! On the way into the car park, we passed an old sign that read, '*Hickman's Granary*', so, once inside, I asked one or two questions. The owners of the shop patiently listened to what must have sounded a strange story and were kind enough to introduce me to Alan Catt of East Guldeford whose knowledge of the area is encyclopaedic. Alan generously gave of his time to characterise the entire area and its way of life to one who knew very little of the Marsh. Alan also gave me a contact number for Frank Palmer of Rye, who I thought might possibly be related to the family of Jack's wife, Ada Palmer. Sadly it was not to be but Frank gave me several valuable pointers in respect of the Rye Town locality.

As Jack Hickman's chosen career path, golf professional, took him initially to the Channel Island of Guernsey, a new and unusual line of enquiry opened before me, one that would meld golf with the island's militia. My first contact was with Mark Bougourd who kindly replied to one of my posts on Chris Baker's impressive '*Great War Forum*'. Mark is deeply involved in the Channel Islands Great War Study Group and he has very kindly allowed me access to the nominal roll of the 9th Divisional Ammunition Column that has been so comprehensively researched by a number of contributors, not least Edwin Parks. Mark also offered valuable advice as to possible pitfalls in researching the Guernseymen and he explained many aspects of the Guernsey Militia and the Great War. Moreover, Mark kindly offered access to several relevant volumes of the excellent GWCI Journal among which, in volume 17 (December 2007) was Liz Walton's excellent article, 'A Case of Mistaken Identity', clarifying the somewhat confusing post-war demise of Emile Blaise. One of the best and most detailed published works on Guernsey and the Great War is Major Edwin Parks, 'Diex Aix – God Help Us (The Guernseymen who Marched Away, 1914-1918)', an impressively researched volume on the island's men who went to fight for 'King and Country' in the conflict. Edwin's book made me believe that it was possible to trace in detail the story of Jack Hickman. Another Guernseyman who kindly offered his help was Steve Foote who clarified my ideas on Jack Hickman's officer in 9/DAC, Lt. Ozanne. Early in the piece, I contacted Priaulx Library in St. Peter Port with a request for help in respect of Jack Hickman in the Guernsey Press and as regards his employment by the Royal Guernsey Golf Club; Elizabeth Gallienne, Research Assistant at Priaulx Library, undertook the task and, although the results were limited, I was encouraged to explore further. Much later in my researches I took a magnifying glass to a

pre-embarkation photo of the Guernsey Gunners in the Edwin Parks book and saw a face that resembled that of Jack Hickman. As the picture credit cited the Priaulx Library I made contact, asking whether it was possible to obtain a copy of the photo; sources were checked and a fine copy arrived in my 'in-tray'. Sure enough, the higher-quality version revealed Jack Hickman on the back row and another piece of the jigsaw fell into place. I thank the Library for their help and for kind permission to use the image – I have been impressed by the Priaulx Library staff's 'can do' attitude. In my efforts to track down any images that reflected even the slightest link to Jack Hickman's time as a golf assistant professional on Guernsey I came across an old picture of the RGGC clubhouse when it was little more than a very classy hut! The picture was posted by Melvyn Morrow of Guernsey but I have not been able to contact him as yet – I offer both my thanks and apologies!

As regards my sources of information in respect of Jack's golfing career, there is one person whose efforts could not go unremarked. In October 2009 while on a family holiday to the East Neuk of Fife, we were spending time where my daughter Vicki obtained her Masters degree – the University of St. Andrews – and we made a chance visit to the British Golf Museum opposite the revered eighteenth green of the Old Course at St. Andrews. There, I enquired about Jack Hickman, not really expecting much by way of results or even interest. How wrong could I have been? Someone on the front desk made a phone call and a while later Jennifer Morton, Museum & Heritage Assistant Curator, came in to see us on her afternoon off. She immediately offered genuine interest and promised to research Jack Hickman's career as a professional golfer. Jennifer provided some excellent and unexpected information: proven dates in respect of Jack's professional career, changes in the place of Jack's employment and permission to access details of Jack's club-making innovation and patent. I was very pleasantly surprised by the treatment received at the home of golf.

As ever, Chris Baker's *Great War Forum* contributed in no small measure to my research. No request is too great or too small for the knowledgeable members of the Forum and, again, plenty of solutions and background colour were forthcoming, not least from Ian Turner who kindly granted me permission to quote from a post in respect of his grandfather's 1919 demobilisation from 9th 'Scottish' Division. Among the published military historians Paul Reed, Trevor Henshaw and Phil Jobson provided advice from their areas of expertise, while I am indebted to Jack Alexander and John Duncan for extra information on the 9th 'Scottish' Division front.

I am delighted to thank my fellow 'grumpy old man', partner in weekly coffee mornings and adviser on all golf-related items, Barry Crutchley, for proof-reading the manuscript. However, any errors that 'made it through' are entirely my responsibility!

My thanks are due yet again to my publisher, Ryan Gearing and his staff at Reveille Press, for their professionalism and patience in answering my occasionally inane questions and requests. Ryan and his team always make a grand job of turning my 'raw material' into a finished product of which I am rather proud! This is our third joint effort.

And, above all, I thank the long-suffering members of my family who have put up with me through the 'labour pains' of yet another book! My wife Sue and daughter Vicki have uncomplainingly accompanied me on numerous visits to the old Western Front, only rarely receiving the inducement of heavy-duty shopping expeditions. Sue also played a key role in helping me to understand our new computer and how to put together the book's maps; I thank my son, David Wayman, for the Royal Artillery image that he created as a centre-piece for the framing of my father's Second World War campaign medals and which is appropriate for another artilleryman, Jack Hickman – Dave's Art and Graphic Design degree has come in useful. He is now a Squadron Leader in the RAF!

To all those many people who have given freely of their time and advice yet have not been mentioned here I can but apologise and plead the ravages of Anno Domini as the cause of my forgetfulness.

INTRODUCTION

'Sir, reference your letter, 89238 was my correct number in the R.F.A. from the 20th of March 1915 until the 19th of March 1919. I served with the 9th Division the whole of that time and from 1st October 1917 until I was demobilised I was on the R.A. Headquarters, 9th Division; my 28 days' leave expired on 19th March 1919. I did not claim any disability of any kind; I left the Army 'A.1.' Hope this will give required explanation.

Yours truly,
John Hickman.'

(Quoted from Jack's reply to official correspondence from the Regimental Document office in respect of his, '...*Protection Certificate*', Army Form Z.11)

Above, in just six lines, Jack Hickman summarised his Great War service. The reality of his experiences, spanning four years of daily uncertainty, danger and separation from home and loved ones, took him to Ypres ('Wipers' in the British Tommy's parlance), Loos, the Somme, Arras, Passchendaele and the German Spring Offensive (known as '*die Kaiserschlacht*'). During the latter struggle, Jack was severely wounded and repatriated to 'Blighty' by hospital ship to spend several months recovering and recuperating in Cumbria.

Unlike so many of his ill-fated contemporaries from the final quarter of the nineteenth century, Jack Hickman lived a long and fruitful life. Born in the hamlet of Broomhill, the son of an itinerant shepherd on the borders of East Sussex and Kent, Jack broke with long family tradition when he qualified as a craftsman-carpenter and also took

up and excelled at the game of golf at the newly-opened local Rye Golf Club, following the example of elder brother, Frank. Little did he know it at the time but this decision was to influence the course of his entire life.

Like Frank Hickman, Jack played golf to a professional standard but went one further than his brother in inventing and patenting a new type of golf-club during the 1920s. It was golf that took Jack to live on Guernsey where, in early summer of 1911[1], an assistant professional's post attracted him to the Royal Guernsey Golf Club located at L'Ancresse on the northern commons of that beautiful Channel Island. Once established at the club Jack, like many young Guernseymen, joined the Artillery & Engineer Company, a specialised branch of the Royal Guernsey Militia and thus received his first taste of military camaraderie just prior to the outbreak of the Great

Jack Hickman's 'Protection Certificate... (A.F. Z.11)...'

War. So he added the skills of the part-time soldier to those of carpenter and emergent professional golfer.

When the storms of war erupted in August 1914, the Guernsey Artillery[2] was accepted as a single unit by the War Office in Whitehall and, after training, was sent to France in May 1915 as the Divisional Ammunition Column (DAC) of 9th 'Scottish' Division. The idea of the *Divisional* Ammunition Column (DAC) was new[3] in 1914/15; the guns and men of the Royal Field Artillery were organised in Artillery Brigades and hitherto each brigade had had its ammunition supply replenished by a dedicated *Brigade*

Ammunition Column (BAC). By May 1916 the scale of the war was such that the BACs were disbanded and their role incorporated into that of the DACs.

9th 'Scottish' Division, 9/DAC's parent unit, was the first of Lord Kitchener's 'New Army' divisions and the Scots, volunteers to a man, set their standards high. This was to be reflected throughout the Great War, with the 'Ninth' being required for many of the toughest assignments, starting at Loos in September 1915; in line with their reputation, their casualty lists were correspondingly high. The official record concludes that the division suffered in excess of 52,000 casualties (killed or wounded) between May 1915 and November 1918. Late in the war, Driver Jack Hickman became one of those casualties.

Against all the rules and regulations, Driver Jack Hickman, out with the first contingent of Guernsey Artillerymen, decided to keep a record of his experiences on the Western Front. Two of the three personal diaries that he produced have survived the ravages of the war years and of the passage of the decades since then to provide a rare insight into the unsung workings of a Royal Field Artillery Ammunition Column. Written almost as the events themselves unfolded, the speculation, optimism, pessimism and dark humour of the ordinary soldier is spiced and broadened by frequent snippets of information of the wider war, apparently passed to Jack by 'his' officer, affording him a panorama of the wider conflict denied to most 'Tommies'.

The first diary charts Jack's journey to the front line in France, his first time under fire and the new unit's settling-in period culminating in its part in the New Army's first major battle – the bloody affair at Loos in September 1915. Following this initiation, Jack obtained leave to England where, in November 1915 he married his beloved Ada – surprisingly, this momentous event warrants no reference in his writings! Sadly, the second diary, recounting the trials and tribulations of the great Somme offensive, is presently, perhaps permanently, missing – however, Jack's progress may be reconstructed

from 9th DAC's own war diary, the Official History, the Divisional History and from other eye-witness accounts. His personal perspective recommences in November 1916 with the third diary and continues through action at Arras and Ypres to Jack's serious wounding in the German Spring Offensive ('*die Kaiserschlacht*') and his subsequent hospitalisation in England. He returned to France in time for the 1918 Armistice and the final six weeks of his story relate to 9th Division's crossing of the River Rhine, their ultimate absorption into the post-war 52nd 'Lowland' Division and playing a part in the Rhineland Army of Occupation near Cologne.

On his return to civilian life Jack resumed his career path of golf professional and club-maker, though now on the mainland, in the 'Garden of England' – Kent – rather than on the lovely island of Guernsey. A skilled and intelligent craftsman, Jack developed and patented new types of golf-clubs, original details of which are held in the highly-esteemed National Golf Museum that stands, appropriately, just a few yards from the eighteenth green of the celebrated Old Course at St. Andrews in Scotland. Running his golf course at Hengrove near Margate, Jack met several celebrities and politicians who played for relaxation at Thanet Golf Club; by 1925 Jack and Ada had four children and all remained rosy until Adolf Hitler's forces invaded France, thrusting the civilian south-east coast of England into the front line. For safety's sake, the area was evacuated of non-military personnel, so Jack Hickman and his family were moved to Hertfordshire to live in Broxbourne. Considered a bit too old to fight a second time, Jack travelled daily to Enfield where he worked in a major munitions factory – 'doing his bit' yet again for the war effort.

Following the successful conclusion of the Hitler war, Jack and his family returned to Kent but his beloved Thanet Golf Course had been so badly neglected, overgrown and damaged by air raids that it had to be abandoned. Jack found work as a golf professional elsewhere in the area where love of his profession led Jack to continue until the ripe age of seventy-five. In his richly-deserved retirement, he lived with each of his children in turn. Then, after a long, varied and productive span of eighty-four years, Jack answered his final roll-call in 1975.

Carpenter, golfer, soldier, inventor and much-loved family man, Jack Hickman's life was full, varied and highly productive. His record of life and death in the front line is unusual in two ways; first, Jack's rank in the Royal Field Artillery was that of 'Driver', the equivalent of 'Private' in the infantry and most personal war diaries were kept by officers; secondly, Jack's diary seems to be unique in that he served throughout the Great War in a Divisional Ammunition Column. The author is currently unaware of a similar example.

---

1   Jack's name appears on the 1911 Census for England but not on that for Guernsey.
2   When war was declared, most of the members of the R.G.A & E., though not compelled to serve overseas, volunteered for such service with the Royal Field Artillery.
3   With the exception of those units then serving in India.

PROLOGUE

Driver Jack Hickman 9/DAC

Saturday, 23rd March 1918
Near Grovetown on the old 1916 Somme Battle-fields. Third day of the fighting retreat.

"Let go the reins!" the voice in his head thundered.

No reaction.

Again the insistent command, *"Let go the reins!"*

Frantically, Driver Jack Hickman 9/DAC fumbled to disentangle the reins that were wound round his arm better to hold the plunging pair of terrified horses.

"Our horses had been tied to old tree stumps and the German shells dropped amongst them. As soon as they started, I got my two horses untied and they were mad with terror; I was just getting the upper hand of them when another shell dropped about ten yards behind me. I felt myself go off my feet with the concussion and at the same time my horses gave a great spring and I flew through the air and landed in a big shell-hole. My left heel stuck in the ground and I heard a sharp crack and I found my left leg out of action. I lay still for a few minutes while several more shells burst around, then I spent about an hour crawling from shell-hole to shell-hole and still under heavy fire. How the pieces missed me I don't know. An officer who tried to get to me was hit in the shoulder. After about an hour and a half of this I managed to get back with the help of a chum and I was carried for about a mile on a stretcher and was then picked up by an ambulance car that was passing. I was taken to the 38th Casualty Clearing Station [at Pont Rémy, on the Somme River just south-east of Abbeville]."

Had he not thrown the reins, Jack would have been blown to pieces as were his unfortunate horses; even so, he had sustained gunshot and shrapnel wounds to his face and to his left ankle, while damaged ligaments in his left leg rendered the limb temporarily useless. Jack's survival was remarkably fortunate – the story of the voices would be repeated through his family down the years. Yet reaching the Casualty Clearing Station did not mean that his ordeal was over – it simply meant that he was likely to survive.

PART ONE

Pre-War World to August 1914

CHAPTER ONE

ROMNEY MARSH: A WAY OF LIFE ON THE EAST SUSSEX & WEST KENT BORDERS

TOWN, VILLAGES AND HAMLETS

In the written records of East Sussex, Jack Hickman's family can with certainty be traced back to the end of the eighteenth century; however, the written history of some of the towns, villages and hamlets featuring in this story stretches much further back into the mists of time. Rye, the principal town of the area, and the village of Iden, birth-place of Jack's great-grandfather William Hickman, both pre-date even the eleventh-century Domesday Book survey ordered by William the Conqueror; East Guldeford, the Hickman family home for much of the nineteenth century, dates back to at least the beginning of the Tudor sixteenth century; Camber village dates mainly to the second half of the nineteenth century, though the name itself pre-dates the village by several centuries: this in respect of the harbour and the castle built on the orders of Henry VIII on the west bank of the River Rother with the aim of protecting the anchorage and the town of Rye from French raids.

Jack Hickman's birthplace, the hamlet of Broomhill, just to the east of Camber village (that was itself 1½ miles east of Rye Harbour), lay on the windswept coast of East Sussex close to the border with Kent. It was described in John Marius Wilson's, '*Imperial Gazetteer of England and Wales, 1870-72'*, thus:

'*Broomhill, a parish in the district of Rye and counties of Kent and Sussex; on the coast, near the Ashford and Hastings railway, 4 miles E by S of Rye. Post Town, Rye. Acres, 3,580; of which 755 are water. Population –*

102. Houses – 22. It is a member of the Cinque Port of New Romney; and has no church.'

The name of Broomhill dates back to at least the twelfth century and during this time the coast has slowly retreated while the River Rother has substantially changed its course. The original hamlet of Broomhill was located on the stretch of Kent/Sussex coast between Camber and Dungeness, approximate to the modern-day Lydd Army Ranges. To a certain extent, many of the smaller ports in that area owed their livelihood

Rye Town, a contrast to the low, flat, agricultural, coastal plain

to the existence of the twelfth century elite association known as the Royal Cinque Ports that comprised Dover, Hastings, Hythe, Romney and Sandwich. Broomhill was one such minor haven, joining towards the end of the 1100s. Extracting a living from the sea at Broomhill was always hard-fought as the exposed hamlet occasionally suffered serious storm damage; two of the worst instances occurred in 1250 and 1252 but it was the Great Storm of 1287 that proved the undoing of Broomhill. Such was the power of the sea that the original outflow of the River Rother at Romney was permanently blocked and the river that previously reached the coast near modern-day Greatstone and Littlestone diverted southwards to Rye and beyond the town into the Channel.

The consequence for Broomhill and its immediate hinterland was an abrupt end to membership of the Cinque Ports and loss of the growing prosperity offered by that elite organisation. As a result Broomhill (then spelt 'Bromehill') and Old Winchelsea both ceased to exist, while the Great Storm of 1287 destroyed numerous coastal and sea-going vessels, drowning many experienced fishermen and sailors. Broomhill was not alone in its misfortunes as, further west, at Hastings the cliff and part of the Norman castle fell into the sea, blocking the port and severely damaging that town's economy.

In its second incarnation, Broomhill hamlet's location is closer to Rye Harbour and the 'new' outflow of the River Rother, nestled on the landward side of the sea wall. Closely associated with Broomhill,

Jury's Gap (first known as 'Jew's Gut') originated as a small fishing settlement that during the 19th Century developed as a watch-house and ultimately as a Coastguard centre. As for the hamlet of Camber, it had no separate existence in the national Census until 1841.

but that population would more than double by 1821. At least until the 1880s, Jack Hickman's branch of the family lived in East Guldeford. As mentioned, his great-grandfather, William Hickman, had been born a couple of miles from there in Iden, and when William had

TABLE 1: LOCAL POPULATION COMPARISON, 1801-1911

Year	Rye	East Guldeford	Camber	Broomhill
1801	2,187	59	–	Unknown
1811	2,681	94	–	18
1821	3,599	124	–	56
1831	3,715	126	–	80
1841	4,031	127	97	123
1851	4,592	137	98	134
1861	4,288	152	101	102
1871	4,366	157	102	129
1881	4,667	182	107	126
1891	4,354	159	112	118
1901	3,900	137	121	145
1911	4,229	167		141

When the very first national census was taken in 1801 the township of Rye dominated the locality, just as it does today, recording even then in excess of two thousand inhabitants. Camber hamlet was not recorded separately and Broomhill appears to have contained fewer than twenty souls, probably just a handful of local fishermen – such small numbers might well be related to the threat of invasion of this stretch of coast during the Napoleonic Wars. However, in 1801 the inland village of East Guldeford was home to fifty-nine people

married Anne Bean in November 1800, the couple had initially set up home in the village. However, by 1806 when Jack's grandfather Henry Hickman was born the family had moved home to the village of East Guldeford, situated on the north-west corner of Romney Marsh. There they remained for several decades although some of the Hickman babies were recorded as being born in other nearby parishes, as was Jack's own father, also named Henry, who first saw the light of day in Broomhill. This may be explained by the hazardous nature of pregnancy and childbirth at that time resulting in expectant mothers often being sent to other family members who would do their best to supervise the confinement.

By 1851, the population of East Guldeford village numbered 137, though the composition of that population had remained similar to that of the 1841 Census. John Offen had taken over the running of the family farm from his ageing mother while George Beeby was running another farm; George Farris had taken up work as a farm bailiff and Thomas Pankhurst still earned his living as a grazier. Employed on those farms was a total of fourteen agricultural labourers. By then there were two shepherds living in the village of East Guldeford: Henry Hickman, now forty-five, who in 1841 had been described as a 'looker', was now called a 'shepherd', although the official returns showed seven 'lookers' where there had been five at the time of the previous census. As in 1841 Mr. Sam Chapman still brewed beer, now with the help of two other men and a drayman to deliver the finished product. Among the domestic workers were six servants and a housekeeper. One sign of the changing times was the presence of two men employed as gate-keepers for the expanding South-Eastern Railway. Three general labourers also lived in the hamlet.

The next census, in 1861, indicated a marginal population increase of just fifteen in ten years, though the composition of the jobs done by those

people had changed little and thus agriculture figured large. Foremost among these were the farmer-graziers Thomas Pankhurst and John Adams; in addition there were fourteen agricultural labourers, two farm bailiffs, six agricultural carters and three carter's mates, eight shepherds, including twenty-seven-year-old William Hickman and his eighteen-year-old brother Henry Hickman and their eighteen-year-old cousin William Hickman – all of whom had been born in East Guldeford. In addition, there were four 'lookers' though, unusually, none of them was a Hickman. There was a shoemaker, a dressmaker and a sawyer; Sam Chapman's brewery was still going strong and he had recently employed a brewer's clerk, Henry Hatcher. There were six servants in the hamlet, again suggesting a slight rise in prosperity. The South Eastern Railway employed two platelayers at the Gate House and a gate-keeper at the crossing, emphasising the permanency and popularity of the latest form of transport.

The population of East Guldeford had remained stable through the 1860's but by 1871 the community contained thirty-two residences of varying size and quality with the village being based on the old Military Road that dated back to the Napoleonic Wars. Two farmers and one grazier were the principal employers in the village – Mr. Pankhurst who lived at the 'Farm House' and farmed 200 acres, employed six men, two boys and two females; William Adams who farmed 51 acres, employed four labourers and one boy; William Dunster the grazier employed a servant, a dressmaker and a governess in his residence. The village schoolmistress was still shown as Isabella Hickman, wife of John Bean Hickman. John Phipps, a farm bailiff, employed one servant while Robert Chapman, a master brewer who had taken over the family business from his father Sam, worked with an assistant brewer and a brewer's drayman. Thus the majority of occupations were still mainly related to agriculture – fifteen labourers and four farm labourers, as well as eight shepherds, a looker and a dairymaid. Domestic

help – general servants, farm servants, domestic servants and a railway servant – accounted for several individuals, while railway-related work still accounted for three (track) platelayers and a labourer. The village also boasted a blacksmith and three carters, essential trades in the local community, and by 1871 even more females were employed in service – a governess, a dressmaker, a tailor and a cook. In view of the fact that Jack's older brother, Edmund, was born in 1879 in Broomhill (as were the next four siblings) it appears that Jack Hickman's parents chose to move to Broomhill hamlet late in the 1870's. They would be nearer the sea but the family would still be in an

St. Mary's parish church, East Guldeford. Jack's parents are buried here

agricultural area on the southern edge of the Romney Marsh.

The 1881 census for East Guldeford suggests that change and expansion was coming to the village. The population had risen to 182, there was a parish church and a parish clerk named Herbert Baker although agriculture still dominated the jobs of the men more than ever – William Adams employed four men at Offen's Farm; farmer George Hemsbey worked 225 acres and employed ten men; William Dunster was still a grazier. Barn Farm, Church Farm and Lamb's Farm were all mentioned by name. There were sixteen agricultural labourers and thirteen shepherds (plus two boys) and a looker. The village was connected to the surrounding areas by three waggoners or carters living in the hamlet. Robert Chapman was the experienced master brewer, employing two apprentices and a drayman with three other men in an expanding concern. The Southern Railway employed one platelayer and a railway porter while domestically in the village there were five servants, a housekeeper, a maid, a cook and also two gardeners; a lawyer's clerk, a barmaid and a shipwright indicated an increasingly diverse population. A ship's captain was, appropriately, away at sea.

From the mid-1880s, the population of East Guldeford entered a period of

The larger cottages at Broomhill Farm, 2010

Broomhill Farm – one of the largest in the Camber area in Jack's youth

sustained decline. An initial ten-year reduction of 23 by 1891 was repeated by the turn of the century, reaching a fifty-year low of 137. This pattern was paralleled by a similar pause in the steady expansion of Camber and Broomhill – possibly explained by a general drift to the rapidly expanding urban centres where industrial wages, though hard-earned, easily outstripped those of the agricultural labourer. However, by the time of the subsequent census in 1911, the population of East Guldeford had recovered to 167, its greatest growth spurt for a century; those of Camber and Broomhill were also showing obvious signs of substantial recovery.

The National Census of 1891 provides a long-surviving snapshot of Broomhill Hamlet in the year of Jack Hickman's birth. Tucked away behind the protection of the coastal ridge and just to the east of Camber, the twin hamlets of Broomhill and Jury's Gap that straddled the East Sussex-Kent border, owed their existence to both the land and the sea. In 1891 the combined population stood at 118 (85 in Sussex and 33 in Kent), distributed across twenty-one families in twelve residences of varying standard. George Frederick Brann Morphett was most definitely the leading light in the hamlet, reflected in the fact that he acted as enumerator for the local census return; Brann Morphett lived in and owned Broomhill Farm, the larger of the hamlet's two farms. The farm encompassed four labourer's cottages, entitling him to the description, '*...farmer and employer*'. His son, George Brann Morphett, lived in nearby Creek House. The smaller Wall House Farm (with just one labourer's cottage) was tenanted by Joseph Miller, described merely as an, '*...agricultural labourer*' rather than the grander title of farmer. Towards and within Jury's Gap were four residences owned by the Admiralty and these were used to house coastguards and their families. Thereafter six properties were occupied by various branches of the long-established Southerden family (traceable in Broomhill at least to John Southerden who was born in 1816), whose principal employ was catching and selling fish. The fishery business was run by the sixty-eight-year-old widowed matriarch Mary A. Southerden but by 1891, the sales side of the business was overseen by an 'outside' fish merchant, Mr. Archie Trollope who, it appears, had married Jane Southerden and thus joined the family business. Nearby, lodging with Charles Southerden in Myrtle Cottage, were builders George Lewis Senior [70] and George Lewis Junior [38] accompanied by a carpenter, Edward Stokes [22]. This suggests that the little outlier of Jury's Gap was in some respects undergoing a degree of expansion.

Within the relatively small community of Broomhill, there were two branches of the Hickman family, each headed by itinerant shepherds, akin to the old style Romney Marsh looker. At Beachbank House, shepherd John Bean Hickman (50) lived with wife Isabelle (47) and their two working-age sons[1], James and Edward, who were both agricultural labourers. When still single back in 1871, Isabelle had earned her living as a schoolmistress. In nearby Cruckfield House lived John's brother, and later that year to be Jack's father, Henry Hickman (48) whose wife Naomi (45) had already borne seven children. The two brothers, John Bean (the elder by two years) and Henry had both been born a couple of miles away in East Guldeford but had chosen to live in Broomhill. Evidence that the hamlet was developing is furnished by the existence of Broomhill and Camber Elementary School that had been set up to serve the local community. In 1911, 29-year-old Mary Jane Booker was head-teacher and she lived at the School House in Broomhill, while her sister Louisa was employed as her housekeeper. Also living in near-at-hand Broomhill Farm was another female school teacher, 21-year-old Gladys Dean.

The single town of any significance in the immediate area is to be found a mile to the south-west of East Guldeford, the ancient town of Rye, one of the mediaeval '*Cinque Ports*' that received special privileges from the Crown in return for providing the King with vital ships and sailors. Now two miles from the sea, Rye was originally on a bay of the sea, affording a haven or 'Camber'.

Rye dates from Roman times as a port and was Norman until mid-thirteenth century and has long been associated with the Wealden iron-making industry. The 1287 Great Storm cut the town from the sea as rivers changed course and began silting the harbour. To make matters worse the French attacked and burned Rye in 1377 – only the stone-built Ypres Tower survived – resulting in the strengthening of the town walls defence. Many years later, in 1540, King Henry VIII built Camber Castle as part of his anti-French defences.

The Cinque Ports association was vital to the prosperity of Rye and over the years the commercial harbour moved closer to the sea but there was a constant struggle to prevent the harbour from silting. Gradually the inning[2] of the marshes effectively 'moved' the harbour wharves even further from the town, leading to a clash of maritime and agricultural interests. The development of bigger ships that could not use Rye harbour took trade away from the town and, locally, greater emphasis was placed upon fishing and smuggling, for which latter activity Rye soon developed a nefarious reputation. By the late 1700s this corner of Sussex and Kent, thanks to its proximity to the French coast, was a stronghold of the smuggler's 'craft'.

In December 1836 Rye town was cut off from the outside world by a huge snowstorm, forcing coach services to be suspended for seven days while a gang of seventy men worked for five days to clear a route into and out of the town. Not only was transport affected but local landowners lost upwards of ten thousand sheep in the deep snowdrifts.

Smuggling apart, Rye was hardly regarded as a hotbed of crime but in 1837 a Rye Borough Police Force was introduced. A principal task was to oversee local beer shops and public houses – in those times such establishments were not permitted to open on Saturday nights or Sunday mornings and afternoons. When the inevitable arrests were made, Ypres Tower was used as a jail and at one stage it had to be expanded by the addition of four extra cells, an exercise yard and a section for women prisoners. The town Police Force lasted until 1889 when it was absorbed by the County Police Force.

By 1841 Rye was a flourishing town of 4,031 people. With its traditional links to sea-going trade and to agricultural land it also displayed most of the occupations that were indicative of a growing and prosperous small town. Associated with the sea were merchants, a rope-maker, chandlers, sail-makers, a shipwright, a ferryman, painters, fishermen and a fishmonger, a customs officer, a preventive officer, a bargeman, mariners and sundry seamen; linked to the land were farmers, lookers, a wool-stapler, a dyer, a cordwainer (leather business), a leather beater, a saddler, a miller, a basket-maker, butchers, grocers and greengrocers, a brick-maker, a potter, general labourers and agricultural labourers; a sluice-keeper was also mentioned – he would ensure that the marsh did not flood unnecessarily in years of higher than average rainfall and that the marsh might be properly irrigated from the Military Canal in drier summers.

Middle-class professions were well represented by solicitors, merchants, bankers, ministers, schoolteachers, a surgeon, an engineer and a registrar – these would have been the principal employers of the servants, charwomen, gardeners, washerwomen and laundresses mentioned in the Census.

Entrepreneurial and artisanal occupations, often good yardsticks of prosperity, included a gun-maker, an ironmonger, a milliner, carpenters, a sawyer, a stone-mason, bricklayers, builders, a plumber, a pipe-maker, a wheelwright, a millwright, a watchmaker, a shoemaker, drapers, dressmakers, a druggist (chemist), an upholsterer, a cabinet-maker, nurses, a chair-maker, bakers, hairdressers, a coal merchant and a coal carter, a stationer, a pawnbroker and an auctioneer. In relation to the several public houses and hotels in Rye there were a brewer, draymen, beer-sellers, inn-keepers, coopers, a spirit merchant and a tobacconist; in keeping with main form of transport of the time, there was a horse agent, an ostler, a coachman, a stable-keeper, grooms and general carriers. Other employment showed clerks, post-boys, a crier, warehousemen, shop assistants, gas workers and even a pedlar. On the night of the fifth National Census, June 6th

1841, the town gaol in Ypres Tower was empty except for the gaoler and his wife – the local constables were evidently not kept very busy!

That year's Census for Rye shows a fair number of people of independent means but, despite the apparent prosperity in the town and the diversity of employment, a small proportion of the local population felt the ravages of poverty. Some form of Poor Relief had existed in law since the reign of Edward III (1327-1377) and had been adjusted and codified in 1601 under Queen Elizabeth I. Following the report of a Royal Commission (1832-33) the Poor Law Amendment Act of 1834 lay the basis for the Rye Poor Law Union and for the organisation of a workhouse that, if already in existence, should be improved. A Rye Town workhouse had been in existence since at least the 1770s and there had also been local workhouses at Iden, Brede, Winchelsea (St. Thomas) and Playden dating back in some cases to Elizabethan times. Outdoor poor relief was still available without entering the workhouse (at least until the late 1840s) but the workhouse would always carry an associated stigma. The Rye Poor Law Union was formed in July 1835 and, in accordance with the new law, was overseen by an elected Board of Guardians. The new Poor Law Union comprised twelve[3] previously separate parishes but assumed the new title of 'Rye Poor Law Union' in deference to the largest centre of population. The 1831 census indicated a population total of 11,418 for the twelve parishes of the Rye area, ranging from the smallest, Broomhill, to the largest, Rye Town itself. Initially, Rye Union made use of existing parish workhouse accommodation at Rye, Northiam and Brede, allowing other buildings to be sold off in the late 1830s.

The 1841 Census shows the old Rye Union Workhouse housing the governor, a matron, a schoolmistress and 125 inmates (42 men and 83 women); by 1844 the average number of inmates was falling, to around 100 men, women and children per annum. During the 1840s building commenced on a new workhouse in Rye Town; when it opened in 1845 it could house more than four hundred 'inmates'. Accommodation was separated by gender and an infirmary extension was added in 1847. However, nothing stood still and by the time of the 1851 Census in Rye, the gaol had closed but the new Rye Union Workhouse was in great demand, containing 202 inmates, though most of them were elderly rather than of regular working age.

Accessibility to Rye greatly improved with the coming of the South Eastern Railway during the 1840s – the period of so-called 'Railway Mania'[4] – and with this accessibility came increased prosperity. The 1841 Census reveals that a number of navvies[5] were living in the Rye area reflecting the putative construction of local railway links; in 1846 building began in earnest on the railway line to Rye Town and beyond it, to Hastings. In return for the right to build a swing bridge over the River Rother, the South Eastern Railway Company (SER) paid the town the princely sum of £4,500[6] and promised to spend £10,000 on the harbour – an offer the town found impossible to resist. Thus, in May 1850, the iron swing bridge over the River Rother (and consequently the railway link to Rye) was formally opened by the Lord Mayor of London who, appropriately, came by special train to '...partake of the hospitality' of Rye. In fact the railway did not actually open to traffic until February 1851 when the arrival of a special train was celebrated by a banquet at the George Inn. With the completion of the railway, the navvies moved on but the coastguard was now moving into the area.

The arrival of the railway brought a number of new jobs to the area, self-evidently those related to the stations themselves and those connected to tourism. Beyond Rye Town, the East Guldeford census return of 1851 records two men employed as gate-keepers for the SER; the 1861 census return for the same hamlet indicates that the SER employed 2 platelayers at the Gate House and a gate-keeper to work the level-crossing. By 1891 there were still 2 platelayers at the Gate House, where a William Kidd was recorded as an SER gateman/porter. Ten years later in East Guldeford the SER contingent comprised a gateman at Star Crossing, a 'points' gateman, and two platelayers, suggesting that railway employment remained stable.

Further transport links developed towards the end of the nineteenth century with the opening in April 1895 of the Monkbretton Bridge and new road to East Guldeford and, in the same month, a 3-foot gauge steam tramway was built from Monkbretton Bridge at Rye to the newly-opened Rye Golf Club, just west of Camber village. In all, burgeoning transport connections, both locally and beyond, would increase the popularity of Rye Town, of Camber Sands and of the new golf links.

So, when Jack Hickman was born in the summer of 1891, Rye was the dominant town of the area but smaller villages and hamlets were flourishing and connections further afield were strengthening.

THE HICKMANS – A FAMILY ON THE BORDERS

Far from the horrors of the Great War that separated Jack Hickman from his beloved golf for three and a half years, the Hickman family's traceable story emerged during the days of another conflict – the American War of Independence (1776-1783). In 1781 in East Sussex, Jack Hickman's great-grandfather, William Hickman, was born in the tiny, pre-Domesday village of Iden that is situated on a low hill in a bend of both the River Rother and now also the

All Saints Church, Iden

Royal Military Canal[7]. The genesis of the village name is etched in the history of England and even linked to the head of state. Twelve years into the reign of the first King Edward, in 1284[8], Edmund de Paseley built a moated, castellated manor house[9]; in itself this was an unremarkable fact but the house was to become the home of Alexander Iden, a fifteenth-century Sheriff of Kent who, in 1450, made his reputation by capturing and killing Jack Cade, notorious leader of the Kentish Rebellion against King Henry VI (1422-1461).

On 3rd November 1800, during Britain's struggles against Revolutionary France, when he was just nineteen years of age William Hickman married Ann Bean of New Romney, who was one year his senior, in Iden's twelfth-century All Saints Church[10]. Over the ensuing eleven years in Iden, William and Ann Hickman had four children: William in 1803, Henry[11] in 1806, James in 1809 and Mary, following whose birth in 1811 the family moved home from Iden to the hamlet of East Guldeford, just two miles away to the south-east but situated on the flat, broad marshes. Once settled in East Guldeford, the Hickman family increased twice more with the births of Elizabeth in 1814 and finally Hannah in 1817. Oldest daughter Mary would survive all her siblings and live even beyond the reign of Queen Victoria. Henry Hickman Sr. – Mary's brother and subsequently Jack's grandfather – was baptised on 9th November 1806, though whether at All Saints Church in Iden or at St. Mary's in East Guldeford is not clear.

In 1838 and at the age of thirty-two Henry Hickman Senior [1806 to 1877], married Martha Pope, the daughter of James and Ann Pope of Broomhill hamlet. Martha was born in Broomhill in 1811 [and lived until 1870], though until 1791 most of the Pope family had been born in East Guldeford. The newlyweds moved to Broomhill where their brood of children included Benjamin, MaryAnn, Sarah, William, James, George, John Bean, and finally their youngest son Henry Junior (later Jack's father) in April-June 1843 in East Guldeford. [Henry Jr. died in Rye in 1920, aged seventy-six].

On 20th July 1868 in East Guldeford, at the age of twenty-five, Henry Hickman Jr. married Naomi Butchers, whose father, Alexander Duff Butchers (born about 1806 in Icklesham, Sussex and who died in March 1891 in Rye), was a farmer in the coastal hamlet of Camber; Naomi's mother, Maria Butchers (née Crowhurst) was born about 1813 in Rye. Naomi, the fourth of six children, was born in Camber between April and June of 1845 and died in Rye in 1909 at the age of sixty-four. Henry Jr., like his father Henry before him, was an itinerant shepherd, as were two of his brothers William (born in 1834) and John Bean (born in 1840). Lookering proved to be a declining way of life as only two more Hickmans, William's sons John F. (born in 1867) and Benjamin James (born in 1871) took up the age-old family skill.

Henry and Naomi Hickman had a traditionally large family, living in East Guldeford until about 1875 and in Broomhill thereafter – Anna Maria, Henry William, George Ernest, Julia, Edmund, Frank, Charles Joseph, Catherine and finally their youngest son, and the principal of our story, John (always known as 'Jack') in May 1891. The youngsters were to tread many a varied and often dangerous path.

Anna Maria (Annie), was born in the early summer of 1869 in East Guldeford. Little is recorded of her life but it is known that she took the immigrant ship to Australia. From the scraps of

Another older sister, Julia

information available, it appears that her younger sister Julia, born between April and June of 1876 in Broomhill, eventually followed Anna Maria's footsteps across the globe to start a new life, hers in Tasmania. As late as 1911, Julia was still living at home in Broomhill with her widowed father Henry Hickman and was described as a 'housekeeper'.

Oldest son Henry William, who was born in the late summer of 1871 in East Guldeford, followed in the male family custom of working the land and the census of 1891 recorded him, aged twenty, as an agricultural labourer. Despite the fact that Henry William was forty-three years old at the outbreak of the Great War he was then already serving in the Royal Navy and served with further distinction as 278363, Stoker First Class, receiving the 1914-15 Star, British War Medal and the Victory

Jack's eldest sister, Annie

Medal. Henry was married and lived in Eastney, Portsmouth, in 1911 – he named the eldest of his seven children Henry William in the family tradition.

By contrast, second son George Ernest, born in 1873, took on a very different way of life from his brother, eventually assuming the licence as landlord of the '*Winchelsea Inn*'. Edmund, born in Broomhill and six years George's junior married a woman from Brighton, eventually set up home in Hurst Green in Sussex and earned a living as a domestic gardener. Three years after Edmund's birth, the first of the family's soldier/golfers was born – Frank arrived in the depths of the winter of 1882 in Broomhill. He became a professional golfer prior to the outbreak of the Great War, working at Ebbsfleet Course, Ramsgate and at St. Augustine

Links when he attested for Army service in December 1915. Frank had married Alice Boultwood in 1908 and the couple had three children prior to his call-up in 1916. From October 1916 he served in the Royal Field Artillery as No.178336, Driver later Signaller after qualifying in, …'*signalling and telegraphy*'.

Next youngest, Charles Joseph (known to all as 'Joe'), was born in Broomhill in the late summer of 1884. His chosen course in life was different again from his three older brothers. Like Frank, Joe married in 1908 (to Esther, a Rye girl), however by 1911 he was described as a groom employed at Streamlands Farm near Tonbridge in Kent. This rural life was exchanged in later years for a more urban existence as Joe decided to run a general grocery store (shown below) in the town of Tunbridge Wells.

Joe Hickman's general grocery store in Tunbridge Wells

Catherine, the youngest of the girls, was born in Broomhill during the late winter of 1888. Information regarding Catherine is sparse, yet the 1901 and 1911 census records reveal that she had left home during the intervening decade, while marriage records show that she wed Ernest Startup in Rye during the summer of 1914.

Finally, born in Broomhill hamlet on 1st May 1891, was the family's second soldier/golfer, John Hickman who was univer-sally known as 'Jack'. From his birth the family lived in '*Cruckfield House*', Broomhill Hamlet (next door to Henry's brother, John Bean Hickman), though by 1901 the family home was recorded in the national census as being '*The Lodge*', Camber. Jack's birthplace, Broomhill Hamlet, lay on the windswept coast of East Sussex (bordering Kent) just to the east of Camber village and 1½ miles east of Rye Harbour. Just as the hamlet had suffered a once catastrophic past, so Broomhill's newest arrival was to experience a chequered but remarkable future.

LAND, SEA AND LIVELIHOOD IN A LONG HORIZON

EXTRACTING A LIVING – SHEEP FLOCKS AND LOOKERING

The hamlet of East Guldeford, for so long the home of the Hickmans, is located on the western edge of the wet, low-lying expanse of Romney Marsh that, down the years, provided employment for several of the Hickman males and thus did the distinctive occupation of 'looker' pass down through at least three generations of the family. Locally, work was not easily come by except as an unskilled agricultural labourer or, better rewarded, as an overseer of the ubiquitous flocks of sheep. Jack's paternal grandfather, Henry Hickman Sr. (born in 1806) and his great uncle James (born in 1809), along with Henry's subsequent sons (thus Jack's uncles) William (born 1834 in Iden), John Bean (born in late 1840 in East Guldeford) and Henry Jr. (Jack's father, born April-June

1843 in Broomhill) as well as nephew William (born 1843 in East Guldeford) all found work as itinerant shepherds known on Romney Marsh at that time as lookers. Even a generation beyond, Henry's grandsons John Francis (born 1867 in East Guldeford) and Benjamin James (born 1871 in East Guldeford) – both sons of William Hickman – and great-nephew William (born 1880 in East Guldeford) earned a living in rain and shine overseeing the hardy flocks on the Marsh.

For four hundred years after the Norman invaders arrived in Kent, much of the present Romney Marsh was either under permanent flood or so wet that agriculture was an unproductive exercise. Up to the 15th century, the principal economic value of the area lay in the production of salt, obtained by isolating and then evaporating pools of sea-water. Salt was an especially valued commodity as it was essential to one of the main preservation processes[12] of meat, fish and some vegetables at that time. Working the marsh for agriculture has always proved a tough challenge for the local population whose numbers often fluctuated in relation to natural and man-made circumstances. Gradually, between the twelfth century and the end of the fourteenth century, the original tidal saltings of Romney Marsh underwent a transformation. This period was known as the 'inning' of the marshes. The process commenced by isolating a section of marsh by raising a sea wall to protect the targeted reclamation from the sea and subsequently by criss-crossing the reclaimed land with a series of drainage ditches and protective dikes or embankments. Thus there slowly emerged fertile, estuarine-type pastures, although unsophisticated Mediæval technology left the land perennially poorly-drained and most difficult to manage.

The present hamlet of East Guldeford became one of the later areas to be reclaimed when, in 1480, Sir Richard (of) Guildford financed the inning of 1,500 acres of marshland. Previously unproductive marsh was thus converted into relatively fertile farmland and the 12 shillings annual rent that Sir Richard paid to the Cistercian monks of Robertsbridge Abbey soon began to seem like a good investment. As was the custom of the day, the wealthy Sir Richard Guildford publicly celebrated his success by raising a church to the greater glory of God. The brick-built St. Mary's Church was built at Sir Richard's behest (and cost) in 1505 and a hamlet, consisting of a few houses, grew around it. Even now, in such a flat landscape, the novel silhouette of St. Mary's Church stands stark against the sky, its twin roofs separated by a stubby bell tower (see page 28). The present church's interior is somewhat basic and was extensively restored during the nineteenth century. The hamlet's name with its unusual spelling, East *Guldeford*, was intended to differentiate it from the same-sounding Guildford in Surrey.

In 1841, two years prior to the birth of Jack's father, Henry Hickman, the National Census recorded that East Guldeford's population totalled just 127 – a rise of only three souls in twenty years. The foremost characters of the hamlet included a farmer, Judith Offen, a grazier, Thomas Pankhurst, a brewer, Sam Chapman, twenty agricultural labourers, two servants and five 'lookers', one of whom was Jack's grandfather, Henry Hickman Senior. From 1841 the population of the hamlet grew slowly until reaching its peak of 182 in 1881, thereafter declining to 137 by 1901. By the latter date, East Guldeford was home to nine agricultural labourers and sixteen shepherds, among whom were four members of the Hickman family – Ben (30), William (67), William H. (21) and John F. (34). Confirming the still-high profile of agriculture, there was a stock-looker George Wratten, a farm waggoner and his mate, as well as a farm carter and a yardman. Specific farms that were named included Wells Farm, Barn Farm Cottages, Collyers Farm, Offens Farm, Worth Farm, Church Farm and the Kent Ditch. Reflecting one of the permanent changes in transport technology, locally the railway employed a gateman, a 'points' gateman, and two platelayers. Domestically, there were two housekeepers, two servants, a cook and a housemaid, mirroring the different social 'classes' within the hamlet. Other skills and professions were represented by a dressmaker and her apprentice, a private tutor and a schoolmistress, a general haulier, a coachman and two men of 'independent means'. Frederick Chapman (succeeding his father Sam)

was an owner-brewer and wine merchant, employing a journeyman brewer. Among the individual 'named' dwellings in the hamlet were 'Rotherview', 'Guldeford Lodge', 'Brewery Cottages', and 'St. Johns Cottages'.

The sheer hardship of attempting to extract a living from such an environment had often been exacerbated by the ravages of lethal and crippling disease[13], so by the early 1500's some of the Marsh's hamlets had been all but abandoned, their buildings left to rot and tumble. As a consequence, rural de-population became the norm, attracting wealthy predators whose inclination was to buy the land in order to extract maximum profit from it. These absentee landlords, resident on higher ground well away

St. John's Cottages, adjacent to Rye G.C., Camber

from the bleak vistas of the marsh, thus developed large estates that offered fewer earning opportunities for the locals, largely because the new landowners put former arable lands to pasture. The wet and windy marshland, criss-crossed by its steep-sided ditches, was unsuitable for cattle and overly damp for arable, so sheep were introduced to Romney Marsh, becoming the predominant sight recognised today. Despite the obstacles to arable farming, local records show that in 1801 Camber hamlet, on the western edge of the marsh and just to the south of Rye Town, still had a surprising amount of land given over to cultivation of which 60% was under wheat, 13% barley, 13% oats, 10% potatoes, 3% peas, 1% turnips.

The introduction of sheep flocks employed fewer people and so contributed to rural decline as elements of the population drifted to the newly-industrialising towns, where the lure of very different work and housing ultimately gave rise to unconscionable squalor and poverty. Rural de-population thus led to urban overcrowding, while those who remained in the broad acres of the marshes had to develop and adjust their skills in order to maintain and feed their families.

Shepherding had long been a respected role on the marsh, but the creation of extensive 'estates' and substantially larger flocks required similar skills with the beasts but an even hardier outlook on life on the part of the shepherd. These 'shepherd-lookers', as they were known, might have responsibility for the oversight and care of several large flocks ranging far across the marsh and encompassing the lands of more than one estate owner. Sheep are voracious feeders and crop the pasture much more closely than do cattle, so the flocks must be frequently moved in order to give the grass sufficient opportunity to regenerate. Of necessity a 'shepherd-looker' needed to be of strong, independent character as he might spend many weeks in his own company; he required mastery of many skills beyond those associated with the direct care of his sheep and must be a 'marsh-man' through and through – it was a bleak and dangerous environment at certain times of the year. He would roam the marsh in pursuit of his chosen profession, usually on foot although some lookers made a living sufficient to fund an equally hardy pony. Such were the distances a looker covered that returning home to his family was a rare treat – his life was the marsh and he usually needed to live near his work, especially during the lambing season or the shearing. Today, visitors who roam the lanes of the marsh occasionally come across what appears to be a small, tumbledown 'shack' that has no obvious function – like as not this building will prove to be an old looker's hut (see page 43), a basic shelter that afforded respite for the roving shepherd who needed somewhere to feed, shelter, store simple tools and personal equipment and above all to lay his head in relative 'comfort',

One of the few remaining Looker's Huts, at Cliff Marsh Farm

close to a warming fire. Sometimes a sick sheep or a weak new-born lamb would share the warmth of the hut while in the adjacent outside pens less serious cases were still at hand for the looker's care. 'Lookering' was a skill that passed down through families, with young lads learning the ropes by taking food and other necessities of life to their fathers and brothers out on the marsh; thus the youngsters themselves became the 'marsh-men' of the future. Today, there is no great likelihood of coming across a former looker's hut, as there are but a dozen left in any recognisable condition – at the height of the looker's day, the huts might be counted in several hundreds. Though no more than occasional shelters, most lookers' huts were brick-built with a chimney and a tiled roof but comprised just a single room of about ten feet by six. By way of a footnote to the way of life of the looker, the knowledge gained by the itinerant shepherd made him a suitable accomplice for many a smuggler who plied their dubious though lucrative trade on the bleaker stretches of the Kent coast. At times such involvement was risky (particularly as the skills of the Revenue Men increased) but the rewards were usually deemed to outdo the dangers.

Just as the man who elected to roam the marsh caring for the flocks required strength of character, so the sheep themselves needed certain attributes in order first to survive and then to flourish – to this end it demanded a special sheep

'Romney' sheep at Salt's Farm near East Guldeford

for a special land and the 'Romney' sheep was bred for this purpose. It could make the most of the least promising grazing and, while generally well-behaved, it was as hardy as was required by the marshes: most important, it was very reluctant when faced with the opportunity to jump an open ditch. These characteristics should be added to a reputation for providing copious amounts of good standard meat and a fleece of quality wool. However, such a creature did not come about by accident of nature, and careful husbandry was necessary for development of the Romney breed as it is presently known.

SAVING LIVES ON A SMUGGLING COAST [14]

Fishing, smuggling, sheep-farming, golf and dangerous seas – these were the bedfellows that at various times shaped the development of coastal settlements from Winchelsea to Jury's Gap and beyond. Around 1800, when smuggling was at its productive height, the Excise or 'Preventive' men were instrumental in establishing the Rye Harbour settlement adjacent to the shore, to the benefit of the harbourmaster and fishermen in general. Excise 'Riding Officers' (first employed before 1700) patrolled the ways and bye-ways of the coast in their efforts to frustrate the illegal importers of spirits, expensive cloth and other luxuries that were often brought into the country at the behest of the local 'quality' and squirearchy. At about that time, 1800, the Excise Men built a Watch House at Jury's Gap (then known as Jew's Gut) between present-day Broomhill Farm and the Lydd Army ranges. In that age of sail, seagoing was so much more dangerous and wrecks at sea were frequent and thus widely feared. With the whole stretch of coast observed by 'The Excise', it made sense in 1803 to locate a lifeboat close to Rye. However, the station did not last long and lapsed for a period of time.

In 1809 the Preventative Water Guard (employing inshore boats) was established, principally to combat smuggling and it was also to help when shipwrecks occurred but not until 1822 did the three elements of the Preventative Water Guard, Revenue Cruisers (seagoing) and Riding Officers (existing on land from 1689) come under control of the Board of Customs to be renamed the Coast Guard. However, change was slow and it was 1829 before the first official Coast Guard Instructions were issued and these included a section on lifesaving and lifesaving equipment, such as the 'Manby' lifesaving equipment that was *already* in standard use. The Coast Guard was made officially responsible for saving lives and protecting property in time of shipwreck. Then, in 1831, after the Coast Blockade that had existed since 1816 also came under the auspices of the Coast Guard, the Admiralty took the opportunity to make the Coast Guard a reserve force for the Royal Navy. The advantages were self-evident.

Coastguards served both on ships and on shore, though men ashore were transferred away from their home region for fear of possible corruption. This likely disruption to family life was mitigated by the fact that Coastguard Stations were equipped with living quarters for married men as well as single – a man could thus take his family with him. Each Coastguard Station was commanded by a Chief Officer, who would normally hold the rank of full lieutenant in the Royal Navy; below the Chief Officer, in descending order of rank, were Chief Boatman, Commissioned Boatman and Boatman. The size of the station determined the number of each rank – by this gauge, the Coastguard at Jury's Gap was regarded as an important station. The Jury's Gap station was re-established in 1833 by the 'National Institution for the Preservation of Life from Shipwreck' (founded in 1824), the fore-runner of the RNLI.

At the conclusion of the Crimean War in 1856 the Board of Customs, that had administered the Coast Guard since its inception in 1822, relinquished control in favour of the Admiralty Board. Smuggling had long been on the wane and the lifesaving role and Naval Reserve aspects had become commensurately more significant.

The lifeboat station changed location several times over the years. In 1856 it transferred to Camber on the eastern bank of the River Rother, though it was still known as the Rye lifeboat. A second lifeboat was also stationed at Winchelsea, reflecting the busy and dangerous nature of that stretch of Channel coast. A new boathouse was built at Rye in 1876 although it would remain open just 25 years until 1901; Winchelsea benefited from a new boathouse in 1882 and the station was renamed Rye Harbour in 1910, yet even that station was closed in 1928 following the loss of seventeen crewmen on one service. It was not until thirty-eight years later, in 1966, that the Rye station re-opened, when an inflatable boat was stationed there.

The frequent changes in location and in the number of lifeboats apparently had little effect on the quality of services rendered to mariners in distress on this coast as between 1831 and 1844 three gold medals and four silver medals were awarded to men of the lifeboat crew. In May 1841 the station was awarded five silver medallions by the King of the French (Louis-Philippe, the *'Citizen King'*) for saving the lives of the crew of the French sloop, *'Le Jeune Victor'*, which was wrecked off Rye in February 1841. On to 1864 and 1891, years that saw two more silver medals awarded for bravery at sea, though the rescue of the *'Thetis'* in February 1864, cost the life of Coastguard Terry. Similarly, in November 1882 the Winchelsea lifeboat capsized during a service and Crewman Edward Robus was drowned. Yet the real hammer-blow came in November 1928 when, on a service to save the vessel *'Alice'*, the lifeboat *'Mary Stanford'* [a non-self-righting 'pulling and sailing' boat with 14 oars], all seventeen volunteers were lost. It was said that,

'...the entire fishing fraternity of Rye harbour perished on that night'.

One member of the principal local fishing family, William Southerden, had been cox'n when the station took delivery of the lifeboat *'Mary Stanford'* and, though William had retired by 1928, his son Charlie was lost on that fateful November night.

Ashore, the 1841 Census reveals that the Rye Harbour lighthouse-man was forty-year-old Sam Russell – a fellow that would remain in the role at least until 1881. By this last census in which he appeared Sam, by then 82 years old and still in charge, was designated the Harbour 'signalman' rather than 'lighthouse-man'. The *'Camber Watch House'* was home to Chief Officer Charles Keating and twelve Royal Navy/Coast Guard boatmen; quite a thirst must have been generated by the sea air as the hamlet boasted both an innkeeper (William Morris) and a 'beer-retailer' (Sarah Toms).

By 1851 Camber/Rye boasted a chief officer CG (possibly Charles Keating), a chief boatman and twelve CG commissioned and ordinary boatmen, hailing from as far afield as Shetland, Cork, Pembrokeshire and Cornwall. Numbers in the Watch House were maintained through 1861 and 1871 – in the latter year, besides the Chief Officer, there was a Petty Officer First-Class, a chief boatman, three commissioned boatmen (including one from Nova Scotia) and five ordinary boatmen. Coast Guard numbers had somewhat reduced by 1881, possibly in the light of the work of the RNLI, showing only six men apart from the Chief Officer

Coast Guard cottages at Jury's Gap

occupying the coastguard cottages. Under the 1891 Census, the Camber Watch House was referred to as the Camber *Coast Guard* Station and the four residences housed the Chief Officer (RN), a Chief Boatman, two commissioned boatmen, five ordinary boatmen and a writer (RN). Ten years later, William Chard of Dawlish was the CG Station Officer in charge of a Chief Boatman, four commissioned boatmen (RN) and at least four ordinary boatmen (RN) and a writer (RN).

By 1911, the year that Jack Hickman moved on from Broomhill/Camber to Guernsey, the Coast Guard Station employed a Station Officer (Admiralty), a Coastguard Chief Petty Officer, two leading boatman and eight ordinary boatmen (all Royal Navy).

"A FINE KEDDLE OF FISH…"

Jury's Gap, which lies just to the east of but close by Broomhill, comprised a number of small, conjoined cottages long associated with the work of the Coast Guard and thus of the Royal Navy. The community seems to have grown up as a small fishing settlement that during the 19th Century expanded into a Coastguard point while maintaining its original character. As far as the fishing aspect of Jury's Gap is concerned, a family by the name of Southerden (occasionally mis-spelt 'Southerton' in various national censuses) dominates the hamlet's past. In 1841, Broomhill (for Jury's Gap was an integral part of Broomhill Hamlet) was then officially described in the census as being, '…*part *of Kent'*. Certainly as far back as 1841 twenty-five-year-old John Southerden's family was fishing those shores, while the presence of sixty-year-old John Greenstreet's family suggested an even longer involvement in fishing. However, the census of March 1851 clearly shows that although the Southerden family was principally concerned with the sea, they could as easily make a good living from the land, attested by the fact that Jane Southerden farmed 150 acres adjacent to the hamlet, employing a total of twelve agricultural labourers. John Southerden was still the main fisherman of the family, remaining so well into the 1870's, though by that time the family was showing more organisation and thus demonstrating its dominance. The sole fish dealer was Eliza Southerden and, of the eight fishermen who supplied her wares, six were family members – John (45), Charles (23), Frederick (21), Daniel (49), George (23) and Daniel Jr. (18). The only family 'outsiders' were Twosign[15] Richardson (24) and James Pope (57). [Coincidentally, Pope was the family name of Jack Hickman's grandmother who was also born in Broomhill.] Ten years later the only apparent changes were that John Southerden Sr. had been replaced by John Southerden Jr. (34) and Samuel Southerden (20) had replaced the younger Daniel Southerden, while James Pope Jr. (45) had taken over from his father. A decade further on, the Southerdens were continuing the logical process of the fishery business being run by a senior female (in this case Mary Southerden) from the family home, *'Seaside'*, though a family 'outsider' Mr. A. Trollope (49) worked there as a fish merchant. Seven Southerden men worked the boats with only nineteen-year-old Thomas Morris representing other local families. As hard as the life of the fisherman was, by the first year of the new century there had been an increase to nine Southerden family members pursuing the valuable catch while the widowed Emily Southerden (57) described herself as a, *'...keddle-net fishing employer'*; the younger Agnes Cooper Southerden (38) declared a, *'...sharehold in the keddle-net fishing business'*. Surprisingly, two 'outsiders', William Henry Wingett (51) and John Booth (44) were also working the keddle net fishery in 1901.

Keddle net fishing (known variously as 'kettle-net' or even 'keddell-net' in Essex) is a beach-based method of fishing that has for centuries been suited to the strong currents off the coast of Camber and Rye. The extensive and shallow Rye Bay is sheltered from all but southerly gales and fish tend to follow the eastward flow of the rising tide. The 'keddle' net itself was about one hundred yards long by four feet wide and was attached to a line of vertical wooden poles stretching out at right angles from the shore and secured at both foot and surface. For the method to succeed, two or more nets would converge with the wide open end towards the beach – tide and panic drove the fish into the trap-like 'purse-end' of the net where they were effectively held until the tide ebbed when the fishermen could remove their catch.

This traditional method of fishing was, as has been shown, still quite popular at the end of the nineteenth century, and had even expanded by the onset of the 1911 census. Two widowed Southerden women, Emily (67) and Agnes Cooper Southerden (48), still shared control of the family keddle net fishing business; father and son, John (65) and John Willie Southerden, worked the keddle nets, while ten more Southerden men fished the area. William Henry Wingett, now 61, still worked the nets and 51-year-old Fred Austen appears to be new to the Jury's Gap fishery. In later years, on 17th November 1930, keddle-netting was mentioned in Parliament by the Minister of Agriculture, "...*sixty-six persons are engaged in keddle net fishing on the south-east coast as a part-time occupation*[16]...", and is still pursued in the present day. Nowadays, keddle net regulations are strictly imposed by the Rother District Council (under the auspices of the Inshore Fisheries & Conservation Authority, Sussex) and keddle net 'stands' are licensed by the council.

THE ROYAL MILITARY CANAL – 'MR. PITT'S DITCH'

Years after the inning of Romney Marsh, a strange thing happened to the area – it was turned into an island. This was not an intended consequence but was incidental to a solution adopted in the face of the threat of invasion in 1804. Britain had been at war with revolutionary France from 1793 until 1802 when the Treaty of Amiens brought hostilities to a temporary halt. In May 1803 the conflict resumed and this is generally regarded as the start of the Napoleonic Wars, as this was the point at which Napoléon Bonaparte seized supreme power in France. By 1804 Napoléon, intending to remove the British thorn from his side, had amassed a huge army of invasion (130,000) replete with the necessary flotilla of boats (2,000) in Channel ports such as Boulogne, opposite Dover and Folkestone. Many ideas were propounded in respect of solving the French threat but the one adopted was that of Lieutenant Colonel John Brown who proposed the construction of a military canal across Romney Marsh between the chalk cliffs of Folkestone in the east, where there was a military barracks at Shorncliffe, and towards the towering cliffs of Hastings in the west where the River Rother would provide an additional natural barrier. The putative nineteen mile long canal was to be just over sixty feet wide and almost ten feet deep, though these dimensions were almost halved in places on account of the pressures of time and cost. On the landward side of the proposed canal that was to be constructed in angled segments, would be a low rampart or 'fire-step' whose military installations would be supplied by a military road that was hidden from plain sight of the enemy by an earthen bank. Thus each section of canal would be protected by cannon whose enfilading fire could supposedly prevent any attempted crossing of the canal line.

The canal itself was never intended to be the sole method of holding at bay any potential invader, at least not one as resourceful as Napoléon Bonaparte. As ever, the first line of defence would always be the fleet – the Royal Navy defeated Napoléon on the high seas and subsequently 'strangled' French trade, thus rendering superfluous the implementation of the second and third lines of defence whose construction was then well under way. The second line of defence, flooding the Marsh, had long been considered an adequate barrier against any invasion – the weakness of the idea was that the full flooding of the entire marsh would, by itself, take too long. The third line of defence was to be the expensive engineering project of the Royal Military Canal and the 'early warning observation' furnished by a coastal chain of Martello[17] Towers.

In order to bring onside the most influential local landowners, the Prime Minister himself, William Pitt the Younger, invited all to a meeting in Dymchurch during September 1804. There he convincingly put forward a plan to defend the country that would incidentally benefit the agricultural community of the Marsh, as the proposed canal could offer a major new drainage system for the perennial winter floods while providing a reservoir for summer irrigation. Recognising a good offer, the local landowners assented – ironically, in the long term, drainage control was to become the major function of the canal. Thus was born the irreverent local name for the canal project, '...*Mr Pitt's Ditch*'.

Commenced at the end of October 1804, construction was carried out by a mixture of civilian 'navvies' who worked on excavating the canal bed, and skilled military men who worked on the ramparts and artillery strong-points. Slowed by floods and the extreme winter conditions that prevailed on the Marsh, progress was initially limited and this was exacerbated by further drains on money and labour. An additional section saw the canal extended from the River Rother to the Pett Levels, just east of Hastings, increasing the overall length to twenty-eight miles. The soil excavated from the line of the canal bed was piled on the landward side to create the parapet that would enable garrison troops to move in both directions while protected from enemy fire. By 1809, after 4½ years, the Royal Military Canal had been completed although, interestingly, the requisite artillery was not available until the summer of 1812; consequently, the defensive line was obsolete prior to its completion. This was compounded by the fact that Admiral Lord Nelson had defeated the Franco-Spanish fleet at Trafalgar on 21st October 1805, so confirming British dominance of the seas, especially the Channel and its approaches.

Coincidentally, in the same year as Trafalgar, work also started on the chain of defensive forts, Martello Towers, along the south and south-east coast of England. However, it was not until 1808 that Romney Marsh technically became an island when the completion of Iden Lock linked the Military Canal to the Rivers Rother and Brede. The overall project reached its completion in April 1809, late but surprisingly just about on price.

In order to accommodate the troops that were to garrison the Military Canal, guard houses, familiarly known as Station Houses, were built at every bridge. Happily for the country at large, neither canal nor its limited garrison were ever called upon to stand against invasion, though the troops were occasionally required to confound the local smuggling fraternity. Ill-regarded and poorly paid, it was not unknown for soldiers of the garrison to accept illicit payment for their 'co-operation' in smuggling operations.

In 1807 the hard-pressed government, eager to recoup some of the huge outlay incurred by the defence works, made the canal available via tolls to commercial traffic. During the years following the conclusion of the wars against the 'Little Emperor', an attempt was made to run a regular barge service between Hythe and Rye, though it did little to offset the canal's ongoing costs. Soon after Jack Hickman's

'Mr. Pitt's Ditch' in 2010

birth in the 1890s, the Royal Military Canal fell into disuse and lay neglected and derelict, except for the Hythe section that was converted into ornamental waters replete with pleasure boating. However, the canal has always provided vital control of winter floodwaters on the marsh and offered irrigation during summer drought. It was a far cry from its original defensive function.

Nevertheless, irrespective of whether or not the Royal Military Canal served its function or was value for the massive expenditure, it became a well-established part of the landscape into which members of the Hickman family as far back as Jack's grandfather, Henry Hickman, were born and grew up.

RYE GOLF LINKS, THE CLUB & THE CAMBER TRAMWAY

Golf was an increasingly popular though necessarily rather elitist sport at the turn of the nineteenth and twentieth Centuries. The club nearest Rye was located as far away as Littlestone, just to the north of Dungeness and the Littlestone Club was at that time not taking on new playing members. The idea was put forward locally that the construction of a new course would benefit both local aficionados of the game and might well attract visitors from far and wide. During the second half of the nineteenth Century, day-trips and longer holidays at the coast had been popularised and facilitated by the development of more accessible rail travel. The South Eastern Railway (SER)

ran through Rye and across the edge of Romney Marsh, crossing the River Rother by the Monkbretton Bridge, so when a new golf course became more than just a pipe-dream, the potential was there to make the club into a real attraction. It was at the end of November 1893 that a formal meeting was held in Rye Town at the George Hotel (possibly in the Benson Room of the old coaching inn of which William Cowtan was then landlord) and those present agreed to proceed with the plans for a new, more local, golf course and that the sandy soil and turf around Camber would lend themselves perfectly to the classic 'links'-type golf course. The name Camber long preceded the development of the village, referring originally to the haven located just to the east of the estuary of the River Rother. Naturally enough the village grew around a cluster of fishermen's dwellings nestling at the waterside where their boats were relatively safe from the weather. However, it was the decision taken in the George Hotel that proved to be the real growth catalyst for the village – the golf links, in turn, temporarily depended on the new 'Royal William' hotel (1894) and the subsequent decisions to develop the course (1895) and to improve access from Rye town via the new tramway (1895) – all encouraged Camber village to expand. What began as an easier way for golfers to transport their gear, would also be found to the liking and convenience of excursionists, fishermen and the public in general.

The original golf links was constructed during the winter of 1893-94, so rapidly that the course could be formally opened on Monday, 5th February 1894 and celebrated by an initial competition – testimony to the assiduous work of the construction committee's chairman, the Reverend John Lockington Bates who incidentally spent fifty-seven years as Rector of Iden. Rye Golf Club itself thus dates from 1894 and it is surprising to consider that, while in 2014 some long-standing and distinguished clubs are still reluctant to admit female members, Rye enrolled thirty-two ladies as early as 1894! Initially there was not even a temporary clubhouse until late 1894, so in the meantime the recently-opened and grandly-named 'Royal William' hotel itself little more than a solid, wooden construction, offered its facilities to golfers. Rye members subsequently enjoyed the facilities of a new, 'temporary' clubhouse that became part of the club buildings still employed today. On the playing front, the original links was superseded in 1895 by an eighteen-hole course laid out by the club's first captain and later secretary, 25-year-old Mr. Harry Colt – his first course design, at such a tender age, was remarkable.

Proximity to the well-established South Eastern Railway accounts for the club's attraction beyond Kent and Sussex, reaching even the hallowed corridors of government and justice in the capital. Yet this burgeoning popularity came about almost in spite of poor local access from Rye station to the golf course – many players, struggling with their gear, had to walk the two miles to Camber, pleasant in spring and summer but less so in winter. Few then owned automobiles and those who did found the road to Camber little more than a slippery track and had involved, back in 1890, passing two tollgates. So the construction of the 1¾ miles of narrow-gauge (three feet) track that constituted the Rye and Camber Tramway was completed in time for a grand opening on Saturday, 15th July 1895. From then, both local and visiting players could reach the Golf Links Station at Camber in less than ten

Rye & Camber Steam-hauled Tramway

minutes and at the cost of just sixpence for a first-class seat on the steam-hauled tram. The general public was quick to realise that the tramway would open up access to the long beaches from the Rother Estuary eastwards towards Dungeness, thus the spur extending from Rye was initially successful enough to make a profit. However, developments in transport saw the popularity of the tramway wane as that of the motor car soared during the 1920s.

Meantime, the club and the course forged ahead. By 1905 membership had all but reached five hundred and the clubhouse was expanded in order to accommodate those increasing numbers. Harry Colt's eighteen-hole links underwent partial redesign in 1907 and the overall yardage of the course was subsequently increased.

The extension of the track to a new terminus at Camber Sands in 1908 encouraged use of the tramway by beachgoers as well as golfers; residents of Rye Harbour on the west bank of the River Rother also used the line as it was quicker to reach Rye Town by crossing the water by ferry and taking the tramway. In many respects, the first twenty years of the twentieth century witnessed the height of the success of the Rye and Camber Tramway. Thereafter decline was at first gradual, then more clearly noticeable. The line actually lasted until the Second World War when it was put to military use following its official requisition in 1939 by the Admiralty and was much utilised for the transportation of parts for the vital Pipe Line under the Ocean (PLUTO) project that would supply petrol to the advancing Allied troops following the D-Day landings in France. However, war took such toll of the line the advent of peace found it so dilapidated that it never re-opened thereafter; the track was subsequently dismantled and the company quietly wound up.

To bring the golf club and its links to

Clubhouse, Rye G.C. in 2010

life, it is vital to examine the evidence that remains of the characters who trod the fairways and worked the club. We have already encountered the Rector of Iden, the Reverend J.L. Bates, without whose inspirational leadership the golf course project might never have reached such impressive fruition. Of equal importance was the club's principal designer, first captain and subsequent secretary, Harry Colt, who went on to forge an ever stronger reputation in the emerging field of golf course construction. Among the early locals who looked to the Rye links for their golfing education would likely have been Frank Hickman and his younger brother, Jack. When the course was opened in 1895, Frank was just thirteen, while Jack was still a toddler of four – both were destined to become golf professionals after their Great War service in the Royal Field Artillery.

Although the course had its own 'temporary' clubhouse by 1901, the '*Royal William*' had long provided many people with refreshment after golf or after a day at the sea, initially as the '*Royal William Inn*' (as run by John Burt in April 1891) or as the '*Royal William Hotel*' run by Frederick Fielder in March 1901. Across the road from the '*Old Billy*', in the golf clubhouse the club steward was 39-year-old Richard Brown of Teynham in Kent, who lived with his wife Rebecca and four-year-old niece Evelyn Mariner in the Golf House. Nearby, in one of the Coast Guard Cottages (not the ones at Jury's Gap) that stood on land owned

by the Rye Golf Club, lived 45-year-old green-keeper Charles Ashment who had been born in the West Indies and whose young son, Alfred (14), born in the Mediterranean on the sunny island of Malta, was one of the club caddies. Next door to Charles Ashment lived thirty-eight-year-old William R. Lonie with his wife and four children. Described as a club-maker and ball-maker, William was born at the home of golf, St. Andrews in Fife, Scotland and moved south to pursue his chosen profession, initially in Cambridgeshire then on the south coast at Rye. By 1911, William would be resident professional at East Mersea in Essex and his twenty-year-old son, John Lonie, would himself be a golf professional at the Bromley and Beckenham Course just outside London. As William Lonie's second daughter, Edith, was born in Rye in 1897, it is quite possible that William was actually Rye Golf Club's first professional. Less directly connected to the club's accommodation was another of the young caddies at Rye, a Welsh lad, fifteen-year-old Frederick Sawyer who was the son of Alfred Sawyer, one of the commissioned boatmen that lived and worked at Jury's Gap Coast Guard Station immediately to the east of Broomhill hamlet.

At the time of the 1901 census, Jack Hickman was still recorded as a nine-year-old scholar, while his nineteen-year-old brother Frank was recorded as an agricultural labourer. It is impossible to know how or why the two Hickman lads took up golf – maybe the prospect of walking the marshes for years was singularly unattractive or maybe the reason was much simpler. The proximity of the new golf links and the opportunity of trying the 'new' game was more than the two lads could resist! Perhaps Frank was drawn to learning the game and Jack wanted to emulate his older brother who, by 1911 was married and earning his living as a professional golfer in Ramsgate, Kent. In 1911, Jack was still living with his widowed father[18], Henry, in Broomhill, and was a young but skilled carpenter and had earned the title 'golf-club maker' – most golf-clubs at that time were hickory-shafted and making a golf club demanded many of the skills of the carpenter. Why had Jack opted for carpentry? At the turn on the century, skills such as carpentry, plumbing, building and decorating were highly valued and recognised as setting a man above the 'labouring' classes – the population was rising so demand for the trades was high, thus work was regular and relatively well-rewarded. Census returns reveal that carpentry was not a Hickman family occupation but there was no shortage of carpenters among the Palmer family into which Jack Hickman would eventually marry in 1915. His future father-in-law, William Palmer, who was born in Rye but later moved to Plumstead by way of Whitstable, was a skilled carpenter and it is almost certain that young Jack knew Mr. Palmer before he and his family left the Camber

area. William Palmer's father-in-law, Edwin Paine of Iden was also a qualified carpenter, as was his own eldest son, Bill Palmer. One thing may be taken as a given – Jack Hickman had qualified as a carpenter prior to adapting his skills to the demands of crafting golf-clubs; in fact, according to the 1911 Census the Hickmans had a twenty-five-year-old carpenter, Samuel Pearce from Portland, Dorset, boarding with them. Doubtlessly, he passed on many useful tips to young Jack. Again, it is fair to assume that at that time Jack was also honing his skills as a golfer on the Rye links at Camber. His first golf job away from the Rye area would, as will be seen, require Jack to cross the Channel.

YOUNG JACK – CHILDHOOD AND SCHOOLDAYS

The fact that in the 1871 Census twenty-seven-year-old Isabella Bean Hickman, wife of John Bean Hickman and so Jack's aunt by marriage, was described as the 'village schoolmistress', suggests that there was already at that time some form of education available in East Guldeford. However, according to information in the East Sussex Record Office, the first East Guldeford school house was the Church of England National School and was built in 1879 on land bought from Mr. William Courtenay Morland of Lamberhurst, Kent. It opened as a mixed entry school in April 1880, catering for about seventy children in its heyday. The school subsequently closed at the

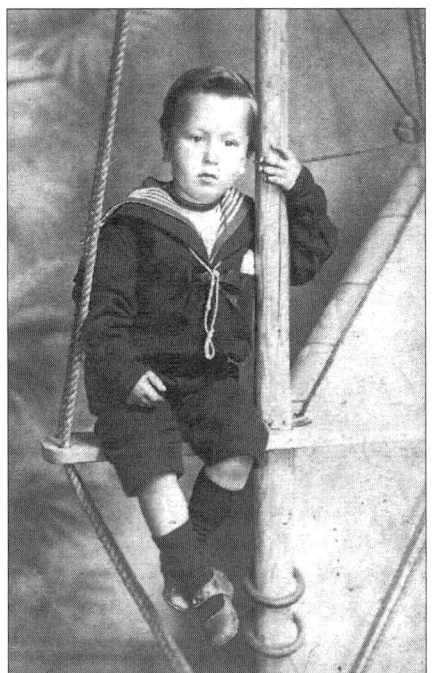

Pre-school Jack in the sailor suit so popular at that time

School. The schoolhouse at Broomhill dated back to at least 1881 when the schoolmistress was Miss Rhoda A. Moffet from West Looe in Cornwall. Jack was attending school by the age of six, a fact that is confirmed by a piece of family evidence, a picture postcard of his class sent to his older sister Julia when she was staying in Kilmarnock, Scotland on 18th November 1897. It appears that the school photograph was taken by professional photographer, C.T. Saunter of Foord Road, Folkestone as part of the celebrations in respect of Queen Victoria's Diamond Jubilee (1837-1897). The photo shows fifty-two children and three adults; this probably represents the whole school population apart maybe from the odd absentee and possibly includes twenty-six-year-old Miss Anna M. Southerden, daughter of Daniel Southerden of Broomhill. Jack (pictured on page 58), then six years old, appears two rows from the back and four children in from the teacher on the left – on the original class photo he is denoted by an ink-spot on his head and ink-spots on each of his white collars, somewhat spoiling the image of his immaculate 'Sunday best'. Four years later, the school population was probably about the same as in the 1897 photo and the National Census of 1901 allows the broad extraction of Jack's possible school contemporaries. It seems likely that one of Jack's teachers was Miss Southerden whose brother, William Daniel Southerden, older by

start of August 1923 when there were only eleven children on the roll at the beginning of the school year. After 1926 the school room took on a new role as the village hall, financed by a local levy of 1/4d per acre. Today, the building exists as a private property, 'The Old School House', on the A259. The 1891 Census reveals that there had lived in the village a schoolmistress and an assistant schoolmistress, while in 1901 there was both a schoolmistress and a private tutor or governess.

Although Jack Hickman's family came from East Guldeford, Jack himself was born in Broomhill and consequently attended the Broomhill and Camber

Camber School photo, 1897: Queen Victoria's Diamond Jubilee. Young Jack is second row from the back, fourth pupil from the left.

Jack in 1897: detail from his school photograph.

three years, would serve in the Great War with 25th Battalion, the Middlesex Regiment and would survive the conflict. The youngsters who were then of an age similar to Jack were Bessie James (6 years), Albert Apps (7), Florence Croft (8), George Brann, William C. Dyer, Richard Chard and Lilian Howells (all 9), Alfred Southerden, Gertrude Godfrey and Alice Sawyer (all 10 years), James Marshall and Arthur George, Kate Sawyer and Annie Howells (all 11), John Southerden, Harry Southerden and Hilda James (all 12), Louie Southerden, Ellen Marshall, Catherine Hickman and Charles Sawyer (all 13) and finally John W. Southerden (14). From among these would later emerge several tragic tales from the war years and, despite the fact that Jack had left his schooldays behind him by about 1905, the stories merit their recounting.

William Daniel Southerden, son of Daniel and Anna Southerden, and a longshore fisherman in the family business, was born in Camber about 1877. His younger sister was Anna M. Southerden, schoolteacher at Jack's old school; most schools would have reverberated with an almost jingoistic fervour for the war but Anna must have spent from 1916 to the end of 1918 in a state of near dread for what might happen to her brother. William enlisted on 17th November 1915 and duly joined his unit, 25th (Service) Battalion, the Middlesex Regiment, as 49331 Private W.D. Southerden. He was soon adjudged medically fit for garrison duty only but in October 1916 he was posted with his unit to Hong Kong, not returning to England until 14th February 1919. While his battalion's task was one of garrisoning the outposts of Empire in order to release better trained units for front-line service elsewhere, William would have been at risk as much from tropical disease as from enemy action but at risk nevertheless. On his return to Blighty in 1919, his unit had been due to serve in Siberia against the Bolshevik Red Army but a medical board at Netley Hospital, near Southampton, adjudged the lad unfit for further military service on account of general debility and badly deformed feet. He was finally discharged on 9th May 1919. Three of Anna's cousins also served in the military – Harry Southerden (born in 1889 and thus a direct school contemporary of Jack's) was a Lance-Bombardier in 142nd Heavy Battery of the Royal Garrison Artillery and fought in France and Flanders; cousins Charles Southerden

(born in 1883) and his younger brother Frederick Southerden (born in 1885) both previously attended Camber & Broomhill School. During the Great War, Charles served with 54th Battery, 39th Brigade of the Royal Field Artillery in 1st Division and survived the conflict.

Péronne CCE: Headstone of Driver Frederick Southerden, killed in action on 1st December 1917 at the age of 33. He was related to the 'fishing' Southerdens.

Frederick Southerden, however, served with 'D' (Heavy) Battery, 63rd Brigade, Royal Field Artillery, part of 12th 'Eastern' Division, fighting on the Somme in 1916 and at Arras in the spring of 1917 but was killed in action on 1st December 1917 near Péronne (where he was buried) when the Germans made a massive counter-attack during the Battle of Cambrai. One of Frederick's brigade officers, Lieutenant Samuel Wallace of 'C' Battery, was awarded the Victoria Cross during the Cambrai[20] actions near Gonnelieu.

At least three of Jack Hickman's school contemporaries lost brothers to the war; Ellen and James Marshall, who were slightly older than Jack but whom he would have known in the playground, lost their younger brother, Robert, in France in October 1915. Very early in the war, perhaps even prior to hostilities, Robert Marshall, who had been born at Broomhill Farm, enlisted at the Rye Drill Hall in 1/5th 'Cinque Ports' Battalion, a Territorial Force unit of the Royal Sussex Regiment. He was initially posted to France with his battalion that in February of 1915 joined 2nd Brigade of the highly-regarded 1st Division; the battalion's role changed in August of that year when it was assigned pioneer duties in 48th '1st South Midland' Division. Robert's was not the 'glorious' battlefield death of *'Boys' Own'* stories but a painful death from one of the many virulent diseases rife in the trenches of France. He contracted enteric fever and, though hospitalised, he died on 10th October 1915 at the tender age of twenty and lies buried in the huge British military cemetery at Etaples, close to the hospital where he was treated. Robert is commemorated on Rye Harbour War Memorial and on the Camber War Memorial.

Another of Jack's classmates of 1901, George Brann, became the brother-in-law of Joe Miller when the latter married George's sister Kate Brann. 21-year-old Joe, then an agricultural labourer, enlisted in Newhaven on 10th November 1914 and reached the rank of bombardier in 45th Siege Battery of the Royal Garrison Artillery. He served with the British Expeditionary Force in France from 31st August 1915. Joe's was one of the somewhat happier stories as he managed to survive the war years.

The final tale, that of 28127, Private Henry Charles Leeds George, held no such pleasant ending. Born at Offens Farm, East Guldeford in 1885 or 1886, Henry was five years older than brother Arthur Leeds[21] George who was another direct contemporary of Jack Hickman. Henry initially joined the 3/Royal Sussex Regiment but was transferred to 'B' Company of the 8th Battalion, the East Surrey Regiment, a 'Kitchener' New Army unit. Henry's division, 18th 'Eastern', was heavily involved in six of the major engagements of the Somme Offensive in 1916 – the Battle of Albert from 1st to 8th July; the Battle of Bazentin Ridge (including the Capture of Trônes Wood on 14th July) from 14th to 17th July; the Battle of Thiepval Ridge from 26th to 28th September; the Battle of the Ancre Heights from 1st to 5th October and from 17th October to 11th November, including the Capture of the Schwaben Redoubt by (Henry's) 55th Brigade on 30th September to 5th October and the Capture of Regina Trench on 21st October; and finally the Battle of the Ancre from 13th to 18th November.

Ironically, Henry survived until the day after the official 'end' of the Somme offensive, when he was killed in action, aged thirty, on 19th November 1916 in the follow-up to the Battle of the Ancre. He is commemorated on the Thiepval Memorial to the Missing and, closer to home, on the East Guldeford War Memorial.

By 1911, some considerable time after Jack had left school and qualified as a carpenter, 29-year-old Miss Mary Jane Booker had been appointed head-teacher at his old school and she lived in the School House, Broomhill where her older sister Louisa (40) worked as her housekeeper. The Census of 1911 reveals that in Camber/Broomhill parish there also lived two young teachers who were just learning their profession – Henry Martyn, 19-year-old son of the Coast Guard Chief Officer at Jury's Gap Coastguard Station and 21-year-old Gladys Dean who was boarding with the Brann family at Broomhill Farm.

1 The two lads were not the couple's only children – Elizabeth was born in Lydd, Kent in 1872 and their first son, Loftus W.B. Hickman, who was eight months in 1881 appears to have died between 1881 and 1891.

2 Reclamation of sea marshes by embankment and drainage.

3 The parishes were Beckley, Brede, East Guldeford, Icklesham, Iden, Northiam, Peasmarsh, Playden, Rye, Winchelsea St. Thomas and Broomhill [then written as 'Bromhill'].

4 Many small, localised railway companies were created in the 1840s but most disappeared through lack of finance or were soon absorbed by larger, stronger companies.

5 'Navvy' was short for 'Inland Navigator', the name originally used for labourers who worked on the construction of the canals or inland navigation at the turn of the eighteenth and nineteenth centuries. Most navvies worked hard, played hard and drank hard, so their local presence was not exactly welcome. Without them, however, the canals and railways would not have taken shape so quickly.

6 Equivalent value today is roughly half a million pounds!

7 The RMC was constructed during the Napoleonic Wars in the early nineteenth century.

8 Some sources put the date of construction at 1318.

9 Only the lines of the moat are clearly visible today.

10 The present-day All Saints Church, much restored over the years, still has a twelfth-century castellated bell tower. Apart from the longevity of the building, its rectors merit a mention in the 'Guinness Book of Records'; across 117 years from 1807 to 1924 All Saints had but two rectors.

11 Henry's birthplace is given as East Guldeford, though the family was then still resident in Iden.

12 In pre-refrigeration days, meat and fish could be preserved by salting, smoking, air-drying or pickling.

13 The most notable and far-reaching in its effects was the Great Plague (often called the Black Death) during the 14th century. In summer, malaria-carrying mosquitoes infested the marshes.

14 Over many years of service, eighteen crew members from the station have paid the ultimate price of their selfless work and crew have earned three gold medals and six silver medals in recognition of their bravery.

15 The name Twosign is probably an English corruption of the French name, 'Toussaint'.

16 Source: 'Hansard', volume 245, c.16.

17 Named after the location of the first such defensive fort at Mortella on Corsica.

18 Jack's mother Naomi died in 1909.

19 Equivalent to about seven new pence today.

20 On the first day of the Tank Attack at Cambrai, 20th November 1917, Wallace kept his battery's guns firing although only five of the gunners remained alive.

21 All the siblings had the same given name preceding the family surname.

CHAPTER TWO

1905-1914: CALLOW YOUTH TO MANHOOD

BORN INTO A CHANGING WORLD

Having been born in May 1891, the youngest of six boys and three girls, Jack Hickman was not recorded on the 1891 Census of England that had been carried out in early April of that year. By the time his name appeared on the next survey in 1901, Queen Victoria's Diamond Jubilee had come and gone in 1897 while the queen's remarkable reign had itself closed on 22 January 1901 on the Isle of Wight. Present by the elderly Queen's bedside were two of Victoria's most privileged and influential relatives, whose lives and decisions would eventually have a grave bearing upon Jack, his broadening family and upon almost every family in Britain, her Empire and much of the known world. With his mother at Osborne House was Albert Edward, the Prince of Wales, soon to inherit the Crown as King Edward VII; in that same room was Edward's nephew and Queen Victoria's eldest grandson, Kaiser Wilhelm II of Germany – together, the two men would later help lift the last of the Hanoverians into her coffin.

More significantly for Europe, the new king had a strong interest in foreign policy and would take a leading role in fostering good relations with France that would pave the way for the Anglo-French 'Entente Cordiale' of 1904. Though not a formal alliance, the Entente would fatefully influence British policy in those vital summer weeks of 1914 between the assassination in Sarajevo of the Austrian Habsburg[1] Archduke, Franz Ferdinand, and the outbreak of the Great War. Edward's nephew 'Willie' harboured grandiose ambitions for his young German state and his intention personally to bring those hopes to

fruition had been clearly evidenced in 1890 when the inexperienced monarch decided to dismiss the long-time German Chancellor, Otto von Bismarck, whose policy had done much to maintain the peace of Europe for almost twenty years. As the two royals stood at Queen Victoria's bedside, the diplomatic routes of their respective governments had many a mile to cover and many a twist and turn to negotiate – King Edward would not survive to witness the catastrophe of war against a nephew whose ambition nor his judgement he trusted.

In April 1901 the new king's inherited Boer War still had a year to run, and the

British army in its colonial policeman role was still suffering in the heat of South Africa. It was learning little that would be of use in the struggles yet to come in the fields of France and Flanders. One revolutionary weapon that might have been better employed by the British army in South Africa, the machine gun, had a forerunner in the 1862 hand-cranked, multi-barrelled Gatling gun, though the first true, automatic machine-gun was the Maxim-Gun, invented by Hiram Maxim in the 1880's. Its water-cooled, recoil-operated firing mechanism could deliver up to 600 rounds per minute. At its best against massed enemy ranks, the Maxim[2] performed with very limited success against the Boers – consequently, the machine gun was regarded more as a novelty than a battle-changer in 1914.

Again, in 1901, two other inventions that would affect Jack Hickman's future were at differing levels of development. On the ground, horse-drawn carriages were in but the early stages of giving way to 'horseless' carriages that, in their turn would be superseded by the purpose-built, *'motorwagen'* designed by the likes of Karl Benz (1888), Gottlieb Daimler (1889) and Wilhelm Maybach (1888). The internal combustion engine notwithstanding, in 1915 Jack Hickman would find himself as a driver in the Royal Field Artillery, controlling a team of four horses and it would be in this capacity that he would be gravely wounded on the Somme in March 1918. In the skies above the Western Front, dogfights

would be fought between fighter aircraft and cities on both sides of the conflict would be bombed and civilians would be killed. Yet in 1901 powered, heavier-than-air flight was considered the stuff of dreamers; wind-dependant kites and hot air balloons had been around for many years and dirigibles had been in existence since the mid-19th century, initially steam-powered from 1852 and electrically-powered from 1884, though neither to great effect. 1900 saw Count Graf von Zeppelin produce the first rigid airship and thus give Germany a valuable lead in the air that would in the Great War translate into the first effective bombing raids on England. Mechanical flight – sustained, heavier-than-air flight or aircraft as we now understand the idea – was still a dream in 1901 and remained so until December 1903 when the Wright brothers achieved the first such verified flight at Kitty Hawk in North Carolina in the USA. It would, however, take until the time of the 1911 Census before Britain officially created the Royal Flying Corps (ironically the Royal Naval Air Service had its own airfield before the RFC was set up) and, certain visionaries apart, the potential of air power would be recognised only with the passage of time.

That Jack was growing up in a rapidly changing world was clearly reflected in the social, economic and political position of women in society. Women's Emancipation was already a movement and phrase that was evoking extreme reactions. In 1892, the year following

Jack Hickman's birth, a Suffrage Bill that would have changed the status of women was put before the House of Commons but, predictably, it failed – ironically, the 1901 Census of England and Wales indicated that there were one million more women than men in the country. Closer to what would prove to be Jack's later choice of profession, in 1893 the Women's Golf Union was created. In much the same vein, Rye Golf Club where Jack would learn the game opened in 1894, admitted female members the same year and the tramway to link Camber to the South Eastern Railway and the rest of the country opened in 1895.

Jack's parents had, in 1901, moved the family home a short distance westwards along the coast to 'The Lodge' in Camber hamlet where Jack was the youngest of four Hickmans still living at home. Nineteen-year-old Frank Hickman was earning a living as an agricultural labourer but had already, no doubt, turned his thoughts towards the game of golf that would later provide his lifetime's profession; sixteen-year-old Joe Hickman, not so long out of the classroom, was also working the Marsh; thirteen-year-old Catherine and nine-year-old Jack were both still at school. Their father, Henry Hickman, was still earning a hard living as a shepherd, though possibly not as a looker – Henry was by then fifty-eight and the life of the Romney Marsh looker was a harsh one. Furthermore, fewer lookers were necessary as agriculture was adapting to the changing demands of the world around it.

Jack's birth in May 1891 coincided with Salisbury's Education Act (5th August 1891) that provided free elementary schooling and two years later, in 1893, the school leaving age was raised from ten to eleven. Jack was but a toddler when the Marquess of Salisbury resigned in August 1892 and the 'Grand Old Man', William Ewart Gladstone, headed his fourth and final ministry (1892-1894). By the time Jack's name appeared on the 1901 census return, the Marquess of Salisbury was again prime minister and Gladstone, at the age of eighty-eight, had died and been buried in Westminster Abbey.

Having left his schooldays at Broomhill and Camber School behind him in about 1905, Jack broke with the tradition of his close family and chose not to work the land but to commit his immediate future as a carpenter's apprentice – it was a decision that would shape not just his near future but his entire life. There is precious little evidence regarding this period of Jack's young life but it is possible to identify trends and, with the aid of a little supposition, offer a plausible scenario.

It is safe to assume that by 1905, with the Rye Golf Club now well established, Jack's brother Frank (his elder by almost ten years) was already steeped in the popular game and maybe encouraging young Jack to swing a club on the nearby links. The most likely way for youngsters to become involved in golf was to offer their services as caddies – the magic of the game certainly soon struck both

Frank and Jack. Jack soon adapted his carpentry skills to the game he was growing to love, so much so that by the time of the 1911 Census, nineteen-year-old Jack was officially described as a 'golf club maker' – it was to last most of his lifetime. According to the census return for 1911, another young carpenter, Samuel Pearce (25) of Portland, Dorset, was lodging with the Hickmans in Camber. It is also possible that learning the skills of carpentry may have brought Jack into closer proximity to the family of a certain Miss Ada Mary Palmer, who would become Jack's wife in 1915. Ada's father, William Palmer, was also a fully-qualified carpenter and, in addition, he had been born in Rye in 1870 and had

'The K.NUTS': Jack, far left, and the Palmer brothers in front of a tipi-style tent.

worked locally until soon after Jack's birth when the Palmers moved north to Plumstead, near Woolwich Arsenal. What is more, William Palmer's father-in-law, Edwin Paine, was born in nearby Iden and also worked as a qualified carpenter. As much as these 'links' may actually be mere speculation, it is also possible that some may bear elements of the truth and it would be fitting if they did! There is no evidence that Jack was ever employed at Rye Golf Club but it is quite apparent that the young man learned the game on its sandy turf. There is conclusive evidence that Jack knew Ada's family well, even after they moved to Plumstead – the above photograph shows Jack and Ada's three brothers relaxing in front of a tipi-style tent. In the picture, Jack Hickman is on the far left of the front row, easily identifiable as the only lad wearing a jacket and tie; Roy Palmer is second from the right on the front row; Will Palmer is on Roy's immediate left and Jack Palmer is seated next to Jack Hickman. All four of the friends were to serve in the British Army during the Great War and only Jack Hickman would survive its effects. This group of friends, like so many other 'dashing' young men of the period, styled themselves *'The K.NUTS'* – note the chalk-written title for the group photograph. The slightly self-mocking term dates from 1911 and refers to a young dandy, a smart, man-about-town. The term was made famous in a music-hall song popularised by Basil Hallam

Detail of 'The K.NUTS': Jack and the Palmer brothers

(who was later to be killed in 1916 in his real name of Captain B.H. Radford of the Royal Flying Corps),

'...I'm Gilbert the Filbert, the Colonel of the K'nuts'.

In truth, it was just young men drawing attention to themselves and indulging in high spirits – much the same occurs in every generation.

TO GUERNSEY AND PROFESSIONAL GOLF

However, it was golf, rather than war that was responsible for Jack Hickman leaving Camber, Broomhill and his familiar, quiet corner of East Sussex. How he came to notice the availability of a job on the beautiful Channel Island of Guernsey was never recorded but he successfully applied for and took up

the post of assistant golf professional at Royal Guernsey Golf Club at L'Ancresse

Royal Guernsey Golf Club emblem

in the very north of the small island. This momentous change in his life almost certainly occurred during the second half of 1911 as he does not appear on the 1911 Census for Guernsey (CI); he would have crossed to the Channel Islands by ship as there was then no alternative, probably sailing from Southampton or Weymouth. As a young man just making his way in the world, Jack would have needed to find rented accommodation on the island and there is evidence that he was taken in by a family in Vale, a large parish[3] in the north-west of Guernsey. He must have been made to feel very welcome at his first lodging as it is the only one recorded for Jack's four-year stay on the island, a stay cut short by the demands of the Great War. However, his new adventure must have been full of mixed emotion for the young man – he was on a beautiful Channel Island for the first time, there to play golf to a high standard on a picturesque links course on L'Ancresse Common. Yet in only 1909 Jack had lost his mother, Naomi Hickman, who died at the age of sixty-four years. She was buried in the parish churchyard of St. Mary's at East Guldeford, close to the homestead where she had spent so much of her family life.

Jack Hickman's 'landlord' on the island was himself an 'incomer' who had married a Guernsey woman. Charles Henry Shipton was born in Southampton in about 1863. His father John had been born about 1830 in Suffolk and had earned his living as a gardener while his mother, Ellen, had been born in Somerset in about 1835. It appears that between 1864 and 1865 the family moved to Guernsey where, given John Shipton's line of work, employment was relatively easy to find. Over the ensuing six years Charles was joined by three sisters – in 1865 Ellen was born, in 1867 Emma and finally in 1870 Amy; all three girls were born in St. Peter Port, Guernsey. However, what seems to have been a happy little family was

devastated over the following ten years. It is not known what accidents or illnesses befell the threesome but by the time of the 1881 Channel Islands Census, John Shipton and two of his three daughters had died, leaving a grieving widow, Ellen Shipton, to raise Charles and younger sister, Emma. In 1881, Mrs. Shipton was living in St. Peter Port at 'Les Canichers' and earning a meagre living as a cook; Charles was seventeen and had already started showing promise as a gardener, while his thirteen-year-old sister Emma was still at school. Within four years, Charles was already making his own way on Guernsey when he married a twenty-four-year-old local girl, Emily (Rachel Alice). By 1891, Charles was earning an independent living as a gardener and the couple had made their home near Bordeaux Harbour in Vale – that no children were mentioned in the census hides another potential family tragedy that does not become apparent until the 1911 Channel Islands Census when the format of the returns was changed to include not only numbers of children born but also numbers who had died. Infant mortality on the UK mainland had, throughout the nineteenth century been alarmingly high, though this often reflected the awfulness of urban industrial living. The 1911 census return showed '3' in the 'children born' column; it also showed '3' in the 'children died' column – what befell these little ones is not certain, probably a virulent disease, but the only certainty is that the Shipton

Royal Guernsey G.C. clubhouse at the time of Jack Hickman's employment there.

family had suffered a second tragedy in two generations. In his professional as opposed to his personal life, things were going well for Charles Shipton; the 1901 census return described him as a "self-employed fruit-grower" who lived at Les Landes, Vale; according to the 1911 return, Charles was an "employer" and "fruit-grower", living at *'Glencoe'* (mis-recorded as 'Glensor Vale' in 1911 summary details), Les Landes, Vale, near St. Sampsons, Guernsey. That the house in which Charles and Emily Shipton lived contained nine rooms suggests that by 1911 his fruit-growing business was very lucrative; yet those nine rooms probably emphasised the sad lack of youngsters to follow in their parents' footsteps and this may explain the couple's eagerness to offer a temporary home to Jack Hickman, a personable young man living away from home for the first time.

Jack's place of work on the island, the Royal Guernsey Golf Club, was founded in 1890, just four short years prior to the inauguration of Rye Golf Club. The course on which Jack Hickman played as an assistant professional in the three years before the outbreak of the Great War was different from the course that was redeveloped after 1918. Part of this resulted from areas of the course being damaged during wartime while it was utilised for military purposes and in part from the post-war construction of houses at the eastern extremity of the course adjacent to the Fort Le Marchant peninsula. Little written evidence remains of Jack's experiences at the Royal Guernsey, though the original club house survived at least into the 1930's and would have been very familiar to the young man from Sussex.

Note: It has proved impossible to

track down an important volume written by A.E. Rose entitled, *'The History of Royal Guernsey Golf Club'*. It would likely have proved invaluable in painting in the environment in which Jack commenced his professional golfing career but, sadly, the book is presently out of print.

INTO UNIFORM

In contrast to the dearth of evidence in respect of Jack's way of life at the RGGC, his time away from the golf course is rather better documented. Whether on account of the rather patriotic, even jingoistic, nature of post-Victorian/Edwardian Britain or whether Jack sensibly identified an opportunity to make new friends on Guernsey, the young man enlisted in the Royal Guernsey Artillery and Engineers. Along with the island's infantry com-panies, the RGA&E constituted the Guernsey Militia, an organisation that had been in existence since the thirteenth century, though it was not formally recorded as such until the fourteenth century.

The very location of the island of Guernsey, in the Channel close to the then Norman coast, dictated that way back into the mists of time it was open to both the threat and reality of invasion from all and sundry – the Dukes of Normandy, Channel pirates, the English Crown, the French Crown, David Bruce the exiled King of Scotland, Royalists, Parliamentarians, French Revolutionaries and Aristocratic Emigrés. And later, possibly the most traumatic of

all, during the Second World War Hitler and the Nazis.

So, from the seventeenth century, each of the Guernsey Parishes was empowered to raise a small company of about 100 soldiers between the ages of sixteen and sixty under the command of a Captain – St. Peter Port, as the only town, was an exception, as it was permitted to raise four companies. By about 1620, in excess of 1,150 men were serving in the Guernsey Militia – by sheer coincidence this number matched the establishment size of a single battalion at the outbreak of the Great War. At the end of the eighteenth century the Guernsey Militia comprised four regiments (namely Town, North, South and West), a troop of horse for intra-island communications, and two companies of artillery; moreover, the British Government was, in its own interests, covering most of the costs.

The French Revolutionary Wars and Napoleonic Wars brought further and substantial change to the Militia and to the island itself. New, stronger defences were constructed, in the shape of sixteen forts and fifty-eight coastal batteries; the vulnerable 'Bridge' area at St. Sampsons was also filled in to stop the northern sector of the island from being invaded and cut off from the rest of Guernsey. The Militia was reorganised in 1803 whereby the North, South and West Regiments were for the first time re-designated Light Infantry units, while the Town Regiment remained a regiment of foot. The Troop of Horse became Light

Dragoons, the Companies of Artillery were raised to Regiment status and a new Pioneer Corps (very useful given the extent of new construction projects) was raised.

The Cloth Hall, Ypres, before and after the 1914 bombardment.

Throughout the nineteenth century, numerous changes were implemented but by 1901 the Royal Guernsey Militia comprised three Light Infantry battalions and the Royal Guernsey Artillery supplemented by two companies of Engineers; together, the gunners and sappers became known as the Royal Guernsey Artillery and Engineers (RGA&E). The latter was the Militia unit in which Jack Hickman would enlist just prior to the outbreak of the Great War.

When, late on the evening of 4th August 1914, the deadline set in the UK's ultimatum to Germany to evacuate sovereign Belgian territory expired, the Royal Guernsey Militia was immediately mobilised. The States of Guernsey offered a contingent of soldiers to help the national war effort. However, Guernsey Militiamen, like their Territorial Force counterparts on the UK mainland, could not be compelled to serve overseas, thus the initial role of the Militia in August 1914 was to relieve the regular British Army garrison on the island. The battalion then charged with the island duty was 2nd Battalion, the Yorkshire Regiment; the 'Green Howards' had served on Guernsey since 1913 but by 28th August 1914 the unit was back in 'Blighty' and ready to join 21st Brigade of 7th Division. The Yorkshiremen were soon to wish they were back on the sunny island as their first major battle was to be the mud, blood and devastation of First Ypres (see left).

Despite the wish of the States of Guernsey to send a contingent of Guernseymen to aid the war effort, there was no existing battalion in the British Army that bore the name 'Guernsey' in its title[4]. So, many impatient Guernseymen went to the mainland to enlist in a wide range of units of the army and in the Royal Navy; while they may not have served with their friends from home, they rendered sterling service to the war effort and many did not survive to return to the island they fought so willingly to defend. However, once the 'Imperial Service' problem had been overcome, volunteers from the Royal Guernsey Militia proved sufficient in numbers to create two complete companies that were absorbed into two battalions in 16th 'Irish' Division – 6th Battalion, Royal Irish Regiment (RIR) and 7th Battalion, Royal Irish Fusiliers (RIF)[5]. 16th 'Irish' Division crossed to France during the autumn of 1915 and took part in the blood-soaked battles of the Somme in 1916.

In November 1916, during the latter days of the terrible struggles on the Somme, the Royal Guernsey Militia was suspended for the duration of the war, conscription was introduced and the Royal Guernsey Light Infantry (RGLI) was reformed as a regiment of the British Army. Upon its formation, nearly all the Guernsey Officers in the 6th Royal Irish Rifles and the 7th Royal Irish Fusiliers were transferred to 1/RGLI.

1st Battalion, RGLI, served on the Western Front for just over a year but suffered nearly a thousand casualties – 327 men killed and 667 men wounded. Most of the original officers and men of 1/RGLI were former members of the Militia but later drafts included a leavening of conscripted men. Having completed basic training in Guernsey the battalion sailed for England in June 1917 for its advanced training before shipping to France at the end of September. The battalion joined 86th Brigade of 29th Division that was commanded by a Guernseyman, Major-General Beauvoir de Lisle. It was the fate of 29th Division to fight in Third Ypres [in the Battles of Langemarck, Broodseinde and Poelcapelle] and at Cambrai [in the Tank Attack and the costly German Counter-Attack]. Losses were such that 1/RGLI was thereafter transferred to Army Troops until end of the Great War.

2nd Battalion, RGLI, functioned as the Reserve Battalion and remained in the Island to raise, receive and train recruits before they were despatched to 1/RGLI for service on the Western Front. Such recruitment was necessarily very limited.

Quarrying being an important element of employment on Guernsey, it is logical that numerous quarrymen were among those who volunteered for overseas service. In January 1917 these volunteers were formed into the 321st Quarrying Company, Royal Engineers. In the apt words of Edwin Parks:

"... The men received Royal Engineer uniforms but no military training."

(Quoted from Edwin Parks: *'Diex Aix: God Help Us'*)

The company landed in France on 15th February 1917, just three weeks after leaving their island home! They were to remain in theatre until well after the war's conclusion.

THE GUERNSEY GUNNERS

Later to be mentioned in dispatches during the Great War, Lieutenant-Colonel Richard Francis McCrea was the pre-war Commanding Officer of the

Members of the Rye Athletic Club, about 1910/11 – note the wide range of ages. Jack is fourth from the right in the back row, sitting on one of the parallel bars.

Royal Guernsey Militia Artillery and Engineers (from 1908 to 1915).

On eventual mobilisation with the Royal Field Artillery (RFA), the officers and men under his command in the RGA & E were formed, with few exceptions, into the Divisional Ammunition Column for the 9th 'Scottish' Division, the senior unit of Kitchener's New Army. During May 1915 it would be the first complete unit of Guernseymen to reach the Western Front. Although the rank and file of the Militia Gunners were ready and willing to serve overseas, they still had to go through the formality of enlisting in the RFA of the British Army. Having climbed the hill towards Candie Gardens, (what thoughts must have been passing through the young golfer's mind?) Jack underwent his army medical on 8th March 1915 in Guernsey's

Town Arsenal. The latter was the main Arsenal[6] for the island's Militia and, while providing quarters for the permanent staff, the Town Arsenal also had a Drill Hall, a clothing store, gun-sheds, officer's stables, armourer's workshops and practice-rooms for the military bands[7]. It is likely that Jack Hickman's enlistment medical took place in either the spacious Drill Hall or in one of the band practice-rooms. The young man would have harboured few concerns about passing the essential tests as he had always kept himself fit during his early youth back in Sussex. Evidence of this is his membership of the Rye Athletic Club in which gymnastics had a high profile. Several photographs show Jack with his club colleagues – it is very likely that the club put on public displays at events in the area local to Rye and even beyond.

Rye Athletic Club, about 1910/11, giving a display – Jack is in the centre, hanging from the bars.

At the time of his medical examination, Jack was twenty-three years and nine months of age; he was described as,

"...five feet one and a half inches tall, 125 lbs. in weight and of good physical development".

(Medical report in Jack Hickman's Army's service record).

Youthful Jack: Rye Athletic Club member.

He had been vaccinated in infancy but already had false teeth and the latter would cause Jack problems early in the new year of 1916. On one of Jack's demobilisation documents[8] it stated that Jack:

'...first joined, on Guernsey, and was medical Class A1.'

However, the same document erroneously intimated that Jack had first joined for service on 3rd January 1915, although his service record reckons his Army service from 20th March 1915, the same date as appears on his attestation papers[9]. The latter also confirms that Jack was part of the...

'[First] Guernsey Artillery Contingent'

...that crossed the Channel to train with 9th 'Scottish' Division from March to May of 1915. His attestation also

First Artillery Contingent bound for England: Jack is capless, left of middle by the ship's rail.

Jack, prior to embarkation for England and 9th 'Scottish' Division.

confirms that Jack served with the Militia, as his answer to the question, *'Have you ever served in any of His Majesty's Forces, naval or military, if so, which?'* was,

"...Yes. R.G.A. & E."

['Royal Guernsey Artillery & Engineers']

The same form indicated that Jack Hickman had become No.89238, and was joining the Royal Field Artillery; more specifically, *'...9th Divisional Ammunition Column'.* His Army Record also confirms that Jack's rank on enlistment was officially given as, *'...Driver'* and this remained so at least into 1918. As for addresses, Army Form 2505 shows that Jack was still boarding with the Shiptons in Vale, while his own father, Henry, was still resident at *'The Lodge'* in Camber. Jack's enlistment was overseen and witnessed by Corporal R. Richings of Royal Guernsey & Alderney Militias and was counter-signed by 2/Lieutenant E. Cowley, officer commanding *'Guernsey & Alderney Recruiting District'.* From 20th March 1915 Jack was under military orders and thus his very life depended on people other than himself.

RGA&E – the Guernsey Gunners prior to departure (courtesy of Priaulx Library, St. Peter Port, Guernsey).

89238 Gunner Jack Hickman RFA appears in the back row, fourth from the left, looking every inch the smart young artilleryman; the pictured was taken prior to the 'Guernsey Gunners' leaving for England to be trained as 9th Divisional Ammunition Column in preparation for joining the British Expeditionary Force on the Western Front.

---

1   Kaiser Wilhelm's Germany had been allied to Habsburg Austria since the signing of the Dual Alliance of 1879 – ironically this alliance had been negotiated by Bismarck.

2   The British developed the Maxim as the Vickers Machine Gun while the Germans employed the Spandau in greater numbers and to better effect.

3   Guernsey contains ten such parishes, divisions similar in some ways to mainland 'counties'.

4   This would be corrected in November 1916 when the Royal Guernsey Light Infantry (RGLI) was re-formed as part of the British Army.

5   Neighbouring Jersey sent a company to strengthen 7th Royal Irish Rifles, also of 16th Division.

6   Town Arsenal was the home of the Militia's 1st Regiment and of the Artillery; in 1882, 'out-Arsenals' were built to house 2nd and 3rd Regiments.

7   Today, the Town Arsenal is home to the Guernsey Fire & Rescue Services.

8   This was Jack's 'Disability Statement' (A.F. Z.22), dated 11th February 1919.

9   This was his attestation for Short Service (for the Duration of the War), Army Form 2505.

CHAPTER THREE
The World Turning Upside Down

THE OUTBREAK OF WAR, 4TH AUGUST 1914

It was heading towards the August Bank Holiday. The summer had been warm with the sun a frequent visitor, making factory and pit stifling places to work, though the harvest promised to be one of the best for years. Many families had booked their rail tickets for a trip to the coast or to the capital – excitement was rising among young and old.

Yet a few dark clouds seemed to be determined to spoil the festivities. For several years now newspapers had carried reports, often tucked away on inside pages because Britain's interests[1] were not seriously threatened, of unrest, even armed conflict at the eastern end of the Mediterranean. Many of the problems seemed to emanate from the decline of the Ottoman Turkish Empire that, from the fourteenth and fifteenth centuries, had expanded to take control of a huge slice of Eastern Europe, Asia Minor and Africa; it once stretched from the gates of Vienna, through the Balkan Mountains, across the narrow entrance to the Black Sea, through the Holy Land and deep into North Africa (and across into Spain). As nationalism took an ever-tightening grip of nineteenth-century Europe, so the old Empires of Austria-Hungary and Ottoman Turkey came under irresistible pressure from their myriad subject nationalities. Strangely, Habsburg Austria remained effectively unchallenged until the rise of Prussia produced the remarkable Otto von Bismarck in the 1860s. Prussia's defeat of Austria's armies in just six weeks of 1866 set a dangerous precedent for an empire in which the dominant Austrians had long been suffered as oppressors; Serb, Bosnian, Pole and Magyar smelt an opportunity. The weakening Ottoman Empire, on the other hand, had long been regarded as the, '…Sick man of Europe' whose demise and fracture was regularly expected [politically, this was usually referred to as the 'Eastern Question']. Each of the Great Powers of Europe had an interest in the health of the '…sick man' and how he dealt with his subject peoples: Russia saw itself as the self-proclaimed protector of Slavs and Christians in the region; Austria-Hungary regarded the borders with the Ottomans as her own prime interest and this led to friction with Russia; France was traditionally sympathetic to Turkey, while newly-fledged Germany sniffed out an opportunity for improved status; Britain wanted, as ever, to protect and strengthen the vital trade routes to India and the Far East.[2]

In 1877, Russia and Turkey came into military conflict over Ottoman treatment of 'Bulgaria', a term that encompassed much of the Balkan region. All but defeated, the Turks sued for peace and it appeared that Russia would set up an independent 'Big' Bulgaria as its client state[3] and would open the Turkish-controlled Dardanelles Straits to allow its Black Sea fleet to exert influence in the Mediterranean. Weight of opinion among the Great Powers was against the Russians and an International Congress was called in Berlin, with the aim of revising the terms of San Stefano. At Berlin in 1878, Russian ambition was thwarted and Austria was bolstered by the frustration of two major rivals; however, the creation of three newly-independent states – Romania, Serbia and Montenegro, (joined by Bulgaria in 1908) – produced a largely unintended long-term problem. When Austria-Hungary announced the formal annexation of Bosnia in 1908, a major European crisis loomed on the horizon as little Serbia perceived a threat to its over-lofty ambitions. Britain, meanwhile, had secured from Turkey the island of Cyprus – imperial trade routes had again been protected but the Balkan problem lingered on.

Subsequent crises in the North African ports of Tangier and Agadir (both in Morocco) and among several of the Balkan states had been settled after an initial round of sabre-rattling. Actual wars had broken out in the Balkans – the First Balkan War, 1912-1913, was between the Ottoman Empire (Turkey) and the Balkan League (Greece, Serbia, Bulgaria and Montenegro); in the Second Balkan War, 1913, Bulgaria alone was fighting her former allies, Greece, Serbia, Montenegro and Rumania. Neither attracted direct British intervention nor many column inches in the British press. Much the same reaction was elicited by the murder by a Serbian student of the Austrian Archduke Franz Ferdinand and his wife Sophie in the Bosnian town of Sarajevo on June 28th 1914. Yet within four weeks, the Great Powers had, '... *staggered and stumbled*' into a war that no-one wanted and no-one intended.[4] The essential difference from the two Balkan Wars of 1912-1913 was that this time one of the Great Powers was involved and the Great Powers were inter-linked within two rival webs of alliances and ententes.[5]

Three weeks had passed before the Austro-Hungarian Government took positive action in respect of the murders; with the support of their ally Germany, Austria sent a strong ultimatum to Serbia.[6] Two days later, on 25th July, Serbia accepted all but one of the terms. Implacably seeking a pretext for destroying Serbia, Austria-Hungary declared war on the Serbs on 28th July. A long-time arch-rival of the Habsburgs, Russia would not allow Serbia to 'go under' and thus mobilised[7] her own troops towards the Austrian border. Germany saw this as a direct threat, tantamount to a declaration of war and, following an ultimatum to Russia (that amounted to, *"...demobilise or fight"*), Germany declared war on Russia on 1st August. Unfortunately for their High Command in particular and Europe in general, Germany's main war plan required a rapid attack to crush France prior to turning on the slow-mobilising Russians – a simple form of divide and conquer. The so-called Schlieffen Plan was first conceived in 1895. Its aim was to invade France via neutral Belgium, thus avoiding the powerful French border forts in the Ardennes Uplands, deliver a knockout blow to Paris from the north and west and attack from the rear the French troops on the Franco-German border. Meanwhile in the east, a small German force would suffice to hold back the slowly-mobilising Russians. Once France was eliminated in the west, the main force would then entrain east to deal a fatal blow to Russia.

So, employing a flimsy pretext, Germany declared war on France on 3rd August then, in order to execute its rather inflexible war plan, demanded passage for its troops through neutral Belgium. The latter naturally refused and was promptly invaded on 4th August. Britain, an original guarantor (as was Germany's predecessor) of Belgium's independence by the 1839 Treaty of London, served Germany an ultimatum to withdraw. The silence of the German government thus ensured that Britain, late on 4th August, became the only country to declare war on Germany. The nightmare had begun.

BRITAIN'S ARMED FORCES IN 1914[8]

THE ARMY IN 1914

In 1914, the army was composed of three main elements – cavalry, infantry and artillery. The following chart shows how the infantry units of the British Army were organised and where the artillery fitted in at the outbreak of war, from the smallest unit (a section) at the top to the largest (an army) at the bottom:-

SECTION – four sections, 12-15 men in each, constituted a platoon.
The section was the smallest unit of the battalion. Four sections, each under the auspices of a sergeant or, more usually, a corporal, constituted a platoon.
PLATOON – four platoons, 50-60 men in each, constituted a company.
Each platoon was commanded by a subaltern (a lieutenant or 2nd lieutenant). Four platoons constituted a company.
COMPANY – four Rifle Companies, 'A', 'B', 'C', 'D' and a much smaller Headquarters company, about 200 men in each rifle company, constituted a battalion.
The company, containing about 200 men, was usually commanded by a major or a captain (even by a lieutenant after battle losses). Each battalion comprised

five companies, usually a headquarters company, four 'line' or 'rifle' companies (generally 'A', 'B', 'C' and 'D') and a machine gun section equipped with two Maxim (later Vickers) heavy machine guns.

BATTALION – four battalions, about 900-1,000 men in each, constituted a brigade. [Reduced to three battalions in February 1918]

Commanded by a lieutenant-colonel, at full strength (which most battalions only ever dreamed about), the battalion contained just over 1,000 men. Every battalion, whether of regular, territorial or war service origin, belonged to a 'parent' regiment that had an established headquarters in the United Kingdom that was responsible for the raising and training of recruits. The regiment had ceased to be the standard fighting unit of the British Army following the Cardwell Army Reforms of 1881 by which regiments' numbers were replaced by (mainly) county-style titles. For example, the old 38th and 80th Regiments of Foot were allied to create the 1st and 2nd Battalions respectively of the new South Staffordshire Regiment. From that time, regiments were 'county' based and recruited from their own region, although a few regiments, such as the King's Royal Rifle Corps and the Guards recruited on a national scale. The majority of regiments had two 'regular' battalions (career soldiers) and these were designated the 1st and 2nd battalions, although some larger regiments like the Middlesex and the Worcestershire could support four regular battalions. Conversely, smaller counties found difficulty in raising and maintaining a single front-line battalion and sometimes had to combine with a neighbouring county, as in the case of the Oxfordshire and Buckinghamshire Light Infantry.

BRIGADE – three brigades, about 4,000 men in each, constituted a division.

Commanded by a brigadier-general, a brigade normally comprised four battalions and a brigade headquarters and thus contained over 4,000 men. Some battalions remained with the same brigade for the duration of the war, whilst others were transferred between brigades several times. The latter often occurred when it was considered necessary to 'stiffen' a particular under-performing brigade with a proven and battle-hardened battalion. Early in 1918, heavy losses and subsequent lack of replacements (trained men were apparently held back in England by the Prime Minister, David Lloyd-George, who believed that Sir Douglas Haig was unnecessarily wasteful of his troops) caused brigade size to be reduced from four to three battalions.

DIVISION – at least two divisions often more, about 18,000 men in each, constituted a corps.

Commanded by a major-general, a division usually comprised three brigades and thus contained about 12,000 infantry. In addition, each division was assigned three field-gun artillery brigades (which in terms of manpower were significantly smaller than infantry brigades), a field howitzer brigade and a heavy battery of the

---

C1: 1914 ARMY STRENGTH

Regulars: 250,000

Reserve: 150,000

Special Reserve: 65,000

TF: 14 Infantry Divisions
        14 Yeomanry Brigades
        23 RGA Batteries
        151 RFA Batteries

Plus Volunteer RE,
RAMC and supply units

Royal Garrison Artillery. These were further expanded by three Royal Engineers companies, field ambulances (not the transport but the RAMC staff themselves), units of the ASC (Army Service Corps), a sanitary section and transport units that totalled another 6,000 men. Adjustments were made during the war, such as the addition of a pioneer battalion, a machine-gun company (1917) and a trench mortar unit; this was partly counter-balanced by the loss (to Corps control) of the heavy battery. During the course of the war the British Army was expanded from just six divisions to seventy-six.[9]

CORPS – at least two corps constituted an army.

Commanded by a lieutenant-general, a corps comprised in 1914, a headquarters and normally two divisions, thus a corps contained slightly fewer than 25,000 infantry and more than 10,000 support troops. As the war progressed and the numbers of troops increased, so the corps could and did contain more than two divisions. The divisions themselves were often moved from corps to corps as battles wore on.

ARMY – one in August 1914 increased to five by November 1918.

This one can be confusing. *The* army refers to the branch of the armed services itself, as opposed to, say, the navy. *An* army, comprising at least two corps, is the largest single unit of the British Army and was commanded by a full general. In August 1914 the British Expeditionary Force that was sent to France was of sufficiently small size to constitute just *one* army. As regular troops were brought back from overseas stations, reservists called up, territorials asked to forego their right to service on home stations only, and Kitchener's volunteers were slowly turned into soldiers, so the original one army grew. By the time of the Armistice in November 1918 it comprised five armies. Such was the scale of the Great War.

Contained within the above structure was a wide range of military functions. The front line fighting troops comprised the infantry (including machine gunners), the artillery and the cavalry, though all the other branches frequently found themselves in the zone of shot and shell. The vital 'support services', if they may thus be described, were the engineers, the pioneers, the medical services and the logistics or service corps – without these, the fighting units simply could not have functioned.

Every soldier (though there were

slight differences for the likes of the artillery, engineers and later the machine-gunners) belonged, in theory, to eight units. In reality, the ordinary 'Tommy' would have struggled to tell you his corps and army numbers, less still the names of those who commanded them. The battalion was the most significant unit in his daily life; he would have known the name of, and would often have seen, the lieutenant colonel who commanded his battalion. More familiar would have been the major or captain who ran the soldier's company of about 200 men; in the platoon of 50 or 60 men, its leader, usually a lieutenant or 2nd lieutenant, would have known the man by name and would have been aware of his strengths and weaknesses as a soldier. The section of about 15 men, which was the largest unit run by a non-commissioned officer (usually a sergeant), would have contained the soldier's closest friends and was the everyday unit to which he belonged and for which he fought.

THE ROYAL NAVY IN 1914

The Royal Navy had a truly powerful, modern fleet, built on the premise that it should be capable of outfighting the combined fleets of its two largest potential enemies.

When questioned in 1798 in the House of Lords as to the likelihood of invasion of these islands by Napoléon's all-conquering 'Grande Armée', Earl St. Vincent (Admiral John Jervis) produced the memorable answer:

C2: 1914 ROYAL NAVY SEA-GOING STRENGTH

22 Dreadnoughts

40 Pre-Dreadnoughts

9 battle-cruisers

108 lighter cruisers

215 torpedo-boat destroyers

28 gunboats

106 torpedo boats

7 minelayers

75 submarines

1 seaplane-carrier

"...I do not say the French cannot come, my Lords
– I only say they cannot come by sea."

Such words explained why Britain still placed its faith, not to say its money and research, in the development of the Royal Navy. Equally, it explains why the British army of 1914 was, in comparison to its continental counterparts, so much smaller and less of a threat in international diplomacy. The principle of the seas providing a natural moat against invasion still held good in 1914. The advent of air power was soon to see the age-old maritime principle come under severe challenge.

AIR POWER IN 1914 RNAS & RFC: RAF FROM APRIL 1918

When the call went out to mobilise in August 1914, the least regarded, except among a perceptive tiny minority, were the brave pilots of the strange machines of the Royal Flying Corps and the Royal Naval Air Service. Even those original few, enthusiastic fliers as they were, could not have believed that within the span of twenty-five years air power would supplant the Royal Navy as Britain's prime defence against invasion. War, or sometimes even fear of it, is often a stimulus to advance in weapons technology – pre-war, the Royal Navy had seen the advent of the 'revolutionary' high-speed, fully-armoured heavy weapons platform in the shape of the Portsmouth-built *Dreadnought* class of battleship. The army was to experience rapid battlefield developments in the form of better machine-guns and more accurate heavy artillery, the terror of increasingly noxious, toxic gasses, the horrors of liquid fire or flame-throwers and the supposed invulnerability of 'land battleships' or tanks. Of course, every effective battlefield development saw the 'boffins'[10] working feverishly to find a military counter-measure. Yet the most rapid advances came in the new field of air power; not only did the technology change at a dizzying pace but also did air power's battlefield tactical role and it even contributed to a change in war strategy by virtue of the introduction of long-distance heavy bombing. After the unreliable 'kites'

> ### C3: 1914 AIR POWER
>
> 1914 Air Power
>
> Royal Naval Air Service
> 93 aircraft
> 6 airships
> 2 balloons
> 727 personnel
> 12 airship stations
>
> Royal Flying Corps
> 63 aircraft
> 900 personnel
>
> The RAF did not exist until 1st April 1918.

and 'string-bags' of 1914, more powerful and efficient engines, stronger airframes, extensive bomb-racks, high-quality cameras and interrupter-gear machine-guns turned aircraft into killing machines that could 'spy' over enemy territory and could 'observe' for the artillery.

Royal Flying Corps (RFC)

Not until 1st April 1911 did the government show strong interest in the military application of powered flight,[11] when the Corps of Royal Engineers was ordered to set up the Air Battalion, (ABRE), based at Farnborough, commencing a long association. The new unit comprised 154 officers and men, divided into No.1 Company (airship) and No.2 Company (aeroplane). The first pilots had to have already obtained a flying licence through private means. On 13th May 1912, just a year after its inauguration, the ABRE was converted by royal warrant into the Royal Flying Corps (comprising an army element, the RFC, and a naval element, the RNAS). As a branch of the Army, the RFC retained army ranks. At the outset, the role of the RFC was to act as the 'eyes of the ground troops', directing artillery fire by rudimentary methods and carrying out photographic reconnaissance. When it deployed to France in 1914 the RFC sent four Squadrons (Nos. 2, 3, 4 and 5) each with 12 aircraft, which together with extra aircraft in depots, gave a total strength of 63 aircraft supported by 900 men. In 1914, the RFC mainly used the de Havilland BE-2, Farman MF-7, Avro 504, Vickers FB5, Bristol Scout, and the Royal Aircraft Factory F.E.2. A year later, in September 1915 at the start of the Battle of Loos,[12] the Royal Flying Corps had 12 squadrons and 160 aircraft in France and Flanders. Therefore, as the French 'Aéronautique Militaire' had 1,150 aircraft available, the vast majority of the early operations on the Western Front had to be carried out by Britain's allies.

Royal Naval Air Service (RNAS)
The RNAS was the naval element of the Flying Corps; ironically, the navy had use of a permanent airfield, the Royal Aero Club's Eastchurch field on the Isle of Sheppey, before the RFC was officially constituted. On 1st July 1914, the Admiralty made the Royal Naval Air Service part of the Military Branch of the Royal Navy so, unlike the RFC, the RNAS opted for navy-related ranks – in the long term, these formed the basis of Royal Air Force ranks in 1918. By the outbreak of the First World War in August 1914, the RNAS had ninety-three aircraft, six airships, two balloons and seven hundred and twenty-seven personnel but not until August 1915 did it come under the direct control of the Royal Navy. Although there was rivalry between the air services, the two co-operated to the benefit of the war effort.

Royal Air Force (RAF)
The Royal Air Force did not exist in 1914, though the RNAS and RFC were both in existence at the outbreak of hostilities. Not until 1st April 1918 did the separate flying services of the army and navy merge to form the new air branch – the Royal Air Force.

ENLISTMENT INTO THE ARMED FORCES

"OVER BY CHRISTMAS!"
This was a phrase that would come back to haunt those who uttered it. It goes some way to explaining the rush to join the Colours when Secretary for War, Lord Kitchener made his plea for volunteers to fight for 'King and Country'. Many an adventurous young man was desperate not to miss the opportunity of being, '...*part of it*'. Some youths were

simply seeking a way out of a badly-paid, grinding job; some just wanted to see a bit of the outside world, having never travelled far beyond the town in which they had been born.

Many of the experts of the time overlooked the American Civil War (1861-1865) where emerged the first massed armies, the first effective machine guns, modern artillery and that nightmare of the Western Front, trench-fighting. It was the first large-scale industrial and economic commitment to a modern war. Coincidentally, the American Civil War lasted four years just as the conflict in Europe would last four years. Field Marshal the Earl Kitchener of Khartoum felt that a three year struggle would be a conservative estimate. It was Kitchener who persuaded Parliament to agree to raise a new 'citizen army'; he disregarded the Territorial Force, created in 1908 by Haldane, because it was controlled by County Territorial Associations rather than the War Office. The Secretary of State's solution was a new, volunteer force, enlisted into the regular army for the duration of the war. Despite criticism and initial problems, it would be Kitchener's 'New Army' that would carry the nation to eventual success.

The regular army was superbly-trained but was used to fighting limited-scale, colonial engagements that depended, in many respects, upon the dominant power of the Royal Navy. A full-scale, continental war would require something on another level entirely. Lord

Kitchener called for 100,000 volunteers over a six-month period; in the event, half a million men volunteered within the first *month*!

The call to arms, 1914: 'Your King & Country Need You.'

So what would Guernsey have known or thought about these events? Everyone would have been familiar with the name of the Prime Minister, Mr. Asquith and even more so with that of the popular Lord Kitchener. The idea that Britain was threatened or in danger would instantly have stirred feelings of patriotic duty in some young breasts, with predictable results; others would have felt strongly but considered their prime duty to be to wife and family, thus enlistment would have been delayed. Some would have been too young but impatient to grow; some would have seen the army as something to avoid at all costs.

Consequently, the pattern of enlistment among the men of Guernsey was typical of those on mainland UK.

Ever since the Army reforms of 1908 the British Army had offered three forms of recruitment – professional soldier in the regular army; part-time member of the Territorial Force committed to serve within the UK; or soldier of the Special Reserve. Britain's system was entirely voluntary, in contrast to the huge conscripted armies of continental Europe.

ENLISTING INTO THE REGULAR ARMY

A regular army recruit had to be taller than 5 feet 3 inches and of an age between 18 and 38 years. He would sign on at the Regimental Depot or at one of several local recruiting offices.[13] The recruit had a choice of army specialism (branches such as engineer, gunner or infantryman) and of regiment. The usual commitment was for a period of seven years full time service with the colours, to be followed by another five on the Army Reserve – popularly referred to as, '...*seven and five.*' These terms were for the infantryman: other arms were slightly different. The artillery, for example, was, '...*six and six.*' When war was declared there were a quarter of a million trained former soldiers on the National Reserve – the British Expeditionary Force would depend heavily upon these men.

Regimental note: Most regiments had two regular battalions (1st and 2nd Battalions) but a very few, large counties such as the Worcestershire and the Middlesex had four (1st to 4th Battalions).

ENLISTING INTO THE TERRITORIAL FORCE

The Territorial Force was created in 1908, the product of the former militia and other volunteer units. The TF offered part-time soldiering with most of the County and national infantry regiments and with each of the Corps of Artillery, Engineers, Medical, Service and Ordnance. Units were recruited locally, men often joining with their mates; men trained at weekends or in the evenings and were required to attend a summer camp. In time of war, they could be called upon for full-time service but they were not obliged to serve overseas. Physical criteria were the same as for the Regulars but the age limit was lower, at seventeen. When war broke out in August 1914, all TF men were 'invited' to set aside their overseas service exemption. Most did, determined to prove Lord Kitchener wrong!

Regimental note: Regiments raised varying totals of TF battalions; 1st line battalions were denoted as 1/5th Battalion TF &c., 2nd line were 2/5th Battalion TF, 3rd line were 3/5th Battalion TF and so forth…. A few regiments comprised only TF battalions, such as the London Regiment, the Hertfordshire Regiment and the Monmouthshire Regiment.

ENLISTING INTO THE SPECIAL RESERVE

As with the TF, the Special Reserve

was another form of part-time military service. Special Reservists enlisted for a term of six years and could be mobilised for overseas service; in such a situation, Special reservists came under the same terms as men of the full Army Reserve. Training commenced with six months full-time commitment, on the same pay as a regular soldier, with three or four weeks training per year to maintain standards. Service could be extended but the upper age limit was 40. A former regular soldier whose army reserve obligation had expired could also re-enlist as a Special Reservist and serve up to the higher age of 42.

Regimental note: Most regiments had one Special Reserve battalion or, if there were a second, it was known as the Extra Reserve battalion. They were always numbered directly after the regular battalions, often denoted as 3rd (Reserve) Battalion or 4th (Extra Reserve) Battalion.

'NEW ARMY' VOLUNTARY RECRUITMENT

As Secretary of State for War, Lord Kitchener barely even considered placing the safety of the realm into the hands of a Territorial Force in which he perceived several fundamental weaknesses. In its then format, the TF had existed only since 1908 and, in Kitchener's view, had yet to prove its worth and reliability; secondly, as things stood, the TF soldier could not be required to serve abroad; thirdly, the TF was administered by

County Associations rather than by the government; fourthly, Kitchener considered that the training of the TF men merely created, '...*part-time, hobby soldiers*' and he wanted fully-trained battalions. When the TF Associations offered the services of the Territorial Force, Kitchener gruffly quipped,

> "...*I don't want Territorials – I want soldiers.*"

While it was true that serving TF men in 1914 had signed up for Home service only and could not be *compelled* to serve overseas, Kitchener almost immediately asked them to sign the Imperial Service Obligation, thus consenting to serve abroad. Any man who exercised his legal right not to sign, whatever the reason, was usually assigned to his regiment's new second-line Territorial battalion. Ironically, TF battalions were serving 'full-time' with the BEF in France and Flanders even before Christmas 1914,[14] and the first complete TF Division – 46th 'North Midland' – would be on the Western Front by 5th March 1915. It would be deep into 1915 before the first 'New Army' units were ready for the front line.

TERMS AND CONDITIONS FOR THE RECRUITS

The recruit of 1914 or 1915 was a volunteer and, as such, he was allowed to join his preferred service – initially army or navy. In the case of the army, a man could, within certain constraints, opt for a branch of the army (infantry, cavalry, artillery, engineers or medics) and choose his regiment. Most men chose a local regiment, to be with their mates or one with a stellar reputation; volunteers were generally assigned to units of the New Armies, although many, once trained, were posted to replace losses in regular army battalions of their regiment.

Given this latitude, a recruit still had to satisfy specific terms and conditions of service and these were clearly outlined on recruiting posters and in newspaper appeals. Every man underwent a military medical examination – as the war progressed and the need for men became more urgent, so requirements were gradually relaxed. The new 'war service' recruits' battalions were accordingly designated 'service' battalions and, salient among these, were the Pals' battalions that allowed for men who lived, played or worked together to volunteer together, train and serve together.

Regimental note: Totals of 'Service' battalions raised by regiments varied from none (among the elite Regiments of Foot Guards) to the forty-five war-raised battalions of the Northumberland Fusiliers. Usually, 'Service' battalions were numbered in sequence after the TF battalions of a regiment.

C4: ENLISTMENT TERMS IN 1914

Age, Height and Fitness
Over 5 feet 3 inches (later relaxed for 'Bantam' battalions): Medically fit: Age19 to 39 (proof not required): Former soldiers up to 45 years

Pay
Ordinary Army pay – 7 shillings43 a week (less 1½d insurance)
Free food, clothing, lodging and medical attendance

Terms
Duration of the war only ('War Service'): 'Then… return to your ordinary employment.'

Separation Allowances (soldier contributed 3s. 6d)
Wife only 12s. 6d: First child, extra 5s. 0d: Second child 4s. 0d: Each extra child, 2s. 0d.

Disablement Pensions
For war disablement – Insurance Benefits plus a variable War Office.

Provision for Widows and Children
Widow – Separation Allowance up to 26 weeks: variable-rate pension would be allowed.

THE MILITARY SERVICE ACTS 1916 – CONSCRIPTION

When other systems of recruitment, including the Derby Scheme of 1915, had been tried and judged incapable of providing the numbers of men required, the government took the bull by the horns and, for the first time in modern British history, introduced conscription. This was enacted in the Military Service Act of 27th January 1916. It was extended and new conditions (including the lowering of the minimum age of recruitment to 18 years) were passed into the law of 25th May 1916, which was known as the Military Service Act, 1916. Together, known as the Military Service Acts, 1916, they marked Britain's final acknowledgement of her commitment to 'total war'. Men were arranged by age groups and called up in turn; single men were called before married men and the right of appeal against 'call-up' was allowed, subject to local decision.

1 With the important exception of the trade routes to India and they were secured by the Royal Navy.

2 The Suez Canal, had been opened in 1869, greatly shortening Britain's major trade routes to Asia.

3 This was confirmed by the Russo-Turkish Treaty of San Stefano in March 1878.

4 The debate over culpability for starting the Great War still rumbles on a century later.

5 An entente was a diplomatic 'understanding' – not binding but indicative of likely mutual support.

6 Serbia was a thorn in Austria's side. A small, independent Balkan state, it had long urged the minority nationalities in the Habsburg Empire to throw off Austrian rule. Austria was thus eager to teach Serbia a lesson.

7 Mobilisation is not a declaration of war; it is an act of putting a nation's troops on a 'war-readiness' alert and moving them rapidly towards the appropriate frontier.

8 This assessment of Britain's armed forces in 1914 (apart from minor adjustments) first appeared in, 'Sorrow into Pride' by Ken Wayman & Barry Crutchley (Reveille Press, 2013).

9 For excellent analyses of this remarkable expansion of the British Army see Martin Middlebrook's, 'Your Country Needs You' and Ray Westlake's, 'Kitchener's Army'.

10 This is a slang term broadly covering scientists, engineers and inventors.

11 …with the exception of balloons and their derivatives. The Air Battalion developed from the School of Ballooning in 1911.

12 Loos, in September 1915, was the first major battle in which Jack Hickman took part.

13 Numbers of recruiting offices increased rapidly after the outbreak of war.

14 Among these were seven battalions of the all-TF London Regiment, including the London Scottish (1/14th Bn), the Artists' Rifles (1/28th Bn), the Queen's Westminster Rifles (1/16th Bn) and the London Rifle Brigade (1/5th Bn). Despite Kitchener's harsh words, all distinguished themselves in battle.

PART TWO

The Great War Diaries
of Jack Hickman

1914-1919

CHAPTER FOUR
TRAINING AND TO THE BEF MARCH TO JUNE 1915

ENGLAND AND BEYOND: MARCH-JUNE 1915

PREPARATIONS

Before Jack Hickman and the Guernsey and Alderney Artillerymen embarked on their long journey into the unknown, they had to undergo a series of inoculations. On Tuesday, 16th March Jack had the dubious pleasure of experiencing his first anti-typhoid inoculation which was followed eleven days later on 27th March by a second. The disease was to become an all-too-common problem[1] in the trenches of the Great War, so the initial discomfort of inoculation was certainly worthwhile. By April, the Guernsey Contingent had crossed the Channel to England and had been embodied at Guadaloupe Barracks in Bordon Camp, near Aldershot. The Islanders and their new Kitchener volunteer colleagues

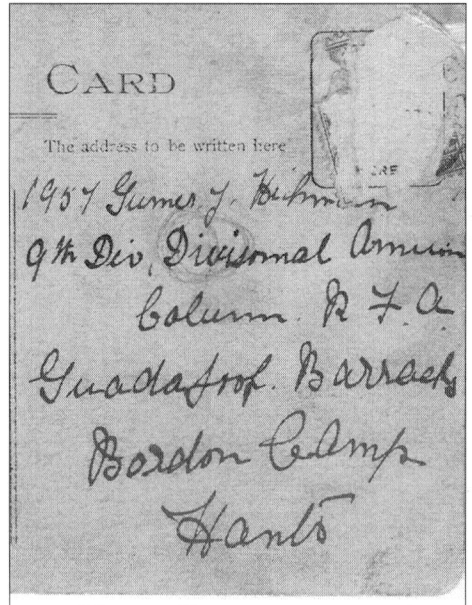

Card from Jack's parents, sent to Bordon training camp and addressed to 'No.1957 Gunner...' 1957 was Jack's Militia number on Guernsey.

would call the Artillery Barracks home only until mid-May 1915 when the entire 9th Division would entrain for the port of Southampton.

Part of the British Army's Aldershot (Southern Command) complex since the 19th Century, Bordon Camp was set in a pleasant corner of North Hampshire. The camp had its own brick-built Post Office and it was from there that a young recruit (sadly unknown to the author) sent home early impressions of his new surroundings:

Royal Artillery Barracks, Bordon.

"This is a lovely part of the country and is great for Route Marching. You would never feel tired on the road. There are about 20 shops in the village of Bordon which is about 5 minutes from camp and a Picture House. Of course there are all the camp stores built for the men in camp here."

Most of 9th Division experienced a full eight months training but the Divisional

Ammunition Column joined later as it was a new unit (like all of its ilk) and… consequently received relatively little specialist training and was therefore committed to learning the job much closer to the front line, often under fire.

Formed at end of August 1914, 9th 'Scottish' Division was the senior of the New Army divisions[2] raised by Secretary of State for War, Lord Kitchener. By September 1914 many of the various units of the division were assembling around Bordon Camp in Hampshire and each unit was experiencing the same difficulties as all the new 'K1' battalions and their support units[3] – rifles and ammunition were in short supply so 'live firing' practice was infrequent; uniforms, webbing, packs and much of the infantryman's equipment were slow in arriving as the various

Bordon Post Office: a lifeline to many a homesick recruit.

industries adapted only slowly to the scale of huge government orders. Billeted in the huts of Bordon Camp's Guadaloupe Barracks and St. Lucia Barracks, the division was fortunate to avoid the necessity of living in tented camps as the autumn weather soon gave way to the rains of winter that turned many an encampment to liquid mud. Ironically, the latter was a foretaste of what would become commonplace during subsequent winters on the Western Front.

Unit training, from platoon level up to battalion level, was followed by divisional field manoeuvres. Fitness and morale were high when, on 5th May 1915, Field-Marshal the Earl Kitchener inspected 9th 'Scottish' on Ludshott Common, 2½ miles east of Bordon. Just two days later, at 11 a.m. on 7th May, Divisional H.Q. received embarkation orders for the Scots to join the British Expeditionary Force in France. The process of entraining and transporting the division lasted several days and had been practised – the first New Army division would always be closely scrutinised – so it was accomplished without a major hitch. The advance parties of the divisional artillery moved off on Saturday, 8th May, to be followed from Monday, 10th May by the infantry brigades. Although 9th Division was under orders eventually to concentrate at St. Omer, travel plans varied according to unit – artillery, animals and transport made the crossing from Southampton Docks to Le Havre, while the infantry made the shorter Channel crossing from Folkestone to Boulogne on troopships that included S.S. 'Queen', S.S. 'Victoria' and S.S. 'Invicta'.

The Royal Artillery stables at Bordon Camp: this would have been a sight familiar to Driver Jack Hickman and his mates.

Accompanying the division's embarkation orders came a timely and stirring send-off from His Majesty the King George V on 10th May,

"You are about to join your comrades at the front in bringing to a successful end this relentless war of more than nine months duration. Your prompt, patriotic answer to your nation's call to arms will never be forgotten. The keen exertions of all ranks during the period of training have brought you to a state of efficiency not unworthy of any Regular Army. I am confident that in the field you will uphold the traditions of the fine regiments whose names you bear. Ever since your enrolment I have closely watched the growth and steady progress of all units. I shall continue to follow with interest the fortunes of your division. In bidding you farewell, I pray God may bless you in all your undertakings."

His Majesty King George V

JACK THE DIARIEST...

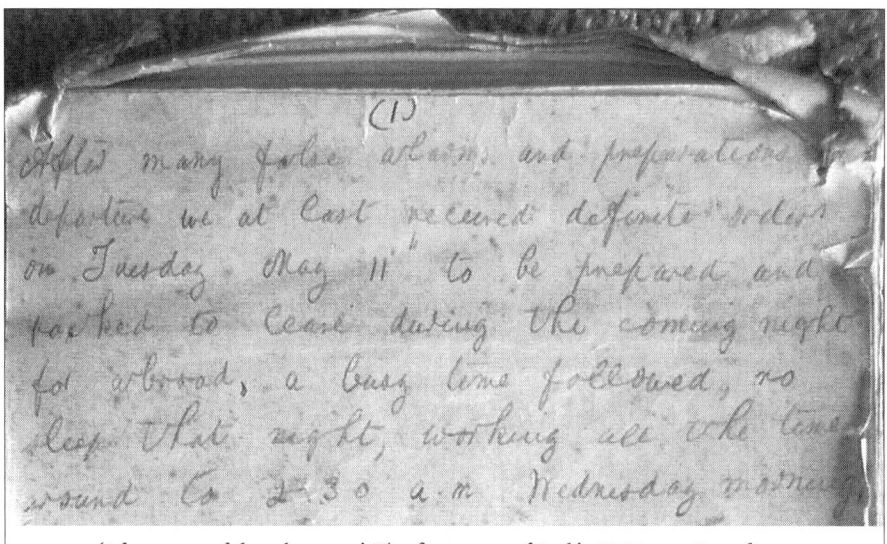

'After many false alarms...' The first page of Jack's 1915 wartime diary.

It is at this juncture that what remains[4] of Driver Jack Hickman's first diary record takes up the tale. The diary itself was a simple reporter's notepad, bound by ordinary, thin string – Jack's handwriting is clear and his diary entries remain, for the most part, lucid and legible. Jack must have been one of the more literate lads among his contemporaries and his writing demonstrates an incisive turn of phrase. Each of Jack's entries, appearing under the sub-heading, **Diary**, is identified by day and date; location has been gleaned from a number of sources.

In this book, as far as is possible, Jack's words have been left as they were written. Infrequently, the odd word is illegible as the lead (occasionally coloured) pencil has faded; an occasional spelling has been altered, most often in place-names. Jack's words appear within speech marks, while extra information, intended for clarification purposes, appears within square brackets or under the direct sub-heading, **Context**.

DIARY

Tuesday, 11th May 1915 [pictured]
Bordon Camp, Hampshire

"After many false alarms and preparations for departure, we at last received definite orders on Tuesday, 11th May to be prepared and packed to leave during the coming night for abroad. A busy time followed, no sleep that night, working all the time around to 2:30 a.m. Wednesday morning."

Wednesday, 12th May
En route, by rail and ship
"Left Bordon Camp Station [most of the infantry brigades departed from Liphook Station for Folkestone] at 6 a.m., being the last to leave of about 17,000 men, mostly Scotch Regiments consisting of Seaforths [7/Seaforth Highlanders], H.L.I. [10/Highland Light Infantry; 11/Highland

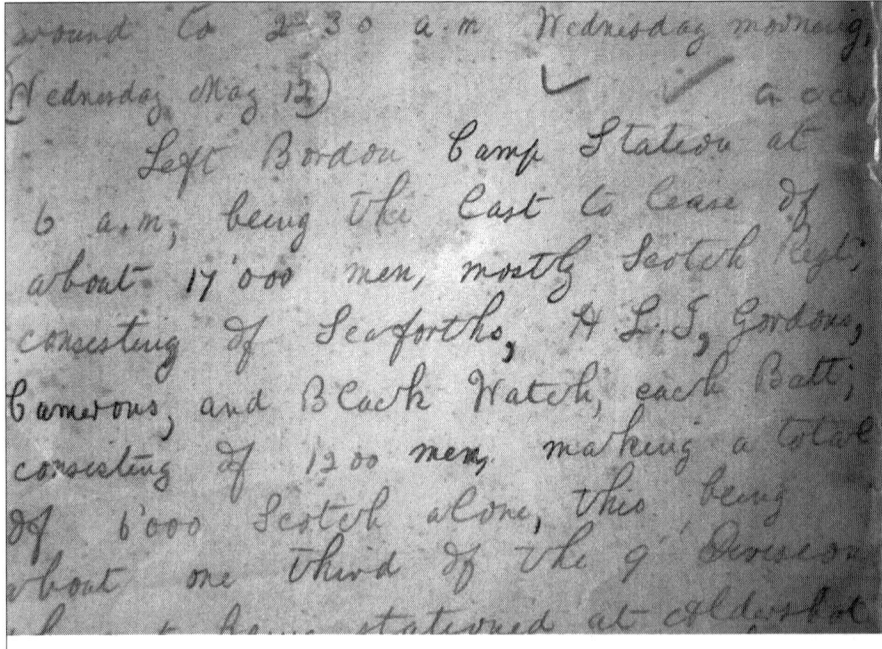

This diary page indicates 17,000 men, probably the entire 9th Division, was en route for the Western Front.

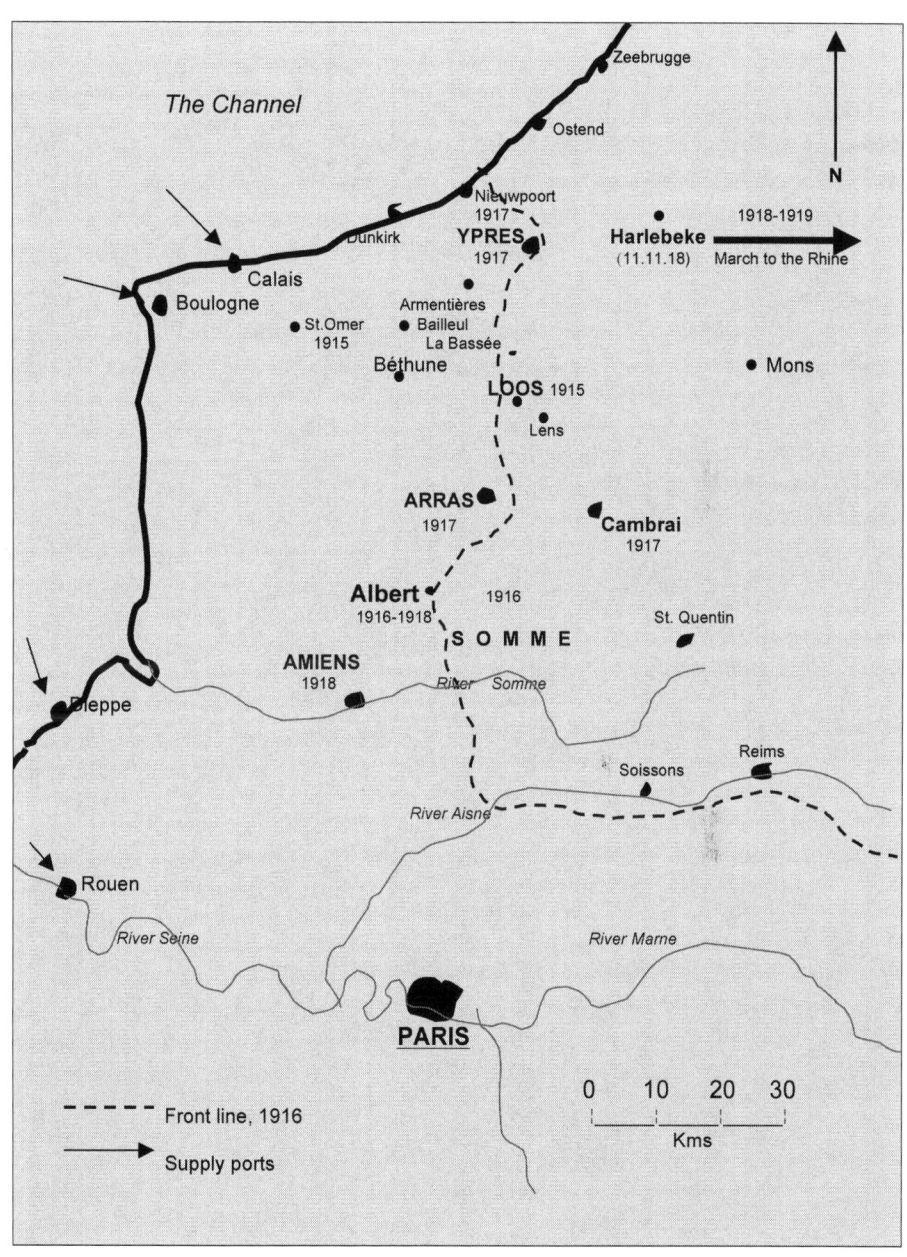

Map 1: 9th 'Scottish' Division on the Western Front 1915-1919

Light Infantry], Gordons [8/Gordon Highlanders] and Black Watch [8/Black Watch]; each battalion consisting of 1,200 men, making a total of 6,000 Scotch alone, this being about one third of the 9th ['Scottish'] Division, the rest being stationed at Aldershot and Bramshott. We [9/Divisional Ammunition Column] reached Southampton just after eight a.m. and spent the day there loading horses and wagons, finally leaving there by troop transport [S.S. 'Minnesota'] at 6 p.m. All the way down Southampton Water we passed a great number of transports loaded with men of the Ninth Division; just past Portsmouth we were stopped by two torpedo boats which accompanied us across to Le Havre [to counter the U-Boat threat]. About 3 a.m. on the 13th, Thursday, we dropped anchor off Le Havre, about two miles out from the harbour."

Thursday, 13th May
Le Havre, France

"First view of France at daylight, Le Havre on a miserable, wet morning; at 8 a.m. we made our way into harbour, finally berthing at about 9:30 a.m. Still raining hard, we spent the day in unloading and landing our stock [a mix of officers' riding horses and draught horses]; about 6 p.m. we proceeded to a rest camp outside Le Havre. We spent the night under canvas in pouring rain, mud everywhere, a foot deep in a good many places; most uncomfortable but everybody was happy but very tired. Le Havre was very busy with our troops, miles of sheds and stores for the Army at the front. The first thing to be seen on every street and post was, '... Keep to the right in France.'"

Friday, 14th May
St. Omer, France

"Up at 4 a.m. and travelled to the railway station at Le Havre, loaded our stock and left by train at 8 a.m. After all day and night in the train [travelling north-east] we arrived at St. Omer at about 6 a.m."[6]

Saturday, 15th May
St. Omer, France

"The weather cleared up just before we reached St. Omer, the first fine spell since we sighted France on the thirteenth. After unloading at St. Omer, we travelled about three miles out to a small village [Tilques, to the north-west of the town] and camped for the night. All the roads we saw were absolutely the worst I have ever seen, holes and loose rock; the houses were very old, red tiled and very low. In the journey up by train, the biggest places we noted were called Abancourt and Rouen; many very large towns were passed a few miles away on either side but too far away to see anything very well. The train journey was awful, having to travel in horse boxes accompanying eight horses,[7] with only straw to sit down upon."

CONTEXT

So, by noon on Saturday, 15th May the 9th 'Scottish' was concentrated in billets to the south-west of St. Omer, among them Boisdinghem, Blendecques and Tatinghem; the division, the first complete 'New Army' division to reach France, would serve on the Western Front in France and Belgium for the remainder of the war and would enjoy a reputation second to none among the Kitchener New Armies.

9TH DIVISION CONCENTRATION AT ST. OMER, FRANCE 15TH MAY 1915

9th 'Scottish' Division that crossed the Channel during the second week of May 1915 comprised the following units and senior officers shown in table 2:

Table 2: **Units of 9th 'Scottish' Division, mid-May 1915**

Gen Officer Comm. 9th Division: Maj-Gen H.J.S. Landon

G.S.O. I:	Lieutenant-Colonel C.H. de Rougemont M.V.O.
A.A & Q.M.G:	Colonel A.V. Payne

Infantry Brigades:
26th 'Highland' Brigade: Brigadier-General E.G. Grogan
8/Black Watch; 7/Seaforth Highlanders;
8/Gordon Highlanders; 5/Cameron Highlanders
27th Brigade: Brigadier-General C.D. Bruce
11/Royal Scots; 12/Royal Scots;
6/Royal Scots Fusiliers; 10/Argyll & Sutherland Highlanders.
28th Brigade: Brigadier-General S.W. Scrase-Dickens
6/King's Own Scottish Borderers; 9/Scottish Rifles;
10/Highland Light Infantry; 11/ Highland Light Infantry

Royal Artillery:
Commander Royal Artillery (CRA): Br-Gen. E.H. Armitage
50th Brigade (A, B, C, D Batteries – each Battery four 18-pounders) + 50th BAC
51st Brigade (A, B, C, D Batteries – 18-pounders) + 51st BAC
52nd Brigade (A, B, C, D, Batteries – 18 pounders) + 52nd BAC
53rd Howitzer Brigade (A [Heavy], B [Heavy], C [Heavy], D [Heavy] –
    4.5in howitzer four-gun Batteries) + 53rd BAC.
All four Brigade Ammunition Columns (BACs) were supplied by the Divisional
    Ammunition Column (DAC).
9th Heavy Battery, Royal Field Artillery (RFA) was with the division for four
    days only.
10th Motor Machine-Gun Battery (MMG).

Royal Engineers
Commander Royal Engineers (CRE): Lt-Col H.A.A. Livingstone
63rd Field Company, RE
64th Field Company, RE
90th Field Company, RE

Mounted troops
9/Division Cyclist Company ⎫ These units were trained to work
'B' Squadron, 1/Glasgow Yeomanry ⎭ together.

Ordnance Section:
Deputy Assistant Director of Ordnance Services (DADOS): Major J.S. Brogden

Pioneers – 9th Seaforth Highlanders, 'The Ross-Shire Buffs' under Lieutenant-Colonel T. Featherstonehaugh

Royal Army Medical Corps:
Assistant Director Medical Services (ADMS): Col C. Cree
27th Field Ambulance
28th Field Ambulance
29th Field Ambulance

9th Division Motor Ambulance Workshop

20th Sanitary Section

Army Service Corps: 9th Divisional Train (Supply Column)
Officer Commanding: Lieutenant-Colonel R.P. Crawley
The divisional train arranged supply between the division and its corps; it worked between the railhead and the divisional ASC. The battalion Quartermaster drew supplies for his unit from the ASC Company attached to his brigade. The ASC of the divisional train used both horse transport and, increasingly, motor transport to excellent effect. In fact, Colonel R.H. Beadon commented of 9/Divisional Train,

"...from May 1915...no single instance occurred of the troops failing to receive their supplies regularly owing to any breakdown of its ASC (companies)..."

9th Divisional Supply Column –
104th Company – divisional troops
105th Company – 26th Infantry Brigade
106th Company – 27th Infantry Brigade
107th Company – 28th Infantry Brigade

Veterinary Section:
Assistant Director Vet. Services (ADVS): Major W.H. Nicol
21st Mobile Veterinary Section

Having reached billets in the area of St. Omer on 15th May, the division remained there for just two days before marching east about fifteen miles to billets near Bailleul [13 miles north-west of Lille], Noote Boom and Outtersteene on the Franco-Belgian border. 9th Division established its General Headquarters [GHQ] at Château le Nieppe.

DIARY

Sunday, 16th May
Tilques and St. Omer, France
"We spent the morning in getting ready for departure again, had dinner and left [from Tilques] at 2 p.m. We went right through the town of St. Omer, where there were large crowds out to welcome us. A lot of British soldiers were there and there was a large hospital [No. 10 Stationary Hospital] full of wounded.[8] It was rather a large town but very old and dirty; most of the houses in the private part of the town had large ditches between them and the roads, each house having a bridge and a strong iron gate to protect them. However, a lot of boating was going on in the ditches or canals or whatever they were called, our Tommies and the girls being the chief occupants of the little punts. We travelled until dark and about 9 p.m. we found a suitable field and camped for the night."

Monday, 17th May
Méteren, France
"We started again about 10 a.m. and travelled [due east through Hazebrouck] to the little village of Méteren [about two miles to the west of Bailleul], camping about a mile outside of the village at about 6 p.m. Here we had our first glimpse of the battlefields of Flanders. Just before we reached Méteren we saw several graves of British soldiers in cornfields by the roadsides – in the church at Méteren, the Germans had had two machine guns mounted and from there had mowed down the Warwicks [an incident that had occurred in mid-October of 1914]."

CONTEXT

There was an eyewitness account of the Méteren Incident[9] that occurred on 13th October 1914.

"The enemy had dashed down and seized the next village, Méteren, and our first task was to drive them out. The place was held by a rearguard of machine-gunners, and could have been encircled and captured, but we were ordered to take it by bayonet.

"We took it at a terrible cost, but found no enemy to bayonet. What

few machine-gunners were there had done their work well and fled in time. Then through Bailleul and Armentières, which the enemy abandoned without a fight."

[Private R.G. Hill, 1/Royal Warwickshire Regiment, 'Diary of an Old Contemptible'.]

Bernard Law Montgomery, later to be the architect of victory over Erwin Rommel's Afrika Korps in North Africa in 1942/3, was a young officer with 1/Royal Warwickshire Regiment during the Méteren incident. At Méteren, near the Belgian border on 13th October 1914, during an allied counter-attack, he was shot through the right lung by a sniper and was injured seriously enough for his grave to be prepared in expectation of his death. Against all odds he survived and was subsequently awarded the Distinguished Service Order for gallant leadership.

DIARY

Tuesday 18th May to Sunday 23rd May
[This page is missing from Jack's diary…]

Monday, 24th May
Méteren
"Nothing happened all day until evening when we again saw the same sort of [aerial] fight." [This entry suggests that an aerial dogfight had also taken place above the camp the previous day.]

Tuesday, 25th May
"Still quiet during the day but again in the evening yet another fight but with more aeroplanes engaged, flying right over the top of us to head off the German and drive him over our guns again. After another terrible fire from our guns without result, he got away chased by our aeroplanes."

Wednesday, 26th May
"A Zeppelin was sighted during the morning at a great distance, though there was rather a doubt about it."

FURTHER SPECIALIST TRAINING IN FRANCE, MAY-JUNE 1915

CONTEXT

During the third week of May, final arrangements were made with established units to train all elements of the division in the specialised techniques demanded by trench warfare. All the Royal Field Artillery brigades (except two batteries of 51/RFA)[10] were attached to the very experienced 6th Division for instruction. 6th Division had been with the British Expeditionary Force (BEF) since mid-September 1914 and had first faced the Germans in the Battle of the Aisne (19th/20th September 1914), subsequently taking part in the Battle of Armentières (13th October – 2nd November 1914). The choice of 6th Division was especially appropriate as the division's artillery was among the most experienced in that sector of the front.

9th Heavy Battery (RFA) landed with the Scots at Le Havre on 12th May but just four days later left the division for Lieutenant-General Pulteney's III Corps[11] for training but the 'Heavies' soon ceased to be part of the divisional field artillery and officially joined the Heavy Artillery Reserve on 18th May. Three weeks later 9th Heavy became Army[12] troops when the Battery joined XVI Heavy Artillery Brigade, thus transferring to the Royal Garrison Artillery (RGA). The logic behind this was that the 'Heavies' could then be more easily deployed when and where the need was greatest – within days, the battery saw its first action at Armentières. 9th Division's Infantry Brigades also received their 'live' trench-training experience under the wing of Major-General J.L. Keir's 6th Division.[13]

Brigade by brigade, the 'new boys' went into the line near Armentières; first up was 27th Brigade on 20th May, followed by 28th Brigade on 22nd May, and finally 26th Brigade on 24th May. All the infantry brigades returned to their parent unit on 26th May.

Once out of the trenches again, all infantrymen received training in 'bombing', the Tommies' familiar name for throwing hand-grenades. Much trench fighting took place at close-

The headstone of Lt.-Col. R.F. Uniacke, killed while riding past an R.E. 'bomb factory' near Nieppe. Seven sappers of 90th Field Company, RE, 9th Division, were killed in the same explosion.

quarters, sometimes even hand-to-hand, so the grenade was a vital element of the infantry's weaponry. At that time there was a variety of grenades or 'bombs', many of them homemade – the latter were nicknamed 'jam tins' as that was what many were made from. Soon, the Mills Bomb was to become the standard grenade used by the British Army. The normal range of the bomb was about thirty yards, though ex-cricketers were said to be highly-valued as 'bombers'. It was not long before the range of the grenade was increased to about 200 yards by the introduction of the rifle-grenade, though this method of launching grenades quickly wore out the Lee Enfield rifles from which they were fired.

The Royal Engineers, commonly known as the 'sappers', went to the III Corps for instruction in trench construction and methods of rapid repair. It also fell to the sappers to set up the early bomb-making factories, notable for their piles of vital jam tins recently emptied by Tommy in the trenches. Bread and jam was a staple that often accompanied Tommy's regular mugs of hot, strong tea colloquially known as 'gunfire'. The men in the front line often groused that the jam was always the same flavour – plum and apple – as the preferred flavours, like strawberry, were supposedly purloined by the men of the divisional supply column or, more likely, by the officers' servants.

On the day (27th May) that the Scots' infantry brigades were returning to their own division, there occurred an horrific, accidental explosion in one of the sappers' homemade bomb-making factories at Nieppe Station. This accident was all the more notable as one of its several victims was Lieutenant-Colonel Robie Fitzgerald Uniacke, a member of the General Staff and who fulfilled the roles of Assistant Adjutant and Quartermaster-General. He was riding past rather than visiting the bomb-making factory of the 9th Division Royal Engineers, specifically 90th Field Company. The explosion was put down to the instability of the explosives. Uniacke is buried in plot B.1 of Steenwerck Communal Cemetery, between Armentières and Bailleul. Lieutenant-Colonel Uniacke's name is also commemorated on the Staff College Graduates' First World War Memorial Tablets at Camberley in Surrey. According to the Commonwealth War Graves Commission, the Colonel died on 28th May 1915, so it is likely that he died the following day from his multiple serious wounds. Seven sappers were killed in the blast (see pages 103–104) while six officers and four other ranks were wounded in various degrees.

DIARY

Thursday, 27th May
Bailleul and Steenwerck

"We left Méteren at 1 p.m. and went just between two villages called Bailleul [actually a town] and Steenwerck. Just as we arrived we were greeted with a terrible explosion and it turned out to be an *experimenting factory at Nieppe Station [about 1½ miles east of Steenwerck] where the engineers were making bombs. The whole place blew up, killing Lieutenant-Colonel Uniacke, a staff officer, and a number of civilians. The explosion was terrible – it was about half a mile away from us and shook everybody in the place. We are now within 3½ miles of the Belgian frontier – on our left, Ypres, on our right, La Bassée. Awful fighting was going on at both places." [14]*

CONTEXT

Jack's observations about the cause of the explosion were accurate but he was less well-informed as to the number and nature of the casualties. He mentions no soldiers apart from Lt.-Colonel Uniacke and asserts that,

"...a number of civilians..." were killed.

The latter claim is very difficult to verify but it is certain that seven sappers were killed in the blast and another of their comrades died the following day from his severe wounds. All of the other ranks who died were Royal Engineers from 90th Field Company, RE – one of 9th Division's three field companies of sappers.[15] Both Steenwerk Communal Cemetery and Bailleul Communal Cemetery Extension (North) were visited whilst the author was researching Jack Hickman's experiences on the Western Front – the seven sappers who died on

27th May 1915 were buried, side by side, in Steenwerk Communal Cemetery, a few feet from the staff officer. They were:

50309 **Lance-Corporal Arthur Richard ANDREWS**, married, aged 31, from London; 90th Field Company, RE; buried in plot B.7, Steenwerk Communal Cemetery.

50344 **Sapper William IMRIE**, single, from Fife; 90th Field Company, RE; buried in plot B.6, Steenwerk Communal Cemetery.

51656 **Sapper Owen KENNEA**, single, from Pembroke; 90th Field Company, RE; buried in plot B.11, Steenwerk Communal Cemetery.

53880 **Driver Alfred KERRY**, single, aged 42, from Nottingham; 90th Field Company, RE; buried in plot B.9, Steenwerk Communal Cemetery.

43826 **Sapper Walter Southwell PEAKE**, married, aged 35, from Brighton; 90th Field Company, RE; buried in plot B.8, Steenwerk Communal Cemetery.

61227 **Driver Frank RIDDLE** single, aged 18, from Northants; 90th Field Company, RE; buried in plot B.10, Steenwerk Communal Cemetery.

49684 **Sapper Lowrie SHARP**, single, from Lanarkshire; 90th Field Company, RE; buried in plot B.5, Steenwerk Communal Cemetery.

Lieutenant-Colonel Robie Fitzgerald Uniacke, married, aged 45; Royal Inniskilling Fusiliers; buried in plot B.1, Steenwerk Communal Cemetery.

The seven sappers killed in the Nieppe explosion, 27th May 1915: comrades in life and death.

One other sapper died of his wounds next day, on 28th May 1915. He was:

43370 Sapper, G.C. CALLAN, married, aged 42, from Manchester; 90th Field Company, RE; buried in plot 1.B.51, Bailleul Communal Cemetery Extension (North).

DIARY

Friday, 28th May
Bailleul and Steenwerck
"Quiet all day. Just before dark, a battery about a mile from us commenced shelling the German lines; German shells pitched all around them about a mile or so away."

[This was a classic case of retaliatory fire].

Saturday, 29th May
Bailleul and Steenwerck
[On this day, Sir John French inspected 9th Division's 27th and 28th Brigades near Bailleul.]

Sunday, 30th May
"Very quiet from Friday to Sunday evening. About midnight, a heavy battery close to us started to open fire – the firing was awful, the ground fairly shook; about 2:30 on the early morning it was like hell on earth but it slowed down before daybreak. This was around La Bassée and Armentières [to the east of Bailleul]."

Monday, 31st May
Bailleul and Steenwerck

"Very quiet except for another aeroplane attack; a German machine crossed our camp at 6:30 a.m. but was followed by one of our own. Several aerial fights were seen during the day. About 7 p.m. an aeroplane was noticed being shelled over the German lines, it being one of ours; two more joined it and the three machines spent nearly two hours in the air over the German lines being shelled the whole time. Just at dark they all three came back and landed on the aerodrome just beside our camp – we gave them a great reception as they crossed our camp very low down. No-one who saw it

Jack, right, and two of his artillery mates; note all three are wearing riding 'spurs'.

will ever forget it – on several occasions we thought the shells had got them but they pulled through."

Wednesday, 2nd June
9/Div. Infantry units at Busnes training grounds
[Training from 2nd June to 25th June]
"Still very quiet from Monday. Great excitement early this morning – about 2 a.m. the alarm was given to turn out the guard and all hands. The same thought struck everybody and everyone jumped from bed in all sorts of dress and grabbed for rifles and ammunition, thinking it was an attack by Germans but it turned out to be a tent on fire. It was soon put out and we returned to bed to dream of the fight we nearly had."

Friday, 4th June
9/DAC still at Bailleul and Steenwerck
"Last night another terrible artillery fight started about 10 p.m. – the firing seemed to shake the whole place, Armentières and La Bassèe again being the scene of operations."

Sunday, 6th June
Bailleul and Steenwerck
"Sunday was quiet until during tea-time a German shell exploded in an oil tank in Armentières. A huge fire flamed for some hours but it burnt out without any further damage. In the morning, about six, I went out on the officer's horse, just close by Armentières and shells were dropping all about the town within a mile of me."
[The officer was most likely 2/Lieutenant

W.H. Ozanne, a Channel-islander, who later earned the Military Cross.]

Monday, 7th June
Marched to Ham-en-Artois
"The day opened with an aeroplane fight which lasted all the morning with occasional rests. On Monday evening we struck camp and left for a fresh one. We left at 5:30 p.m. and passed some ruined towns on the way. The largest one was Merville [five miles east of St. Venant], the biggest and most up-to-date which we have seen in France, also St. Venant [halfway between Hazebrouck to the north and Béthune to the south]. Both these towns were badly knocked about, especially the church in each place, huge buildings were nothing but bare foundations. The most noticeable thing was that, though the church was in each case a mass of ruins, the part that had a statue of the Virgin Mary stood up alone, untouched. In both of these towns we saw a lot of the Indian Ghurkas,[16] very fine men they were to look at. We stopped for the night about 10:30 p.m. by the roadside and, after tending to the horses, we slept on the road until daylight."

THE SIGNIFICANCE OF ARTILLERY ON THE BATTLEFIELD

CONTEXT

But for underestimating the importance of the Russian winter in the east and failing to understand the importance of the Royal Navy and sea power in the west, it is reasonable to suggest that Napoléon Bonaparte's domination of Europe might have lasted far beyond a 'mere' dozen or so years.

A strange way to introduce a piece on artillery in the Great War you may think but much of Napoléon's success resulted from his peerless understanding of artillery and its deployment on the battlefield. While his massed columns of infantry, not least his Imperial Guard,[17] terrified and defeated many a foe (often by their sheer reputation), as a military commander Napoléon clearly knew the value of efficient artillery and how to employ his cavalry to exploit gaps in the enemy line. During the Great War, cavalry played little part beyond the early skirmishes of 1914 – it was to develop into a war dominated by artillery. Even in Napoléon's time the received wisdom was that on the typical field of battle, cavalry beats infantry and artillery defeats cavalry – as a trained artilleryman, Napoléon recognised the power of the guns, commenting,

> "...Great battles are won with artillery..."

...and

> "...God is on the side with the best artillery."

It was not *always* so but it does indicate the value of skilfully-managed, powerful guns. He also had a clear idea of the main role he expected his cavalry to play,

> "...It is the business of cavalry to follow up the victory, and to prevent the beaten army from rallying..."

Even so, Bonaparte was generally flexible in his deployment of cavalry yet he also recognised that,

> "...Good infantry is, without doubt, the sinew of an army; but if it is forced to fight for a long time against.... superior artillery, it will become demoralised and will be destroyed."

Napoléon made his reputation as an outstanding artillery commander in lifting the British siege of Toulon in 1793 and further came to the attention of the Revolutionary government two years later when he dispersed rioters outside the Tuileries in Paris by employing what he termed:

> "...a whiff of grapeshot [also known as canister or shrapnel]..."

By the outbreak of the Great War, Europe had been largely urbanised and mechanised by the effects of the Industrial Revolution and, at sea, on land and even in the air weaponry and transport had made strides forward. Where Napoléon's artillery pieces had fired only relatively small, solid round-shot, basic explosive shell or canister (grapeshot) and were effective to about two-thirds of a mile, industrial developments had immensely improved the artillery pieces along with the variety and weight of shells they could fire. John Terraine summed up the significance of artillery in the Great War thus,

> *"...The war of 1914-18 was an artillery war: artillery was the battle-winner, artillery was what caused the greatest loss of life, the most dreadful wounds, and the deepest fear."*

[John Terraine, 1921-2003]

By the time of the 1918 Armistice, the range of guns would be measured in tens of miles, the heaviest shells would weigh in excess of one ton and fuzes would allow shrapnel (known to Bonaparte as grapeshot) to burst a hundred feet above troop concentrations for maximum killing effect. Moreover, chemical-filled shells would be able to render enemies ineffective even before a battle commenced. Heavy and light machine-guns would further mechanise the battlefield as would increasingly powerful trench mortars, grenades, flame-throwers and the new tanks. Cavalry would be employed as supplementary and emergency infantry, while the latter's role was reduced to trench occupying and holding – the epithet, coined by J.F.C. Fuller (later Major-General),

> *"...Artillery conquers, infantry occupies..."*

...was never more valid than during the Great War. The experience of the infantry under an artillery attack was lucidly described by the German author of *'All Quiet on the Western Front'*, Erich Maria Remarque,

> *"...An artillery barrage is a terrifying thing..."*

Few men who served in France and Flanders would likely disagree.

Often regarded as the most talented artilleryman in any army during the Great War, Oberst Georg Bruchmüller rose from the *Landwehr* (Germany's equivalent of the Territorial Force) to attain the role of Supreme Artillery Adviser to General Erich Ludendorff from the time of the Verdun Offensive (1916). His German nickname *'Durchbruchmüller'*[18] ('Breakthrough Bruchmüller') indicates the esteem in which he was held as anything resembling a breakthrough on the Western Front was as rare as hen's teeth. Bruchmüller was renowned for his meticulous, innovative methods and for an intuitive knowledge of weight, type and length of barrage needed to prepare or soften any target. First, he demanded that intelligence-gathering must be accurate and comprehensive. Secondly, the early disruption of the enemy's ability to fight was of paramount importance, thus surprise was of the essence as was the concealment of specific attack intentions and preparations.

Bruchmüller's strategy depended initially upon disruption of the enemy's prepared positions and their lines of re-supply and reinforcement. He demanded tight control of all artillery assets, micromanaging the specific fire missions of each battery of each type of weapon available for the barrage. His artillery plan involved the following three stages of delivery of fire,

Stage 1 depended heavily upon surprise; the principal targets were headquarters, command posts, communications lines, gun-lines, and infantry positions. The barrage should be sudden, concentrated, and make extensive use of gas to inhibit the enemy's ability to resist. In short, stage one was intended to damage enemy morale.

Stage 2 specified concentration upon counter-battery fire. The intention was to destroy the enemy's most potent defensive weapon, its own artillery.

Stage 3 reverted to fire on designated targets according to range. Some lighter batteries would continue to target infantry positions while heavier batteries would engage long range targets with the aim of inhibiting the forward movement of ammunition supplies and infantry reinforcements.

The artillery plan for the German Spring Offensive of March 1918 was drawn up by Oberst Bruchmüller. The plan was exploited by specially-selected and trained *Sturmtruppen* ['thrust troops'], resulting in the war's greatest breakthrough, forty miles, before the advancing German infantry ran out of steam and was first held outside Amiens then subsequently pushed back across the Somme battlefield. Both sides suffered very heavy losses in the Spring Offensive or *'Kaiserschlacht'* ['Kaiser's Battle']. Incidentally, during the early days of the offensive, Driver Jack Hickman was wounded by a shell near St. Quentin on the Somme while carrying out his duties with 9th Divisional Ammunition Column. He was fortunate to survive, yet as J.F.C. Fuller once observed,

"Surviving is the only glory in war."

AMMUNITION SUPPLY & THE ROLE OF THE DAC IN 1914/15

As powerful as were the guns of the Great War, they were nothing without an adequate supply of shells and spare parts to replace those that were rapidly worn out or expended. Divisional Ammunition Columns (DACs) did not exist prior to the outbreak of war in August 1914 and up to that time most of the work of ammunition replenishment was carried out by Brigade Ammunition Columns and then Battery carts attached to and manned by the individual batteries of each RFA Brigade. Although the Army expected the artillery to play an important role on the war, the scale of the conflict left every branch of the services, Royal Navy apart, short of all types of weapons and equipment. There had certainly been change since 1902 but the lessons learned by the Army on the plains of South Africa against the mobile Boer Commandos were somewhat unlikely to apply to the rigours and methods of static trench fighting.

Anticipating the expected expansion of the artillery, the introduction of DACs put yet another demand on manpower and so, initially, they were composed of reservists or drivers from the Special Reserve units – in the case of 9th 'Scottish' DAC, most of the gunners were Guernsey militiamen but volunteers to a man.

At the war's outbreak in August 1914, the official war establishment of a Divisional Ammunition Column was 548, comprising:

15 officers

533 other ranks

709 horses

101 General Service Wagons

3 carts

6 bicycles.

Over and above this, in the first year of the war each Royal Field Artillery brigade and each Royal Garrison Artillery heavy or siege battery formed its own ammunition column for the direct supply of forward ammunition dumps that were usually temporary during offensives. The task of ammunition supply to the infantry was also the responsibility of the BACs and DACs; each DAC had a Small Arms Ammunition section – initially, fourteen four-horse wagons loaded with sufficient SAA to replenish an infantry brigade.

1914 THE AMMUNITION SUPPLY CHAIN

Ammunition rounds were held in theatre, at stages between railhead and gun line, to about the following totals, though this increased massively when preparing an offensive:

18-pounder field guns	1,000 rounds
4.5in howitzer	800 rounds
60-pounder	500 rounds

Notes: As the war effort progressed, so 'old' guns such as the 13-pounder field gun and the 60-pounder were phased out and replaced.

As a general rule, ammunition dumps decreased in size in proportion to their proximity to the front line.

DEPOTS, PARKS AND DUMPS

An Ordnance Depot was a *permanent* storage area run by the RAOC, close to the port of entry but beyond a substantial buffer zone in case of accidents. Such depots were generally beyond the range of enemy artillery, yet increasingly attracted the attentions of German aircraft. The RAOC were the ammunition 'experts', so most Ordnance Depots supported a workshop formally known as the Ammunition Repair Facility; this would necessarily be located close to the destruction area where defective or obsolete explosives could be detonated safely.

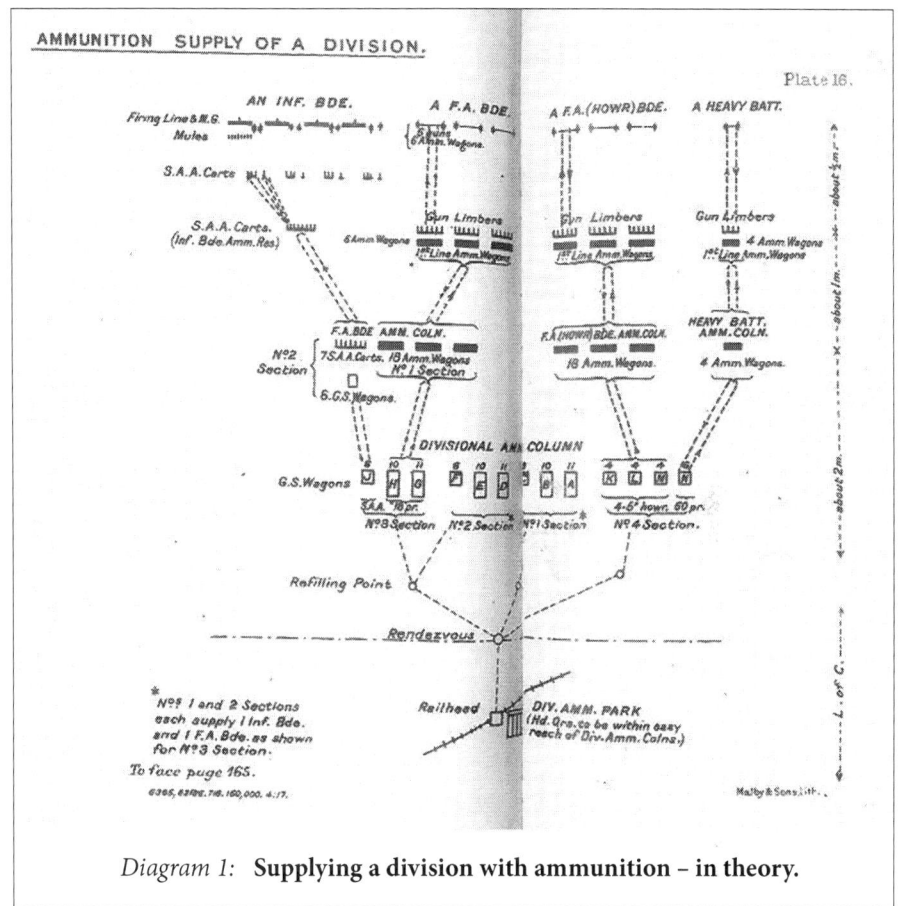

Diagram 1: **Supplying a division with ammunition – in theory.**

An Ammunition Park was huge but was intended to be mobile in relation to movements of the front lines it served. Such parks were run by the ASC.

A Divisional Dump was temporary, usually close to a railhead, and fed divisional refilling points. Brigade Dumps were even more mobile as they existed closer to gun positions for the collection of ammunition by each battery's carts. Divisional and Brigade Dumps were run by the division's RFA personnel and occasionally came under enemy artillery fire. The dumps, as Jack Hickman recorded in his diaries, increasingly became prime targets for enemy bomber aircraft.

Inside a dump, ammunition was stored in tarp-covered racks or stands that were divided by heavy, sandbag traverses, employing the same blast-limitation principal as the construction of traverses in a front-line infantry trench. The largest dumps even had secure, reinforced magazines where the more volatile explosives were held.

Although camouflage was occasionally used on the huge ordnance dumps and ammunition parks to confuse enemy bombers, it was an essential piece of kit for smaller dumps nearer to the front line – the dumps deployed the same kind of screens and netting that were present around gun-pits and over the guns themselves. Common to all dumps, even refilling points, was a loading area for transferring stored ammunition to and from transports of various types.

In areas adjacent to the front line, transport routes used to reach the infantry and the gun line were often under constant enemy artillery

Diagram 2:   **Division's Front Lines & No Man's Land**

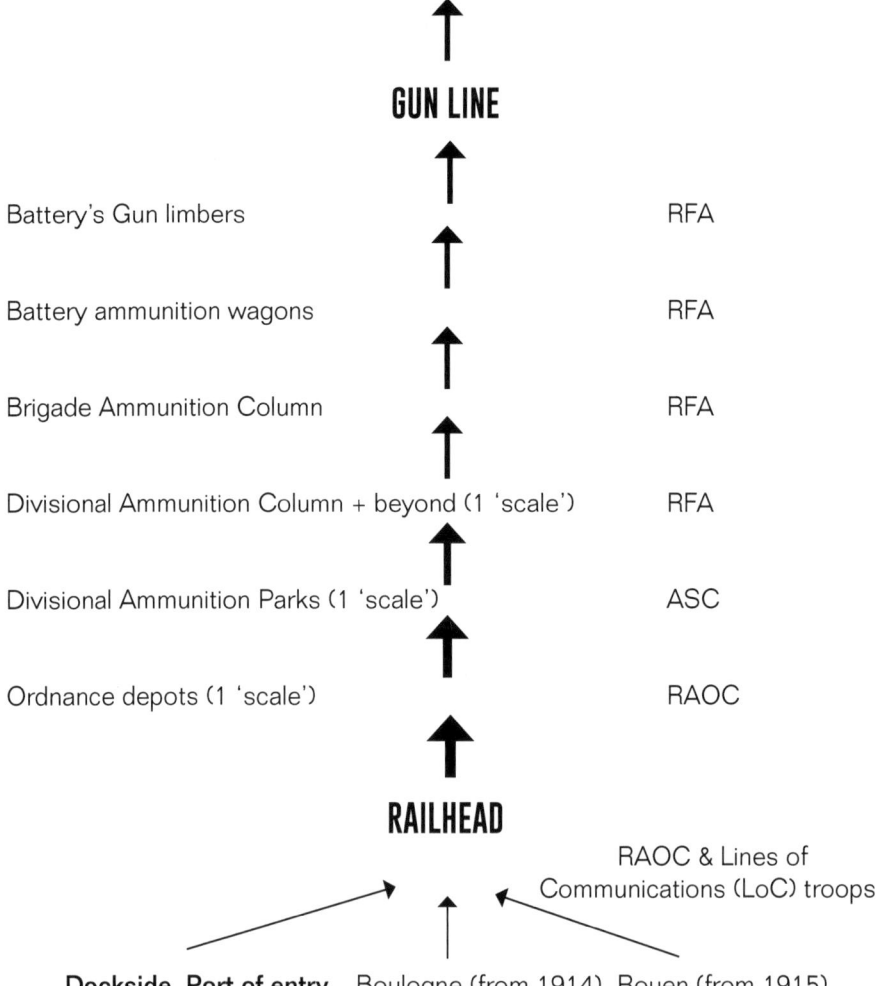

GUN LINE

Battery's Gun limbers   RFA

Battery ammunition wagons   RFA

Brigade Ammunition Column   RFA

Divisional Ammunition Column + beyond (1 'scale')   RFA

Divisional Ammunition Parks (1 'scale')   ASC

Ordnance depots (1 'scale')   RAOC

RAILHEAD

RAOC & Lines of Communications (LoC) troops

Dockside, Port of entry – Boulogne (from 1914), Rouen (from 1915)

observation; here, the men responsible for ammunition re-supply thus became night-workers. Even then the German artillery had the range of the supply routes and tended to drop short, speculative barrages on roads in forward areas in order to disrupt the working of the British artillery. The two sides both employed their new air forces in aerial scouting and photography, searching for the location of larger ammunition dumps in the rear areas, ever hopeful of disrupting enemy shell supplies through artillery barrages and aerial bombing. Jack Hickman witnessed the dramatic effects of a successful German 'hit' [19] – such was the living nightmare for men of the DACs.

Notes: In the ammunition supply diagram on page 112, a 'scale' of ammunition refers to the officially-designated allocation for the whole division. Thus the forward 'scale' was held among the elements of the DAC and the artillery and infantry brigades; a support 'scale' was stored and thus available in the divisional ammunition park; a third 'scale' was stored in the RAOC ordnance depot near the port of entry. When the divisional artillery was involved in a 'shoot' or the infantry was attacking or under attack, two full scales of ammunition were, in theory, available for forward movement. The theory did not always work so efficiently in practice on account of bad weather and enemy shell-fire.

As an indication of the size of the DAC's task during an offensive, the Somme campaign of July to November 1916 (a twelve-mile front) required the daily onward distribution of about 20,000 tons of ammunition. This was over and above the several weeks of shell-dumping to build the vast stocks necessary for the preparatory bombardment – in the case of the Somme offensive, the artillery barrage lasted seven days and nights. This was massively expensive of shells, exhausting for the British gunners and terrifying for the enemy recipients.

Even though the war, by June 1915, had been underway for nearly ten months, the role of the DAC was still evolving while transport links, mainly railways, were still being constructed or extended. Separated from ordinary stores, ammunition supply was delivered by full train loads that were sent forward to ammunition railheads for onward distribution.

Ammunition, both shells for the artillery and Small Arms Ammunition for the infantry and the machine-gunners, was usually loaded directly onto goods wagons in railway sidings that connected the UK munitions factories to the main rail routes. The hazardous cargo was thus transported to docks where supply ships were loaded for the short passage across the Channel. At the French port, the ammunition was offloaded to the continental dockside railway-yard for onward despatch to

C5: DAC Manpower and Animals in April 1915

The official **War Establishment of a 'New Army' DAC**, such as 9th 'Scottish', stood at 528 – slightly lower than in August 1914:

> 12 officers
> 1 Warrant Officer
> 10 sergeants
> 32 artificers
> 473 Other ranks
> [140 in each of sections 1, 2 & 3]
> [84 in section 4]
> 683 horses.
> Note: Brigade ACs were still in operation at this time.

A **DAC Headquarters** was small – in early 1915 the standard comprised:

> Lieutenant-Colonel (O/C, DAC)
> Adjutant
> Sergeant-Major
> Artillery Clerk
> Battery Quartermaster Sergeant (BQMS)
> Clerk
> Gunner
> 2 Medical Orderlies
> 6 Drivers for vehicles
> 1 Driver for spare horses
> 1 spare Driver
> 6 officers' batmen

> A total of 23 personnel.

huge Army Corps ammunition 'parks' in each of the various Army areas, thence forward to Divisional Parks – this was under the auspices of men of the ASC (Army Service Corps) and RAOC (Royal Army Ordnance Corps). From there, artillerymen of each DAC, organised into four numbered sections, utilised GSWs[20] (General Service Wagons), to collect the required ammunition from specified 'refilling points' at or close to their Divisional Park.

The staple transport of the DAC was the horse-drawn General Service Wagon (GSW). Each wagon had the following capacity:

SAA ammunition	40 boxes (1,000 rounds per box)	*or*
18-pounder	108 rounds	*or*
4.5in howitzer	66 rounds	*or*
60-pounder	40 rounds	

[Source: *'Field Service Pocket Book, 1914 (reprinted 1916)'*, General Staff, War Office]

Until May 1916, 9th Divisional Ammunition Column like all its counterparts comprised four sections, numbered 1, 2, 3 and 4. Sections 1 to 3 handled ammunition for the18-pounder field guns and small-arms ammunition (SAA) for the heavy and light machine-guns as well as for Tommy's trusty .303 Lee Enfield rifle; 4 Section transported a 'howitzer portion' for 4.5-inch and, very briefly, a 'heavy portion' for the 60-pounder battery (thereafter, the 'heavies' were under Corps or Army command). From May 1916 9/DAC, again like its counterparts, was organised in two 'echelons', A and B, the former to fetch ammunition from the ordnance depots and parks, while the latter was responsible for onward supply to the gun line and the infantry.

So, the DAC's function during the early years of the war, was to ensure supply to their division's brigade ammunition dumps and refilling points where each BAC (Brigade Ammunition Columns[21]) would take care of its own infantry battalions and Field Artillery brigades; Howitzer brigades and Heavy batteries had their own dedicated ammunition supply column. Transport for siege batteries, including ammunition supply, was carried out by Mechanical Transport (MT) Companies of the ASC. One such company was included within each Army and Corps. Each Corps also had a Corps Ammunition Park, also an ASC (MT) unit, which received and held re-supply stocks of ammunition. In addition, all Royal Garrison Artillery (RGA) batteries at Corps and Army level would each have their own dedicated ammunition columns.

HORSES & MULES

Before the advent of the powerful motor lorry and tractor, the task of all types of military haulage was the lot of the humble but ever-reliable horse. The Army's requirement of such beasts in August 1914 was upwards of 150,000 – numbers required increased as new divisions formed and newer and heavier artillery pieces were produced. Under the stresses and strains of war service, the effective working life of a horse was greatly foreshortened, thus remounts

Table 3: Six Grades of Army Horse

1) **R1**   Cavalry mounts (15 hands 1½ inches – 15 hands 3 inches)
2) **R2**   Yeomanry mounts (14 hands 2 inches – 15 hands 1½ inches)
          Every unit had a proportion of riding horses (R1 & R2) for their officers who might have to visit widely distributed companies.

   Note: Cavalry mounts required extensive training and so could not immediately provide remounts in the numbers needed.

3) **LD 1** Light Draught for field artillery teams. Field artillery used LD1 Horses (six per gun team) but in 1918, shortages meant that all BEF six-horse teams were reduced to four.
4) **LD 2** Light Draught (but heavier than LD1 for transport vehicles (i.e. General Service Wagons, baggage, supplies, ammunition and gun limbers). Used six-horse teams. A horse (LD 1&2) could draw half a ton in fair country (including weight of transport).
5) **HD**   Heavy Draught. Shires, Clydesdales and Percherons. A heavy draught horse (HD) could draw one ton (including weight of transport). Maximum load for a four-horse (Heavy Draught) General Service Wagon was 3,000 lbs load (excluding weight of transport). Medium artillery required LD2 and HD teams.

   Note: Draught horses required little training by the army as most were accustomed to working under harness or between cart shafts.

6) **P**   Pack animals (mules and horses). During wetter stages of battles where roads had been all but destroyed, such as Third Ypres (Passchendaele) pack mule trains were among the few methods of re-supplying the guns.

R = riding	two standards	R1, R2
D = draught	three standards	LD1, LD2, HD
P = pack	one standard	P

were ever more greatly in demand. Back in 1908 the Army began making contingency plans for its equine needs, though this first scheme was less than successful; so, the 1911 Army Act handed over responsibility of a horse census to the Territorial Force.[22] By 1913 this census recorded over half a million horses for requisition if war should come. A requisitioned horse still had to be paid for by the Army, so the 135,000 beasts required at short notice in August 1914 constituted a major outlay for the Army. With beasts obtained from field, town, factory-yard and coal-pit, after just a single year of fighting, one in four of the country's lighter horses had been requisitioned, as had 70,000 heavy horses, to the temporary detriment of agriculture. Consequently, representatives were sent abroad in the widening search for remounts, enjoying most success in Canada, the United States (until 1918 when the Americans required horses for their own army in France), Argentina and Australia. The last of these also supplied mules as did the two Iberian[23] nations. In order to offer some idea of the scale of the horse and mule supply problem, below are given establishment requirements for certain units.

A DAC [August 1914]	709 horses [a few Riding]
A DAC [April 1915]	683 horses
A Royal Field Artillery Battery	172 horses [122 Draught, 50 Riding]
A Royal Field Artillery Brigade	748 horses
A Howitzer Brigade RFA	679 horses
A Royal Horse Artillery Battery	228 horses
A Cavalry Regiment	608 horses
A Pioneer Battalion	75 horses [57 Draught, 6 Riding, 12 Pack]

Bearing in mind that 9th 'Scottish' included three RFA Brigades, one Howitzer Brigade, a DAC, a divisional supply column, a squadron of Yeomanry, three engineer companies dependent on horse-drawn transport and a requirement for officers' riding horses, there was a large number of beasts that needed feeding, watering, grooming and veterinary care.

ARMY VETERINARY SERVICES (AVC)

Although the draught horses that were used by the artillery and supply transport sections required minimal training, many of the men of these units were unaccustomed to working daily with horses and thus further training was necessary for the soldiers.

In August 1914, veterinary services almost immediately came under near-unsupportable volumes of work in order to keep acceptable numbers of horses and mules in the field.

Initially, the Army Veterinary Corps that accompanied the British Expeditionary Force to France and Flanders comprised 122 commissioned AVC officers and 797 other ranks whose joint task was the welfare of the BEF's 50,000 horses. A Mobile Veterinary Section was attached to each division to meet needs in the field – 9th 'Scottish' Division's Assistant Director of Veterinary Services (ADVS) was Major W.H. Nicol who commanded the 21st Mobile Veterinary Section. Over the course of 1914-1918, temporary commissions were granted to nearly

Table 4: Veterinary Units (AVC) by 1918	
Schools of Farriery open (one in France, three in UK)	4
Mobile Veterinary Sections	80
Field Veterinary detachments	2
Base Depots of Veterinary Stores	6
Veterinary Field Bacteriological Laboratories	4
Horse hospitals + support units	20
Veterinary Hospitals for 2,000 patients each	18
Veterinary Hospitals for 1,250 patients each	10
Veterinary Convalescent depots (1,200)	5
Veterinary Evacuation Stations	16

all the country's civilian vets, thus the manpower of the AVC and the facilities available to it increased dramatically. By the Armistice, the core of 122 commissioned officers had expanded to 1,356; in the same time span 322 warrant officers, non-commissioned officers and men had expanded to 26,146. Many improvements, both specific and general, improved the welfare of the Army's many horses and mules – by the end of the war, contagious disease among military animals had been all but eradicated thanks to scientific knowledge and surgical treatments. Further innovations included the use of Motor Horse Ambulances, Veterinary Evacuation Stations, Field Veterinary Laboratories with each Expeditionary Force, Central Veterinary Research Laboratories based at Aldershot and more Veterinary Hospitals in the UK.

LINES OF COMMUNICATION & AMMUNITION SUPPLY FROM THE FACTORY TO THE FRONT

As the war progressed in both time and scale, so weaponry and supply systems became more sophisticated (if such a word may be used in relation to methods of killing).

The process began with the sourcing of raw materials and their arrival at the munitions factory. Ideally, there would be one factory per division and it was calculated that the output of each factory should approximate to 2,000 tons for every day its division had its guns in action. This standard could not be attained early in the war and this was reflected in the 1915 'Shell Scandal'.

In March 1915 the British offensive at Neuve Chapelle exposed the short-comings and weaknesses in the system of munitions production. It was not until David Lloyd-George was appointed to the new role of Minister of Munitions that the situation showed any major improvement. Initially, tonnages were low but changes in munitions policy and organisation resulted in greatly enhanced production – gradually, the industry was effectively put on a war footing and another element of 'total war' fell into place.

The demands placed on the munitions factories were of course determined by rate of shell expenditure at the front. For example, an 18-pounder field gun might access an extra thousand rounds between Boulogne and the front line but if that gun were in action for three half-hour 'shoots', firing at about ten rounds per minute, the entire reserve supply would be exhausted in an afternoon. The same was true, pro rata, of the heavier artillery pieces.

The finished munitions were usually loaded directly onto wagons in rail sidings at the factory; the shells were then transported to the mainline railhead en route for the Channel ports of Southampton, Dover and Folkestone where the ammunition was loaded on to transport ships in the port. Cross-Channel transports were both valuable and vulnerable and so they were usually escorted by destroyers or torpedo boats to protect them from possible U-Boat attack. The enemy threat apart, a Channel crossing was also at the mercy of weather, sea transport availability and

railway capacity (at home and in France and Flanders).

Initially, all ammunition moved through Boulogne but as the war progressed the BEF expanded and so demand increased in proportion such that by 1915 a second port of entry was required. Rouen was the logical choice for the southern ammunition route since, at the behest of the French, the BEF had extended southwards to the Somme River the section of the front line for which it was responsible.

Once the ammunition transport had berthed at, say, Boulogne, the vital yet dangerous cargo was offloaded by Lines of Communication troops to the dockside railhead and thence either directly into ammunition trains or to a huge, nearby Royal Army Ordnance Corps depot. These port ammunition dumps had to be available for temporary storage that was easy to reach from the port but which would pose only a limited threat to the local civilian population should an accident occur.

Standard-gauge railways would then move the ammunition to extensive Army/Corps ammunition parks, run by men of the Army Service Corps (horse and motor transport). Their task was to ensure the ammunition's onward transportation to railheads in rear of divisional operating areas. From the divisional dump the ammunition was then taken, usually by motor transport (ASC, MT) or rail to the divisional refilling point. Such locations, in rear of the area where the division was operating, had to be mobile and thus were under canvas rather than in permanent buildings.

It was from the divisional refilling point that the Divisional Ammunition Column manned by Royal Artillery personnel took control of the ammunition for the first time and distributed it as required to units, parks or dumps. The Divisional Ammunition Column employed General Service Wagons pulled by four-horse teams though, as the war progressed, increasing numbers of light, narrow-gauge railways and motor-lorries became available. Until May 1916, the DACs would distribute the shells among the four brigade refilling points from where the Brigade Ammunition Columns would deliver the shells to Battery Refilling Points for carts to replenish the guns and limbers themselves. Forward transportation depended upon terrain, road surfaces and enemy action – on occasions, ground and weather conditions stymied wheeled transport so packhorse and pack-mule ruled the supply lines, moving eighteen-pounder ammunition in eight-shell canvas carriers despite the thick, glutinous mud. Slow, maybe, but far better than no shells at all. In the case of Small Arms Ammunition (SAA), wooden boxes filled with cartridges were usually manhandled through narrow communication trenches into the front line, not infrequently under sometimes deliberate but generally speculative enemy fire.

From mid-1916, 60cm light railways[24] began to replace the early, unreliable Motor Transport in the onward supply of ammunition, even as far as the brigade areas and on to the front lines.

EFFECTS OF WEATHER ON AMMUNITION DISTRIBUTION

Cross-Channel weather could affect the delivery of ammunition to the distribution ports of Boulogne and Rouen although railway transportation from the ports to the railheads was generally immune from all but the worst snow and ice. Undoubtedly, the element of the transport system most vulnerable to weather disruption was the point at which the main railway (the ASC Ammunition Parks) gave way to light railways, motor-lorries and, more frequently, horse-drawn General Service (G.S.) Wagons under the auspices of the DAC's 'A' echelon. The often cobbled French and Belgian roads were not particularly suited to the movement of heavy loads of ammunition aboard motor-lorries and G.S. wagons though even the pavé was better than nearer the front where forward dumps were accessed by difficult roads that had been reduced to little more than heavily-muddied tracks.

Beyond the forward dumps, transportation to the batteries was increasingly under the shadow of German artillery that, during especially wet offensives like the Somme and 3rd Ypres ('Passchendaele'), occasionally rendered impassable to wheeled vehicles approaches already deep in glutinous mud. It was then that the hard-pressed men of 'B' echelon's four sections turned to horses and mules that laboured stoically under the weight of full saddle-packs and canvas ammunition-carriers, the beasts struggling through mud that was sometimes indescribably deep and sticky.

The classic image during 3rd Ypres of men fighting to extract trapped guns from the morass of Flanders mud, following persistent rain that had flooded agricultural land whose drainage system had been obliterated by the massive preparatory bombardment, applied equally to men and horses that slipped from the mud-covered walkways. While men suffered a slow death by drowning, horses were usually shot to curtail their suffering. At such times, if batteries occasionally ran short of shells, the gunners' understandable frustrations were probably matched by the drivers' aggravation at dragging crushing weights and frightened beasts through the slime. Yet while the battle was maintained, both gunners and drivers would strive to keep their respective teams working effectively.

In warmer, drier times, the heavy mud turned to dust and this brought the other problem of observation by the enemy – heavy ammunition wagons threw up tell-tale clouds of dust that quickly drew down German artillery fire.

ARTILLERY UNITS SPECIFIC TO 9TH 'SCOTTISH' DIVISION

9th Division – RFA Brigades (50th, 51st, 52nd and 53rd)

Just as the battalion was the basic tactical unit of the infantry, so the RFA Brigade was the basic tactical unit of the field artillery. Like most other divisions, 9th 'Scottish' Divisional Artillery was composed of three brigades of field guns, a brigade of howitzers and, briefly, a battery of heavy guns. At full establishment, a brigade of 18-pounder field guns comprised four batteries, each of four guns, 795 men (including 23 officers), 748 horses, 60 General Service Wagons and 36 carts. A 4.5-inch howitzer brigade comprised four batteries, each of four howitzers, 755 men (22 officers), 679 horses, 57 General Service Wagons and 5 carts. 9/Division Artillery comprised three brigades of field guns – 50th 51st and 52nd), a brigade of howitzers (53rd) and a single battery of heavy guns, old 60-pounders that soon came directly under Army control. Each of the four artillery brigades had its own dedicated ammunition column (50, 51, 52 and 53/BACs) with eight ammunition wagons in addition to the 9/Divisional Ammunition Column.

9th Division – An RFA Brigade HQ

9/Division's CRA (Commander Royal Artillery) until May 1916 was Brigadier-General E.H. Armitage. Each brigade, however, was directed by an RFA Brigade HQ that was commanded by a Lieutenant-Colonel and which usually comprised about 45 personnel, not all of them Royal Artillery.

Captain or Lieutenant (Adjutant – in charge of administration)

Captain or Lieutenant (Orderly Officer – responsible for stores and transport)

1 Royal Army Medical Corps officer (RAMC),

1 Army Veterinary Corps officer (AVC)

Sergeant-Major

2 Corporals

2 Bombardiers

9 Drivers

7 Gunners

1 Clerk

1 Trumpeter.

Between them, the above men executed the roles of signaller, telephonist and assisted with range-taking tasks.

9th Division – RFA Batteries

Table 5: 9/Divisional Artillery

Three brigades of field guns:

    50th Brigade (A, B, C, D Batteries – each of four 18-pounders)

    51st Brigade (A, B, C, D Batteries – each of four 18-pounders)

    52nd Brigade (A, B, C, D Batteries – each of four 18-pounders)

    Each RFA Brigade had its own dedicated ammunition column:

    50th Brigade Ammunition Column, 51st BAC and 52nd BAC.

There was also one brigade of howitzers:

    53rd (H) Brigade (A [Heavy], B [Heavy], C [Heavy], D [Heavy] Batteries –

    each of four 4.5in howitzers) with its dedicated 53rd (H) BAC.

[Initially, 9/Division had a battery of heavy guns, old 60-pounders. Within days, the latter was removed to Army Corps control.]

1 Corporal and 3 privates of the RAMC were attached for water-cart duties – safe, clean water was vital.

8 Gunners acted as officers' batmen

2 Orderlies for the Medical Officer.

Brigade HQ commanded four Batteries and a Brigade Ammunition Column.

Ideally[25] or at full establishment, each battery of field guns numbered 198 men, 172 horses and six wagons:

Major or Captain[26] (O/C Battery)

Captain (2 I/C)

3 Lieutenants or Second-Lieutenants (in charge of 2-gun sections)

Battery Sergeant-Major (BSM)

Battery Quartermaster Sergeant (BQMS)

Farrier-Sergeant

4 Shoeing Smiths (one a Corporal)

2 Saddlers

2 Wheelers

2 Trumpeters

7 Sergeants

7 Corporals

11 Bombardiers

75 Gunners

70 Drivers

10 Gunners (as officers' batmen)

6 ammunition wagons

122 draught horses

50 riding horses

9th Division – Brigade Ammunition Columns (BACs)

The allotted task of the Brigade Ammunition Column was to bring ammunition and other supplies to the Battery positions from the Divisional refilling points. A BAC was divided into two sections – one to re-supply the field guns and howitzers: the second Small Arms Ammunition. The BAC units of 9th Division were,

50th BAC, 51st BAC, 52nd BAC and 53rd (H) BAC

In theory, each Brigade Ammunition Column numbered 163 officers and men.

Captain (O/C BAC)

3 Lieutenants or Second-Lieutenants

Battery Sergeant-Major (BSM)

Battery Quartermaster Sergeant (BQMS)

Farrier-Sergeant

4 Shoeing Smiths (one a Corporal)

2 Saddlers

2 Wheelers

1 Trumpeter

4 Sergeants

5 Corporals

5 Bombardiers

30 Gunners

96 Drivers

3 Gunners (as officers' batmen).

Notes on Ammunition Columns

In action, the brigade ammunition columns were on the battlefield itself, subject to both direct and indirect fire from enemy lines. Operating further to the rear were the divisional and corps columns, whose principal tasks in battle were to replenish the refilling points for the forward columns and to draw fresh ammunition supplies from the depots nearer the railhead. An unspoken but accepted function of the officers and men of the Royal Field Artillery employed with the ammunition columns was to act as immediate replacements for casualties among the gunners in the batteries – this explains why at least twelve men who originally enlisted in 9/DAC were recorded as 'killed in action' with one of 9th Division's gun batteries or even with another division's guns. The dozen men so far identified in this category are:

89301	Sergeant de la Mare, T	C/53	died 19th Dec	1915
89325	Gunner Baker, CP	B/51	died 14th Nov	1916
89231	Gunner Keyho, JM	C/51	died 20th Nov	1916
91389	Gunner Marquand, CWJ	C/23	died 27th Dec	1916
89321	Gunner Bichard, A	D/51	died 17th April	1917
89210	Gunner Luxon, JH	50/Bde	died 20th April	1917
91218	Gunner Green, SS	D/51	died 22nd April	1917
90886	Gunner de la Rue, CM 4.5in	How	died 29th April	1917
89193	Bombardier, Nicolle, WH	C/50	died 29th April	1917
89223	A/Bdr, Le Noury, JW	A/232	died 1st July	1917
89167	Gunner Strappini, B	D/175	died 9th July	1917
89239	Gunner Herring, WH	52/Bde	died 28th August	1918

1 There were more than 7,000 cases of typhoid-type diseases on the Western Front; of these, more than 250 proved fatal. See the comment in Jack's diary for Saturday, 3rd July 1915.

2 Originally, the senior 'K1' Division would have been 8th 'Light' Division but the return from overseas garrisons of further battalions of 'Regulars' led to the 8th Division title being used before the New Army men were fully trained. The first of the 'Light' divisions was thus numbered 14th.

3 Qualified instructors for this 'civilian army' were also in very short supply.

4 Given the age of the diary entries and the fact that they are pencil-written in ordinary notebooks, it is difficult to tell whether one or two of the initial pages have been lost. Two of the diaries are simple reporter's notebooks held together by strong, string knots.

5 These were not the infantry battalions as they crossed from Folkestone to Boulogne.

6 Landing at Boulogne, the infantry battalions enjoyed a much shorter journey to St. Omer.

7 Many Great War Tommies have commented on the signs that adorned many troop trains in France, '8 chevaux ou 40 hommes' – 'Eight horses or forty men.' In Jack's memory, eight RFA horses were accompanied by several gunners/drivers. It must have been somewhat crowded!

8 Jack's description, "…full of wounded", might be explained by the fact that on 9th May the Battle of Aubers Ridge had been fought and on 15th May the Battle of Festubert had commenced. No. 10 Stationary Hospital at St. Omer was due west of these battlefronts and would have been 'fed' wounded from No.10 Casualty Clearing Station and No.54 C.C.S, both at Hazebrouck.

9 For further details please see Appendix 6.

10 51/RFA is easy notation for 51 Brigade, Royal Field Artillery.
51/BAC is same for 51 Brigade Ammunition Column.
9/DAC is 9th Divisional Ammunition Column.

11 Referred to traditionally as the 'Three' Corps rather than the 'Third' Corps.

12 'Army' here is used in the sense of 'First Army' commanded by General Sir Douglas Haig or General Sir H.L. Smith-Dorrien's 'Second Army' rather than 'the' Army as opposed to the Navy.

13 On 27th May 1915, 6th Division was taken over by Major-General Walter Congreve V.C.

14 On 27th May, the battles of 2nd Ypres were coming to a close (to the north of Jack's position), while to the south the Battle of Festubert had recently concluded.

15 The two other RE companies were 63rd and 64th Field Companies, Royal Engineers.

16 In the Indian Corps, there were two battalions of Ghurka Rifles with 3rd (Lahore) Division and four with 7th (Meerut) Division that took part in the Battle of Festubert in May 1915. Problems of acclimatisation and reinforcement caused most of the Indian infantry to be withdrawn from the European theatre of war from October 1915.

17 Napoléon's Imperial Guard is generally acknowledged as the elite infantry of its time; it marched tirelessly, foraged effectively and fought en masse or in column like men possessed.

18 The German nickname is a pun – 'Durchbruch' means breakthrough.

19 This description may be found in a later chapter, reference: 17th September 1917…

20 Do not confuse 'GSW' in this context with the way it is used in soldiers' service or pension records, where 'GSW' is a regular simplification of 'Gun Shot Wound'.

21 The Brigade Ammunition Columns were absorbed into the DACs in May 1916.

22 The Territorial Force cavalry branch was known as the County Yeomanry and therein were many men who knew what to look for in a good horse.

23 Spain and Portugal together constitute the Iberian Peninsula.

24 The sole example of a military-constructed light railway remaining from the Great War is to be found at in the southern end of the old Somme battlefield. The Froissy-Dompierre railway is now a tourist attraction, known locally as, 'Le P'tit train de la Haute Somme'. Though the track is relatively short, the journey into the past is endless.

25 No unit was ever 'at establishment', except maybe when it left its depot, or in the most optimistic dreams of the adjutant.

26 Once in the field, promotion, either temporary or permanent, was necessarily rapid.

CHAPTER FIVE
LOOS & YPRES 1915

<u>AUTUMN INITIATION</u>

WAITING FOR THE PUSH

DIARY

Tuesday, 8th June   **Berguette, north of Lillers**

"At 3 a.m. we were up and on the move, travelling until 11:30 a.m., when we reached our camp, not quite sure of where we are but rather near La Bassée [a dozen miles to the east]. The heat for the last week has been almost impossible to bear; this morning was the worst and it finally finished with a thunderstorm that started about 1 p.m. and lasted until four. Torrents of rain fell and cooled the air a lot; it was still raining slightly at 6 p.m. We have received no post at our camp for nearly a week and have been unable to send any letters off. On Sunday a new lot of 'Kitcheners' [men] followed us up – Royal Fusiliers of 12th ['Eastern'] Division, they were fairly knocked up with the heat and were dropping by the roadside. Four died from over-exertion and we had a busy job helping to bring the others around. I met some of the Royal Sussex Regiment, including two chaps from Rye called Openshaw [30070 James, 263127 Albert are the only two men of that surname who served in the Royal Sussex[1]] but did not know them. I am expecting to meet Burgess [he is never identified nor mentioned again] as they are believed to be at La Bassée."

Thursday, 10th June

"Dinner time and it has just come on to rain again. Just had news of a big move on our part if possible. Our officer just told me the reason of our sudden shift to this part of the line. The French have made an advance near Arras and want English troops to help them. The 9th Division has been sent here to carry out a big move which is hoped to do a lot towards ending the war by breaking the line by La Bassée and forcing the Germans to retreat near

Ypres. The enclosed map [this had been removed from Jack's diary, possibly by the 'censor'] is cut from the 'paper of Tuesday 8th [June] – 'x' shows our present camp at the time of writing [near Berguette]."

Thursday, 17th June

"Still in the same camp but under orders to leave at any moment. Nothing much to mention since 10th June except on Monday night [14th] when a terrific artillery battle started close to us. All

Monday night and Tuesday it went on, on Tuesday night it increased and the terrible din kept everyone awake. On Wednesday morning all was calm and not a gun could be heard. Orders came for us to move at an hour's notice – the camp went mad, expecting it was the beginning of the great advance that we have been waiting so long for. We all knew the great battle we had heard raging was our division at work but just as we were ready to start an order came for us to stand by. Later we discovered that we had had a severe reverse and that the French had lost all the ground they had taken. This meant that we must stay here until our lot advance again. It's a very quiet camp tonight but we may go forward at any hour now. News is very hard to get but we have had a very bad time of it during the last few days, or rather the French have, which means the same thing to us at the present time. For now, we can only stand fast and await orders."

CONTEXT

Joffre, the French commander, had planned consecutive attacks for the first half of 1915. In February, the French Fourth Army assaulted strong German defences in Champagne, advancing some two miles at a cost of more than 40,000 casualties; the French First Army's support attack near Saint-Mihiel was similarly unsuccessful and costly. Joffre's second attack plan was intended to assault the relative heights of Vimy Ridge; he wanted the British to take over full responsibility for the Ypres Salient, thus releasing an entire French Corps for use on the Ridge, and to execute a diversionary attack on La Bassée. Sir John French (commander of the BEF) refused to co-operate, instead sanctioning a British attack at Neuve Chapelle on 10th March. Joffre put off the March offensive until May but, as would occur opposite the French at Verdun in early 1916, a major German attack on the British in the Ypres Salient in late April necessitated a change of French start date on Vimy Ridge. Coincidental with the British assault on Aubers Ridge,[2] 9th May saw the opening of the French offensive in Artois between Arras and Lens, aimed at capturing Vimy Ridge and thus dominating the Douai Plain. Initial success on the ridge was soon reversed and the fighting became attritional – by 18th June French casualties in the offensive exceeded a quarter of a million for negligible gains in what was known as the Second Battle of Artois.

DIARY

Sunday, 20th June
La Ferme Château, Berguette
(Fine and warm)
"Still at Berguette [three days after the previous diary entry] and quiet. Last night [Saturday, 19th June] another hard battle with artillery took place but we have not yet heard the result. Today has been an easy one for me – I spent the afternoon

in the shade of a cherry tree and had a nice sleep. We are camping in a field full of cherry and pear trees that are loaded with fruit. An hour ago the news came in that our batteries had done splendid work during the last two days and had regained a lot of the ground the French had lost last week – that means we will soon move. Everybody in camp is feeling high-spirited at the prospect. Will we be disappointed?"

Tuesday, 22nd June
Berguette
"Outside the shops; I spent an hour wandering round. Quite a smart place, not much sign of war here, except for the soldiers, mostly British, who are in the town, either billeted or passing through. In the evening I had a walk around a very large, dense forest [possibly le Bois d'Amont, a couple of miles to the north of Berguette] and had a swim in a stream that we found there.

"Still very quiet during the last couple of days. Just had tea. Another big artillery fight started close to us. There's no sign of us moving yet but cheerful news has just come through that the French have broken through the German line [near Souchez] and in another place have 15,000 Germans in a four-mile wedge and are shelling them from three sides. Our officers expect it to be a great victory for us; everybody in camp is greatly excited awaiting the order for the move that is a long time coming. Our Colonel told us today we would be home for Christmas

dinner [over by Christmas, yet again?]. I hope he is right."

Friday, 25th June
Ecquedecques   **West of Lillers**
(Heavy rain)
"Yesterday [Thursday, 24th June] the whole section had a route march. We left at 7 a.m. and travelled until 10:30, stopped for dinner just by a camp of the Indian Cavalry – a lot of Bengal Lancers – and A.W.L.A.R. [this seems to be a slight confusion here – possible explanations are as follows. There was an 'Ambala' (3rd) Cavalry Brigade in France in 1915 with the 1st Indian Cavalry Division and later in the conflict there was the 46th '1st Alwar' Cavalry that formed in 1918 from the Alwar Lancers. During the Great War the Alwar Lancers served on the North-West Frontier.]

"...After dinner we left at 2:30 p.m., reaching camp at 6:30. We had a fine outing. On arriving back, orders were waiting for us to move off in a few hours – a big advance was coming along the line from La Bassée to Souchez. As I write this [11:30 a.m. today] the Scotch infantry are passing on the way to the trenches – we follow at three this afternoon. All our division is on the move today and big things are expected. It is pouring with rain and mud is everywhere but we have got to go through it. The Scotch look happy enough, despite the weather, and we give them a cheer – they are the boys to give the 9th Division a good name. We are just packing up – I wonder where we shall sleep tonight?"

Friday evening – 9:30 p.m., 25th June
Lillers
(Warm then thunderstorms)
"At last we have made the long looked-for move. We left Berguette at 3 p.m. and just as we left a heavy thunderstorm and rain squall caught us, like drowned rats. We travelled on through Ham-en-Artois and camped just outside Lillers [three miles south of Berguette], wet through to the skin. We don't take much notice of the town as we pass through."

Saturday, 26th June
Lillers
(Fine, dry, warm)
"A lovely morning. Our clothes dry, we now feel very pleased with ourselves after our little excursion through the rain. During the morning I went into the town of Lillers to do some shopping and quite enjoyed it. It is one of the best and biggest towns we have seen in France – it reminded me of Woolwich Square. It was market day and the town was full of stalls."

Sunday, 27th June – 10:30 a.m.
Lillers
(Heavy rain)
"Rotten morning, just come on to rain like mad and we have orders to stand ready for another shift in a few hours. We are to relieve the 2nd Division [an experienced 'regular' unit that had been 'out' since August 1914] who have been getting a very warm time of it all around this way. Our batteries have just gone into action and our infantry are moving up the line to relieve at dark tonight. All we can hear at the present time is bagpipes as they go marching along."

Monday, 28th June
Chocques
(Rain)
"Left Lillers at 3 p.m. – spent the night four miles from Béthune [near Chocques or Annezin]. Shells were falling all over the town but business was going on as usual."

Tuesday, 29th June
Bivouacs in Robecq
(Rain)
"Again shifted camp. Went a little further away from Béthune to a little place called Robecq [east-north-east of Lillers]."

Wednesday, 30th June
Robecq
(Heavy thunderstorms)
"Very quiet all day until evening when three aeroplane fights took place in half an hour. Weather rotten, rain every day during the last week, heavy storms, very little sun. Thousands of soldiers all around this way; last evening they were passing from tea time all during the night until daylight this morning. A number of them were just out of the trenches at La Bassée and a lot were showing slight wounds and limping."

CONTEXT

During the nights of 1st/2nd July, 26th and 27th Brigades relieved 7th Division in the line east of Festubert; 28th Infantry

Minenwerfer or 'Moaning Minnie' – the German heavy mine-thrower.

Brigade was in reserve. They remained in the line until 18th August, experiencing a 'proper' initiation into the ways of trench life. As the Germans held the ridge line, only their artillery could fire by direct observation. Part of the line was a salient [in the Bois Grenier sector], known as 'The Orchard' and was regularly under fire from artillery and mortars – there was a high casualty rate here.

"Our artillery could do little at that time to help the infantry – for every shell that we had, the Germans had ten and each attempt to retaliate resulted in a fiercer and heavier bombardment. Until our gunners were supplied with enough material to enable them to compete with the enemy, the best policy was to refrain from annoying him.

"The infantry particularly disliked our feeble artillery efforts because they alone felt the consequences. For a similar reason all trench mortars were unpopular – when a mortar was fired, that section of trench was drenched by the enemy with '[Moaning] Minnies.'"

[This was a clear indictment of the shell shortage at that time.]

[John Ewing: *The History of the Ninth 'Scottish' Division, 1914-1919'.*]

DIARY

Friday, 2nd July
Near Lillers, north of Béthune
(Very hot)
"Shifted camp again [from Robecq] in the afternoon, advancing three miles just to the left [north] of Béthune. During the evening, about 8 o'clock, a very exciting time started when three of our aeroplanes were hovering over our lines. The German guns at once began to shell them – about one hundred shells were fired at the three for half an hour. The air was full of bursting shells with the aeroplanes dodging about amongst them as if it was nothing. Weather is scorching hot. Flies by daytime and mosquitoes by night make it unbearable to live as one can't breathe without swallowing them."

Saturday, 3rd July
Lillers   **Shells and Insects**
(Very hot)
"Very quiet all day, about 9:30 p.m. A big battle started just over Béthune, the ground shaking with the reports of the big guns while the bursting shells lit up the place like electric lights flashing up – it is a splendid sight to see from a distance. Weather still boiling hot with the insects being bigger pests than ever. I am one mass of swellings and hard lumps after being bitten by them – it's a good thing we were inoculated or there would have been a few deaths before now. The day has been marked by a drowning fatality in

No.2 section [of 9/DAC], a driver named Steel being drowned in the canal[3] while bathing."

[He was actually 58396 Gunner Herbert Walter Steeley, 9th Division Ammunition Column, RFA, aged 27 years. Records show that he died on 3rd July 1915. He is buried in grave 11 of Robecq Communal Cemetery,[4] five miles north-east of Béthune, in the Pas de Calais. He was the son of Mr. and Mrs. C. Steeley of Old House Lane, Corley, Coventry, Warwickshire. He was married to Elizabeth Steeley of Stone House, Red Hill, Fillongley, Warwickshire].

"That's two of our column gone since we have been here – last Sunday one of the men from No.1 Section was shot accidentally by his chum. It's No.3's turn to lose one now."

[In fact, Driver Herbert Steeley, RFA, was actually the third 9th Divisional Artilleryman man to die recently, after: 60497 Sergeant E.G. Ling, 'C' Battery, 53rd Brigade RFA died on 26th June 1915 and is buried in plot 1.A. 168 of Longuenesse (St. Omer) Souvenir Cemetery

33434 Bombardier Frederick Pennington of 'C' Battery, 53rd Brigade RFA died two days later, on 28th June 1915, and is buried in plot VIII.F.1 of Brown's Road Military Cemetery, Festubert].

CONTEXT

As it became ever more apparent that air observation, bombing and aerial fighting was an important aspect of this war, demand for Anti-Aircraft gun batteries increased apace. GHQ in France ordered that not only should there be one AA Section per division, but another fifteen gun Sections to cover the lines of communication. In July 1915, two Searchlight Sections [organised by the Royal Engineers] were stationed in Saint-Omer. By August 1915, there were in all 13 Searchlight Sections in France.

DIARY

Tuesday, 6th July

Gonnehem   **Shell shortages**

(Very warm and thundery)

"Very quiet for the past two days but today has been our nearest to the dangerous region – we are now about three miles or less to the north-west of Béthune [near Gonnehem] and that town has been shelled by the Germans all day today. At the present time, 6 p.m., the shells are shaking the ground and overhead, about the same distance to the north of us, three of our aeroplanes are being shelled within a mile of each other – it is a grand sight. A very bad thunderstorm is lurking around us so we are in for a lively time tonight. At 7:30 p.m., if it is fine, we are holding a concert in our section – it will be a strange contrast to the guns banging, with

'ragtime'[5] going on at the same time. Extra guards are on and everything is ready for a possible retreat as things are looking very black around this part of the line. We are short of ammunition[6] and the Germans are massing fresh troops along from here towards Ypres. Our leaders here are very uneasy and our batteries have orders to hold their part of the line at any cost – no retreat to be thought of at any price. If only the people at home realised what it feels like to know that if we only had the ammunition we could go forward but instead of that we look like going back. We have so many troops here we don't know where to put them – because of shortness of ammunition we can't put them in action. Thousands of our troops are all around here and have never been in action because of no shells to help them. At the present time retreat seems almost certain; if so, Heaven knows how it will finish."

CONTEXT

Thursday, 8th July

Lord Kitchener's inspection

Lord Kitchener inspected 26th Brigade (in divisional reserve) and detachments of 9th Division between Locon and Hinges, three miles north of Béthune.

[John Ewing: *'The History of the Ninth 'Scottish' Division, 1914-1919'.*]

Throughout a rather hot month of July, 9/DAC War Diary reports a consistent shortage of decent drinking water; this must have been most unpopular with the men, though no doubt strong, sweet tea – 'gunfire' – was still available.

DIARY

Saturday, 10th July
Gonnehem

"Nothing to mention except the third man has died – three Saturdays running, a dead man. The Quarter-Master died suddenly this morning."

[The soldier who died was 89613 Battery Quarter Master Sergeant James Thomson Turnbull Milne of 9/DAC who actually died on Friday, 9th July 1915; Milne, who had been born in Hawick, Roxburgh was a married man whose home was in Warrington, Lancashire. He is buried in plot I. D.28 of Chocques Military Cemetery.]

Friday, 16th July
Gonnehem   Dogfights and balloons
(Unsettled, rainy)
"Everything has been very quiet during the past few days except for a great number of aeroplane fights and three visits from German aeroplanes – one has been just over our camp three times in the last two days. This morning about 6 a.m. a number of fights took place between them just over Béthune, three miles from us. Today I had my first experience of a German 'Jack Johnson' [nicknamed after the black American heavyweight champion of the world from 1908 until 5th April 1915. The name became a slang term for

German 15cm mortar and 21cm howitzer shells that gave off a lot of black smoke on detonation. A howitzer was a short-barrelled, usually heavy, gun that fired a shell in a high trajectory – it derived from a German word for catapult].

"I went into Béthune for the officer and while there the Germans fired twice at an observation station, which was a captive balloon, about a mile high right over the town. The two shells burst just short of the balloon about five hundred yards over our heads. It was a bit of a shock, the first one that went off, though the next was looked for but only two came – we looked for more but did not get them. The weather has been unsettled and it is raining now."

Sunday, 18th July
Gonnehem   A dark, dangerous ride
(Wind and rain)
"Very quiet today but last night a big battle raged nearly all night. I went into Lillers which is about seven miles away and had a most exciting taste of a strange country after dark. I went as groom to our officer and, leaving camp at six and doing the journey in quick time on a pair of very spirited horses, we reached Lillers at seven. At 9:30 p.m. we left for camp [at Gonnehem] again, black as pitch, blowing and raining, we could not see a yard in front of us. The horses took all our time to manage, while the bursting shells and flares thrown from the firing line about three miles away gave us a time we are not likely to forget. For about three miles we had to

travel along a narrow towing path by the side of the La Bassée Canal and how we got home safely I don't know. It was a grand sight to see the firing line – for five or six miles it was a long line of flashes which lit up the country for miles. Then we would get a minute or two of darkness when it was impossible to see at all – it took us 2½ hours to do the journey back, though we were going as fast as we dared. We had several narrow escapes from a bath – I was twice over the bank with one leg but managed to pull him [the horse] back in time. I don't know where my heart was for that two hours but it was certainly not in the right place. I don't want another journey like that – I would sooner dodge the shells."

CONTEXT

During this period the divisional artillery was very short of shells but as salvoes merely encouraged retaliation, a tacit *'live and let live'* attitude developed. British use of mortars and artillery drew down German fire on the trenches, especially by *'Minnies'* [*'Minenwerfer'*] or mine-throwers.

The Prince of Wales occasionally visited the trenches, often into dangerous forward saps, in search of souvenirs, much to the displeasure of divisional officers. On one such visit, no steed had been provided for His Royal Highness, so he proceeded to borrow one from a divisional officer – the mount was thereafter dubbed, *'Prince'*.

[John Ewing: *'The History of the Ninth 'Scottish' Division, 1914-1919'.*]

DIARY

Monday, 19th July

Gonnehem   **A fire fight**

"Very quiet today after another attempt to break through last night by the Germans, one that ended in failure for them. Last night's battle was the heaviest we have seen since we have been here. It started about ten and lasted for about two hours, during which time there was not a quiet moment. Heavy artillery and machine guns were going as fast as they could be worked and during the scrap fire-bombs[7] were dropped on Béthune from some type of aircraft that could not be seen. According to what we see and hear around this way, the end of the war seems to be very near at the present time but it is very hard to say. Early this morning several shells were dropped on Béthune by the 'Hun' big guns but the people still stay and carry on their business, which is ample proof of the confidence they have in our troops. Kitchener's Army is just showing them what they are made of and I think everybody is satisfied (except the Germans)."

Friday, 30th July

Gonnehem   **A deadly accident**

(Clear and calm)

"Still at the same camp and nothing very exciting in the firing line but a terrible accident happened in our column last night about 12:30 a.m. An explosion took place

in the guardroom of No.1 Section – the guardroom was composed of ammunition packed in a square and nobody knows how it happened but it is thought that a man must have dropped a lighted cigarette. It caught some cordite in the place which instantly went up; four men were badly injured and one has just died from his injuries." [In fact, at least two men died from their wounds. They were – 27732, Driver Raymond Godfrey, aged 19 years, 9th Divisional Ammunition Column; he was the son of Louisa Godfrey and the late James Godfrey of 6, Greenbank Crescent, Darlington, County Durham. Also killed was 84793, Driver James O'Neil, 9th Divisional Ammunition Column. The two men are buried beside each other in Lillers Communal Cemetery, Raymond in plot IV.A.7 and James in plot IV.A.8].

"The other three are in a very bad way; though it was a quarter of a mile away it woke the whole camp, everybody grabbing respirators thinking it was a German aeroplane dropping bombs – as we are expecting that we have orders to grab for respirators at the first sign of aeroplanes. It was a lovely night, bright moonlight and not a breath of air, ideal for air raids. It's a very serious camp this morning, in spite of the lovely weather."

Lillers Communal Cemetery Extension: final resting place of Driver James O'Neil and Driver Raymond Godfrey, RFA, 9/DAC.

Saturday, 13th August
Gonnehem   Front line trenches
"Today I had my first look at the trenches. I went into the Red Cross Hospital by the firing line, east of Béthune – all that could be seen was a bare wasteland with not even a tree standing as far as the eye could see. Everything was very quiet, no fighting for a couple of days around that part."

Sunday, 14th August
Cantrainne rest camp, near Lillers
"Shifted from our camp by Béthune, gone back just close to Lillers at a place called Cantrainne [two miles east of Lillers] for a ten-day rest. The next move after a short spell is to be to the south of Béthune. There's nothing to be heard of the guns here – we are about ten miles from the line."

CONTEXT

On 18th August, 7th Division relieved 9th Division in the line, releasing the latter to go to the training grounds near Busnes where, on 19th August, 9th 'Scottish' was again inspected by Lord Kitchener who complimented the division on their efforts thus far. 9th Division remained in the Busnes area, training hard and practising rapid trench assaults until the end of the month. Up to then, the division's overall casualties had been relatively light and their trench skills had been honed to a pitch; the Scots wondered when they would be tested. [John Ewing: 'The History of the Ninth 'Scottish' Division, 1914-1919'.]

DIARY

Sunday, 29th August
Cantrainne rest camp, near Lillers
(Hot then stormy)
"A miserable night after a lovely week of boiling hot weather. Tomorrow we expect to shift back to the firing line and at last the long-expected advance is to come off. I was told last night by the officer [2/ Lt. W.H. Ozanne] after a visit from the General that on 8th September we shall attempt to break the German line and commence what we hope and think will be a victorious move. Every confidence is in the move being successful. We have taken over thirty-five more miles of the line from the French,[8] which will leave them nearly one million men to reinforce the French line. Whether successful or not, we have got to do something to take the continual pressure off the Russian line [that was retiring rapidly before the Germans and Austrians near Warsaw].

"The plans of months[9] are about to be put into action under General Joffre and everybody is glad to get a move."

Monday, 30th August
Cantrainne rest camp, near Lillers
(Cold after a hot week)
"The next month will show what will happen towards ending the war – expert opinion seems to be divided as to a quick finish but everybody is certain of striking a very big blow at the main German army.

Yesterday two of our largest batteries came by on the way from England to La Bassée where the most important part of the advance is to be attempted. We have had a fortnight resting in this camp and every man is now eager to get to the fighting point once more. It is raining hard at present and mud is everywhere. Yesterday we did not know where to go for coolness; tonight we want big coats on."

TOUGH INITIATION AT LOOS

CONTEXT

On 2nd September 9th 'Scottish' Division relieved 1st Division in trenches to the east of Vermelles, adjacent to what would become, during September and October 1915, the battlefield of Loos as part of a double-edged attack. In Artois, the French aimed to advance due east, towards Valenciennes and from Champagne towards Mauberge; the British I Corps (Lieutenant-General Hubert de la P. Gough) and the IV Corps (Lieutenant-General Sir Henry S. Rawlinson) were to advance towards the Haisnes-Hulluch line to protect the left flank of the attacking French. Short of artillery pieces and ammunition, the British plan would rely heavily on the release of gas prior to the infantry attack.

[John Ewing: *'The History of the Ninth 'Scottish' Division, 1914-1919'.*]

DIARY

Friday, 3rd September
Ammunition Dump, Béthune Town sports fields
(Heavy evening rain)
[In the town district of Annezin]

'La Grande Place, Béthune', prior to major damage from shelling.

"Yesterday, 2nd September, we left our rest camp at Lillers and proceeded on the first stage of the expected advance. We left at 1 p.m. and camped at Béthune about 5:30 p.m; our camp is on the town sports fields. It covers a large space, being a racecourse, football pitch, tennis courts, bowls, skittles with huge grandstands and waiting and dressing rooms. A very pretty place in peacetime but at the present time all to pieces with shellfire and soldiers being billeted here. We are now closer to the

actual fighting than we have been at all. The batteries are close beside us and we are just close enough that a shell could just about reach us. A number of shells fell here a few weeks ago and we are sleeping alongside of a hole big enough to put at least four men in. One tennis court has been blown all to pieces by a shell only just lately. On Tuesday we all are looking for the first real big move towards the advance. On the way up yesterday we saw hundreds of new motor transport wagons loaded with shells for the five large siege batteries that have just come out [The heavy siege batteries were under Corps and Army control] and which we all look to for the first and most important thing of paving the way for our infantry. Our [divisional artillery] batteries are proceeding on to the line today to get their positions and tonight we shall start work once more in grim earnest. The band is about to play on our side? We mean to have those hills at the back of the German lines, if we don't go any further. As they have much drier positions than ours for their trenches, we hope to go on much further before the winter stops us. Great excitement runs high along the British lines for it is pretty well known that we are now on for something, though not many know quite what. As usual, when we shift it rains – it has pelted in torrents since about five last night and it's still coming down hard. Everything is wet through; every time we make a shift we get bad weather. We don't know where to turn for a dry place – we only found one dry place

and that was playing bowls in one of the recreation rooms next to our camp. We spent an hour there until our fingers had the skin off the tips. We now have to wait on the watch for what happens and our next move will be towards Berlin (I hope)."

Tuesday, 7th September
Béthune Town sports fields
(Hot) **Rumours of an advance**
"The day has dawned at last. Sometime during the next 24 hours we commence the first attempt at a real advance. The next few days will show what will happen. It is a long, hot day and everybody is strung up to concert pitch waiting for the enemy, as we believe darkness will start the ball. Thousands of troops are passing up the line and everywhere is hustle and bustle. Our camp is simply an arsenal of shells and bombs. All is ready except for the hour to start motors with the officers. Aeroplanes are everywhere; a dozen can be seen at the present time, flying within a radius of about five square miles and passing each other like traffic in a wide street."

Friday, 10th September
Béthune Town sports fields
Artillery duel
"Last evening closed with some very exciting aeroplane fights close over our heads. We saw eight at one time being shelled within two miles of each other; one shell burst right on one 'plane and we all thought he was done but he righted his machine again and managed to get well

behind the line before coming down. At ten last night the bombardment by our troops started all along the line; during the day they threw one or two big shells at a small hill where the Germans had a lot of communication trenches – a few shells from 9.2in howitzers blew the whole hill to ruins. This was only a small start. Last night we gave them a terrible bashing – the thundering of our artillery and the German shells dropping kept us all awake all night. This morning, about 8:30, we began to bring some very heavy guns into action and now, 10:30, the banging is terrific. Every shot seems to jar our heads on our shoulders and the windows in the houses keep up a continual chatter. The real thing has not yet commenced in earnest; this is only a slight beginning. We are still waiting for the big move which has been delayed by waiting for a move up of the French line from La Bassée away towards the Swiss frontier."

Wednesday, 15th September
Under fire   Volunteer forward labour
(Warm but dull)
"10:30 a.m. – Today has opened very quiet, a fine, warm morning but very dull. Yesterday I went up to within three-quarters of a mile of the German trenches – volunteers were asked for to go up and help build bridges and lay telephone wires. I went with fourteen others and it was a very exciting time. We passed up through three lines of our own artillery and went to work on a bridge. All was quiet when we first arrived but we had orders to go in

open order and keep low for fear of shell fire if we were seen by the enemy. We got to our position with a row of 18-pounders on our right and a 9.2in howitzer battery on our left – we did not know the 9.2ins were there until they suddenly let go. From ten in the morning up to 4:30 p.m. we worked with three batteries of 18-pounders and one of 9.2ins firing over our heads – it was a trying experience for the first hour but after that it was nothing. The Germans did not reply until about 3:30 p.m. when I was on the top of a dugout digging out a large plank; suddenly a shell burst about half a mile up, right over our heads. I was soon pulled off the high position but we found that the shell had been fired at one of our aeroplanes that was over us. After that, about thirty shots were fired at the machines that kept flying over us but none was returned at our batteries that kept up a continual fire all day."

Evening, 15th September
Béthune Town sports fields
Fire alarms
"9:30 p.m. – Today has been very quiet at the camp but tonight as it grew dark a big glare was seen in the direction of Annequin. As it got darker, the glare seemed to get brighter and at the present time it is a big glare for miles up in the sky. Our captain thinks it must be a village at the back of the German lines as it is too far away to be on our side. A heavy bombardment is going on, to our left, towards the coast, but our own batteries are all quiet. We shall no doubt find out

in the morning what the big glare means. Last night we were called out at 9:30 p.m. by the fire alarm; a fire had broken out in the billet of the Scotch down the road but they got it under [control] before we got there. On Monday a farmer close to us lost the whole of his year's crops, every stock was burnt to the ground – the fire lasted nearly three days and is not finished yet, the ashes still being bright. The glow in the sky is not so bright now; the morning will show why, no doubt. I am now off to bed."

Saturday, 18th September
Béthune Town sports fields
(Very hot)
Bombs and 'whizz-bangs'

"Today has opened very quiet and up to now, 12:30 p.m., nothing has happened except for shelling of our aircraft that has been going on at intervals all the morning. All last night a terrific battle raged in the direction of Neuve Chapelle – rifle and machine-gun fire was terrific and about two in the morning a heavy explosion shook the place. This morning we learn that it was an enormous bomb dropped at Neuve Chapelle, which is about eight miles north-east of us. About one o'clock the Germans sent us a souvenir in the shape of a lovely whizz-bang dropped about a quarter of a mile away after passing over us. We were all getting ready to dress but no more came, so we stayed in 'kip' until six. The night was one unbroken battle, the most severe being at Neuve Chapelle or in that direction. We have not been able to get any news of the big fire that we saw in

the direction of Annequin on Wednesday night. Today is very hot, so after dinner I am going to have a dip in the stream that runs through our camp."

Sunday, 19th September
Béthune Town sports fields
(Calm and warm)
Preparing ammunition supplies

"Last night was again a very exciting time. At about eleven, the Germans made a very heavy attack on our lines away towards Neuve Chapelle. Our guns were all turned on to the spot and completely cut them to pieces. Just before dark last evening a sudden order came in for all the [General Service] wagons to fill up at once. Today, the whole of the ammunition park is going to load all ammunition into our column and then refill in readiness for us to draw, as we have about ten times the amount we are supposed to have. There is no doubt that the extra big move is going to start in a very short time. We are getting tired of waiting for the big thing that we know is coming but is such a long time about it. The firing last night, though very heavy, is not a bit of what is going to be heard. Today is very quiet and rather warm, though we have a nice, cool breeze blowing."

Monday, 20th September
Béthune Town sports fields
(Clear)   **Artillery duel**
"Last evening was again a very exciting one from an aerial point of view. At five o'clock fifteen aeroplanes crossed over our heads in a bunch making for the coast

A lifting bridge on La Bassée Canal: the waterway was a frequent target.

direction. *They were much larger than any we had seen before and were very high up – it was a splendid sight, not a cloud in the sky, the noise being heard before they were anywhere near us. After that the rest of the evening was taken up by aeroplane fights all along the line as far as we could see each way. Hundreds of shells were fired from the anti-aircraft guns but apart from a great waste of ammunition, nothing happened. This morning, ever since daylight, a terrible artillery fight has been on – the booming seems to jar one's head down into one's shoulders. I forgot to say that last night, after the aeroplanes passed over, we saw a wonderful blood-red light which seemed to explode; we heard no noise but a huge flash illuminated the sky for miles. This was about 7:15 p.m. and in the direction of Neuve Chapelle."*

Evening, 20th September
Béthune Town sports fields
Eve of Loos artillery barrage

"8:30 p.m. – Tonight at 5:30 another fleet of eleven aeroplanes of the large pattern [probably Gothas] crossed over us making straight for La Bassée. It is very hard to get news but it must be some very special thing. There is a good amount of firing going on down the French line but our own guns are fairly quiet. The officer has just told me that we start tomorrow morning at five to bombard the German lines with all of our bigger guns – the bombardment will last for five days. Then will come the attempt to encircle the vast army that is opposing us. The plan is to drive around from the French lines and come in around La Bassée and Lille and drive the Germans in towards Ypres

where we shall catch them on three sides. Saturday next will see the commencement of this great movement. The encircling movement is entrusted to three divisions[10] – 2nd Division [Regulars], 7th Division [Regulars] and ourselves, 9th 'Scottish' Division [Kitcheners]. We, the first full division of Kitcheners to come out, are to be in it from start to finish."

THE BATTLE PLAN FOR LOOS

CONTEXT

The French commander, General Joseph Joffre, judged that July 1915 was a propitious time for Britain, France and Belgium to make a breakthrough on the Western Front and to give Russia some room for manoeuvre after a summer of defeat and retreat in the face of German-Austrian combined forces. The French intended to attack again in the Lens-Arras sector while the British were required to make a holding assault on the German lines in the La Bassée-Loos sector. In addition, the French would make a parallel attack in the Champagne region and a number of diversions would also inhibit German reinforcements from being moved up to the main target areas. A reluctant participant, Sir John French requested a deferral to late September, while subordinate British generals strongly criticised the choice of battleground – the IV Corps commander for the assault, Lieutenant-General Sir Henry Rawlinson, commented tersely,

"...my new front at Loos is as flat as the palm of my hand. Hardly any cover anywhere. Easy enough to hold defensively but very difficult to attack. It will cost us dearly and we shall not get very far." [He would not be proven wrong].

Still noticeably short of artillery and ammunition, the British High Command opted to commit to their first use of chlorine gas as a precursor to the assault at Loos – the decision was justified part as 'payback' for the Germans' Ypres gas attack the previous April and part to compensate for the relatively feeble artillery barrage that would be available to the British guns. On the other hand the infantry, though containing several 'New Army' units, of which 9th 'Scottish' Division was one, was deemed to be up to scratch in both standards and numbers. Nevertheless, planning for what was to be known as the Battle of Loos, was noticeably over-ambitious. The offensive was entrusted to the French Tenth Army and to the British I and IV Corps. The main French attack would occur in Champagne, aiming for Mauberge beyond the front lines; the British attack would occur between Haisnes and Loos to its south (on a front of 3½ miles), heading for Valenciennes. The overall hope was for the two strikes to link – 'breakthrough' was still the aim of army planning.

On the British front, the I Corps would strike for Haisnes in the north while the IV Corps would strike for Hulluch in the south, beyond the Loos-La Bassée road; subsidiary, diversionary attacks elsewhere were intended to disrupt and distract reinforcements from the main field of battle.

The weakness of the British Artillery was tacitly acknowledged by the intention to hinge the initial assault on a release of gas that would be cancelled if the wind was unfavourable, whereupon the entire attack would be scaled down. In any event, the German second-line wire proved too distant to cut by the limited artillery barrage, so early successes were difficult to exploit effectively on such an 'open' battleground.

In the centre of Lieutenant-General Hubert de la P. Gough's I Corps, 9th 'Scottish' Division's task was to establish a northern defensive flank, so it was imperative to capture the line 'Railway Works > Fosse 8 > Haisnes' and then to push on towards Douvrin. On the right front of the I Corps, the Regulars of 7th Division were expected to establish a southern flank facing Loos – if both corps enjoyed success then they were expected to forge ahead. To 9th Division's left and on the I Corps left wing, 2nd Division was tasked to capture the Givenchy Salient and take the German front line before moving on Auchy in order to forge an even stronger northern flank.

On 2nd September, 9th 'Scottish' took over the line east-north-east of Vermelles and opposite the imposing Hohenzollern Redoubt, with the aim of preparing for the coming battle. The division's frontage

was 1,600 yards of what was to prove the toughest sector of the entire Loos battlefield – and it was entrusted to the only 'Kitchener' division alongside three divisions of regulars in the I Corps (2nd, 7th and 28th Divisions). The terrain over which the Scots would advance was essentially open – to the west and behind them was a railway embankment that afforded some cover to reserves; ahead, the only heights or cover were the pit-head gear and spoil-heaps that would be familiar to the lads from the mining areas of Central Scotland. But on this battlefield the few heights were in enemy hands and the Scots' infantry advance was both overlooked and covered by German machine-guns.

As the role of the artillery was to demolish enemy defences, the acute shortage of guns and ammunition was a major drawback from the outset. The preliminary bombardment was set for 21st September and in this all the artillery, including divisional brigades, was initially controlled by the I Corps CRA, Br-Gen. J.F.N. Birch. The four-day bombardment employed 18-pounders using mainly shrapnel in an attempt to cut the enemy wire; defensive strong-points were shelled by the few 'heavies' available;[11] divisional howitzer batteries were targeted to the night shelling of tracks, roads, communications trenches and buildings. To attempt to neutralise defensive rifle fire and machine-gun nests, to interdict enemy movement and to prevent the repair of wire during the night of 24th

September, indirect fire from British machine-guns was used extensively.

On the morning of the battle, British artillery bombarded the German front line then re-directed to the back areas of Haisnes and Cité St. Elie. Once the assault commenced, control of the artillery reverted to divisional CRAs, with two batteries assigned to follow up any successful infantry attack. Trenches were to be pre-bridged and all necessary materials were to be carried by the batteries, a vital factor in the re-supply of ammunition.

DIARY

Tuesday, 21st September
Artillery Start of the Battle of Loos

"AT LAST, [Jack's emphasis] the great thing for which we have waited for months has finally made a commencement. This morning, about 6:30, a huge explosion just away to our left told us that the Marine Artillery had opened the ball with a 15-inch shell;[12] immediately from then on the bombardment[13] has kept on and will keep on until Saturday next. The terrible noise that is going on cannot be described, it is the most unholy noise one could think of – those who live through this lot will never forget it even if they try. The gun fire during the last month has been awful but this is the most nerve-trying of the lot. It is terrible to see the Red Cross motors pass by with the wounded Tommies on the way to the base hospital – [they appear to be…] a mass of blood, it is hard to tell if they are dead or alive. We have seen hundreds pass by here during the past month but how many are going down in the next month? The time of some poor devils is getting short now."

Wednesday, 22nd September
RFC artillery 'spotting'

"3:30 p.m. – last night was again a very busy one for the Royal Flying Corps [RFC]. We saw some very clever range-finding and marking for our guns – one aeroplane circled around over the German lines with shells bursting all the time for quite half an hour. A very big gun they had somewhere there was giving us a lovely time and we had to stop it. This particular aeroplane kept over their position until he spotted the gun which was cleverly hidden; then, out came a fire ball when he was directly over the gun. A little to the right he found another gun and dropped another fire ball over it. He then came back over us to the aerodrome and as soon as he was out of the way our guns began to play on the spot the flyer had shown us. About a dozen shots were fired and then we heard no more from the German guns. This morning we bombarded the enemy lines very heavily from 7:30 up to twelve; since then things have been very quiet except for a row of 18-pounders that keep up a slow fire at intervals." [The latter comments confirm the limitations placed upon the British Artillery by the insufficiency of ammunition].

Thursday, 23rd September
Bombardment continues

"Today nothing special has happened except for the usual heavy bombardment lasted all the morning. During the afternoon everywhere was very quiet."

Friday, 24th September
Loos – Eve of infantry assault
(Heavy rain)
"10:30 p.m. – All day today has been the usual bombardments. About three this afternoon they broke out with greater force – this, we all know, is the final touch before our infantry make an advance. Tomorrow we shall go forward or be blown to blazes and no-one feels like sleep tonight. It has been the most trying work of my life – about ten hours' sleep in a week and working hard all the time. Millions of rounds of ammunition have gone out during the past seven days and tonight we have just finished the last lot for this bombardment. We have been loading ammunition from 3:30 this afternoon until ten tonight and now I am off to bed. Early morning tomorrow we will see the start of our advance – it remains to be seen how far we will get."

CONTEXT

Saturday, 25th September
Loos – Opening infantry assault
(Variable winds)
The attack orders of 9th 'Scottish' for 25th September were as follows. Their overall task was to establish a strong, northern defensive flank; with 2nd Division to their left, the Scots' task

appeared achievable. They were ordered to go to the assault with two brigades, each with two battalions 'up' and one in reserve. 28th Brigade occupied the left front (10/Highland Light Infantry and 6/King's Own Scottish Borderers) – their objectives were to secure the railway line from the Corons[14] de Marons to the junction with Les Briques (roughly parallel to the British front line), Train Valley (that crossed No Man's Land towards Les Briques from the British lines) and Madagascar ('Mad') Point and trench. 26th Brigade occupied the right front (5/Cameron Highlanders and 7/Seaforth Highlanders) – their objectives were the daunting Hohenzollern Redoubt ('Hohenzollernwerk', shown on pages 146–147), Fosse Trench and Dump Trench (the original German front line at rear of the Redoubt) then Fosse No.8, Les Trois Cabarets and the Corons de Pekin. These were intended to be the 'First Line Objectives' of 28th and 26th Brigade – such targets turned out to be wildly optimistic, though not on account of the Scots' want of courage. Brigadier-General Bruce's 27th Brigade was in flexible reserve, 2,500 yards behind front line – their intended role was either to support the attack on Fosse No. 8 or to add weight to the hoped-for advance towards Haisnes or Douvrin. The latter did not materialise.

In preparation for the assault, new forward, 'jumping-off' trenches were dug just 150 yards from the German line; new communications trenches linked the lines to aid reinforcement, re-supply and

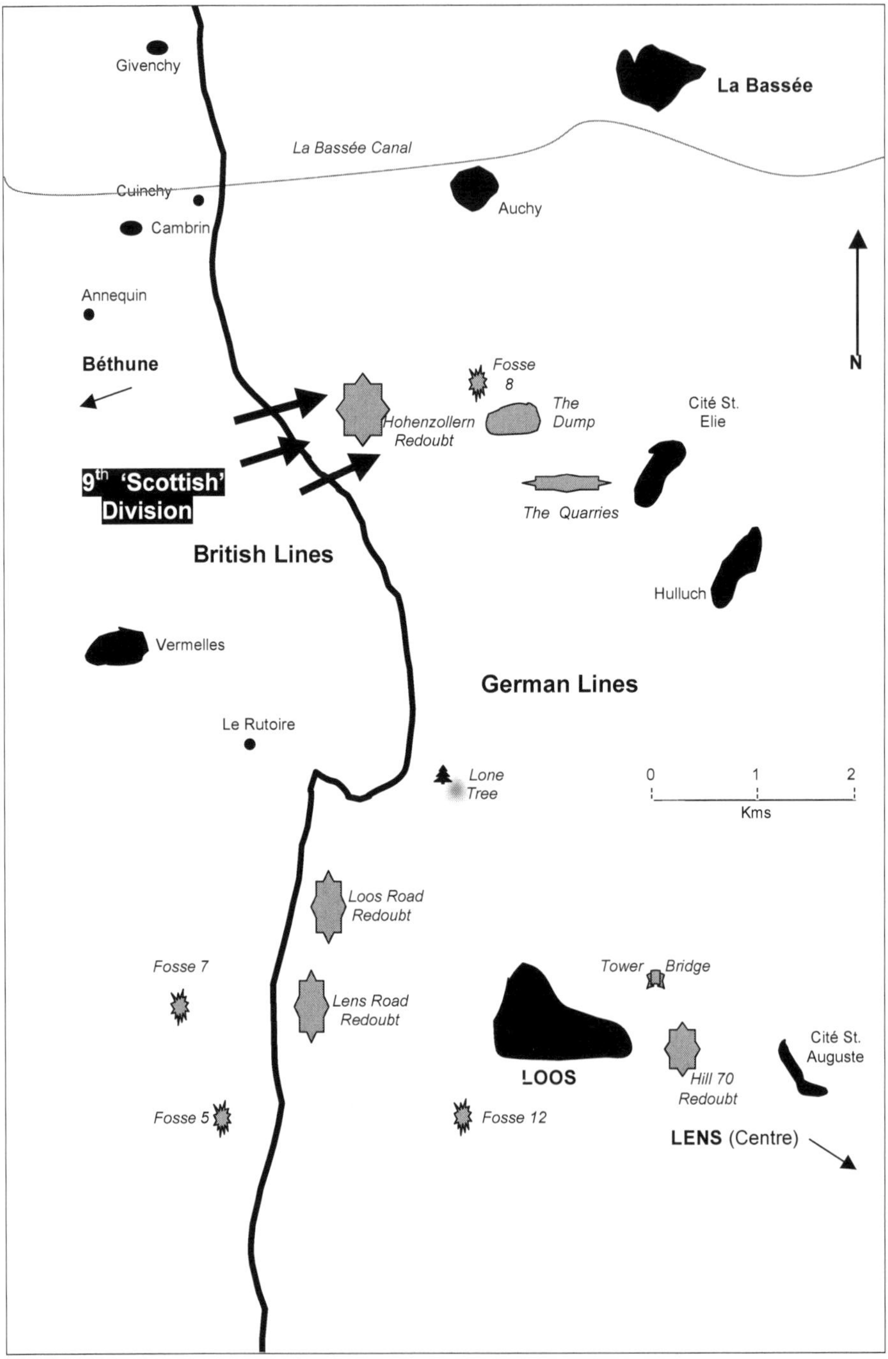

Givenchy

La Bassée

La Bassée Canal

Cuinchy

Auchy

Cambrin

Annequin

Béthune

Fosse 8

The Dump

Cité St. Elie

N

Hohenzollern Redoubt

9th 'Scottish' Division

The Quarries

Hulluch

British Lines

Vermelles

German Lines

Le Rutoire

Lone Tree

0 1 2

Kms

Loos Road Redoubt

Fosse 7

Tower Bridge

Lens Road Redoubt

Cité St. Auguste

LOOS

Hill 70 Redoubt

Fosse 5

Fosse 12

LENS (Centre)

Map 2: 9th 'Scottish' Division at Loos, 25th September 1915

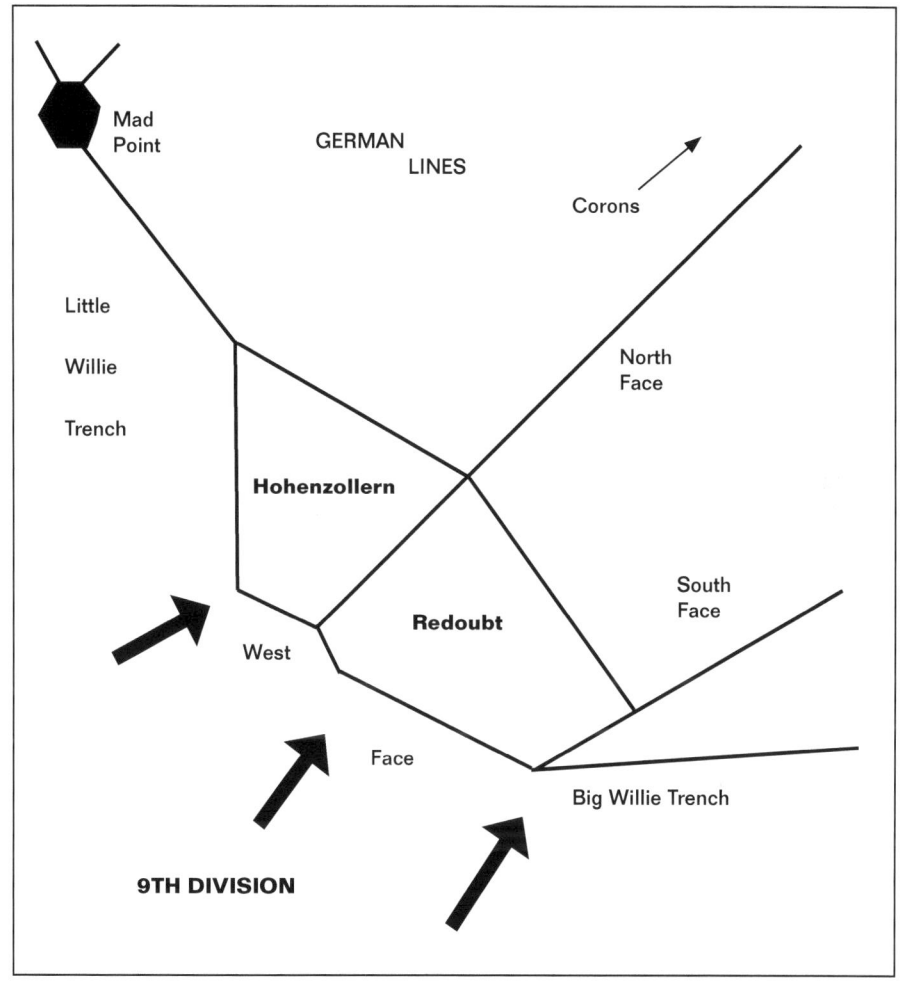

Diagram 3: **9th Division at the Hohenzollern Redoubt**

evacuation of the wounded. In all, 12,000 yards of new trench were constructed. Ammunition, stores and tools were dumped all along 9th Division's front; special 'bomb' dumps were created to cope with the large amounts of grenades required; Small Arms Ammunition (SAA), picks and shovels, water and medical stores were all held in forward dumps; dumps had to be well forward as communications trenches would be needed to move the inevitable numbers of wounded men. Each infantryman was given 200 rounds SAA but had to dump his haversack in order to carry his ammunition.

In the event, the Loos offensive was so nearly a success but the initial advance on 25th September was not properly exploited, with the result that three weeks of attacking left the front line just over a mile forward, either side of the town of Loos at a cost of some 60,000 casualties. Above all, Loos was the first real 'blooding' of Kitchener's 'New Army' divisions and some of the Territorial divisions – in fact for many Scottish, southern and midland regiments, the battle was a grim foretaste of the slaughter on the Somme in the summer of 1916. In view of the ammunition shortage, 150 tons of chlorine gas were released at sunrise, 5:50 a.m.; the infantry assault, timed for 6:30 a.m. (Zero-hour) was preceded by a limited artillery barrage. The gas cloud, augmented by smoke candles, drifted towards the German lines but the wind was light and fluky; a shift in direction caused the gas to 'stall' in No Man's Land, even drift back to British lines – some assault battalions had to advance through chlorine and, despite wearing rudimentary 'smoke-hoods', a number of the attacking infantrymen suffered the debilitating effects of gas.

DIARY

Saturday, 25th September
Ground attack – forward the Ninth!
(Heavy rain)
[9/DAC War Diary spoke of, *'...heavy rain swamping the ground...'*, and described the camp as being, *'...a foot deep in mud.'*]

"12:30 p.m. – At last we have made a start this morning. Our division advanced just over two miles and we are all packed and ready for the order to move on after them. It is a pretty bad sight this morning to see the wounded going by on the way to the hospital. It is hard to get any definite news but we do know that we have had a splendid success – our big guns will again have some work to do to open the way for the infantry. They have gone so far forward that we can't hear them at all. If one of our 15-inch guns lets go then we can just hear the report but our 18-pounders have gone clean out of earshot altogether but we will be on them before night comes."

CONTEXT

Saturday, 25th September
Heavy Scots' Losses
At 6:29 a.m., the lead battalions of 26th Brigade advanced and by 8 a.m. both the 7/Seaforths and 5/Camerons were established on the east side of Fosse No.8. An hour later, at 9:10 a.m., 28th Brigade on the left divisional front had been repulsed although 26th Brigade was reported as, *'...making good progress,'* against the German 117th Infantry Division. 28th Brigade made a determined second attack but this too was repulsed; by now this brigade had lost two-thirds of its effective strength and had to be withdrawn to their start line. Speed of reinforcement in mid-morning was crucial to the outcome – 27th Brigade had difficulty moving

forward while the enemy managed to reinforce with the Guards Reserve Division, the 10th Bavarian Regiment and one battalion of 123rd Division – the day hinged on this aspect. Forward movement of the guns depended upon the capture of Fosse No.8, The Dump and the Double Crassier, all of which could provide vital observation points for the enemy; in the event, by late afternoon artillery support consisted of 52nd Brigade RFA and one Howitzer battery, both of which were withdrawn at night as their positions were too exposed. By the end of the day on the 25th, 28th Brigade had been repulsed whereas 26th Brigade still held the Dump and Fosse No.8; the reinforcing 27th Brigade had managed to hold on to Fosse Alley.

During a long day 9th 'Scottish' had soaked up fearful punishment; the worst battalion casualty lists were:

8/Black Watch	511 (killed, wounded or missing)
5/Cameron Highlanders	406
7/Seaforth Highlanders	378
11/Royal Scots	267
8/Gordon Highlanders	249
12/Royal Scots	197
	Total: 1708

Sunday, 26th September
Withdrawal of the Ninth
Early on 26th September, the Highland Brigade was relieved by 73rd Brigade. By 6 a.m., all three brigades were back in their original front lines. Throughout the night long-range enemy artillery fired on Madagascar Trench and Les Briques Trench, Cam Alley and Pekin Alley. During Sunday afternoon, 27th Brigade filled the gap between 9th and 7th Divisions by occupying Dump Trench.

[John Ewing: 'The History of the Ninth 'Scottish' Division, 1914-1919'.]

DIARY

Sunday, 26th September
German counter-attacks
(Bright and sunny)
"2:30 p.m. – Our move up after the batteries did not come yesterday, after all. We packed up in the rain at breakfast time and waited about all day in the wet expecting the order to move on. At three o'clock the order came to move at four, so we finished up everything but it commenced to pour hard as soon as the order came in. At four we were ready to shift off and, soaked to the skin, we waited in the pouring rain until seven when the

La Guerre 1914-15-16
Visé Paris

Panorama de Loos (P.-de-C.)
The Panorama of Loos

Edition Deschamps à Béthune

Loos battlefield showing the structure nicknamed 'Tower Bridge'.

order came to remain where we were. In our wet clothes we lay down to sleep with nothing to eat since eleven in the morning. At 2 a.m. I was called up to get the officer off with his horse – an order for 1,200 rounds of shells had come in, wanted at once. We've had hardly any sleep for over a week, in 'bed' at night soaked to the skin, on the wet mud. I wonder how some at home would like to change their fancy socks for this. The 9th Division has done wonderful work; with the 2nd and 7th Divisions we were carrying out the most important move of flanking. Our division was first through the enemy's lines and led the advance for three miles then held that position until 7th Division came up, then started on again. We have

had great success so far but the price we have paid has been shocking; for two days, ever since the attack began, we have had wounded passing us on the way to hospital. All sorts of wagons and motors are being used, the large supply of ambulance motors not being enough. This morning one of our batteries had to fall back and we are at the present moment meeting a heavy counter-attack by the Germans to recover the lost ground. The firing is so heavy that we can now hear it quite plainly. Owing to the stop we are still awaiting orders to move. Fortunately today has turned out a lovely day and the bright sun is drying us all up nicely. We expect to move tonight but do not know will happen now."

CONTEXT

Monday, 27th September
A V.C. earned, a C.O. killed

'For Valour'. A line drawing of the Victoria Cross.

At 2:30 a.m. a second attack on The Quarries was repulsed. The CO of 9th Division, Major-General George Handcock Thesiger (from a long-established military family), the Rifle Brigade, was killed by German shellfire at Loos while he was reconnoitring the Hohenzollern Redoubt that was in imminent danger of being lost to the enemy. Killed in action 27th September 1915, Thesiger had been in command of the Scots for just a few days. The immediate situation was rescued by 26th Infantry Brigade which, at 10 a.m., sent forward to the Redoubt seventy men of 8/

Black Watch (the Royal Highlanders) and thirty men of 5/Cameron Highlanders. Among these reinforcements who rallied the flagging defenders was Corporal James Dalgleish Pollock, 5/Cameron Highlanders, who earned the plum-ribboned Victoria Cross in this action – despite being wounded several times and against the odds, he held his position. The citation for his award reads as follows:

> *"...On 27th September 1915 near the Hohenzollern Redoubt, France, at about noon the enemy's bombers in superior numbers were successfully working up 'Little Willie' Trench towards the Redoubt. Corporal Pollock, after obtaining permission, got out of the trench alone and walked along the top edge with complete disregard for danger, and compelled the enemy bombers to retire by bombing them from above. He was under heavy machine-gun fire the whole time, but contrived to hold up the progress of the Germans for an hour before he was at length wounded."*

Corporal Pollock was later commissioned and rose to the rank of Captain.

The Scots' active infantry involvement at Loos ended on 27th September; in just three days the division lost close on 6,000 casualties. Despite limited successes, such as 28th Brigade's capture of Fosse 8 Dump – that was widely hailed as a great feat of arms – the division had not really lit the fuse to their eventual reputation. The divisional artillery remained in support of 28th Division until 1st October and continued to take casualties. By the time of their full withdrawal, 9th 'Scottish' had sustained 6,058 men killed, missing or wounded. For the record, in the IV Corps, another 'New Army' Division, 15th 'Scottish' sustained 6,896 casualties during the Battle of Loos. For the Scots, Loos would rival the opening of the Somme offensive in the summer of 1916.

The restricted allocation of ammunition and the limited artillery to fire it hindered Allied chances of success. Logically, the Divisional Ammunition Column and most of the BAC units were at their busiest in the build-up to and during the preparatory artillery barrage. Having dumped shells and SAA as far forward as was practical, the prime business of the DAC was to maintain shell levels at the forward dumps from which each BAC and the gun-battery carts could replenish stocks at the guns and their limbers. 9/DAC War Diary indicates that between 26th and 29th September there were constant requests for replenishment of supplies of hand grenades, suggesting a high degree of close-quarter fighting.

9th Divisional Artillery fired as part of the I Corps, providing twelve batteries of 18-pounder (QF[15]) guns, namely:

A, B, C and D Batteries of 50th Brigade RFA [Lt.-Col. Brooke]

A, B, C and D Batteries of 51st Brigade RFA [Lt.-Col. Carter]

A, B, C and D Batteries of 52nd Brigade RFA [Lt.-Col. Perreau]

And three batteries of 4.5 inch howitzers, namely:

B, C and D Batteries of 53rd Brigade RFA [Lt.-Col. Knapp].

Initially under Corps control for the four-day barrage, as soon as the infantry assault commenced control of the divisional artillery reverted to the 9th Division CRA[16], Brigadier-General Armitage.

Even when the Scots' infantry brigades moved out, their divisional artillery remained on the gun-line, supporting 28th Division until that division's own guns arrived on 1st October. Again, the DAC and the associated BACs remained with their prime attachment, the Scots' artillery.

The initial gas release of 25th September was ineffective as the wind was fluky and smoke candles, intended to 'bulk out' the gas cloud, caused loss of direction among infantry. 26th Brigade's trench mortar teams were all knocked out early in the assault and thus attempts at exploitation were soon frustrated. Medical support and transport arrangements for the wounded were wholly inadequate, so many men were left on the battlefield for several days to die of exposure, shock, thirst or even despair. Any failure or mistakes on the part of 9th Division may be set at the door of their general inexperience of battlefield tactics under fire. It was not their courage under fire that failed them – the 2,824 lads who never returned from the field of battle at Loos testify to that.

[Principal sources: John Ewing: *'The History of the Ninth 'Scottish' Division, 1914-1919'*; Niall Cherry, *'Most Unfavourable Ground – Loos 1915'*; Michael Gavaghan, *'Forgotten Battles, Loos, 1915.'*]

DIARY

Tuesday, 28th September
"Since Sunday no change has, as yet, taken place in the artillery – heavy firing with occasional rests and slow but sure advance by our infantry. We have surrounded La Bassée and are now only awaiting an order to take it entirely. The French have taken Souchez and are still making great progress. The wounded are not as plentiful past us as on Saturday, Sunday or Monday. On the first three days the losses were terrible in lives and wounded, though very few of the wounded were very bad, being arm and head wounds. One this morning was taken past with his leg off and one had an explosive bullet burst in his thigh [these 'dum-dum' bullets[17], as they were known, were internationally illegal]. The 9th Division has lost heavily but has done splendidly – everywhere around us we hear our infantry and artillery being praised up to the skies."

CONTEXT

Wednesday, 29th September
Infantry move to Ypres
The infantry brigades that had cleaned themselves and their gear had been ordered north to the Ypres Salient by means of route marches and slow railway journeys.

DIARY

Wednesday, 29th September
(Rain)
"Our artillery is rather quieter today but our infantry [here Jack refers to the British rather than the 9th 'Scottish'] is still holding the ground gained and in one or two places has pushed forward a bit. Not much news can be obtained, except that everything is going well for us. Very few wounded have passed here now for two days but the fighting is very severe along the whole front. The weather is very bad, mud and water impeding the progress of our troops a good bit."

CONTEXT

Thursday, 30th September
Thus did 9th Division come out of the line at the end of September; the divisional infantry leaving first, followed by the divisional artillery. The I Corps commander, Lieutenant-General Hubert Gough, paid 9th 'Scottish' fine compliments:

"On leaving the I Corps, the GOC wishes to tell the Ninth Division that he thinks their conduct in the assault on the German lines [at Loos] was beyond all praise and no words can express the value of their gallantry and self-sacrifice to our country. They showed during the heavy fighting not only a great dash and courage but endurance and discipline and the highest qualities of a soldier. He can only wish them the best of all fortune in their future efforts and he is sure that they will maintain the high standard as soldiers and men that they have already reached."

[Order from I Corps HQ dated 30th September 1915 – John Ewing: *'The History of the Ninth 'Scottish' Division, 1914-1919'*.]

TO YPRES. OUT OF THE FRYING PAN…

DIARY

Thursday, 30th September
Striking camp (North to Ypres)
"Nothing very exciting today. About tea-time an order came through that we were to pack up and get off to Ypres."

CONTEXT

Thursday, 30th September
The news of a move to an Ypres Salient that already held terrors (the Salient was notorious for German mining under Allied trenches) for many British units was akin to the Ninth jumping from the frying-pan directly into the fire. Even so, many of the Scots battalions felt that they had not done themselves justice at Loos and that the Salient offered an opportunity for the Ninth to announce themselves on the Flanders front.

Friday, 1st October
A New C.O. for the Ninth
9th Division now received a new Divisional Commanding Officer, Major-General W.T. Furse [to be widely known, though not to his face, as, *'Windy Bill'*]; following Loos, there were at least nine new battalion COs and one new brigade commander. In the Salient, the division came under the auspices of the V Corps (Lieutenant-General H.D. Fanshawe).

Demarcation Stone, Locon, near where Jack recognised Colonel McCrea.

DIARY

Friday, 1st October
Steenwerck
"This morning at nine we left Béthune on our way to Ypres. Passing through Locon [immediately north of Béthune], I saw Colonel MacCrea, the president of the Royal Guernsey Golf Club." [Richard Francis McCrea was Commanding Officer of the Royal Guernsey Militia Artillery and Engineers from 1908 to 1915; he was mentioned in dispatches during service in the Great War; after the war he was made Aide-de-Camp to King George V.]

"We passed a lot of Indian troops, a lot of them being Ghurkas. Reaching Steenwerck [immediately south-east of Bailleul] about 4 o'clock in the afternoon, we camped for the night close to one of our old encampments where we pitched up after we first came over."

Saturday, 2nd October
West of Poperinghe/Ypres
(Cold and frosty)
In camp here for the month
"Today we left Steenwerck at 2 p.m. and travelled through Bailleul, which is a very large town and by far the best I have seen since I left England. We passed over the Belgian frontier about 4:30 p.m. and the first Belgian town we passed through was Locre [Loker]. We had an awfully cold journey and finally reached our camp, five miles from Ypres, at 9:30 p.m.

The past week has been very cold and at Steenwerck we had to sleep out and woke in the morning covered in frost – much of the last month's programme will soon lay out the weak ones and one or two have already packed up for a rest."

CONTEXT

Sunday, 3rd October
Hill 60 trenches
On Sunday, 3rd October, 9th Division's 26th & 27th Infantry Brigades relieved 17th 'Northern' Division in the trench lines near Hill 60. 9th 'Scottish' Division's front line commenced south of Zillebeke and extended north of Hill 60 to a point south of the Ypres-Comines Canal near Oosthoek. The Germans held the advantage of occupying the higher ground, while No Man's Land varied in width between 25 and 400 yards. The main feature of the division's location was the was hotly contested Bluff, on the north side of the canal – this man-made spoil-mound rose steeply and dominated the entire sector. Divisional Headquarters were established at Hooggraaf, two miles south of Poperinghe.

During this tour of duty, 9th 'Scottish' was in the Ypres Salient for three months, experiencing copious amounts of rain and mud – even the 'surfaced' roads were coated ankle-deep in mud. Consequently these roads were, "…choked with transport and often shelled…", thus 9/DAC had a more than usually difficult task on their hands to re-supply the gun batteries and to satisfy the infantry's small arms needs.

When out of the line, rest huts for the infantry were at Canada Huts in Dickebusch – a ten-mile march from the front line back through Ypres; moreover, the hutments were of poor quality, draughty with leaky roofs and located in a sea of liquid mud. This period saw four-day tours, alternating between front-line trenches, support and *at rest* (which often meant, '*...hard at work fetching and carrying*'). The trenches that the troops occupied were usually part dug and part sandbag breastwork on account of the high water table in the Salient. During the months October to December, the Division gradually shifted position in the front line from south to east of Zillebeke. This period of the division's service in the Salient was described by John Ewing as,

"...a time of almost unmitigated gloom and discomfort".

[John Ewing: *'The History of the Ninth 'Scottish' Division, 1914-1919'.*]

DIARY

Tuesday, 5th October
West of Poperinghe   Big gun duel
(Wet, clearing cold)
"Things have been quiet from Saturday until last night when the Germans began bombarding Poperinghe. They kept it up heavily for two hours then were quiet until about four this morning when they had another go for about two hours, and

now, 2:30 p.m., they have started again. The guns on our side are very heavy and the German shells that come over are from very big siege guns – each explosion shakes the buildings all around us. The weather is very cold at night and miserably wet, with mud everywhere."

[According to the War Diary, the 9/DAC 'camp' at Poperinghe was a mixture of billets, tents and bivouacs.]

Wednesday, 6th October
All quiet on the.....
"Very quiet, except for an occasional shell bursting within a mile or so. Nothing exciting."

CONTEXT

Thursday, 7th October
9th Divisional 'Training School'
General Furse opened the 9th Divisional 'Training School' at Poperinghe – an officer school for training and 'esprit de corps' (morale). It was cross-company and encouraged inter-battalion socialising and training.

[John Ewing: *'9th Divisional History'*]

DIARY

Thursday, 7th October
Tour of Duty   (On Colonel's escort)
"Things [are] still very quiet. I had a decent outing this morning when I was put on the Colonel's escort for a trip

to the outlying points of our division. The Colonel [the Lieutenant-Colonel in command of the DAC] and five other big 'pots' composed the party, with three of us as escort and a trumpeter. We had a good ride, about fifteen miles, stopping at a place called Abeele [south-west of Poperinghe] and also at Poperinghe. The last-named place is shelled nearly every day but on this occasion we were lucky enough to get in and out without any little German souvenirs being sent over."

British troops in 'La Grand'Place, Poperinghe', before the worst shelling.

Saturday, 9th October
Burning barns…spies?
"Nothing happened yesterday until the evening about eight when a big fire broke out at a farm about a mile from us. Our fire alarm went and we turned out but it was past doing anything to – three big barns where the Royal Engineers were billeted were burnt to the ground. Spies were suspected but no-one was caught. It was a bit of excitement. We went across country like a paper chase party over country we had never seen before and plenty of fun was caused – through ditches and hedges, over turnip fields and all sorts of unexpected obstacles, all of which were got over or through with plenty of sport about it."

Sunday, 10th October
"Still very quiet along our line except for the occasional artillery duel, generally during the night."

Monday, 11th October
Poperinghe bathtime
"This morning we all went into Poperinghe for a bath. It is a very pretty little town but badly knocked about in the part nearest the firing line."

Wednesday, 13th October
Hohenzollern Redoubt
"Very heavy fighting has been going on during the past few days around Loos and La Bassée. Big attacks were made by the Germans to recapture the Hohenzollern Redoubt, which is a very heavily fortified position but our guns mowed down the whole lot as they advanced in close formation – over 8,000 were lying between their trenches and ours after the attack

had been completely repulsed. *Reports came through that the Germans along that line are completely finished and are giving themselves up at every chance; according to these reports the end seems to be well in sight but it is hard to say." [In fact, the attack on the Hohenzollern Redoubt was made by the British 46th 'North Midland' Division, an action that cost them dear on 13th October 1915.]*

Thursday, 14th October
Artillery duel
"Last night a very heavy artillery duel went on from about 8 p.m. until the early hours of the morning. The numbers of shells sent over by each side must have been in the thousands – it was almost as bad as the artillery bombardment before the advance at Loos. No news may be had yet but a heavy fight must have taken place all around Armentières." [Again, this was part of the five day October postscript to the Loos battles. During the early hours mentioned in Jack's diary entry the random nature of trench warfare would strike at 9th 'Scottish'].*

CONTEXT

Friday 15th October
Trench mine casualties
At about 4 a.m. the Germans detonated a powerful mine twenty-five yards in front of a trench occupied by 10/ Argyll & Sutherland Highlanders near The Bluff. However, the mine threat was well-known to the defenders so the front line had been cleared but the casualties sustained, 15 men killed and 50 wounded, were in the support and communications trenches. The casualties were among the twenty-eight 10/Argyll & Sutherland Highlanders who died on 15th October 1915. The only Highlander to be identified for his burial was:

S/1575 Lance-Sergeant James Neil (plot I.H.18 Spoilbank Cemetery, Ypres)

All the other Highlanders (Scots unless indicated) are commemorated on the Menin Gate in Ypres,

S/9345 Private John Robert Armstrong [English] (33)
S/10164 Private William Baird [Canadian]
S/8337 Private James Brown (27)
S/1816 Private David Burt
10113 Private Henry Charles Chinnery [English] (21)
S/8248 Private Peter Crawford (19)
S/2470 Private Thomas Easdale (23)
S/8742 Private Alear Faulds
S/5944 Private Arthur N. Gillespie (24)

S/2294 Private William Gillespie

S/8755 Lance Corporal Thomas Cuthbertson Gold (24)

S/7687 Lance Corporal Anthony Grady

S/6222 Private Lawrence Heenan

S/8563 Private William Humphrey [English]

S/2563 Private Judge, William [English]

890 Private Frank Kennedy (22)

S/8086 Private Duncan MacColl

S/8398 Private Thomas McBride (28)

S/1573 Private John McDonald

S/1990 Lance Corporal John McGowan [English]

S/8885 Private Neil McGregor (20)

S/9592 Private Kenneth McLean

566 Private John Miller [Northern Irish]

S/1670 Private John Nairns

S/1864 Private William Penman

S/7907 Private Donald White

S/4336 Private James Woods

At 1:30 a.m. on the same morning, the Germans had also detonated a small mine near the trenches of the 5/Cameron Highlanders, killing eight men,

S/18461 Private George Aitken (22)

S/18234 Private Albert John Collins (19)

S/18797 Private Alexander Gray (24)

S/18384 Private George Hall (19)

S/18454 Private David C. Pritchard (20)

S/18392 Private Walter George Richardson (26)

S/13543 Private Peter Robertson

S/18444 Private James Merry Scoular (18), resident of Ontario, Canada.

The eight highlanders were all buried in plots C.15-23 of Blauwepoort Farm Cemetery, 3 kilometres south-east of Ypres town centre

[John Ewing: *The History of the Ninth 'Scottish' Division, 1914-1919'*; Naval & Military, CD-Rom *'Soldiers Died in the Great War'*; Commonwealth War Graves Commission.]

CONTEXT

Sunday, 17th October
Armagh Wood
By this date the division had been moved to the sector just east of Armagh Wood, towards Observatory Ridge.

[John Ewing: '9th Divisional History'.]

DIARY

Sunday, 17th October
First close view of Ypres
"Yesterday I paid my first visit to Ypres and it as worth the walk to see the sight. On the way up, about four miles from Ypres we passed through a small village called Vlamertinghe and it was smashed to a pulp, houses down for hundreds of yards, just heaps of bricks, shell holes in all the fields – one huge hole was about fifty feet across and twenty feet deep. The railway station and all around was ploughed up; the railway, being the line of our supplies, is of course the target but as fast as the line is smashed the Royal Engineers put it right. Ypres is just a heap of broken walls and bricks – quite a big place in ordinary times. It is now as quiet as the grave. We got in and out under cover of a thick fog but just as we left the Germans started to shell the place but none was very close. We were very lucky."

Monday, 18th October
Heavy fighting

"Very heavy fighting has been going on all day today. Heavy artillery has been going all day without a stop and now, 7:30 p.m., they have put on a spurt and are firing rapid-fire. Machine-guns and rifles are going at it for all they are worth. Last night there was also very fierce, close-quarter fighting."

Tuesday, 19th October
"All last night, until daylight this morning, a terrible battle raged all around Ypres. Not much artillery was used after about nine last night but the machine-gun and rifle fire was very fierce throughout the night."

Thursday, 21st October
Slightly injured
"Everything very quiet all along our line since Tuesday night. Today I went to Poperinghe with my officer to see him off on seven days' leave. I tried to break my neck – the streets are paved with cobblestones, very dangerous things – when my horse slipped and turned a somersault, while I did the same thing across the road. A motor lorry loaded with timber missed me by inches but I knocked my knee rather badly and at present have rather a stiff leg. I expect I shall be a cripple tomorrow!"

Saturday, 23rd October
West of Poperinghe/Ypres
"Very quiet today all along our line. This afternoon I had a trip into Poperinghe on my own. Spent the afternoon looking around the town – it's a very pretty place,

much bigger than it looks at first glance. It has been badly knocked about all around the station but it's business as usual."

Tuesday, 26th October
Dogfight

(Bright then rain later)

"Today opened with very bright weather after twenty-four hours very cold with heavy rain. As soon as daylight came on, action started all along our line. Heavy artillery fire on both sides went on up to dinner time; our aircraft were very busy and also the enemy all along the line. Our anti-aircraft guns kept up a heavy fire at hostile aircraft. At about ten in the morning we saw our guns shelling away at a German machine; one of the aircraft from the aerodrome close to us (Abeele) went up and a sharp fight followed for about twenty minutes. Finally the German came down very quickly inside our lines, so we scored another point for our side. At the present time, 6:30 p.m., heavy machine-gun fire is going on all around Ypres, the artillery being very quiet. Slight rain is falling again – another wet night."

Wednesday, 27th October
King's Tour

(Heavy showers)

"Today has been very quiet on the fighting line. Heavy showers all day, very cold at times and awful mud everywhere. This morning the King [George V] passed through on a tour of inspection – we turned out a guard but it only fell to a very few lucky ones to see him."

Friday, 5th November
Rain, Mud and Artillery

(Unsettled then bright and cold)

"10:30 a.m. – Nothing to report since 27th of last month except rain and mud. Occasional artillery fire and during last night rather a heavy fight about midnight which lasted until about two this morning. Still the same weather – about two fine days in three weeks."

Saturday, 6th November

(Calm but foggy)

"Yesterday about twelve the weather suddenly cleared and we had bright sunshine all the afternoon. The fine weather was the signal for aeroplanes to get to work. For two hours we had a continual bombardment of our machines over the lines. At nightfall a heavy fight commenced between our big guns and the enemy. It lasted all night until early dawn and then fell off into quiet. Very frosty and cold; today has been fine but rather foggy. Very quiet now [7:30 in the evening]."

Tuesday, 9th November
Shelled in Ypres

(Strong winds)

"Today I again paid a visit to Ypres, no change except a few more shells had helped to do more damage. The Germans started to shell us so we did not stay long – our usual luck was with us and we got away without mishap of any kind. The railway station had received another heavy bashing since I was there last, a number of houses being a complete mass

of ruins. A few shells were dropped at an open piece of road where we could be seen from the enemy observation station but we had got well away before they came along. One or two Army Service Corps [ASC] wagons got knocked out but we got safely away. Weather still bad, very strong wind blowing and every sign of our house going over before the night has gone by."

CONTEXT

Wednesday, 10th November
Sanctuary Wood sector

(Cold and wet)

By this date the division had shifted to front line trenches east of Sanctuary Wood (then still an actual wood with thick undergrowth). The sappers and pioneers worked ceaselessly in trenches that nevertheless remained poorly-built with the rain regularly collapsing and flooding both trench and dugout. This situation made thigh-length gumboots or waders invaluable; even so, the cold and wet was perpetual, giving rise to the dread condition known as 'trench foot'[18] so the application of whale-oil and anti-frostbite grease was daily overseen by the officers. As with the sector of The Bluff, there was much mining in this latest sector – it was a practice in which the Germans were at that time superior.

A light railway was used for bringing forward rations and stores to an extended front line that stretched from The Bluff to Sanctuary Wood, a distance of some 5,000 yards. This was a long

divisional line for a unit as far below strength as was 9th 'Scottish' Division. Along the entire front to the east of the ruined city of Ypres, movement was possible only after dark and even then the German artillery had the range of important cross-roads and exposed sections of road. The sterling efforts of the ASC and DAC transport was highly regarded and, despite casualties, mud and choked roads, they delivered the rations and ammunition as regularly and reliably as was possible. Running the gauntlet of shells every night while suffering the wear and tear on limbers, carts and wagons was as unsupportable as the drain of horses and men.

Given those stated dangers, General Furse attempted to establish artillery dominance and thus 'buck up' the troops by introducing a 'retaliation tariff':-

For one enemy mortar shell = one salvo of 18-pounder High Explosive

For one enemy torpedo = two salvoes 18-pounder High Explosive and two of 4.5in.

For one enemy 5.9in = one 8in shell

This made the gunners and infantry feel better but did not silence the enemy.

[John Ewing: *'The History of the Ninth 'Scottish' Division'.*]

DIARY

Thursday, 11th November West of Poperinghe/Ypres

(Rain) *(Lt. Ozanne's near miss)*

"Nothing very exciting except more rain and more mud. Very heavy artillery firing yesterday and today Vlamertinghe is being very heavily shelled. Our team had some very narrow shaves but got off lucky. Four Royal Engineers were badly wounded in the legs; one driver lost both legs – the mule he was riding got a shell right in the stomach blowing him in pieces and taking off the driver's legs with it. Our officer, Lieutenant Ozanne[19], had a narrow one today – a 9.2in shell burst about a hundred yards away and a large piece dropped by his feet, missing his head by a couple of feet."

Sunday, 14th November
Trouble in the Channel

(Fine but cold)

"Very wet from Thursday up to last evening when it suddenly cleared and commenced to freeze. The artillery immediately took advantage of the fine weather and the Germans dropped about forty shells on Poperinghe during the middle of the night. Today has been lovely and fine but very cold all day and every prospect of a frost again tonight. There has been no post, owing to the boats being unable to cross, with mines and enemy submarines in the Channel. In addition, all leave has been cancelled owing to those troubles."

[Albeit Jack does not say so but he must have been slightly concerned that similar cancellations might affect his wedding plans that were set for 30th November.]

Wednesday, 17th November
Poperinghe

(Rain, hail and snow)

"Heavy fighting all day yesterday around Ypres. I was in Poperinghe all the morning and a great number of wounded were brought through. The artillery fire all day was very heavy on both sides, lasting up to about midnight then calming down. At the present time [12:30 a.m.] they are shelling Poperinghe and Vlamertinghe and have been at it for about half an hour – it looks like the start of a big attack. Weather very changeable, three nights very hard frost and this morning rain, several hailstorms and one little attempt to snow but couldn't."

Thursday, 18th November
Serious air raids

(Hard frost, mist)

"Today started lovely and fine after a very hard frost and it soon developed into one of the most exciting days we have had for a long time. About eight o'clock, as the mist was clearing, three German aeroplanes were seen over us. Our guns opened fire and kept at them for about twenty minutes but without any good results. After dropping three bombs on Poperinghe they vanished again. About 11:30 we again heard aeroplanes at which point our guns again let fly – looking up we could see six

large, German planes that came right over us, well spread out, then the fun began. Without warning, one dropped a bomb in the next field to us and within five minutes they dropped ten more. Six fell in 'C' Battery, 50th Brigade, two were aimed at our aircraft sheds and the next fell on the No.17 Casualty Clearing Station Hospital at Remy Sidings, about half a mile from us. It was very exciting while it lasted – 'C' Battery was rather badly knocked about but the damage is not yet known, though it seemed very slight."

"8:30 p.m. – heavy fighting that commenced about noon is still going on, the artillery on both sides very active."

Monday, 22nd November
West of Poperinghe
(Wet)
"Very heavy firing during the past four days – both night and day the artillery kept up heavy fire and each night machine-gun and rifle fire was very fierce for some hours."

Thursday, 25th November
West of Poperinghe
(Wet)
"Very quiet since Tuesday night, occasional artillery fire for an hour or two but otherwise rather quiet. Last few days wet and muddy but not quite so cold."

Friday, 26th November
Vlamertinghe visit
(Snow and hail)

"Tonight I will finish the first edition of this diary for tomorrow, if all's well, I begin seven days' leave." [This is a somewhat low-key diary entry, considering that the week's leave would include Jack's wedding to Ada Palmer!]

"I have had a good finish to an eventful six months – two hours' ride at a stretch gallop in a blinding snowstorm and hailstorm. I had to go to Vlamertinghe with the officer on business. On the way, as soon as we left, we got stuck behind a number of wagons blocking the way owing to one being in the ditch. The only way out was across the ditch, so we did it, and we then had to cross about three miles of ploughed fields and ditches which we managed. It snowed and hailed almost all the time – I was frozen…"

[Here, Jack's diary entry ends abruptly, mid-sentence. Apparently, Jack's notebook diary for December 1915 and the whole of 1916 is currently missing; whether this fact was down to it being lost or confiscated by his company officer, who acted as censor, has never been established. This situation is unlikely to change.]

CONTEXT

Sunday, 28th November
Commenced home leave
On Sunday, 28th November Jack Hickman commenced his home leave to England, '…with ration allowance,'

Ada & Jack around the time of their wedding late in 1915.

(granted by the OC 9/DAC, according to Jack's Army Record). So began seven days that would change Jack's life far beyond the course of the Great War.

Monday, 29th November
Wedding Day

The day following his arrival back in Plumstead, twenty-four-year-old Jack married his fiancée Ada Mary Palmer (aged 22) at St. James's Church, Plumstead.

Jack's bride, Ada, was born in 1893 in Plumstead, Kent, the third child of William Palmer[20] and Mary Ann (known as 'Polly') Palmer, who were both born in Rye, Sussex in 1870. Mary Ann 'Polly' Paine was the daughter of Edwin Paine (a carpenter, born in Iden, Sussex in 1849) and Johanna Paine (a dressmaker, née Donovan in Rye, Sussex in 1839). At the time of Jack and Ada's wedding in November 1915, William and Polly Palmer were living at 29, Raglan Road, Plumstead with Polly's elderly parents, Edwin and Johanna Paine – it must have been a fair-sized dwelling as

Jack and Ada were added to the family roll that November!

Ada Palmer, who was always known by Jack as 'Flick', had three brothers – Will (born in Whitstable, Kent in 1892), Roy (born in Plumstead, Kent in early 1893) and Jack (born in Plumstead, Kent (in 1894 or 1895), along with a younger sister, Kate (born in Plumstead, Kent in 1899 or 1900). All three of Ada's brothers served in the army during the Great War and, tragically, all three died during or as a result of their military service. Given William and Polly's birthplace and William's craft as a carpenter, it is more than likely that Jack and Ada had been acquainted since their childhood. The couple were to be blessed with four children: Jack (born in 1919), Maisie (born in 1920), Ronald (born in 1921) and Barbara (born in 1925). Despite getting married while on leave from the army, Jack was expected to return promptly to his unit.

Ada Palmer, who was always known to Jack as 'Flick'.

Tuesday, 30th November
Weapon reorganisation

Meanwhile, back on the Western Front, change was afoot with the infantry's weaponry. The Vickers Gun was a heavy, water-cooled machine-gun; it was deadly when efficiently employed on the battlefield, whether using direct or indirect fire, but it required a gun-team to make it effective and demanded much training. Hitherto, each infantry battalion had been allocated two, then later four, Vickers Guns. The introduction of a new, light machine-gun, the Lewis Gun, initially allowed for four per battalion – men were selected for special training (just two weeks was required) on the new light weapon. The Vickers Guns were withdrawn from battalion control and formed into Machine-Gun Companies (MGC) with each company comprising four two-gun sections, and one MGC available per brigade. One Vickers Gun was rated the equivalent of approximately thirty rifles.

Sunday, 5th December
Back with the Ninth

(Heavy rain, over two weeks)
On Sunday, 5th December Jack rejoined 9/DAC from home leave.

Sunday, 12th December
Infantry relief commenced

The relief by 50th 'Northumbrian' Division commenced – on account of the conditions, it was not completed until 20th December! Men of the Ninth reckoned the Salient was their worst sector of the entire front line during the war.

Wednesday, 15th December
Artillery barrage

Fearing a German gas attack, the artillery pounded the German lines in an attempt to hit possible gas cylinders.

Sunday, 19th December-20th December (night) German gas attack

German artillery bombarded then released gas but no infantry attack materialised as the 9th Division artillery was ready, shelling the German lines relentlessly.

Tuesday, 21st December
Borre

(Rain)
No.2 Section, 9/DAC marched [14 miles] to Borre to relieve a section of 50/DAC. [Source: 9/DAC War Diary]

Wednesday, 22nd December
Artillery relief

(Rain)
9th Divisional Artillery was relieved by 50th Divisional Artillery and departed the front area gun-lines. Remainder of 9/DAC marched out to Borre and rest billets. [Source: 9/DAC War Diary]

Wednesday, 22nd to Sunday, 26th January
'At rest' & training – Watten (Artillery) and Merris (Infantry)

The artillery was based at the Artillery

Training Camp near Watten (north-north-west of St. Omer) where it underwent a 'vigorous' training course – the artillery 'billets' remained at Borre. The infantry and other branches were billeted around Merris (due east of Hazebrouck) where they bathed, cleaned, smartened-up, drilled, replenished and trained. The infantry practised bombing, rifle-shooting and more general training for 5 hours per day.

Football matches were played daily and there was a single rugby match for the officers between 26th and 28th Brigades, though the match was drawn. The divisional band and concert party, 'The Thistles', entertained the men during the evenings. Another point of interest, even curiosity, was the fact that at the start of January 1916, Winston Churchill took over command of one of the division's battalions – 6/Royal Scots Fusiliers.

[John Ewing: 'The History of the Ninth 'Scottish' Division, 1914-1919'.]

1 …according to Medal Record Index Cards.
2 The British would follow up this attack on 15th-25th May with an assault at Festubert.
3 Steeley died in Le Canal d'Aire, which further east became La Bassée Canal.
4 One of only fourteen British burials from the Great War.
5 'Ragtime' was, and still is, a popular style of swing music.
6 The ammunition shortage would continue at least until the Battle of Loos (September/October 1915). Gun batteries were limited in the shells they could expend per hour. At Loos, the shell shortage was cited as a reason for Britain's first use of poison gas.
7 Incendiary bombs…
8 During the summer of 1915, the length front under the control of the BEF stretched from the northern sector of the Ypres Salient to the village of Hébuterne, twelve miles north of the River Somme.
9 This refers to the planning for the Battle of Loos (the BEF) and a double spearhead into Artois and Champagne (the French).
10 The other division in the I Corps, the Regulars of 28th Division, were in reserve.
11 At Corps there were just twenty 6in Howitzers and 12 of higher calibre.
12 This was one of three 15-inch howitzers available for the British offensive.
13 7 a.m. was the official start time for the artillery bombardment on 21st September.
14 'Corons' were rows of terraced miners' cottages and presented major problems to assaulting troops.
15 'QF' indicates 'Quick-Firing' gun.
16 'Commander Royal Artillery'.
17 A term for hollow-nosed or soft-nosed bullets that expand on impact to cause extensive tissue damage. The first were manufactured at the Dum-Dum arsenal in Calcutta. The design was declared illegal by international agreement in 1899 at the Hague Convention.
18 Trench foot was caused by constant exposure to wet and cold – feet would discolour, swell and begin to rot unless dried, cleaned and treated with a water-inhibitor like whale-oil.
19 Jack's officer, 2nd Lieutenant W.H. Ozanne of 9th Divisional Ammunition Column, was commissioned from the Royal Alderney Artillery. He was commissioned on 14th August 1914 and subsequently earned the Military Cross and was also mentioned in dispatches.
20 William Palmer's grandfather was another William Palmer, a mariner who was born in Rye, Sussex, c.1845.

CHAPTER SIX
PLOEGSTEERT INTERLUDE

'CALM' BEFORE THE STORM

THE MISSING DIARY

Jack Hickman's diary record for 1916 is presently, probably permanently, missing. The narrative for 1916 relies heavily, therefore, upon the Divisional History (John Ewing: *'The History of the Ninth (Scottish) Division, 1914-1919'.*), Jack's Army Service Record, the 9/Divisional Ammunition Column war diary (WO95/1753), the Official History, *'Military Operations in France & Belgium 1916 Volumes I, II with appendices'*, and sundry other sources.

Friday, 14th January
29th Field Ambulance
According to the surviving pages of Jack Hickman's Army Service Record, he was admitted to 29th Field Ambulance for the repair of, *'...defective dentures'*. 27th and 28th Field Ambulances were also part of 9th 'Scottish' Division.

The 'Field Ambulance' was a mobile front line medical unit (not the vehicle of modern connotation). Most came under command of a division, and had special responsibility for the daily sick list and for care of battle casualties of one of the Brigades in the division – the FA usually assumed the same number as its brigade thus, normally, a division had three Field Ambulances. The expected capacity of the Field Ambulance was 150 casualties but, in battles such as those on the Somme, many FAs would simply be overwhelmed by those requiring treatment. Much of the work of the Field Ambulance lay in the organisation of an effective evacuation chain; usually, this would be set up as follows:

Chart 6:   **Evacuation and Treatment of Casualties**

Each Field Ambulance was composed of 10 officers & 224 men, RAMC.
Each Field Ambulance comprised three Sections
Each Section had Stretcher Bearer and Tented subsections

Regimental Aid Posts (RAP) one per battalion – first point of contact

Advanced Dressing Station (ADS) one per brigade

Main Dressing Station (MDS) one per division

Plus a Walking Wounded Collecting Station for the division

Throughout January

The men of 9/DAC were in billets in Borre.

Monday, 24th January to Monday, 31st January

Ploegsteert sector

Between these dates the division completed the relief of 25th Division in trenches in the Ploegsteert sector, a few miles south of Ypres. 9th 'Scottish' Divisional Headquarters was at Nieppe, south-west of Ploegsteert, until 13th February when it moved to Steenwerk, south-west of Nieppe, on account of extensive shelling. The front line itself was east of Ploegsteert Wood where the standard tours of duty were six days 'in', six days 'out'. The main compensation for the move was that billets for reserve and rest were excellent – a great relief after the cold, leaking Canada Huts at Dickebusch just south of Ypres. The trenches in the Ploegsteert sector were manned by 9th Division until the end of May 1916. It was described at that time as:

'...One of the pleasantest areas along the British Front'.

A TIME OF CHANGE

Tuesday, 1st February

New CRA 9/Division

The men of 9/DAC were in billets at Borre for the whole month, though a half section was at an advanced ammunition dump at Nieppe. Brigadier-General H.H. Tudor took over as 9th Division's Commander Royal Artillery (CRA) from Brigadier-General E.H. Armitage. Later in the war Tudor was promoted Major-General and took command of 9th 'Scottish' Division, which post he held at the Armistice. Once the British Army of the Rhine was established, Tudor took command of the Lowland Division that subsumed 9th 'Scottish' and was part of Godley's IV Corps in Germany.

April 1916   Artillery Reorganisation

During April 1916 three RFA batteries, D/50, D/51 and D/52, were extracted from their 9th Division artillery brigades to re-form 53rd Brigade (comprising 18-pounders only). 50th, 51st and 52nd Brigades each then had three 18-pounder batteries and one howitzer battery; 53rd Brigade had three 18-pounder batteries only. (Note: all batteries were still on a 4-gun basis).

May 1916

Brigade and Divisional A. C. Reorganisation

In May 1916 Brigade Ammunition Columns of 50th, 51st and 52nd Brigades were broken up and their personnel largely absorbed by the Divisional AC. The official 'establishment' of a Divisional AC now increased to sixteen officers and about 800 other ranks but overall the reorganisation released surplus Royal Artillerymen and some were transferred into RFA brigades in order to make good recent losses. The DAC assumed the following structure – the 'A' echelon of three sections of GS wagons under brigade control remained with the division at all times to transport re-supply ammunition (shells and SAA) to dumps that were accessible for each gun battery's wagons; the 'B' echelon of a single section was held at corps level even though it was still a divisional asset, transporting divisional ammunition. Of course, the DAC continued to re-supply the various units with hand-grenades, rifle-grenades and mortar rounds where appropriate. In practice, this system proved most effective.

Early 1916

Trench Mortar Reorganisation

As with the field artillery, trench mortars were reorganised in early 1916. The standard infantry trench mortar was the Stokes Mortar as it was very mobile and could fire 30 shells per minute. Each brigade's personnel for the mortar battery came from battalions in that brigade – an advantage of this arrangement

was that the men in the mortar battery would think twice before drawing down enemy retaliation on the heads of their own Scots mates. The 9/Medium Trench Mortar Brigade (comprising three batteries, 'X', 'Y' and 'Z') was formed by the end of April. Heavier mortars came under Royal Artillery control manned by men from the RGA and also by pioneers of 9/Seaforth Highlanders. Initially there were three mortar types – 1½in, 2in and 3.7in though, after a few months this was reduced to 2in mortars only. Finally, in April 1916, an even heavier 9.45in mortar (nicknamed the *Flying Pig*') was introduced, leading to the formation in May of the V/9 Heavy Trench Mortar Battery.

April-May 1916

Infantry Brigade Reorganisation

Then, at the end of April and beginning of May, it was the turn of the infantry to undergo substantial change when the infantry brigades were reorganised in order to accommodate the arrival of the tough South African Brigade. 28th Brigade was entirely broken up, though it was not transferred *en bloc*. 8/Gordon Highlanders (26th Brigade), 6/Royal Scots Fusiliers (27th Brigade) and 10 & 11/Highland Light Infantry (both 28th Brigade) were transferred to 15th 'Scottish' Division. 10/ Argyll & Sutherland Highlanders were moved from 27th to 26th Brigade; 6/King's Own Scottish Borderers and 9/Scottish Rifles (The *'Cameronians'*) replaced the Argyll & Sutherland Highlanders and

Royal Scots Fusiliers in 27th Brigade. At the end of April, the South African Brigade replaced 28th Brigade (29th Field Ambulance was also replaced by the South African Field Ambulance). 4th Battalion of the new brigade was the 'South African Scottish' Battalion, replete with Atholl-tartan kilts. The entire division was inspected by General Haig (Commander of the BEF) on 29th April.

Throughout May 9/DAC was based in the area of La Crèche, Schaexken and Nieppe. At the end of the month, the AC marched to Borre.

Saturday, 6th May
South Africans 'up the line'
In early May the South African Brigade took over trenches in place of 28th Brigade. Although it was their first taste of the trenches on the Western Front, they had previously served in Egypt and the unit brought with it the reputation of the South African as an implacable fighter. This would soon be amply demonstrated.

Saturday, 13th May
The 'Bird Cage' Incident
11/Royal Scots were holding an area of Ploegsteert Wood abutting the 104th Saxon Regiment-held salient known as the 'Bird Cage', on account of the amount of wire. There were considerable mining works proceeding, aided by a number of infantry working parties. That evening, following heavy shelling and mortaring, sixty attackers crossed No Man's Land and entered the Scots' trenches where they were repulsed and a counter-attack sent out. The Royal Scots lost 16 killed, 8 missing and 61 wounded. Only fifteen of the dead have been definitely traced:

11930 Private Robert Armour, (29), I.B.9 Rifle House Cemetery
26715 Private John Bell, I.D.6 Rifle House Cemetery
16851 Private John Cargill, I.B.5 Rifle House Cemetery
10717 Private Andrew Dewar, I.C.5 Rifle House Cemetery
23144 Private Robert Duff, (25), I.E.4 Rifle House Cemetery
13230 Private John Keenan, (31), I.A.7 Rifle House Cemetery
26152 Private James Mahoney, I.D.4 Rifle House Cemetery
16830 Private Michael Mannion, (19), I.A.5 Rifle House Cemetery, [English]
22802 Private William Nesbitt, I.A.6 Rifle House Cemetery, [Northern Irish]
13141 Corporal Thomas Penman, I.E.1 Rifle House Cemetery
15067 Private James Robinson, (20), I.C.8 Rifle House Cemetery
22991 Private Philip Tubman, 1.B.6, Rifle House Cemetery, [English]

All the above were buried in Rifle House Cemetery that was initiated by 1/Rifle Brigade during First Ypres in November 1914. Rifle House Cemetery is located in Ploegsteert Wood, south of Ypres.

Died of wounds on 13th May 1916
15348 Private John Skinner, (35), II.B.90, Bailleul Communal Cemetery Extension
(Nord) [he was a Boer War veteran].

Died of wounds on 14th May 1916
2514 Private James Robertson, plot II.B.92, Bailleul Communal Cemetery Extension
(Nord).

Died of wounds on 15th May 1916
10648 Private Thomas William Anderson, plot VIII.A.111, Boulogne Eastern
Cemetery, Pas de Calais.

Saturday, 27th to Tuesday, 30th May   Relief
9th Division was relieved by 41st Division and thus a relatively 'happy' interlude for
the division came to an end. 9/DAC moved to camp at Borre.

THE EFFECTS OF THE PLOEGSTEERT EPISODE

It was during this period at Ploegsteert that 9th 'Scottish' Division became a particularly
good sniping and raiding division. It was also here that machine-gun companies began
the practice of indirect fire (towards general rather than specific targets), sweeping
across roads and other likely places in the German lines at night.

CHAPTER SEVEN
JULY 1916:
HARD FIGHTING ON THE SOMME

TOWARDS ARMAGEDDON

DIVISIONAL TRAINING
Again the narrative for the 1916 Somme offensive relies heavily upon the Divisional History, the Official History and the 9/DAC War Diary (WO95/1753/2/3).

CONTEXT

Training & Recreation
Roquetoire
On 1st June, 9/DAC marched seventeen miles to Roquetoire where, between 1st and 14th June divisional training took place.

9th 'Scottish' Division concentrated at Bomy (13 miles south of St. Omer) where the Divisional Headquarters was set up. A period of training and recreation was organised and this began to revive enthusiasm after the disaster and losses of Loos in the previous September. Even a horse-show was planned, to include riding and transport but it had to be cancelled as orders were received to rejoin the XIII Corps under General Rawlinson in the Somme sector. The move south commenced on 13th June.

THE MOVE TO THE SOMME
Tuesday, 13th June

En Route from Bomy
The remainder of the division moved from Bomy by rail.

Thursday, 15th June
Near Vaux-en-Amiénois
9/DAC entrained at Berguette and at Lillers for the move south to the Somme. The Scots concentrated near Vaux-en-Amiénois (its DHQ), 3 miles north-north-west of Amiens. From the first day near Amiens, the evidence of a coming 'Big Push' was apparent – huge numbers of men were concentrating, ammunition and supplies were moving forward at night, many new R.E. and ammunition dumps had been set up, hospitals established and aerodromes developed. 9/DAC marched to camp near Bray-sur-Somme.

Orders for battle were received on this day. The XIII Corps would be on the British right flank and 9th Division would be in the XIII Corps reserve while the assault would go in with 30th

Division on the right and 18th 'Eastern' Division on the left. All three divisions were New Army divisions; Haig did not have full confidence in his new troops and consequently tried to keep their instructions as basic as possible. In some cases, this proved lethal.

Saturday, 17th June

The war diary shows that three drivers of 9/DAC were wounded and five killed by shell fire.

Wednesday, 21st June

Two gunners were killed and five wounded by shell fire. Those killed in action were:

89156 Gunner Thomas Charles Waterman (33)

109588 Gunner Sidney William Neighbour

Both are buried in Chipilly Communal Cemetery Extension.

Among the wounded was:

89167 Gunner Bert Strappini (19).

THE BROADER PICTURE

On the downside, the Russians had been driven from Poland in a crushing defeat; Germany and Bulgaria drove the Serb army from its land until it reached the sea, effectively committing Great Britain and France to the Salonika expedition in Serbia's support; the Gallipoli naval actions and troop landings had ended in a long, drawn-out, abject failure while Mesopotamia (present-day Iraq) saw the siege and surrender of British troops in Kut in April 1916. On the plus side, Italy had joined the war on the side of the Allies in May 1915 but its efforts were principally limited to its own self-interests on the Southern Front, mainly against Austria-Hungary. Making strategic gains in this region was the main reason for Italy switching sides.

THE SOMME BATTLE PLAN IN OUTLINE

STRATEGY

The Somme offensive emerged from the Chantilly Conference of December 1915. Whereas Germany had, for decades, feared a war on *two* fronts, the Allied intention for 1916 was to launch near simultaneous assaults on *three* fronts against the Central Powers. The overall strategy would comprise:

- A major Russian offensive against Germany's eastern flank.

- An Italian offensive in the Isonzo River sector of the Southern Front.

- A joint Anglo-French assault on the German lines in the previously 'quiet' region astride the River Somme.

Summer 1916 was to be the chosen timing for three principal reasons – the Russians needed to replenish both manpower and equipment following their ordeals of 1915; the inexperienced British 'New Army' divisions lacked battle-training and time in the front-line trenches; also the British had taken over from the French the front line around Arras so the British Army now held a continuous, eighty-mile front from north of Ypres to the Somme, thus troops on the ground were spread ever more thinly; above all, a midsummer offensive should enjoy more reliable weather than had the previous one at Loos in the late autumn. Despite hindsight delivering scathing attacks on the thinking behind the initial assaults, the background reasoning was quite sound. The theory of a co-ordinated attack on three fronts offered good chances of success but, in war, account must always be taken of the enemy's ability to take his own action and thus disrupt the most promising of plans.

VERDUN AND THE TRENTINO

From the German side of the wire, no major offensive had been launched since the gas-fuelled attacks on the Ypres Salient in late April of 1915. Having made an attempt on the British symbol of defiance, the German army commander Erich von Falkenhayn now turned his attention towards a symbol of French pride and military commitment, the fortress town of Verdun. His aim seemed to be to draw in French troops to the town's defence and thus essay to, '...*bleed the French army*

to death'. This relentless succession of attacks was the war's first overt example of a campaign of attrition rather than one aimed at a breakthrough – 'wearing out' rather than 'breaking out'. The first of a protracted series of assaults towards Verdun was launched on 21st February, throwing the Allies' careful planning into disarray. The Somme offensive would have to be rethought.

On the Southern Front the situation was further complicated during May by the Austrians' Trentino Offensive that drove back the Italians, inflicting considerable losses upon them. The Austrians' success compelled Russia to change the timetable of its intended attack from late summer to early June. In a bid to relieve their Italian allies, the Russians prematurely launched the '*Brusilov*'[1] Offensive against the Austrian troops, throwing them back and capturing nearly 200,000 men by mid-June – it was to prove to be one of Russia's most successful offensives. To avert the imminent disaster, Falkenhayn directed German divisions to the Austrians' support and prevailed upon General Hötzendorf to move numbers of Austrian troops away from the Italian Front to reinforce Galicia against the re-energised Russians. At least the first element of the Allied plan had met with success.

NECESSARY DELAYS

Despite this strategic relief, the 'mincing machine' of Verdun ground on remorselessly, committing increasing numbers of French troops to the town's defence.

Therefore the British Commander, General Sir Douglas Haig, now forced to shoulder the greater share of the Somme offensive, was urged by his French counterpart, General Joseph Joffre, to advance the starting date. Such a major attack required massive tonnage of military supplies and matériel; set for 25th June, the initial assault was postponed until 29th June. A second postponement, this one of 48 hours, was forced upon Haig by several days of wet and stormy weather that flooded some trenches and severely hindered transport movements. Yet some of the assault troops had already started for their assembly trenches. From 24th June, all troop and supply movement had been carried out to the terrifying sound of the greatest artillery barrage the world had ever witnessed. The second delay forced the Royal Artillery to eke out existing supplies of shells for an extra two days. Zero-Hour was finally set for 7:30 a.m. on Saturday, 1st July – after early fog, the weather would be glorious for the supposed 'walkover' advance.

THE TACTICAL PLAN

The planned five-day artillery bombardment by over 1,500 guns (comprising 1,010 field guns and howitzers, 182 heavy guns and 245 heavy howitzers – just about every artillery piece available in that theatre of operations) was intended to cut the German barbed-wire and destroy their trenches, rear transport and headquarters areas. At 7:28 a.m., two minutes prior to zero hour on 1st July, seven large mines and numerous smaller ones (the product of many months of tunnelling) packed with explosives would be detonated under sectors of the German front line, enabling the first waves of British troops to walk across No Man's Land with rifles 'at the port'. Weighed down by extra equipment, the inexperienced 'Kitchener' men were told that they would simply occupy and consolidate the 'undefended' German trenches – here again surfaces the old adage, '…artillery conquers, infantry occupies'. The British would attack, initially with fifteen divisions of General Sir Henry Rawlinson's Fourth Army, on a sixteen-mile front from Serre in the north to Maricourt in the south while the French would attack with five divisions on an eight-mile front instead of the originally-planned forty divisions on a twenty-five mile front. The British attack involved four 'Regular' divisions [4th, 7th, 8th and 29th], eight of Kitchener's 'New Army' divisions [17th 'Northern', 18th 'Eastern', 21st, 30th, 31st, 32nd, 34th and 36th 'Ulster', with Jack Hickman's '9th 'Scottish' and 19th 'Western' in reserve] and three Territorial divisions [46th 'North Midland', 48th 'South Midland' and 56th 'London', with 49th 'West Riding' in reserve].

On the northern (left) flank of the British line, two of the Territorial Force divisions, 46th and 56th of General Sir Edmund Allenby's Third Army, were tasked to engage the enemy in a diversionary attack on the strongly-held Gommecourt Salient, with the intention of attracting potentially devastating enfilading fire away from the main assault further to the south. As Sir Douglas Haig was not fully confident of the abilities of his 'New Army' divisions, he thus determined to make their orders as straightforward as possible, hence the 'walkover' and 'occupy' instructions – it would, however, cost many units dear.

Once the infantry in the main attack was established in the German lines, Sir Hubert Gough's three cavalry divisions were expected to exploit the breakthrough to capture Bapaume and, in company with the infantry, would wheel north towards Arras. Unfortunately, no military plan of attack ever really survives contact with the enemy and the Somme was to prove no exception.

In this case, some of the problems were possibly avoidable – the British had too few heavy guns (and these were too widely spaced rather than in concentrations) to destroy the strongly-built, German trenches and dugouts; worse still, up to a third of British 'heavy' shells proved to be duds; the shrapnel shells intended to cut the German wire were not up to the task, thus much of the thick wire faced by the infantry assault remained uncut; ordered to walk across No Man's Land instead of using the usual 'rush' tactics, the heavily-laden and largely inexperienced infantry gave the German machine-gunners enough time to race up the steps from their safe, deep dugouts and to set up their devastating weapons; finally, once many first waves of infantry had been cut down like stalks of ripening corn, lack of information (most methods, including flags, metal discs on soldiers' backs, telephone lines and runners, were destroyed by enemy fire or simply swallowed up by the 'fog of battle') reaching battalion, brigade, division, corps and army headquarters led to subsequent infantry waves being sent forward into the teeth of the gale. Where successes did occur, it was in sectors where it was easier to send back intelligence but the overall picture was either unknown to H.Q. or distorted. Nevertheless, the assault would continue, in varying degrees of strength and in different sectors of the Somme, until 18th November. Fortunately, the British army would learn its costly lessons on the Somme.

LOGISTICAL DETAILS

The tactical plan for the Somme offensive was thus relatively straightforward. The logistical plan that was being executed behind the lines, was necessarily much more complex as division after division poured into the sector; veteran regulars, Territorials and 'Kitchener' men found themselves side by side in the gently rolling landscape of the Somme – to put a single division's 12,000 infantrymen (twelve battalions), 3,300 artillerymen (three field gun brigades, one heavy brigade and a divisional ammunition column), four trench mortar batteries, three field companies of Royal Engineers (650 men) and one battalion of Pioneers (1,000 men) in the field and to maintain them there required the unstinting and unsung work of a divisional supply train (administered and manned by the much-derided Army Service Corps), three field ambulances (manned by the Royal Army Medical Corps), a divisional Signal Company (manned by a mixture of 162 Royal Engineers and infantry) and a Mobile Veterinary Section (manned by the Royal Army Veterinary Corps). A note should be added here that the divisional troops were responsible for moving supplies only from the Corps-administered railhead dumps; those in turn arrived at Corps from the Army-administered re-supply ports. In all, many and complex logistical problems had to be overcome on the grand scale before a single man could go over the top. Fifteen such divisions were intended to take the field on 1st July 1916.

Ninth 'Scottish', the proud senior of the new Army divisions, moved forward from Vaux-en-Amiénois (north-west of Amiens) on 23rd June to concentrate around the town of Corbie, beside the River Somme and to the east of Amiens. Next day, all and sundry moved eight miles further upriver to Etinehem, then on 27th June to a small, bleak railway 'station', two miles south-east of Méaulte, known then to the Tommies as Grove Town[2] Camp – or the 'City of Dumps' as military material (guns, ammunition, food and water, medical supplies and spare kit) was transported remorselessly forward for the coming offensive. Rail transport (main lines, branch lines and narrow-gauge), road transport (motor and horse) and the mainstay of the infantry, the 'Mark One' hobnailed boot, all played their parts in preparing the 'Big Push'. Billets, good bad or indifferent, all had to be earmarked and allocated to every battalion that moved into the Somme sector; field hospitals, and the means of transporting the wounded to them and often beyond, had to be established and filled with a plethora of medical supplies; aerodromes, re-plete with accommodation, mechanics and supplies had to be set out – four squadrons of aircraft and one kite balloon squadron had been made available to Fourth Army; thirty aircraft were tasked to vital counter-battery operations, sixteen to reconnaissance and nine to special missions, including increasingly valuable aerial photography.

Artillerymen, among them Jack Hickman, were among the busiest of those preparing for the offensive. Divisional artillery (each comprising three brigades of 18-pounders and one brigade of 4.5in howitzers controlled by divisional staff) generally travelled with the horse transport of their own divisions but medium and heavy Corps artillery (60-pounder guns, 4.7in and heavy howitzers controlled by corps staff) and the even heavier Army artillery ('super-heavies' controlled by Army staff) had to be moved independently either by teams of draught horses (Clydesdale, Suffolk Punch, Percheron or Shire) or by the new Holt tractors that used the caterpillar-type track (these spread the weight of heavy vehicles over a larger area to prevent the vehicle from sinking into the mud – vital in the great battles of 1916/17/18) or by rail. Consequently, existing 'normal' roads leading to the front had to be repaired and strengthened, while many new roads had to be cut. This gruelling work was carried out by engineers, pioneers and understandably reluctant infantrymen.

Not all divisional artillery was in direct support of its own division for the bombardment – for example, the CRA of 9th Division Artillery, Brigadier-General H.H. Tudor, commanded 50th and 51st Brigades RFA of 9th Division with 4th Divisional artillery in support along with all the batteries of 29th and 32nd Brigades RFA of 4th Division and with a call on the 23rd and 52nd Army Field Artillery Brigades if required.

The range and quantity of guns and howitzers available for the initial British bombardment was unique for the time and all had to be hauled to their gun-lines, then gun-pits dug and camouflaged; battery ammunition dumps were created adjacent to the guns while ammunition re-supply lines and dumps had to be established between the railhead and the guns. Philip Gibbs, the outstanding war correspondent of his generation, reported on this impressive artillery build-up[3],

"Travelling along the roads we saw new guns arriving – heavy guns and field guns, week after week. We were building up a great weight of metal."

The artillery pieces employed on the Somme comprised low-trajectory guns and higher-trajectory howitzers; they were available in the following numbers:

Divisional Field Artillery:

18-pounder guns	808
4.5in howitzers	202

Corps Heavy Guns & Howitzers:

4.7in guns	32
6in guns	20
60-pounders	128
6in howitzers	104
8in howitzers	64
9.2in howitzers	60

Army Heavy Guns & Howitzers:

9.2in guns	1
12in guns	1
12in howitzers	11
15in howitzers	6

French support Artillery:

75mm guns	60 (gas shells)
120mm long guns	24
220mm howitzers	16

This provided 1,537 guns and howitzers – one field gun per 20 yards and one heavy per 58 yards of the front. The consequent build-up of huge stocks of ammunition for the artillery as well as

Small Arms Ammunition (SAA) was, for the first time prior to a major offensive, properly planned and arrangements for its forward movement to the (expected) advancing guns were carefully co-ordinated. The ammunition re-supply plan was as follows:

Dumped at the Guns:

18-pounders	– 354 rounds per gun
6in howitzers	– 200 rounds per gun
8in howitzers	– 90 rounds per gun

Dumped near the Guns:

18-pounders	– 1,000 rounds per gun
6in howitzers	– 650 rounds per gun
8in howitzers	– 500 rounds per gun

At Divisional Dumps:

18-pounders	– 250 rounds per gun

At Corps Dumps:

6in howitzers	– 200 rounds per gun[4]

Saturday, 24th June
The artillery barrage opens
So intensive a build-up of ammunition required the services of seven trains a day over several weeks until, by 20th June, the vast majority was in place for the commencement of the initial counter-battery bombardment on 'U-Day' – 24th June – assuming 'Z-Day' to be 29th June. Six days' water and rations had to be brought forward and distributed for the sustenance of men and horses during the bombardment; gun-pits (along with a number of false such positions) were carefully sited and the guns dug-in, often reinforced by steel, timber and dozens of sandbags; the establishment of forward observation posts, vital for spotting the fall of shell and relaying appropriate adjustments, required the laying of almost 50,000 miles of telephone cables. All had to be achieved before the counter-battery bombardment commenced on 24th June and the work thus required was back-breaking and executed by engineers, pioneers and infantrymen.

Once arrived at their lines and strongly dug in, the guns had to be ranged on their prospective targets:

"The guns spoke one morning last week with a louder voice than has yet been heard upon the front and as they crashed out we knew that it was the signal for the new attack. Their fire increased in intensity, covering raids at many points of the line, until at last all things were ready for the biggest raid." [Philip Gibbs]

Wednesday, 28th June
9/DAC marched out to camp at Sailly-le-Sec, remaining there until 9th July.

THE SOMME OFFENSIVE UNDER WAY

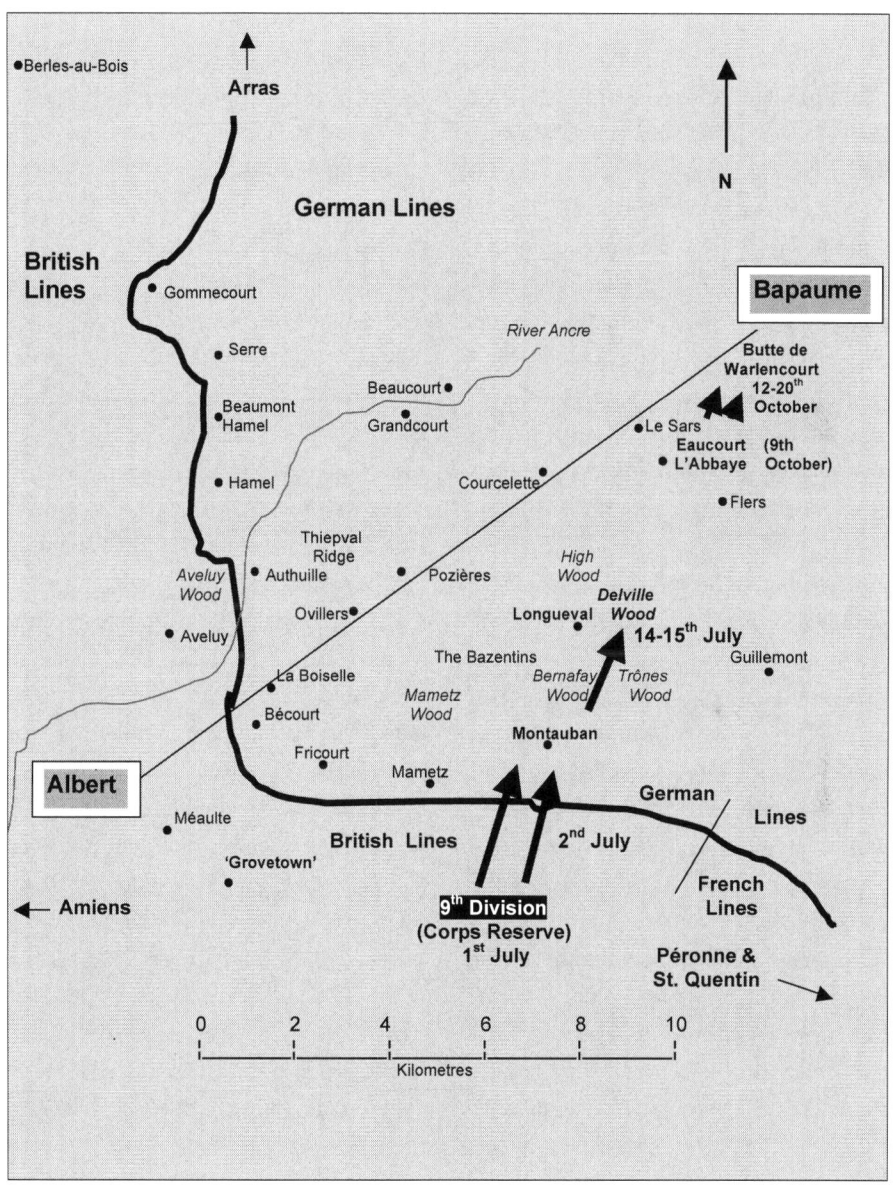

Map 3: 9th 'Scottish' Division on the Somme, June to October 1916

'Z'-Day, originally set for Thursday, 29th June, was set back two days on account of the severe summer storms that ranged across the Western Front on 26th and 27th June (and incidentally turned Grove Town into a sea of mud), lasting into the early hours of 28th. By 11 a.m., despite the morning's hot sunshine, a 48-hour postponement had been enacted, in order to give roads, trenches and men a chance to thoroughly dry out ahead of the assault. It meant stretching ammunition supplies for an extra two days but that also meant a longer period available for wire-cutting and destroying enemy trenches and support systems.

Thursday, 29th June
On the divisional gun-lines
(Hot, sunny)

Back from the front-line troops opposite Mametz and Montauban, the artillerymen of 9th Division (50th and 51st Brigades RFA) must have viewed with mixed feelings the extension to their work; for four days and nights the guns had been thundering and the men were tired but they knew that the longer they fired, the better were their infantry mates' chances of success. Dug in on the gun-line beside 9th Division's guns were those of 4th Division (29th and 32nd Brigades RFA) and those of 18th and 30th Divisions for the bombardment as well as the 23rd and 52nd Army Field Artillery Brigades. Despite the inevitable squeeze on ammunition supplies, the guns spoke for two more days until 'Z'-Day, Saturday 1st July, dawned misty then clearing sunny and warm (72°F/22°C) – a day more in keeping with cricket than the blood-letting that was about to intensify beyond imagination.

Saturday, 1st July
'Advance, rifles at the port...'
(Fog clearing to warm sun, 72°F)

9th Division's infantry was held in reserve on 1st July behind 7th, 18th 'Eastern' and 30th Divisions opposite the villages of Mametz and Montauban at the southern extremity of the British front and adjacent to the troops of their French Allies. Prepared to be moved forward whenever needed, the battalions of 9th Division were readied like those of the assault battalions – 20 officers were to go into battle while the remainder were to remain behind as the core of any necessary later reorganisation; 200 rounds SAA were issued per man; every man of the four rifle companies was to wear coloured shoulder bands to facilitate recognition in the fog of battle[5] ('A' Company = red, 'B' Coy = yellow, 'C' Coy = blue and 'D' Coy = green); a number of other ranks were selected from each brigade to remain out of the line in order carry out the replenishment of stores such as SAA, Stokes Gun shells, machine-gun ammunition, R.E. stores and tools to be used for the 'reversing'[6] and consolidation of captured trenches.

9/DAC's War Diary for once gives a clear picture of the unit's job from the outset:

'....'A' Echelon at Sailly-le-Sec, 'B' Echelon at Vaux-sur-Somme, all in bivouacs. Commenced sending ammunition up to battery positions daily from 'A' Echelon and twenty wagons daily from 'B' Echelon for... fatigues with CRE (Royal Engineers).'

Saturday, 1st July 1916
Artillery crescendo
(72°F, sunny)   (Infantry assault) Philip Gibbs observed the crescendo of artillery fire that preceded the infantry assault[7],

> "The full power of our artillery was let loose at about 6 o'clock this morning. Nothing like it has been seen or heard upon our front before and all the preliminary bombardment, great as

it was, seemed insignificant to this. I do not know how many batteries we have along this battle line or upon the section of the line which I could see but the guns seemed crowded in vast numbers of every calibre and the concentration of their ire was terrific in its intensity."

> "Shells were rushing through the air as though all the trains in the world had leapt their rails and were driving at express speed through endless tunnels in which they met each other with frightful collisions."

> "High explosives were tossing up great vomits of smoke and earth all along the ridges (around Thiepval). Shrapnel was pouring upon these

Sketches of Tommy's life Up the line — N° 6   Waiting for the barrage to lift. It makes you feel small and sort of lost !

A cartoonist's impression of waiting for the barrage to stop. Created by Private Fergus Mackain (Royal Fusiliers).

places…*The enemy was being blasted by a hurricane of fire."*

"Every five minutes or so, a single gun fired a round. It spoke with a voice I knew, the deep, gruff voice of old 'Grandmother', one of our 15-inch guns, which carries a shell large enough the smash a cathedral with one enormous burst."

[This 15-inch BL (Breech-Loading) Siege Howitzer, weighing in at over ninety tons, was a 'super-heavy' produced by the Coventry Ordnance Works that had developed the proven 9.2-inch (BL) Siege Howitzer. Six such 15-inch Howitzers (among 427 heavy guns and howitzers) were available for the preliminary barrage on the Somme. Throughout the war these 'super-heavies' were operated by detachments from the Royal Marine Artillery. This type of howitzer (often referred to as 'Grannies' or 'Grandmother') fired a High Explosive shell that weighed 1,450 lbs and produced an effect that was described as 'rhythmical obliteration'; its maximum range was marginally in excess of 10,500 yards, similar to the Coventry Ordnance Works' 9.2-inch (BL) Mk. I Howitzer but 1,000 yards less than the 12-inch (BL) Howitzer manufactured by Vickers. The howitzers were moved to Mailly Maillet between 5th and 12th June and were mounted. All

Silk postcard, 'Albert 1914', depicting the damaged Madonna and Holy Child.

the howitzers took part in the preliminary bombardment prior to the opening of the Somme offensive. Initially the targets were Beaucourt and Grandcourt but on 6th July the howitzers were remounted and re-targeted to Thiepval and Pozières.]

At last,

"It was 7:30…The guns lifted and were firing behind the enemy's first lines….there were trench mortars at work along the whole length of the line before me….the men were out of their trenches and the attack had begun."

On the right-hand sector of the XIII Corps, the artillery bombardment had successfully cut much of the German wire and the infantry of 30th Division, one in which General Rawlinson, commander of Fourth Army, had earlier professed little confidence, swept over its objectives and quickly consolidated its gains.

In the left-hand sector of the XIII Corps, 18th 'Eastern' Division encountered stiffer opposition though the artillery had again done its wire-cutting work very effectively and had supported the advance with a type of creeping barrage[8]; by early evening most of the two divisions' objectives had been taken and consolidated, including the ruined village of Montauban. In retrospect, the only major disappointment on the XIII Corps front was the failure to exploit the shallow, weakly-held remaining German line, a line manned by the battered remnants of four beaten and scattered battalions, reinforced by, '...a scratch force of clerks, cooks, batmen and 200 recruits'[9], behind whom the artillery was shattered and the 'door', seemingly, wide open. In their attacks, 18th and 30th Division together had sustained fewer casualties (6,126) during the day than had 34th Division (6,380) in front of La Boisselle and were certainly buoyed by their success; however, 9th 'Scottish' Division, eager to erase the painful memories of their abortive assaults at Loos in September 1915, was left kicking its heels in reserve. Furthermore, three

The beautifully refurbished Basilica spire gleaming in the sunshine.

divisions of General Gough's cavalry was within striking distance of the vulnerable Montauban battlefield but for whatever reason, consolidation rather than exploitation was the order of the afternoon and, by midnight, fresh German battalions had plugged the gap.

Its divisional artillery apart, 1st July had proved to be a frustrating one for 9th 'Scottish'. Divisional HQ, established at Grove Town Camp since 27th June, just south-east of Méaulte, was supported by two companies, one from 7th Seaforth Highlanders and one from the South African Brigade. The assault divisions of the XIII Corps, 18th 'Eastern' and 30th, were assembled to the north of the Albert-Péronne road. In Corps reserve to the south of that route, two miles from the front and hidden from the enemy by Maricourt Wood, the battalions of 9th Division's 27th Brigade were divided among Billon Valley, Copse Valley and Trigger Wood Valley; those of 26th Brigade, further back, were split between Grove Town and Celestins Wood (near Chipilly on the River Somme). Throughout what must have felt like an interminable day the 'Jocks' sat tight, awaiting the order to move up and through the assault troops but the only order to advance was limited to 12/ Royal Scots and 6/King's Own Scottish Borderers, whose instruction on the evening of 1st July was to join 18th Division for trench-digging and other consolidation work!

Sunday, 2nd July
The Scots support goes in
(75°F, sunny)
27th Brigade relieved 90th Brigade of 30th Division in Montauban but as the communications trenches were so congested this relief was not completed until 3 a.m. the following morning. The South African Brigade replaced 27th Brigade in their former position but the remainder of 30th Division stayed in place.

Monday, 3rd July
Bernafay Wood taken
(68°F, fine, some thunder in SE)
On a warm evening and under orders from 30th Division, 12/Royal Scots and 6/King's Own Scottish Borderers of 27th Brigade followed a twenty-minute bombardment to attack and capture, at minimal cost, Bernafay Wood which lay

500 yards to the east and north-east of Montauban.

Tuesday, 4th July
Holding the Wood
(70°F, overcast, thunder)
Easy to take, Bernafay Wood proved a hot place to hold as both the wood and Montauban village were heavily bombarded day and night.6/KOSB lost more than 150 men in less than twenty-four hours in the wood. Late on the 4th and into the small hours of the 5th, Ninth Division relieved the remainder of 30th Division that was due a hard-earned rest yet it would be shorter than anticipated.

The Calvary now erected on Maltz Horn Ridge.

Friday, 7th July

9/DAC's War Diary recorded that a DAC driver[10] died of wounds inflicted by shell fire. He was a Yorkshireman, 84661 Driver Tom Kay who is buried in plot I.A.10 of Péronne Road Cemetery, Maricourt.

Saturday, 8th July

Trônes Wood, back and forth

(73°F, overcast, 8mm. rain)

Just a grenade's throw east of Bernafay Wood was the German-held Trônes Wood whose capture was crucial to any advance into Delville Wood; yet to attack Trônes Wood was to invite heavy enfilading fire[11] from Delville Wood to the north and from Maltz Horn Ridge to the south. Units of 30th Division,

assisted by 9th Division, commenced the attacks on the wood which they took but later lost to German counter-attacks, so beginning a process of gain and regain that cost numerous lives on both sides.

Sunday, 9th to Tuesday, 11th July

Attacks repulsed

(68°F-82°F, cloudy but dry)

DAC HQ and 'A' Echelon marched to Bois des Tailles and 'B' Echelon moved to Sailly-le-Sec. On 11th, one driver was wounded, again by shell fire as the enemy sought to disrupt supply to the guns.

Three more 9th Division attacks went in, partly succeeded and were then later repulsed, causing the planned major offensive into Longueval and Delville Wood to be postponed for at least four

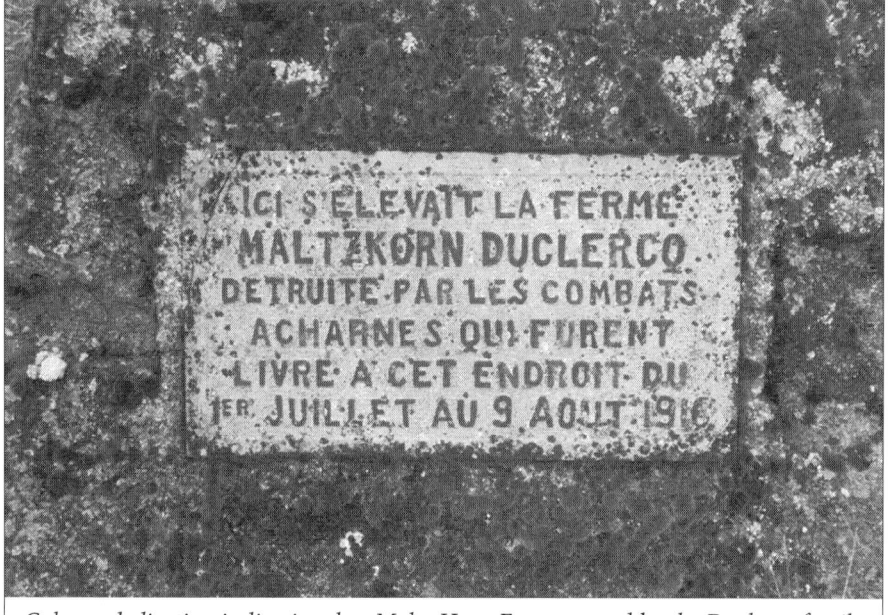

Calvary dedication indicating that Maltz Horn Farm, owned by the Duclercq family, was destroyed by battles from 1st July to 9th August 1916.

days; when it commenced, Trônes Wood was still in German hands.

Wednesday, 12th July

Two more drivers were wounded by shell fire.

Friday, 14th July
Battle of Bazentin Ridge
(14th-15th July)

(70°F, overcast but dry)

3:25 a.m. – 26th Brigade (right) and 27th Brigade (left) assaulted the German line in a well-executed night attack, quickly reaching the edge of Delville Wood and carrying two lines of trenches but they were unable to take the sugar refinery of Waterlot Farm a short distance to the east of the wood. The advance was undoubtedly eased by 18th Division's remarkable clearance of Trônes Wood by 9:30 a.m. on 14th July – a success that had eluded many previous attempts; in addition, the enemy had been confused as to the timing of the assault by heavy shelling each morning in the run-up to the attack and by a carefully-applied, original artillery plan. Wire was cut by accurate, regular fire over several days prior to the attack; there was just a five-minute opening barrage preceding zero-hour, comprising three minutes of shrapnel to discourage enemy movement and then two minutes of High Explosive with delayed fuze; the first would be followed by seven further barrages of varying objectives and duration over the ensuing four or so hours. This novel idea of 9th Division's CRA, Brigadier H.H. Tudor, was intended to avoid the premature explosion of shrapnel shells that hit the wood's trees above the leading British assault troops; from 'Z'-Hour, the barrage was timed to lift 50 yards every one and a half minutes to 'shelter' the advancing battalions. The success of the infantry clearly reflected the effectiveness of the artillery plan, one that would thereafter be employed time and again throughout the war.

Saturday, 15th July
Battle of Delville Wood
(15th-19th July)

(72°F, misty then sunny)

9/DAC lost another driver wounded by shell fire today. For 9th 'Scottish', the first day of the Bazentin Ridge attack morphed into the first day of the Battle of Delville Wood. At daybreak, one company of 5/Camerons and later two of 4/South African made attack after attack on Waterlot Farm, eventually taking it but being shelled out by German barrages of such ferocity that the farm could not be finally occupied and consolidated until the 17th July.

12/Royal Scots twice unsuccessfully attempted to take Longueval village but withdrew during the evening.

The South African Brigade was tasked to clear Delville Wood from the south-west and by evening, despite repeated counter-attacks and heavy shelling that persisted all night, the South Africans held the wood. The divisional artillery laid down an accurate barrage behind the wood and gravely hindered the forward movement of German troops.

Sunday, 16th July
Longueval defiant
(73°F, overcast, 4mm. rain)

Despite heavy mortaring of the village, 11/Royal Scots' and 1/South African's further attempts to take Longueval were largely unsuccessful. 9/DAC lost one driver killed and seven wounded by enemy shell fire. [The 9/DAC driver killed was 160 Driver Hector MacMillan (26) from Campbeltown, who is buried in plot II.A.8 of Dive Copse British Cemetery, Sailly-le-Sec.]

Monday 17th July
Waterlot Farm taken by the Ninth
(70°F, misty and overcast)

At 9 a.m. and following a preliminary bombardment, 26th Brigade captured and held Waterlot Farm. Further efforts to advance were again repelled by the Germans – machine-guns and an artillery duel caused heavy casualties on both sides. All the following night Delville Wood was shelled mercilessly and drenched with gas, with 9/DAC losing Lieutenant Guy to the effects of gas.

Tuesday, 18th July
Delville Wood lost
(72°F, overcast)

Both Echelons of 9/DAC marched out to Grovetown, south of Albert. Mid-afternoon saw strong German counter-attacks against Delville Wood – waves of Germans from beyond the Givenchy Road, were held off by British artillery and South African machine-guns but another assault from the north of the wood succeeding in finally squeezing out the South Africans; a third attack, intended to re-take the village of Longueval, met with only partial success.

Wednesday, 19th July
Out of the line

Ninth Division, depleted and exhausted, was ordered out of the line. The relief of 26th Brigade (by 8th Brigade of 3rd Division) and of 27th Brigade (by 95th Brigade of 5th Division) began on 19th July at night; most of the surviving South African Brigade were similarly relieved.

Thursday, 20th July
Artillery still in line

By the morning of the 20th the relief was complete, the last small detachment of gallant South Africans having been replaced in the line. The artillery of Ninth Division remained in the line until 27th July, supporting attacks by 3rd Division and 2nd Division on Longueval and Delville Wood. The Ninth's experienced CRA, Brigadier-General H.H. Tudor, acted as CRA for both the relieving divisions. Throughout the actions since 1st July, the 9/DAC along with the entire transport section of the division never failed to deliver the ammunition, rations and stores, always under heavy fire and often at heavy cost – without

The South African Memorial Museum that is located, most appropriately, in the heart of Delville Wood where the South African Brigade fought so gallantly and at such heavy cost in the summer of 1916.

those unsung heroes the bloody struggle in Delville Wood could never have been maintained. The artillery itself was superbly run by Brigadier-General Tudor, whose insistence on the use of high explosive rather than shrapnel, was warmly supported by the infantry. Even so, the fighting had extracted a terrible toll – in three weeks of bitter fighting against three top-class German divisions (3rd Guards Division, 7th and 8th Divisions of the Magdeburg Corps), 9th Division lost 7,617 officers and men, a figure that represented almost fifty per cent of its existing strength. It was a dreadful price to pay for the division's

hard-fighting reputation. In 9/DAC the price on the 20th was proportionally high as eight drivers were wounded by the enemy's artillery.

At the end of July 1916, the composition of 9th 'Scottish' Division had changed considerably from the unit that had crossed the Channel in May of 1915. The most obvious and far-reaching change was the arrival of the South African Brigade that had replaced the Scottish battalions of 28th Brigade – the four South African infantry battalions had formally joined the division on 11th May 1916, followed by a Trench Mortar Battery and a Field Ambulance.

Table 6: Units of 9th Scottish Division on 31st July 1916

26th Brigade	8/Blk Watch	7/Seaforth H.	5/Cam'n. H.	10/A&S H.
27th Brigade	11/R. Scots	12/R. Scots	6/KOSB	9/Sco. Rifles
S. Africa Bde	1/S.A. Inf.	2/S.A. Inf.	3/S.A. Inf.	4/S.A. Inf.
Artillery Bdes	50th Bde RFA	51st Bde RFA	52nd Bde RFA	53rd Bde RFA
Batteries	A,B,C; D (H)	A,B,C; D (H)	A,B,C; D (H)	A,B,C
Mortars [Div]	X.9	Y.9	Z.9	V.9 (Heavy)
[Bde]	26th TMB	27th TMB	S.A. TMB	
Amm. Col.	9/DAC			
M/Gun Units	26th M.G. Coy	27th M.G. Coy	28th M.G. Coy	
R. Engineers	63rd Coy.	64th Coy.	90th Coy.	
Pioneers	9/Seaforth H.			
Signal Serv.	9/Div Sig Coy			
Fld Amb.	27th Fld Amb.	28th Fld Amb.	SA Fld Amb.	
Div. Train	9th Div. Train			
Mob Vet Sec	21st Section			

1   The offensive was named after the Russian General who planned it, Aleksei Brusilov.

2   There was no 'town', merely a siding with no proper platform, a huge open space with endless tents, dozens of dumps and a barbed-wire 'cage' for German prisoners of war. During September and October 1916, as the Somme battles progressed, Casualty Clearing Stations (2/2nd London C.C.S., No.34 C.C.S. and No.56 'South Midland' C.C.S.) were established in Grove Town, explaining the existence of Grove Town Cemetery with its 1,395 burials (of which only four were unidentified).

3   Philip Gibbs, 'The Battles of the Somme', (1917, Heinemann).

4   Artillery piece numbers and ammunition re-supply sourced after General Sir Martin Farndale KCB, 'The History of the Royal Regiment of Artillery – The Western Front 1914-18'. (1986, Royal Artillery Institution).

5   'Fog of battle' was both a literal and figurative term in 1916. Artillery fire produced smoke and detonations across the battlefield, hurling earth, men and equipment into the air; equally, most forms of communication from the front-line troops back to their commanders were rapidly destroyed or inhibited and thus a figurative 'fog' descended upon the field of battle.

6   A captured enemy trench was, by definition, facing the 'wrong way', so the fire-step had to be reversed and the parapet strengthened and built up. Later, the ground beyond the trench had to be wired if the trench was to become the new front line.

7   Philip Gibbs, 'The Battles of the Somme'. (1917, Heinemann)

8   This was not a true creeping barrage as it lifted from trench to trench rather than by fixed time and distance 'lifts' with the infantry following as close to it as possible, thus keeping the enemy in his deep dugouts. Where applied as advised, as at Fricourt (7th Division, XV Corps), attacks were successful; elsewhere, as commanders 'adapted' the plan, near-disaster ensued as at Serre (31st Division, VIII Corps) and at La Boisselle (32nd Division, III Corps).

9   Martin Middlebrook, 'First Day on the Somme', (1971, Allen Lane)

10   97650 Driver Richard Brown of 'C' Battery, 53rd Brigade RFA (9th Division), died of wounds the previous day and is buried in plot III.F.7 of Péronne Road Cemetery.

11   Enfilading fire originates from the flanks of the line of attack and is thus very damaging to any assault.

CHAPTER EIGHT
REST, REPLACEMENTS AND RETURN TO THE SOMME

INTO REST BILLETS

THE REPUTATION GROWS
Wednesday, Thursday 19th/20th July
Rest at Last
(Very warm, dry)

The three brigades of Ninth Division made their way back from the front line, variously to Méaulte (26th Brigade), Citadel Camp (27th Brigade, near Fricourt) and Happy Valley (South African Brigade, near Bray-sur-Somme). The artillery had a week further to work at their gun-line and 9/DAC paid a heavy price. Praise forthcoming from senior officers was both fulsome and deserved. In his detailed assessment on 21st July of his division's achievements in and around Delville Wood, that had justifiably come to be known by the 'Jocks and South Africans' as '*Devil's* Wood', General Sir William Thomas Furse observed:

"The Ninth Division is being withdrawn from the battle line. It has played a conspicuous and honourable part in one of the greatest battles in the world's history...

"The demands made on all branches of the division have been great and right well have they been answered...

"...the infantry, I am sure, will be the first to recognise the assistance they have received from the artillery, who have been working at the highest pressure day and night since the 24th June and are still in the line..."

From higher still up the chain of command, G.O.C. Fourth Army, General Sir Henry Rawlinson, commented four days later:

"The attack ....on 14th July was a feat of arms which will rank high amongst the best military attainments of the British Army...

"Not only has the fighting spirit of the infantry of the Division been admirable but the manner in which the artillery has helped and supported the infantry shows that a high degree of training has been attained."

Wednesday, 19th to Sunday, 23rd July
Rest and Training
(Warm, mainly sunny)
Under a warm, healing summer sun, the sadly depleted battalions of the 'Jocks and Springboks' were allowed a few days to recuperate – during the mornings 'training' was light, while kit replenishment was thorough; afternoons were spent swimming in the River Somme near Bray. Steadily the gaps in the ranks were reduced by small but frequent drafts of replacements.

Sunday, 23rd July
Artillery Support
(Warm, overcast)
While the artillery maintained its support of 2nd and 3rd Divisions, the infantry left the Somme, trudging long, hot, dusty roads to Pont Rémy, five miles south-east of Abbeville.

Tuesday, 25th July
Bruay-la-Buissière – Rest & Training
(Warm, overcast)
The division was soon transferred north to the IX Corps, First Army, concentrating around Bruay-la-Buissière, less than ten miles east of Loos where 9th 'Scottish' had been so harshly blooded in September of 1915. A mining area not easy on the eye, Bruay nevertheless provided the rare luxury of hot-spray baths at the pit-heads; moreover, fresh clothing and unusually copious leisure time filled with a variety of entertainments allowed the veterans of Loos and the Somme,

such as remained, to remember what civilisation was like. After a few days the battalions were dispersed into the local countryside where the raw replacements were initiated into the ways of training and into the ways of their new comrades. This interval of recuperation lasted just a fortnight.

Friday, 28th to Sunday, 30th July
'A' and 'B' Echelons marched out, moving camp to Vaux-sur-Somme on 28th, to Allonville on 29th and then to L'Etoile and Bouchon the next day.

Tuesday, 1st August
9/DAC entrained from Longré and Pont Rémy for Bryas and Diéval, then marched to Magnicourt-en-Comté where they remained under canvas for a week, until 9th August.

SIX WEEKS ON VIMY RIDGE

Saturday, 12th August to Monday,
25th September
Vimy Ridge
Still short of manpower, on 12th August 9th Division relieved 37th Division on Vimy Ridge, the north-south crest of which was firmly in German hands. In late 1916 the area was relatively quiet apart from the constant threat of mining and the daily 'mortar hate' but the arrival of the divisional artillery quickened a few German pulses as the batteries 'registered' their most likely targets. Locally, snipers posed a regular threat to

the unwary – one, nicknamed 'Cuthbert', was a menace in the Carency sector until he himself was shot by a British sniper. Trench raids[1], intended to disrupt the enemy and to gain 'intelligence' from any prisoners that were taken, became a frequent and productive aspect of life on Vimy Ridge. 9/DAC remained at Caucourt, Hermin and Héripré until the end of September. Two officers were seconded for trench tramway work at Mont St. Eloi.

THE SOMME BECKONS AGAIN

Tuesday, 26th September to Sunday, 8th October
Somme again
On 5th October, the Column moved back to Magnicourt, then on 8th to Rebreuviette and by 11th had reached Béhencourt. They were moved to a training area under Third Army, later joining the III Corps, once again under General Rawlinson's Fourth Army on the Somme where the British line had moved forward considerably since the Scots' experiences in Delville Wood.

[In September the artillery was re-organised to six-gun batteries. To achieve this, 53rd Brigade RFA was broken up and thereafter the divisional artillery consisted of three brigades, 50th, 51st and 52nd.]

Monday, 9th October
"…a vast waste of wilderness"
(64˚F, fine)
By the time of the return to the Somme,

each battalion had been supplied with ten Lewis Guns, so increasing the volume of ammunition to be moved up to the infantry by the DAC. Also by this time the British had taken the ridge from Thiepval north-west to Combles and the Germans were back to their fourth line of defence. The 9th Divisional History described the terrain as,

"…a vast waste of wilderness created by three months of savage warfare… covered with the debris of battle and of camps…the entire area was intersected by rutted roads barely able to stand the stupendous amount of traffic passing over them…"

[John Ewing: *'The History of the Ninth 'Scottish' Division, 1914-1919'.*]

Following long marches over badly broken terrain in appalling weather, two infantry brigades of 9th Division relieved 47th '1st/2nd London' Division in the line near Eaucourt l'Abbaye (1½ miles east of the Albert-Bapaume Road at Le Sars, a ruined village that had just been captured by 23rd Division). On the left of the sector was the German-held, fifty-foot high, chalk outcrop of the Butte de Warlencourt – a feature, protected by numerous machine-guns, that the 'Scottish' would soon enough come to know and detest. The South African Brigade relieved 140th and 142nd Brigades (of 47th Division) in preparation for 9th Division's assault on the deadly Butte. This blot on the rolling landscape would never be captured by assault – it would be evacuated by the Germans in the tactical withdrawal to the Hindenburg Line[2] of February-March 1917. Moreover, successive artillery barrages in the area had left the gun-line accessible for ammunition re-supply by pack animal only – a slow and difficult procedure for the DAC.

[John Ewing: *'The History of the Ninth 'Scottish' Division, 1914-1919'*.]

Tuesday, 10th October
Battle of the Transloy Ridges, 10th-18th October
(68°F, sunny)

Wednesday, 11th October
'Feint' Attack
(61°F, dull, damp)
A *'Chinese Attack'*[3] was carried out by 9th Division's infantry to deceive the enemy into revealing artillery and machine-gun positions prior to the main attack on 12th October. This one successfully discovered several machine-gun nests that were duly targeted by the artillery.

Thursday, 12th October
Attacks on the Butte de Warlencourt
(61°F, dull with drizzle p.m.)
(12th-18th October)
Zero-hour was set for 2.05 p.m. and was to be preceded by a High Explosive barrage creeping forward at the rate

of fifty yards per minute; in this, 9th Division artillery was supported by the whole of 47th '1st/2nd London' Division artillery and by two brigades of 1st Division's artillery.

The Western Front Association's memorial to the struggles for the Butte de Warlencourt.

9th 'Scottish' was tasked, along with 30th Division, to take Snag Trench and then the Butte de Warlencourt, including a trench called The Tail (that ran back from Snag trench to the Butte) and also a mound called The 'Pimple' at the western end of Snag trench. The preliminary bombardment was inaccurate, missing the German front line trenches and their machine-gun posts (this was proven by later aerial photos), so the infantry attacked towards Little Wood and the Butte under cover of numerous smoke candles ignited by 4th Special

Company, RE. Minor gains were made and the attackers dug in but there was a strong defence by enemy; apparently, British preparation had been rushed and 9th Division's commander, General Furse, had in vain pleaded for a 48-hour postponement of the assault.

Friday, 13th October
The 'Pimple'
(61°F, dull, dry)

When troops of the South African Brigade reconnoitred The 'Pimple' it was found to be more or less unguarded, intelligence that was put to good use the following day. The Ammunition Column:

> '...arrived at Bécourt...encamping near Bécourt Hill. Unit HQ briefly set up to south of Mametz Wood... finally settling just south of Bécourt Wood on 15th.'

HQ remained there to the 24th November while the men were bivouacked on Bécourt Hill, two or three miles to the south-east of the town of Albert.

Saturday, 14th October
The 'Pimple' Taken
(61°F, overcast)

3/South African Battalion, under Captain L.F. Sprenger, captured The 'Pimple' and part of Snag Trench, incorporating them into the South African lines despite German counter-attacks.

Sunday, 15th October
(57°F, 3mm. rain a.m., then clear)

Monday, 16th October
(54°F, frost then sunny)

Tuesday, 17th October
(55°F, frosty then sunny but 3mm. rain at night)

Wednesday, 18th October
Snag Trench
(57°F, 4mm. rain a.m.)

Another major attempt was essayed, by 9th Division with 30th Division on the right, to take Snag Trench – it was preceded by an artillery barrage of Stokes trench-mortars on the front-line, with smoke and tear-gas on the 15th 'Scottish' Division front. The attack commenced at Zero-hour (3:40 a.m.) in heavy rain; success was limited so another attack was sent in at 5:45 p.m. that this time took much of Snag Trench except 100 yards either side of The 'Nose'.

Thursday, 19th October
'Flammenwerfer!'
(57°F, 4mm. rain)

In torrential rain at 5:30 a.m. 9th 'Scottish' was counter-attacked by infantry with *'flammenwerfer'*[4] causing terrible wounds to the defenders; unsurprisingly, 9th Division's line was pushed back. The South African Brigade was relieved by 27th Brigade and, hampered by terrible conditions of mud and rain, the relief was not completed until 6 a.m. on 20th October.

> *"Magazines for Lewis Guns were carried in buckets, like nosebags, each*

holding four. *The usual weight for a man was two buckets but that was a Herculean task on such a night…One Lewis gunner of 6/King's Own Scottish Borderers was so firmly embedded beyond the waist in mud that when he was finally extricated with ropes, both his ankles were broken."*

[John Ewing: *'9th Division History'*]

Friday, 20th October
The 'Nose'
(48˚F, fine but very cold)
At about 4 p.m. 6/King's Own Scottish Borderers took, lost and retook the 'Nose'. 11/Royal Scots took 250 yards of The 'Tail', advancing under an artillery barrage that lifted 50 yards every time the infantry fired a green light.

"A man too seriously wounded to walk had to wait hours for a stretcher – the usual number of men to a stretcher was two but eight was scarcely sufficient at the Butte de Warlencourt."

[John Ewing: *'9th Division History'*]

Nevertheless, the Butte de Warlencourt remained in German hands.

Late October
9th 'Scottish' Relieved
In late October, 9th 'Scottish' Division was relieved and the infantry brigades came out of the line, though it appears that the artillery remained in place until the end of that month. Subsequent infantry training and refurbishment took place near St. Pol.

[Chris McCarthy: *'The Somme, 1916 – the Day-by-Day Account'*, 1993, Arms & Armour Press]

THE DIARY RESUMES

Jack's diary entries resumed in November 1916 Perhaps he had been waiting for the chance to obtain a notepad to replace the original that may well have been lost during the Somme battles, especially in the mud of the Butte. However, the first surviving entry is undated. For whatever reason, the six pages preceding the entry for 9th November have been removed or lost. By the latter date the infantry, but not the artillery, of 9th 'Scottish' Division had already moved north towards Arras. The dateless entry reads:

"…the surrounding villages had many old houses [that had been] shaken down and not a pane of glass was left in place anywhere."

Thursday, 9th November 1916
Air raid
(54˚F, frosty, bright)
"Today has been a fine one and tonight is as light as day. It is about 9:30 p.m. and a German air-raid that started about six is still in progress; for over three hours the guns have been blazing away all around

us. *Our own planes are up and machine-gun fighting has been going on all around. Fire bombs have just been dropped about three hundred yards away from us – it seems we are in for a lively night."*

CONTEXT

Further air combat

Air combat was intense throughout 9th and 10th November; each side carried out bombing raids on enemy ammunition dumps; in each instance, numbers of defending fighters led to intense combat. The daylight raid by BE2 bombers of 12 and 13 Squadrons RFC, escorted by fighters of Nos. 11 (FE2bs), 29 (DH2s) and 60 (Nieuports) Squadrons RFC was attacked by around thirty German machines, leading to the loss of or serious damage to, seven British aircraft. A mid-day patrol by DH2s of 29 Squadron RFC ran into the new Albatros D-IIs of Jasta 1 and the British consequently lost three aircraft. German air defence was especially strong as their High Command was desperate to conceal the construction of the massively powerful Hindenburg Line to which the German troops would retreat in the early spring of 1917.

DIARY

Friday, 10th November
Still 'on the Somme'
(50°F)
[This day brought bad news to the lads

of 9/DAC – two DAC men temporarily attached to 'D' Battery of 51st Artillery Brigade were killed by enemy shell fire. The two lads could not have originated from places much further apart in the British Isles. 143564 Gunner Alexander M. MacIntosh was just nineteen years of age and hailed from the town of Thurso in Caithness; mortally wounded the previous day, he died of his wounds on 10th November and is buried in plot IV. A. 38 of Dernancourt Communal Cemetery Extension, not far from Albert on the Somme. 89185 Gunner Henry Rupert Rabey was a thirty year-old Guernseyman from St. Peter Port who originally served as No. 1256 with the Artillery Company of the Guernsey Militia and had travelled out in April 1915 with the First Guernsey Contingent to join 9th 'Scottish' Division at Bordon in Hampshire. He too was mortally wounded serving the guns of D/51 Brigade, only to succumb to his injuries on 9th November; he is buried in plot I.Y.4 of Bécourt Military Cemetery at Bécordel-Bécourt near Albert. The two men came from homes separated by nearly 500 miles but served and died as comrades-in-arms in France.]

"The raid of last night reached rather serious proportions for us during the early hours of the morning. The Germans dropped a bomb in the next camp to us and when everybody came out to look the Huns swept low and turned machine-guns on to them – one man was wounded

and our stable roof was perforated with bullets. More news of the explosion of last Monday has just come through – seven hundred French civilians were killed along with a great number of German prisoners who were in a camp close to the dump."

[This last statement in respect of the, "... explosion of last Monday", clearly suggests that Jack had previously mentioned it in his notebook diary, thus the diary must surely have existed at some point.]

Saturday, 11th November
Strafes and shells
(55°F, frosty and misty)
"Last night the Germans made another raid on our camp – they were all around from just after dark until two in the morning. The machines shut off their engines and planed [glided] down on to the crossroads with its transports and riddled the countryside with bullets; they also riddled our ammunition dump with hundreds of bullets and now tonight, being too misty for aeroplanes, they have just dropped over a dozen six-inch shells alongside of us. One fell in No.2 Section officers' cookhouse, wounding the cook and the Captain's servant. They say there is no peace for the wicked – well, we are not getting much anyway."

Sunday, 12th November
(50°F, overcast)
"We had no more fun last night after the shells. They allowed us to pass a peaceful night, for a change. The French have today

had another success, taking the village of Saillisel [south-east of Le Transloy]."

Monday, 13th November
"More bad news followed, with shells falling into No.2 Section's camp and wounding two men."

Wednesday, 15th November
Beaumont-Hamel captured
(46°F)

63rd Royal Naval Division's memorial at Beaucourt in the Ancre Valley.

"Today has been our day. North of Thiepval we advanced on an eight-mile front, taking over 5,000 prisoners and three villages – St. Pierre Divion [captured by 39th Division on 13th November 1916], Beaumont-Hamel [stormed by 51st 'Highland' Division on 13th November 1916] and one other not yet named in our

'In Memory of the Officers and Men of the RND who fell in the Battle of the Ancre, November 13th-14th 1916.'

telegram [probably Beaucourt, captured by 63rd 'Royal Naval' Division on 14th November 1916]."

Thursday, 16th November
Under fire again
(41°F, clear, frosty)
"Today has been another very cold and frosty one. About nine this morning the Germans threw over about a dozen very large shells – three fell about four hundred yards away from our camp and the noise of the burst shook everything for a mile around. The hole made by one of them was big enough to put a small house in. During the early hours of the morning, aeroplanes again attacked the camps and roadways with machine-gun fire."

Saturday, 18th November
(54˚F, snow then 8mm. rain)
[On 17th and 18th the Column's HQ and sections moved nearer the Albert main road.] *"We awoke this morning to find the ground covered in snow but as the air was much warmer, about nine it turned to rain and the snow soon cleared. We are now back to our usual two feet of mud again tonight!"*

SNOW AND MUD BUT SOME RESPITE

The Somme Campaign drew to an official close on 18th November as snow fell, melted and deepened the sticky, chalk-mud that covered the battlefront. Fighting on the Somme had been exceedingly difficult for several months but the weather now rendered it impossible. 9th 'Scottish' DAC was soon to experience the cold on its slow journey to a rest camp north of Arras.

DIARY

Tuesday, 21st November
"Not much doing for a couple of days on our front. There's every possibility of us leaving here for a few weeks for a rest – we expect to move in a few days."

Saturday, 25th November
Towards the Arras Front
[The various branches of 9th Division moved north and were reunited near Arras.]

Saturday, 2nd December
Rest Camp – Rebreuviette
"After a week of cold travelling we are at a rest camp, a place called Rebreuviette (north of Doullens), near Arras. We left the Somme on 25th November and stopped on the journey for the nights at Béhencourt [south of Contay], Talmas [north of Villers-Bocage] and Barly [south of Avesnes-le-Comte] finally reaching here where we expect to stay for a week or two and then go into action near Arras. [The men went into billets]. We then expect to take part in a new push, joining up the Somme near Thiepval."

CONTEXT

Tuesday, 5th December
North-east of Arras
9th Division took over the line north and east of Arras. Despite the damage done to Arras in 1914, the city was still in fair condition late in 1916.

DIARY

Thursday, 7th December
Rest Camp – Rebreuviette
"We are still in a rest camp at Rebreuviette but expect to go into action at Arras to relieve the 35th Division, 'The Bantams'. [Jack was wrong as the Column remained at Rebreuviette until 27th December and thus spent Christmas Day out of the line]. A very heavy attack has been made by the Germans to break through between Vimy Ridge and Arras but the attack was stopped."

Tuesday, 12th December
(Heavy snow then rain)
"This morning we awoke to find it snowing heavily. It went on at intervals during the day with occasional showers of rain. We are still at Rebreuviette."

DEATH IN ACTION OF BROTHER-IN-LAW WILL PALMER

CONTEXT

Sunday, 17th December
Thiepval Ridge

Will Palmer, 16/Rifle Brigade, first born, first killed. 'Missing in action' near Ypres.

Jack himself was unaware of Will's death until possibly weeks later as Will was posted, 'missing in action' rather than 'killed in action'. A telegram would have informed Will's parents of the situation but there would have been little hope of a happy outcome. Jack's subsequent home leave at the end of January 1917 would have proved very tense at Raglan Road with Ada's parents.

Jack's brother-in-law, William Charles Palmer, was born in January 1892 in Whitstable, Kent. 5ft 3in, a similar height to Jack, he volunteered in December 1915 in Woolwich and was embodied on 22nd May 1916. Married to Alice, he lived at 26, Speranza Street, Plumstead and earned his living as a carpenter. Joining Kitchener's 'New Army', Will became S/19346, Rifleman, 16th (Service) 'St. Pancras' Battalion, the Rifle Brigade, a unit that was part of 117th Brigade, in Major-General G.J. Cuthbert's 39th Division. Will landed at the port of Le Havre on 27th August 1916, though he did not join his unit in the line until 7th September. Plunged directly into the Battles of the Somme on Thiepval Ridge, Will's brigade was in support to 118th Brigade's capture of the powerful Schwaben Redoubt on 14th October. 117th Brigade attacked Stuff Redoubt on 21st October, sustaining 138 casualties. During the second week of November (the 15th) 39th Division was moved north to the Ypres Salient via St. Omer (Bollezeele). The shift was fatal for Will Palmer as he was killed in action near Ypres on 17th December 1916; initially declared 'missing in action', Will's death was not confirmed until a much later date. Consequently, he is commemorated

1916, only drawing to a close in the coldest French winter in living memory. Following initial German successes, the French army had fought back doggedly through the late summer and, during the autumn, had pushed the German line backwards – Fort Douaumont was recaptured at the end of October, soon to be followed by Fort Vaux and, in a final push on 15th December, the enemy was driven three miles beyond Douaumont. Verdun had been saved but at the cost of fearsome French losses to the order of 350,000 men[5]. However, the dreadful Battle of Verdun would have an unexpected consequence in that the hero of the hour was an artilleryman, General Robert Nivelle, who would subsequently be appointed C-in-C of the French forces. Nivelle's idea to replicate his Verdun success in Champagne and the Artois during the spring of 1917 would lead to disaster and, ultimately, the French army mutinies that would threaten the entire Allied war effort.

Will Palmer's name engraved on the Menin Gate Memorial to the Missing at Ypres in Belgium. His memory, along with that of over 53,000 comrades, is honoured every evening by the sounding of the 'Last Post'.

on panels 46-48 and 50 of the Menin Gate Memorial to the Missing in Ypres. He was awarded the British War Medal and the Victory Medal (Medal Roll M/102B22, Page 2886).

DIARY

Wednesday, 20th December

Rebreuviette

(Cold with snow)

"Yesterday was a very cold one and in the afternoon there was a snowstorm which is still left lying in many places. Today has been very clear and it has been freezing since dinner. Not much news except for the French advance north of Verdun during December."

CONTEXT

The French army's struggle to save the iconic town of Verdun lasted from February through to mid-December of

---

1 Trench raids varied in scale, from an officer and a few other ranks to assaults comprising several platoons.

2 What the British knew as the Hindenburg Line was, to the Germans, the 'Siegfried Stellung'.

3 A 'Chinese Attack' was a lifting artillery bombardment similar to that which precedes an actual infantry assault; however, in this type of attack the artillery suddenly switched back to the front line to hit reinforcing troops that had manned the fire-step to repel the 'assault'.

4 'Flammenwerfer' were the German flamethrowers that had first been used near Hooge Chateau in the eastern sector of the Ypres Salient in July 1915. A terrifying weapon.

5 German losses were but slightly lower, at 330,000, however Verdun was safe.

CHAPTER NINE
HINDENBURG LINE, ARRAS, LENS

JANUARY TO AUGUST 1917

PLANS AND PULL-OUTS

CONTEXT

November 1916   **Chantilly – Allied plans for 1917**

At the Chantilly Inter-Allied Conference of November 1916, strategy for 1917 was determined by the Allied leaders, presided over by the French General Joffre along with

General de Castelnau; the main decisions were taken by Joffre and the British C.-in-C. Sir Douglas Haig[1] (along with Sir William Robertson). The original intention of the British was for a follow-up offensive on the Somme but the replacement of General Joffre by the rising star of General Robert Nivelle[2], who was newly promoted to the post of commander-in-chief of the French Armies in the north and north-east, led to a re-drawing of the plans. Nivelle's promised French breakthrough was intended for the Chemin des Dames on the Aisne, while Haig's troops would attack from Arras, intending to sweep south-east towards Cambrai.

   Thus the British army was destined to provide a diversionary offensive that, by opening several days prior to the French attacks, was intended to attract German reserves; then the French assault might more easily achieve a breakthrough in the Champagne.

Jack's Christmas card, 1916, sent to 'Flick'. This card was produced by 9th 'Scottish' Division and bears the unit's thistle logo.

DIARY

Tuesday, 26th December
Wanquetin, 7½ miles west of Arras
"Boxing Day. Christmas is now over and after spending a month in Rebreuviette in a good billet, we ended up with a good Christmas Day and then, today, we have left it all behind and are once more in action. We have just arrived at a village called Wanquetin [halfway between Avesnes and Arras] near Arras and according to all reports and signs, we are here as usual for a big affair. Huge loads of ammunition and lots of big guns are being taken up every day and night. There is no doubt that Arras will be the place of the next big push and it will be before very long."

CONTEXT

27th December
Wanquetin
[9/DAC War Diary]
The Column marched to Wanquetin rest camp to the west of Arras.

Jack's message to his wife suggests that 9th Division had had problems with their card producer as the much-sought-after cards arrived late and in short supply.

DIARY

Sunday, 31st December
Wanquetin
"The last day of the year – a rumour

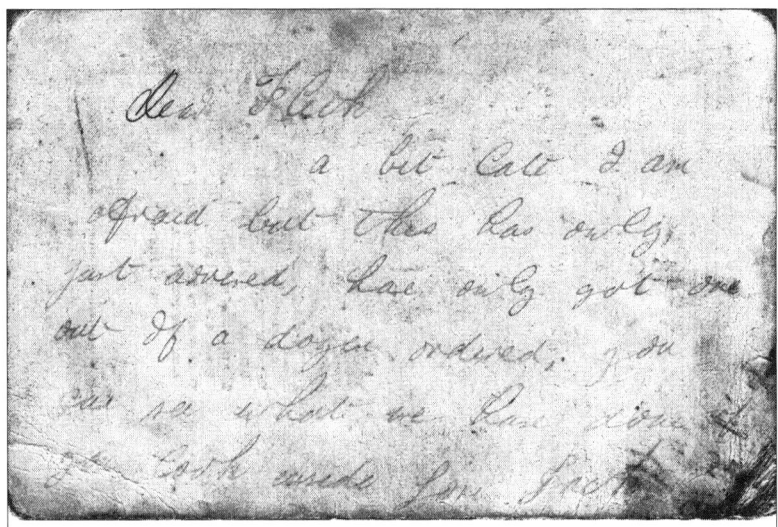

'Dear Flick, a bit late I am afraid but this has only just arrived, have only got one out of a dozen ordered. You can see what we have done if you look inside. Love, Jack.'

has just come through that tonight, at midnight, we intend to give the 'Hun' a welcome for the New Year. We don't quite know what form it will take – it will be a big artillery bombardment but whether it is to be a big push onwards, we don't know. We are all anxiously awaiting the night to come to see what happens."

1917

DIARY

Tuesday, 2nd January
Wanquetin, 7½ miles west of Arras
"Two days of the New Year gone by. The attack on Sunday midnight did not come off – it was given away in some respect and so it is postponed but before this month is out we shall make a big attack on this front."

Sunday, 7th January
Artillery barrage
"Last night was a very lively one. We put over 1,000 rounds a gun followed by an infantry raid which penetrated to the Germans' third line, bringing back a number of prisoners and valuable information. Preparations for the big push are going on fast. Today, a number of Indian troops arrived in the village [according to F.W. Perry, 'Order of Battle of Divisions, 1914-1918 (Part 5B)' the only Indian troops in France in 1917 belonged to the cavalry Divisions]; numbers of cavalry[3] are coming up as well, while heavy guns are going up night and day."

Thursday, 11th January
(Cold, snow)
"Today has been a very cold one and a little snow has been falling at intervals all day. Very heavy artillery work has been going on all week just around Arras; a lot of gas has been released, both by shells and otherwise. Preparations still go on for the big move that we all expect very shortly."

Wednesday, 17th January
Successful raid
(Heavy snow)
"During last night quite a lot of snow fell. We awoke this morning to find three inches on the ground. Our division carried out another raid to the south-east of Arras on Monday night, bringing in a large number of prisoners."

CONTEXT

1st to 22nd January
In rest at Wanquetin

'The men occupied billets, huts and barns; the horses [and mules] were on prepared standings [under cover]. A detachment of one officer and forty men was sent to the Divisional Bomb Store at Duisans.'

[9/DAC War Diary entry for this three week period of 'rest'].

Monday, 15th January
Divisional A. C. Reorganisation
The DAC was further reorganised in

January 1917 when divisional artilleries were reduced from four to two brigades [leaving 50th and 51st Brigades RFA as the 9th Divisional Artillery]; logically, the numbers in the DAC were reduced to 15 officers and about 700 men, and later in the same year numbers of other ranks came down to about 600 men.

> '*DAC now consisting of 'A' Echelon composed of H.Q., No.1 & No.2 Sections; and 'B' Echelon.*'

[9/DAC War Diary entry for the 15th January changes to the A.C.]

Monday, 22nd to 31st January
Frévin Capelle & Bray-sur-Somme

> '*…'A' Echelon moved to Frévin Capelle (in huts and billets)*
> *….'B' Echelon moved to Bray-sur-Somme (in barns).*
> *Horses and mules under cover in 'A' Echelon, majority*
> *of animals under cover in 'B' Echelon.*'

[9/DAC War Diary entries for 22nd to 31st January.]

Wednesday, 24th January to Saturday 3rd February
On home leave Jack was granted home leave by, '*…O.C. 9/DAC*' from Wednesday, 24th January to Saturday, 3rd February 1917, '*…with ration allowance*'. What was originally seven days' leave was extended of necessity resulting from

the dearth of boats crossing the Channel – Jack does not specify whether this was a consequence of the weather or simply a logistical problem. However, by skipping forward to his diary entries of 6th and 12th February, there is an indication that the weather was very wintry at that time.

[Jack Hickman, Army Service Record]

February
Bray

> '*Men of 'B' Echelon at Bray in barns remaining there the whole of the month.*'
> '*Men of 'A' Echelon moved from Frévin Capelle to Larrisset (HQ), Ourton (1&2 Sections); a week later the sections moved to Pernes…for the remainder of the month.*'

[9/DAC War Diary entries for February.]

DIARY

Sunday, 4th February
Return to France
"*Should have returned from leave but there were no boats.*"

Tuesday, 6th February
St. Martin's rest camp, Boulogne
(*Snow and ice*)
"*Returned from leave but got hung up at Boulogne until Saturday 10th. Spent four awful days at St. Martin's rest camp in snow and ice. I arrived back at our camp about midday.*"

Tuesday, 6th Evening

"…heavy fighting on our front around Mont St. Eloi."

[The hamlet of Mont St. Eloi is four miles north-west of Arras.]

Sunday, 11th February
Larrisset, west of Arras

"Today we have shifted a few miles nearer the line and nearer to Arras. We left Frévin-Capelle [two miles due west of Mont St. Eloi] and have camped in a little village called Larrisset [under a mile north of Agnez-lès-Duisans]. The preparations here for the big push are being carried on at a great pace – huge dumps of ammunition are growing and new roads are being cut. There is no doubt that the big push will be here [in the Arras sector]."

Monday, 12th February
Larrisset

(Warmer; rain)

"Today has been much warmer and a thaw has set in for the first time in over a month – there is every sign of rain tonight. Should the thaw keep on, operations will no doubt start very soon, as most everything seems to be ready."

Sunday, 18th February
Artillery build-up

(Warmer)

"The thaw still lasts and there is mud everywhere. Nothing big has started except raids every day on some part of the line. Day after day fresh, heavy guns are being brought up all along the line but I can get

no details [Jack could evidently elicit no information from his usual source] of when we are likely to commence." [Jack would not have been allowed to include such information in a letter as it would have been deemed likely to have been of aid to an enemy; he would certainly have been in trouble if his notebook had been discovered.]

Wednesday, 21st February
Larrisset

(Clear and fine)

"It is still very quiet on our own front, nothing much on except preparations for the big thing. On the Somme we are doing great things[4] still and we expect to have Bapaume very shortly if the weather holds fine. Roads are still very bad and muddy owing to the thaw but it seems to be clear overhead."

RETREAT TO THE HINDENBURG LINE

CONTEXT

(February-April, 1917)
Operation *'Alberich'* **– Shortening the line**

The vulnerable salient in the German line at Bapaume was a prime reason why the German High Command chose to shorten their defensive line by means of the construction of the *'Siegfried Stellung'*. Commencing in late February and reaching its completion in early April 1917, German divisions on the Somme implemented Operation *'Alberich'*, a strategic withdrawal to a newly-constructed and massively powerful defensive system. The strategy was simple. The German army on the Somme, severely weakened by the five-month British offensive, chose to shorten the line they had to defend by creating what became known as the 'Hindenburg Line'[5], that stretched its seeming impregnability from near Lens in the north towards Reims in the south – the saving in troops, matériel and supplies was hoped to afford Ludendorff's armies a respite that might be exploited by the burgeoning success of the German U-Boat campaign. Officially, the main withdrawal took place between 16th and 19th March, when thirty-five German divisions relocated from the tortuous Somme sector front line to the new defensive work, deeply built on reverse slopes[6] and supported by impressive blockhouses. Although construction had begun during the latter months of the 1916 Somme battles, the German High Command accessed more time in late March by issuing a general order that:

'...the whole zone between the present fighting line and the new position will be made a desert.'

In executing this order, retreating German soldiers destroyed habitation, felled trees, killed or carried off livestock, poisoned water sources, wrecked transport systems and booby-trapped the entire area. Consequently, the incredulous British filled the military void in a measured, even slow advance. Ludendorff's 'scorched earth'[7] policy thus served its purpose and the legend of the 'impregnable Hindenburg Line' was established from the outset; equally, in the propaganda war, the German soldiers' alleged reputation for heartlessness and viciousness grew apace.

The initial construction of the *'Siegfried Stellung'* had been spotted by Royal Flying Corps reconnaissance patrols in late October 1916. Further RFC patrols began to report the withdrawal of small numbers of German units from the Somme from 22nd February 1917 though subsequent detailed photo-reconnaissance of the defensive construction was greatly inhibited by the introduction of two legendary fighter aircraft to the German squadrons – the Albatros D. 'III' and the Halberstadt D. 'V'. As a result, the work of 59 Squadron RFC's RE8 reconnaissance patrols was severely limited or executed at high cost; the expected bombing of the construction work by BE2s of Nos. 8, 12 and 13 Squadrons RFC was equally restricted as the British escort fighters were inferior machines compared to the Albatros and the Halberstadt.

DIARY

Sunday, 25th February
Rumours of German retreat
(Sunny)
"Today has been a very bright, sunny day. Big things have happened, at least

according to rumour. *The Germans have evacuated several parts of the line on the Somme – we have sent out patrols at places and no enemy is found within three miles but as yet no confirmation of the report is obtained though it is official that it is so at one or two points."*

[Jack Hickman's diary entry suggests that the 'rumour-mill' was as active then as it is today, even though it was then fed by far fewer sources! On this occasion such rumour proved to be accurate.]

Monday, 26th February
Rumours confirmed
(Late rain)
"The rumour of yesterday is correct – the Germans have retired on a ten-mile front to a depth of roughly two miles. We have taken four more villages and straightened out our line from the left of Bapaume towards Arras."

Tuesday, 27th February
'One man working at the Divisional Bomb Stores was wounded by shell fire.'

[9/DAC War Diary]

Thursday, 1st March
Maroeuil
(Fine; rain later)

'...Men in huts and horses under cover.'

[9/DAC War Diary]

"The retirement of the enemy on the left of Bapaume[8] is still going on steadily – how far they intend to go is uncertain. There is practically nothing now to stop us walking into Bapaume and no doubt in a few days this will have been done. Heavy artillery work went on last night on our front between Arras and Vimy. For about three hours we thought the big push had started but it turned out to be a big raid by the Canadians. The enemy has properly got the wind up over our raids – each night their artillery puts up a heavy barrage in No Man's Land to stop us in case we intend to raid them. Two more villages have fallen to us on the Somme [most probably Grandcourt and Bucqouy] and there is a lot of aircraft business around Arras – it looks like big business soon. The advance on the Somme will no doubt postpone our offensive for some weeks, as all our heavy artillery positions will have to be moved and that will take some time. Weather fine today but there was rain last night and there are signs of more tonight; the roads are in rather bad condition."

THE AIR WAR OVER ARRAS

CONTEXT

British losses of men and machines during March 1917 were equal to those incurred in the whole of 1915; of these, eighty per cent were from air combat as opposed to the ground fire that had claimed proportionally more victims earlier in the war. The cause of this change in balance of power is to be found in the arrival of two outstanding German fighter aircraft – from January the Albatros D. 'III' and from February the Halberstadt D. 'V'. In addition, new German photo-reconnaissance aircraft, such as the two-seat Rumpler C. 'IV' had an operating ceiling (21,000 feet) that was substantially higher than the British fighters sent to intercept them – it was also the first aircraft to carry oxygen equipment to cope better with the greater operating ceiling.

The new Bristol F2a fighters of 48 Squadron RFC flew their first operations on 5th April; the squadron encountered Manfred von Richtofen's Jagdstaffel ('Jasta') 11 of Albatros Scouts. Four F2a fighters were lost, two shot down by the *'Red Baron'* himself. One of the Flight Commanders of 48 Squadron RFC, and leader of the first Bristol patrol, was none other than Captain William Leefe Robinson VC. He had won the Victoria Cross by becoming the first pilot to shoot down a Zeppelin – his victim was army airship 'SL11', shot down by Robinson's outdated BE2c, in a ball of flame over Cuffley.[9] This success on 2nd September 1916 not only made great headlines in the propaganda war but also, more tangibly, deterred a night raid on London by sixteen Zeppelins, thus affording civilians the first obvious evidence that their fliers were fighting back over England. It was a much-needed victory

Table 7: Principal RFC/RNAS squadrons (showing 'home' aerodrome and types flown in March 1917) involved in the air war over the Arras sector during the same month

Squadron	Aerodrome	Type	Losses/Victories
8 Sq –	Soncamp aerodrome	BE2e	5 losses
11 Sq –	Izel-le-Hameau aerodrome	FE2b	8 losses
12 Sq –	Avesnes-le-Comte aerodrome	BE2e	2 losses
13 Sq –	Savy aerodrome	BE2e	3 losses
29 Sq –	Le Hameau aerodrome	Nieuport 16	2 losses, 1 victory
48 Sq –	La Bellevue aerodrome [arrived on 5th March, flying the new fighter-recon Bristol F2a]	Bristol F2a	no losses
59 Sq –	La Bellevue aerodrome	RE8	4 losses
60 Sq –	Filescamp Farm aerodrome	Nieuport 16, 17, 23,	2 victories
6(Naval) Sq	La Bellevue aerodrome; attached to the RFC from 15th March Nieuport Scouts		no losses

in the wake of the nation-wide grief over so many casualties on the first day of the Somme offensive. The capture of 'Robbie' was an ominous prelude to 'Bloody April'[10] in the skies above the Arras sector.

DIARY

Monday, 5th March
Maroeuil
(Snow)
"*Awoke this morning to find the ground covered with snow and it is still at it. Rough luck for us as it may stop operations once more. There was a very heavy bombardment during each of the past three nights but not much excitement during the daytime except air-fights when the sky has been clear.*"

Tuesday, 6th March
Maroeuil
(Sunny, cold)
"*Today has been a most remarkable one owing to the number of our aeroplanes that have been up all day since about eight this morning. During one period, from about nine until twelve, there were forty-odd flying over Arras. The enemy fired hundreds of rounds but with no effect on our chaps who carried on as if nothing was happening.*"

[There were no British air losses in the Arras sector on this day although nineteen losses occurred elsewhere on the Western Front].

"*It was a bright, sunny day and just the kind of weather for observation work. Rumours of the enemy's retirement on our front have not yet been confirmed.*" [Such confirmation of the German Retreat to the Hindenburg Line would soon be made official, not least for its propaganda value.]

Thursday, 8th March
A rare quiet day
(Cold winds, snow showers)
"*The last two days have been very bitter – terribly cold winds and today very heavy snow squalls at intervals. The ground is covered and it is freezing hard. Nothing to report from the line.*"

CONTEXT

7th-8th March: the poor weather at least temporarily prevented enemy air reconnaissance and bombing sorties.

DIARY

Sunday, 11th March
Maroeuil
"*At last we feel that some great move is close. Last night the orders came through for vast quantities of ammunition to go up [forward] and infantry is going up the line. It means only one thing – it is only a matter of days before the 'big bang' starts. Everywhere is feverish and methodical preparation and we are all on thorns to know what day and hour the din will commence.*"

Saturday, 17th March
Bapaume captured
(Sunny but cool)
"Today we have had the official news that Bapaume has been taken at last – now we look for Péronne to be the next one. Still very busy on our front at Arras, lots of ammunition going up daily but the start date of the big push is still unknown, though very close. Weather splendid today with bright sunshine and a drying wind."

Monday, 19th March
Péronne captured
"Today has developed into a very rough and ready one. During the afternoon we had the news through that our troops had taken Péronne [it was captured by a Royal Warwickshire battalion of 48th '1st South Midland' Division on 18th March 1917] and the French are also making a very big attack at Soissons and are still attacking as we receive this news. Last night for about two hours round about midnight our own artillery kept up a terrific bombardment on our own front to the left of Arras but details are not in as yet. This evening about 5:30 word came through to say that the Germans had evacuated three lines of trenches from Arras to the Somme – our main army is out of touch with them but the cavalry

has gone through and has found them at various points. Details not to hand – great news expected at any moment."

CONTEXT

16th to 19th March
German withdrawal completed
16th to 19th March 1917 were the days when the bulk of the German army on the Somme front withdrew to the newly-constructed 'Siegfried Stellung' defensive lines. Judging by the diary entries made by Jack from late February, it appears that the ordinary Tommy, starved of good news of Allied advances, somewhat eagerly misinterpreted the German withdrawal as a great victory. Even so, the fact that the German High Command felt obliged to shorten their defensive line did indicate that the Somme offensive had drained German resources. During the 'retreat', the German High Command had ordered that anything that might be of use to the Allies be destroyed and that many 'booby-traps' be set to slow down the Tommies clearing individual buildings in villages and hamlets. Thus the coming offensive at Arras was to prove remarkably important in many respects.

THE PLAN OF ATTACK FOR THE ARRAS OFFENSIVE (9TH APRIL TO 17TH MAY 1917)

The town of Arras, similarly to its Belgian counterpart Ypres, had been in Allied hands for the first three years of the war. Like Ypres, it was situated just a few miles from German lines and formed a salient, thus offering an inviting target to German artillery. Like the mediæval Flanders town, the centre of Arras with its ancient town hall and belfry had been pounded to barely-recognisable rubble. In yet another similarity, Arras was overlooked by a German-held ridge from which accurate artillery fire could inhibit any Allied breakout onto the Douai Plain; while Ypres was dominated to its south by the German-held Messines Ridge, so Arras was dominated to its north by the steep, fortress-like Vimy Ridge. Therefore, in each case, a major Allied attack from such a salient demanded the neutralisation of a seemingly impregnable enemy-held ridge as a pre-requisite for success.

A second consideration, in the interests of public and troop morale, was to ensure that the casualty lists of 1916 on the Somme should not be repeated. The new Prime Minister, David Lloyd-George, believed that General Haig was too willing to accept high casualty rates so in its preparation for the Arras offensive, the much-maligned British High Command went to great lengths to protect its assault troops. Several months prior to 'Z' Day (9th April 1917), a series of mediæval, even Roman, quarries, cellars and caves in the limestone beneath the city of Arras had been worked into a system of tall caverns and inter-linked tunnels under the south-eastern Arras suburbs of Ronville and St. Sauveur. Shaken by the losses on the Somme in 1916, the British High Command's intention was to protect many of the battalions going into battle by threading them through tunnels that emerged into the daylight close to the front line, thus reducing the time spent under the deadly hail of German machine gun fire while crossing No-Man's Land. To achieve this,

'...a series of subterranean, mediæval quarries on the edge of the town (beneath…Ronville and St. Sauveur) would be linked by tunnels to create the most extensive underground network in British military history.[11]'
As Robert Hardman points out, 'In a matter of months they [the tunnellers] had created two inter-connected labyrinths, twelve miles long and capable of hiding 25,000 troops.'

[Robert Hardman, 'Daily Mail', 2008]

This underground world was lit by electricity, enjoyed running water, was protected by gas-proof doors and even boasted a 700-bed hospital, several chapels and a sixty-centimetre, light railway. The northerly of the two tunnels, the St. Sauveur Tunnel, ran from the massive Crinchon Sewer (linking the system to the cellars under the Town Hall and the Cathedral) to the front line on the Cambrai Road, to the east of Arras; the more southerly of the tunnels[12], the Ronville Tunnel, ran from the Crinchon Sewer to the front line on the Bapaume Road. This network was accessed from a series of manholes in Arras, the principal ones being located under the town hall, in front of the railway station and beneath the French military barracks. At the other extremity, on the front line, several branch tunnels led via long flights of steps to the surface – a remarkably safe approach to the inevitable dangers of No Man's Land for so many soldiers on 9th April.

PREPARATIONS FOR THE SPRING OFFENSIVE

The tunnelling works were completed on time – the caves and quarries under the town were capable of concealing more than 25,000 soldiers from enemy gunfire. The network of tunnels was divided into two main sections. The first, situated under the Cambrai Road, was the domain of the Scots of 9th 'Scottish' Division, who baptized their galleries with familiar names such as Carlisle and Glasgow, and the English of the 35th 'Bantam' Division, who likewise named galleries after their home towns of Manchester, Liverpool and Chester. The network of tunnels under the Ronville district of the town was, from February 1917, occupied by New Zealanders who named their galleries after home towns such as Wellington. The total length of the tunnels amounted to an impressive twelve miles.

Prior to the assault of 9th April, the troops had to spend long periods of time in the tunnels and so the latter were equipped with kitchens, water supplies from the mains or wells, and electric lighting throughout. The tunnels provided a high degree of safety compared to the surface trenches at a comparable distance from the front and this must have eased some of the fears as men waited to go into battle. Also installed and less reassuring was a hospital capable of treating 700 wounded. It was fitted out like a normal hospital with waiting rooms for the wounded, an operating theatre, a rest area for the stretcher-bearers and the reserves, and a mortuary. It was even equipped with signposts to ensure users could find their way around.

Preceding the assault of 9th April there was to be an exceptionally intense preliminary bombardment. Aerial reconnaissance since late 1916 had identified vital targets in enemy territory while larger trench raids gathered as much information as possible on the structure of the German defences. Large models were constructed so that the officers and company leaders could familiarize themselves with the terrain they were expected to capture.

The assaulting troops were to receive additional support from new weapons. Tanks were to be used for only the second time (following their trial on the Somme) as well as a recent development called the Livens Projector – a steel tube, similar to a mortar, which could fire cylinders great distances and thus be able to deliver poison gas into the enemy lines without fear of the wind blowing it back. Moreover, on 6th April 1917 troop morale was given a major boost when it was announced that the United States had entered the war.

Z DAY

On Monday 9th April 1917 at 5.30 a.m., after a fierce bombardment lasting four days, the British First Army (actually comprising four *Canadian* divisions under the command of General Henry Horne) set out to capture Vimy Ridge. Control of the ridge would facilitate General Allenby's Third Army advance towards the Douai Plain beyond the ridge. Allenby's objectives also included Monchy-le-Preux, a German artillery stronghold just a few miles to the east of Arras that commanded the Scarpe Valley. General Gough's Fifth Army, on the right wing of the offensive, was tasked to capture the village of Bullecourt in the Hindenburg Line.

In summary the objectives were:

- Pre-requisite – to take the high ground of Vimy Ridge.
- To advance onto the plains below the ridge and to capture the transport junction of Douai.
- To take control of Monchy-le-Preux so as to ease the task of advancing eastwards along the Scarpe Valley.
- To assault and capture the village of Bullecourt, thus making an initial inroad into the powerful *'Siegfried Stellung'* or Hindenburg Line.

DIARY

Tuesday, 20th March

Ammunition build-up

"The fall of Bapaume has been confirmed and is much better than we at first supposed. Over a dozen villages have been taken, including Achiet-le-Grand, the main German railhead for the Arras-Somme salient. An advance was made over about eleven miles of ground at a depth of two and three miles. The French are also advancing on a twenty-two mile front at Soissons and great news is expected at any hour. No details are yet to hand concerning the German evacuation near Arras, meanwhile our own preparations for a very big offensive are still in full swing. For ten days now we have taken up about 15,000 rounds of 18-pounder ammunition while hundreds of [motor] lorries are running day and night, carrying the heavy gun ammunition; thousands of infantrymen are still going up at night."

Wednesday, 21st March
Good news!

"Today great news has come through regarding the French attack. From Péronne running south, the French and British have advanced on an eighty-mile front to a depth of ten miles at some points. The cavalry has been through and many important villages [actually towns] have been taken, including Roye and Noyon; more details are expected during the day."

Saturday, 24th March
'...one vast dump of munitions'
(Hard frost, biting wind)
"The past few days have been chiefly

heavy artillery duels at intervals but they never lasted long. This morning a German aeroplane came over our lines in a perfect clear blue sky – he was flying high up and had a splendid view of our huge dump of ammunition. We are living in a huge camp which is one vast dump of munitions. Only one bomb or shell amongst them would put the whole place up, so we did not quite appreciate the presence of 'Fritz' above us. The guns commenced to let fly at him and he was soon tossing about like a cork among the puffs of smoke. Our shells and machine-guns at our dump opened up on him and for about twenty minutes it was all excitement watching for him to come down but he got clear. Shortly after, several big shells fell around the dump but no luck for 'Fritz' as yet. About midday, the guns commenced to speak all along the line on either side of Arras. Away to the south, where the bend in the line joins the retreat from the Somme, the artillery bombardment was awful. About 3:30 this afternoon, the guns on our own front as fiercely as the guns to the south and now the whole line is going as hard as the Somme on the first of July last. Has the push started, we are all asking? But wait and see – I think it has. Ammunition is still going up the line in large quantities – somebody will soon get hurt! News of the French and British advance is quite scarce today but we think the Germans will make a big stand soon, then we hope to give him the knockout blow and finish it, but much has still to be expected in heavy fighting."

CONTEXT

Jack's entry for 24th March reveals the abiding fear, almost nightmare, of those involved in the manufacture, transportation and firing of munitions – the constant threat of ignition, by whatever means, of huge quantities of explosives. For the artilleryman in a theatre of war, aerial bombing and artillery bombardment were the most likely culprits. Members of an Ammunition Column, by the very nature of their re-supply task, had to live with such a shadow over their daily lives. In the gun-line, all artillerymen were effectively at the mercy of the efficiency of the munitions-worker, the rate of wear of the gun itself and the accuracy or otherwise of the enemy's own gunners.

Thursday, 22nd to Saturday, 31st March

The build-up towards the opening of an artillery barrage presaging a major offensive in the Arras sector is supported by an entry in 9/DAC War Diary:

> *'All available horses and wagons engaged in carrying ammunition up to battery positions.'*

DIARY

Sunday, 25th March
Build-up continues
(Warmer than previously)

"The bombardment is still going on in a great commotion during last night – it eased up for a bit but at dawn it broke out again. We don't quite know what to make of it. It is hardly heavy enough to be the big thing but it is far above the average attack bombardment. The weather today is much warmer, after two very hard frosts and cold winds. There are large quantities of ammunition still going up."

Wednesday, 28th March
(Cold with snow and rain)
"The last three days have been noted for very heavy artillery work but not much news has come through. We have had a few very exciting half hours since Sunday. 'Fritz' has just found out that we are here and has just popped over a few beauties but has only knocked the earth about so far. Weather very cold, with snow, rain and sun at intervals."

CONTEXT

The British artillery bombardment of 25th to 28th was facilitated by air observation carried out by the likes of 48 Squadron RFC's newly-arrived Bristol F2a fighter-reconnaissance machines. Even so, German artillery fought back to inflict losses among the British lines.

'One man attached 64th Coy RE killed by [enemy] shell fire [on 28th].'

[9/DAC War Diary]

The 9/DAC man killed on 28th March was 168882 Driver Harold Edward Buss who was born in Tonbridge, Kent. He was killed in action (aged 22) while serving on attachment to 64th Field Company, RE, from 9/DAC near Arras. He is buried in plot II.L.3 of Faubourg d'Amiens Cemetery, Arras.

DIARY

Sunday, 1st April
Maroeuil dump shelled
(Persistent rain)
"Nothing very exciting has happened in the past few days, except plenty of work by the artillery and lots of munitions and guns going up the line day and night. The weather is terribly wet, leaving mud everywhere. Last night the Germans put a fifteen-inch shell into a dump at Maroeuil [north-east of Agnez-lès-Duisans], setting it on fire. I was only about half a mile away and the crash nearly shook me off my horse. About midnight, the Germans shelled the same spot again and drove out the ammunition column of the 4th Division, killing three men, wounding three and killing many horses. They have now camped by us for a time."

CONTEXT

In fact, the men killed were not of the 4th Division but belonged to 17th 'Northern' Division whose guns were also to play a major role in the coming Arras offensive that would open on 9th April. They were:

6929	Driver Neil Buchanan (22)	D/79, RFA.
55357	Driver Herbert Algy Hasler (27)	D/79, RFA.
2689	Driver Edgar John Nicholas (20)	D/79, RFA.

All three men belonged to 'D' (Heavy) Battery, 79th Brigade, 17th 'Northern' Division and were almost certainly at the dump with horse-drawn wagons to collect a load of shells for their guns. They were in the right place at the wrong time. The three lads were buried in plots IV. C. 4, IV. C. 3 and IV. C. 7 respectively, of Maroueil British Cemetery, four miles to the north-west of Arras.

9/DAC War Diary records the following observations:

'1st to 7th April: Column at Larisset. Engaged in carrying ammunition from two XVII Corps dumps to gun positions.'

DIARY

Tuesday, 3rd April
Larisset
(Snow and cold)
"The weather again is awful. Yesterday afternoon it snowed from about three until after six and it was as bad as at any time this winter – this morning we awoke to the

Maroueil British Cemetery, where the three lads of D/79 are buried.

same thing again. It is awful – ever since last September it has been one terrible winter of bad weather. Last night, about nine, a Zeppelin was reported over Arras; all lights were out and the guns manned but it did not reach us, so we look forward to a visit from them on a finer night. On the new German line south of Arras our troops have again advanced, taking eight more villages – great developments are expected from that quarter if the weather will hold fine. Tonight everybody is whispering, 'It starts tonight'; we don't quite know but it seems as if the start of the big push is close at hand. An unusual calm and quiet rests everywhere, the first time for weeks that the traffic has actually stopped. We are all excitement, waiting and wondering. About 7:30 this evening, a German airman came over and put down two of our balloons in flames – we have not found out whether the men escaped."

Wednesday, 4th April
Artillery barrage, Arras
(Cold but clearing)
"At last it has started! This morning at three all the field guns began to bombard the German barbed wire – they have been going all day and are still at it. So far the big guns are quite silent, not one half of the whole lot are in action as yet but we shall hear them at any minute now. We have discovered today that the two balloons that were brought down last night at Arras were German balloons, not ours (cheers!). The weather tonight looks finer and everybody is more cheerful."

[The air offensive in support of the Battle of Arras commenced on 4th April].

Thursday, 5th April
Barrage continues
(Heavy rain p.m.)
"Last night, about midnight, our heavy guns commenced to work; all night long they carried on until daylight this morning. They then quietened down and the field guns have carried on alone all day. Rumours today tell us that the heavy guns have done great things, smashing up the German artillery in good style but it is early to judge the result as yet. Tomorrow we expect the infantry to go over, so we should get good news very soon."

Saturday, 7th April
Kite balloon down
(Fine)
"Today has been finer after the heavy rain of yesterday afternoon. Tonight about six p.m., a German aeroplane came over and set fire to one of our kite balloons that was up over our camp – the two observers came down safely in parachutes but the balloon was burnt to a cinder. The Royal Scots have all gone up [the line] tonight; we understand they are the first to go over, followed by the South Africans. Tomorrow we move our headquarters up to our forward positions – the next few days should bring great things."

Sunday, 8th April
Eve of battle, Maroeuil, north-west of Arras

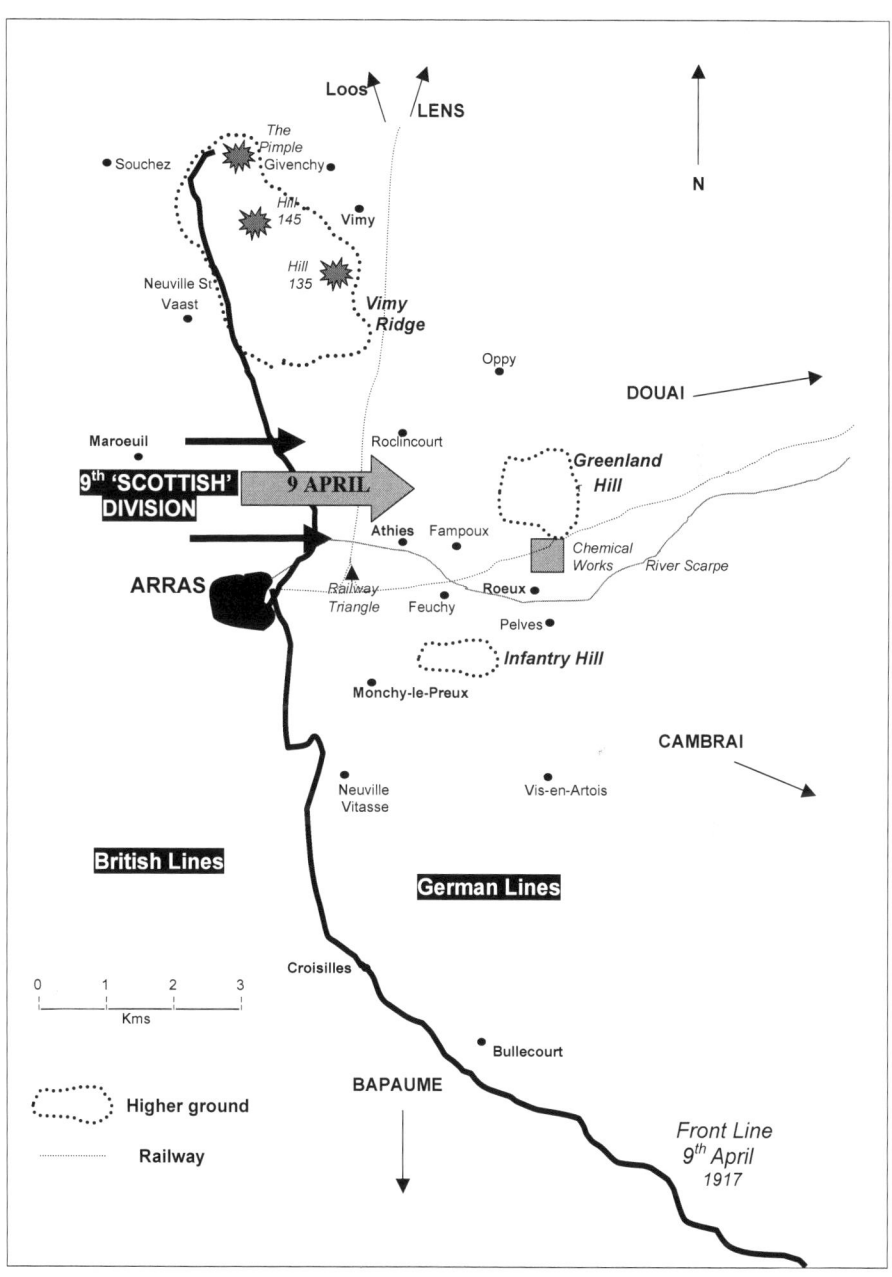

Map 4: 9th 'Scottish' Division at Arras, spring 1917

"This is Easter Sunday. Today we have moved up to our advanced positions at Maroeuil [four miles north-west of Arras centre] and thousands of troops are here. We are by a railway on which are five super-heavy guns on armoured trains; they are only about two hundred yards from our camp and the crash of them is terrible. We have been peppered with shrapnel from anti-aircraft guns and from German shrapnel as well but so far nobody has been hit. At the moment things are quiet but we expect a terrible racket tonight for tomorrow morning the infantry go over the top, so the guns will soon be on the job again, preparing the way for them. No sleep tonight."

Monday, 9th April
Vimy Ridge & 1st Battle of the Scarpe
(9th-14th April, 1917)
(Very cold with heavy snow showers)
"This morning at 5:30 the infantry went over the top to the tune of a terrible bombardment. At two o'clock we had the news over that they had taken the first two lines and five hundred prisoners; at three this afternoon they had the third line with 1,100 prisoners. On our left, on Vimy Ridge, the Canadians made a fine advance, taking a lot of prisoners [not yet counted]. At the present time, 8:30 p.m., a terrific bombardment is in progress on the Vimy front – all the heavy guns on our front are turned on the Canadian front and the din and flashes are enough to frighten anybody. It has been a great day, so far. The cavalry went through on

our front during this afternoon but no report has been received from them as yet, except that they have gone a good many miles. The 4th Division is going through us tonight to give us a rest; everything has gone splendidly up to now but the next day or two will have to pass before any opinion can be formed on the result. The weather today has been terribly cold, a gale of wind and a lot of rain and sleet. This morning, one of our captive balloons was torn away from its moorings – the last we saw of it was up in the skies ravelling at a terrible rate of speed. The observers escaped with parachutes. Tomorrow is looked forward to with great eagerness by us all to see what it will bring forth. All the troops are moving up and tomorrow we shall follow them."

Tuesday, 10th April
Moving up the gun-line
(Very cold with heavy snowstorms)
"Today we have moved forward again near Arras – we are in old gun positions with shell-holes all around us but at present things are quiet as regards German shelling. Two rows of very heavy guns are just behind us and some all around us; in about half a mile of us there are about fifty guns of monstrous size – we are in the centre of them."

[This comment reveals that the very heavy artillery pieces fired from positions well back from the front lines. The dual reasons were that the heavier guns covered a greater range than the field pieces and their heavy weight made them more difficult and thus slower to remove from the field of battle should worst happen and the front lines be overrun.]

"The noise and swish of the shells over our heads make one creep about but we have got to stick it. The news today is still good – our infantry have gone further and our cavalry are again at work. Prisoners taken yesterday from the neighbourhood of Vimy to Arras number about 35,000 according to the latest information – our [9th] Division alone took 14,000 on the first day. It is hard to get news as yet but the next day or two should bring in great tidings. The air is full of rumours – Lens is reported as taken; also a big French advance further south but that we shall no doubt hear about tomorrow. The weather today has been awful – heavy snowstorms then freezing hard, as bad as any part of the winter."

CONTEXT

10th to 30th April
Anzin

'Column remained at Anzin and was engaged in carrying ammunition to gun positions. On various dates German guns that had been captured were brought from their positions into [our] camp. Quantities of ammunition were also collected. Captured guns included: seven 7.7cm guns; one

9cm gun; five 5.9cm howitzers; one 10.5cm howitzer.'

[9/DAC War Diary]

DIARY

Wednesday, 11th April
Living under the 'Heavies'
(Very cold with persistent snow showers)
"One more day of the big push has nearly gone and what a time it has been! Last night all the guns around us opened up and kept on until eleven this morning. It then stopped and the 4th Division infantry went over to attack the Germans' fourth line. As yet the news of the attack has not come through. The bombardment, while it lasted, was terrible as we are only about one hundred yards in front of the heavy guns and the shock of the reports almost stuns one. At present they are quiet except for an occasional shot. Just on our right, in Saint Catherine [in the north-western sector of Arras], the heavies bombarded for about an hour but they have now eased off again. Everything has so far gone splendidly and the Germans are in full retreat with our cavalry after them." [This report, in respect of the use of cavalry, proved to be fanciful.]

"The weather is still cold and it is snowing at present."

Thursday, 12th April
(Snow thawing; clearing skies)
"Still we continue to push on with almost

unbroken success. All along the line of attack we have carried every objective – the 4th Division is reported to have taken a position and then lost it again and our own infantry have gone in to retake the lost ground but the real truth of it all has not come through as yet. The work of the artillery near us has not been as heavy as yesterday but the positions in front of us have been very active all day and at present they have broken out again afresh but what the trouble is this time we do not know – possibly another counter-attack on the position we attacked this evening at five. Today the weather is much finer. At dawn this morning we had about six inches of snow but it has all disappeared during the day."

CONTEXT

Thursday, 12th April
South African Brigade, towards Roeux

"*At 3 p.m. on the 12th April the 1st, 2nd, and 4th South African Regiments [actually battalions rather than regiments of 9th 'Scottish' Division] assembled in Fampoux. The enemy was evidently prepared…this movement was… subjected to a heavy and steady bombardment, which cost us many casualties. The prospects of success were not bright. All three brigades of the 9th Division…..had had no sleep for four nights, three of which they had spent lying in the snow without blankets and many without greatcoats. There was no chance of an adequate bombardment and there was no time to reconnoitre the ground: the country between Fampoux and Roeux station was perfectly open and was commanded in the south by a high railway embankment and three woods, all of them held by the enemy… while in the north it sloped gradually to the inn around which the Germans had organized strong-points. It was impossible, therefore, to prevent the movement of troops being observed by the enemy…..As the different [South African] companies began to deploy from the shelter of the houses in the east end of Fampoux they were met with heavy machine-gun and rifle fire.*

"*The attack was timed for 5 p.m., when our guns opened fire. Unfortunately our barrage dropped…..behind the first enemy line of defence, so that the South Africans had a long tract of open ground to cover…Our artillery, too, seemed to miss the enemy machine-gun posts on the railway embankment which, combined with the flanking fire from the woods in the south and the south-east and from the direction of the inn, played havoc with both the attacking brigades. The result was a failure. A gallant few of the South Africans succeeded in reaching the station, a point in their objective, where their bodies were recovered a month later when the position was captured. For the rest, only one or two isolated* parties reached points as much as 200 yards east of the line held by the 4th Division. But as a proof of the quality of the troops, it should be recorded that before the attack was brought to a standstill, the casualties of the 2nd Regiment, who went in 400 strong, amounted to 16 officers and 285 men, while the 1st Regiment lost two officers and 203 men, and the 4th, six officers and 200 men. Among the dead were Captain Grady, who commanded 'A' Company of the 4th; and Lieutenants J. M. Ross, Lees, and Porteous. Since the first part of the assault had failed, the 26th Brigade, which was waiting to advance on Roeux, was not called upon. That night it took over the line from the Scarpe to the Hyderabad Redoubt, where it linked up with the 4th Division, and the South Africans withdrew to the Green Line. They were finally relieved on the night of the 15th April having suffered, in the three days since the 12th April, 720 casualties."

[John Buchan, 'The History of the South African Forces in France'.]

DIARY

Friday, 13th April
A degree of success
(Clearing during the day; calm)
"Last night our infantry went over and retook the position lost by the 4th Division – it was rather a big scrap while it lasted and our South African 'Scottish' [1st, 2nd, 3rd and 4th Battalions, the South African Infantry that had replaced 28th Infantry Brigade on 6th May 1916 when the latter brigade was broken up and disbanded] got rather a nasty mauling but got what they went over for. The artillery has been fairly quiet today – the big guns near us have nearly all moved up. It was a great sight about sunset to see the aeroplanes; scores of them were up at once and after hovering around above us they headed away over the German lines at a great height. Some of our latest machines were among them – a very large 'plane that can go straight up instead of having to go up in circles. A big raid is evidently on somewhere behind the German lines tonight. The weather is a lot better today and looks finer tonight – very still, no wind and fairly clear. Many rumours of great happenings on the French line keep coming through."

CONTEXT

Below are details of the raids of 13th April mentioned by Jack Hickman.

"On 13th April daylight bombing raids were carried out over Essigny-le-Petit, Busigny Station and Henin-Liétard Station that was used by the Germans for de-training troops."

[Chaz Bowyer, Communiqué No.83, 'Royal Flying Corps Communiqués, 1917-1918.']

Table 8: 'Bloody April' 1917 in the skies over Arras

2 Sq	Hesdigneul aerodrome	BE2c, BE2 d, BE2 + AW FK8 (from April 1917)	4 losses
5 Sq	Savy aerodrome (La Gorgue to 6 Apr)	BE2e, BE2f, BE2g	5 losses
8 Sq	Soncamp aerodrome	BE2d, BE2e	5 losses
10 Sq	Chocques aerodrome	BE2e, BE2f, BE2g	4 losses
11 Sq	Savy aerodrome	FE2b	16 losses
12 Sq	Avesnes-le-Comte aerodrome	BE2d, BE2e	13 losses
13 Sq	Savy aerodrome	BE2d, BE2e	14 losses
16 Sq	Bruay aerodrome	BE2f, BE2g	17 losses
19 Sq	Vert Galand aerodrome (Fienvillers to 1st April)	Spad S.VII	6 losses, 1 victory
25 Sq	Lozinghem aerodrome	FE2b, FE2d	7 losses
27 Sq	Fienvillers aerodrome	M'syde G100/102	6 losses
29 Sq	Le Hameau aerodrome	Nieuport 16, 17	15 losses, 1 victory
35 Sq	Savy aerodrome (St.-André-aux-Bois to 4 April)	AW FK8	1 loss
40 Sq	Treizennes aerodrome (Auchel from 25th April; Bruay from 29th April)	Nieuport 17	5 losses, 1 victory
43 Sq	Treizennes aerodrome	Sopwith 1½-Strutter	6 losses
48 Sq	La Bellevue aerodrome	Bristol F2a	12 losses, 2 victories
55 Sq	Fienvillers aerodrome	DH4 (ops 23rd April)	10 losses
56 Sq	Vert Galand aerodrome	SE5 (ops April 22nd)	1 loss
57 Sq	Fienvillers aerodrome	FE2d	13 losses
59 Sq	La Bellevue aerodrome	RE8	15 losses
60 Sq	Filescamp Farm aerodrome	Nieuport 16, 17, 23	19 losses 1 victory
66 Sq	Vert Galand aerodrome	Sopwith Pup	3 losses
70 Sq	Fienvillers aerodrome (Vert Galand to 1st April)	Sopwith 1½ Strutter	1 loss
100 Sq	Izel-le-Hameau aerodrome	FE2b+BE2c, BE2e	2 losses
6(Naval) Sq	La Bellevue aerodrome	DH4	4 losses
8(Naval) Sq	Auchel aerodrome	Sopwith Triplane	2 losses

'Victories' and 'losses' both include shot down, badly damaged, forced to land, crew killed, wounded or captured.

"13th April was the first day since the offensive began that weather was clear enough for a full day's work in the air, especially a resumption of bombing. 38 machines, from 19, 25, 27 40 and 66 Squadrons, gathered to raid Henin-Liétard."

[Trevor Henshaw: *'The Sky Their Battlefield.'*]

DIARY

Saturday, 14th April
German balloon downed
(Clear; less cold)
"Today has been a fine one and not much doing in the way of fighting on our front. The heavy guns have now nearly all moved up past us but the fighting has been nil. Last night we put down another German balloon."

Sunday, 15th April
Lens captured by the French
(Persistent rain)
"Today has been a rotten, wet day but good news of the fall of Lens [in the French sector, to the north] has helped to buck us all up a lot. Heavy artillery work was the chief thing of the day; just on the right of us the artillery has been going ever since the middle of last night and since dark the guns on our front have been going heavily. The Germans have also been shelling very heavily all day at different points of the line. There is evidently some very hot work going on away towards St. Quentin [in the Somme sector]."

Monday, 16th April
An artillery day
(Persistent rain)
"Today has been another wet one and marked by artillery work only. The Germans gave us some reminders that they have some big guns – they shelled the battery beside our camp several times and dropped some fifteen-inch Silent Sues [a 'Silent Susan' was a trench-soldier's nickname for a high velocity shell as it exploded almost before it was heard] into Etrun [immediately north-east of Duisans]. Apart from that there was not much doing apart from artillery work all along the line, heavier in some parts than others."

Tuesday, 17th April
Another artillery day
(Sleet, snow, very cold)
"Another day of rain, snow and freezing cold. Not much doing, only heavy artillery work all day without any stop. Early this morning another captive balloon broke away from her moorings and was swept away out of sight in the clouds. No news can be obtained, we are cut off from the outside world – no papers since we left civilisation a week ago last Sunday. There are many rumours of what has happened at other parts of the line but none of them has been confirmed."

Thursday, 19th April
News of captures
(Clearing during the day)

"Today has been a bit finer but yesterday was as usual wet and cold. The usual artillery work is the only thing on our front but great news has come through from the French line – they are making a big attack on a twenty-five mile front and have taken over 10,000 prisoners and a lot of guns of different sorts and sizes. Our total on our front from Arras to Lens since the ninth of the month is 14,000 prisoners, 194 guns and a large amount of stores, ammunition and machine-guns, plus two Engineers' dumps. All the matériel is very valuable. Everything is going well on the whole line so far."

Even so, the 9/DAC War Diary reported:

'2/Lt. A. Delves was wounded while collecting these guns.'

Saturday, 21st April
9/DAC covers 51st 'Highland'
(Fine and warmer)
"The past two days have produced very fine weather and everything has bucked up as a result of it. On our own front artillery work has been very heavy but not much in the infantry line. Our own infantry is out of the line and we are covering the 51st ['Highland'] Division Scottish Territorials. Today has been a very busy one in the air. At about five o'clock this afternoon the Germans put down one of our kite balloons over Arras – it was burnt to a cinder.

"...the RFC aircraft also put down three German kite balloons."

[Trevor Henshaw: 'The Sky Their Battlefield.']

About seven in the evening a big air fight took place over our lines between two large squads of 'planes...

"...nearly fifty 'planes were patrolling at one point; though there were few reports of combat, 16 Squadron RFC sustained three losses of Be2s, while 29 Squadron RFC lost three Nieuports and their two-man crews – Jasta 11 claimed the 'kills'; there were no others recorded."

[Trevor Henshaw: 'The Sky Their Battlefield.']

...two came down from one lot and three from the other but so far we do not know if we 'scored' or the enemy did as it was too far to see which was which. One came down nose first with a terrible crash; the others just floated down like large pieces of paper. Weather still fine and the artillery work is terrible to listen to."

Sunday, 22nd April
Yet another barrage
"Last night was the biggest bombardment since the counter-attack by the Germans at Delville Wood [on the Somme] in July 1916; the crash for an hour was terrible to live through. Tonight again the guns are going at the same rate but it is all along the line. Early tomorrow morning

the infantry are going over all along the line in the biggest attack ever yet carried out. This present bombardment is the preparation for that attack. It is a great sight and tomorrow we hope to get great news."

Monday, 23rd April
2nd Battle of the Scarpe
(23rd-24th April, 1917)

"A night never to be forgotten! All during the hours of the night the guns kept up a terrific din. At four this morning they suddenly burst out in all the full force of every gun all along the British front. Never has anything like that from four to six this morning been heard, it was absolutely terrible. Up to last evening, the heaviest bombardment of the war had been the attack on Delville Wood in July last. None of this present push had come close to the first fortnight on the Somme but the two hours at dawn this morning was far beyond any that has ever taken place before. We have not yet got much news through except that we have taken the Chemical Works [at Roeux on the River Scarpe], a very strong fortress in the new German line. Ever since the attack by the infantry at six this morning, the guns have been going without a stop – at the present moment the Germans are making desperate counter-attacks to regain the lost ground."

"Late evening – The heavy work by the artillery is still going on. We cannot get any definite news through but things are not going any too well for us – we have got all we wanted but at rather heavy losses. Tonight we have heard that we have lost part of what we gained this morning but we are making another attack tonight. It is a terrible battle – it makes one feel that this must be the final battle. It is raging from the Somme to Loos and is a case of 'neck or nothing'. Tonight is the second night of this battle – we wonder when it will stop."

That day's 9/DAC War Diary entry reported:

'Two drivers wounded whilst taking ammunition to Battery positions.'

Tuesday, 24th April
Taking Casualties

(Clear skies, hot)

"Still the battle rages, as fierce as ever. Last night our two wagons went up with ammunition. One was blown up, killing one man and four horses while one man and two horses were wounded – the man had two fingers and his knee-cap torn off."

[The fatality was 12498, Driver Charles Henry Ashworth, 9/Division HQ, aged 40, married, born, lived and enlisted in Liverpool, died of wounds, buried in plot IV.E.20 of Duisans British Cemetery, Etrun.]

"The fight all night was terrific; we took and lost a fortified position three times and our own infantry were brought back

Headstone of Driver C.H. Ashworth in Duisans British Cemetery

Duisans British Cemetery, where Driver Charlie Ashworth is buried.

from rest camp to go over again after the same objective. We have heard that they succeeded but we have no official news to that effect. At about nine this morning, enemy aeroplanes dropped two bombs on our camp after some big guns but no damage was done. Just after dinner a German aeroplane attacked the balloon over our camp but one of our machines came up and they fought for several minutes just above our heads. Own machine was winged and had to come down and the German made off amid shells from our anti-aircraft guns. Last evening we saw four divisions of Germans massing for an attack. Our guns turned on them and blew them to nothing – those not hit scattered at once. Even so, the enemy is massing thousands of men to stop our attack – the tide of battle still ebbs and flows. Ironically the weather is glorious, hot sun and clear skies."

Wednesday, 25th April
German counter-attacks

"The great fight has ceased, for a time at least and it is all in our favour. We have taken and now hold the two-mile advance which we were after on Monday. We held it all night against terrific attacks all of which we stopped with huge losses to the Germans. Last night and today have been fairly quiet and we have moved up our heavy guns and have prepared for whatever comes – and it seems to have come, for about 9:30 tonight our batteries suddenly opened up all at once and blazed away like mad for half an hour. They have quietened down now so I suppose we have once again stopped their counter-attack."

Thursday, 26th April

"Today has been another......fairly quiet one along the line but the news of the great battle is beginning to come through. It was the greatest battle of all history and it seems now to have ended and it is in our favour. The Battle of Arras has given us an advance of over two miles and the capture of an important height [Vimy Ridge], nearly 4,000 prisoners and the losses of the Germans have been terrible – we estimate to have destroyed twelve divisions; in the same battle we destroyed, in two days, sixty-one aeroplanes and seven kite balloons."

[Trevor Henshaw in 'The Sky Their Battlefield' does not confirm the air successes – the RFC appears to have lost far more aircraft than their enemies].

"We are now preparing for another big blow at them, which we expect will start about Saturday or Sunday. This morning we had an exciting few minutes. A kite balloon was just over our camp but no observers were in it; suddenly a German aeroplane darted from the clouds and flashed round and around the balloon. After three attempts he finally put it down in flames. All afternoon the Germans have been shelling Arras with seventeen-inch shells – they make a terrible crash, produce clouds of smoke and do a lot of damage. They caused a fire which burned all afternoon – the guns have just put in another shell after about an hour's rest."

Friday, 27th April
A Lucky Escape
(Fine)
"Another fine day and fairly quiet along our front. Preparations are in progress for the big push which is coming off again on Saturday or Sunday. This afternoon I had to go up to the village of Blangy and I had the most terrible time of my life. My Boss went to our artillery headquarters and left me in the road with the horses for over an hour and the whole of that time the Germans were shelling like blazes at the village. The first five shells were within ten yards but owing to the depth of soft brick and dust from the ruins the shells buried too deeply to do much damage. After that they carried on until we left. About two hundred shells were put all around me, the farthest one not more than one hundred yards away and some within less than twenty yards. I learned today the real meaning of the phrase, 'getting the wind up' – I never want another experience like it. There were plenty of dugouts and everybody else was in them but I could not leave my horses so I stood there, a target for anything that came. How I was missed is something I shall never understand."

Saturday, 28th April
Battle of Arleux
(28th-29th April, 1917)
(Fine but thundery)
"All last night the guns carried on heavily. At dawn this morning, just after four, the whole lot broke out into that terrible barrage fire like the early morning of the

23rd [April]. During the day the news came through that we had taken that ridge called Greenland Hill that has cost so many lives. Later came the news that we had lost it again, so tonight we have the task before us once more. The fighting is still very fierce and the cost to the Germans is terrible – the fight they are making for this ridge shows how important the position is to them. This weekend should alter many things on our front. The weather is still fine but it's looking likely to thunder."

Monday, 30th April
(Fine)
"The past two days have been lovely and fine but not much doing in the fighting line – occasional bursts of artillery fire for an hour or so. The most exciting incident of the last two days was an amazing air fight over our camp this afternoon – thirty machines took part but none came down that we could see. Our planes chased the others away as far as we could see them."

Tuesday, 1st May
(Sunny and warm)
"Today has been another bright, sunny one and the chief incidents have been air work. Many fights have taken place and one German was brought down just by our camp. It was fetched down from about a mile up and came down over and over, like a wounded bird. Within about two hundred feet of the ground the pilot again got control of his machine but he had to come down; the two German officers were taken prisoner. The 'plane's petrol tank was

riddled with bullets and one of the men tried to destroy the machine but dozens of Tommies were on the spot in a few minutes and the Germans got 'rough house'."

[Trevor Henshaw states in 'The Sky Their Battlefield' that there was a big air-fight to the east of Arras, involving as many as forty aircraft, although unusually there were no British casualties.]

Thursday, 3rd May
3rd Battle of the Scarpe
(3rd-4th May, 1917)
"All yesterday was quiet until evening. The first little incident was a dud shell going off just by our camp – it had been lying there for some time and we have no idea what set it off but nobody was hurt. Then just about sunset the artillery broke out and their firing carried on all night. Just on ten o'clock, just as most of us were getting to sleep, a buzz of aeroplanes was heard. Then a burst of machine-gun fire broke out and several 'planes came down low and raked our camp all around with bullets. This went on at intervals all night and about half a dozen bombs were also dropped but no damage has been done as they all fell in open country. The guns kept at it noisily all night and at daylight this morning they doubled in intensity – for about an hour it was the same terrible barrage fire as we had on the 23rd of last month. We have not heard that the infantry went over but no doubt they did. No news is to hand but the guns are still going heavily."

'One driver killed and two wounded (one has since died) transporting ammunition.'

[9/DAC War Diary]

[The soldier killed in action on 3rd May was 33508 Driver James Rafferty (37) 9/DAC. He was born in Warrington, Lancashire. Commemorated on bay 1 of the Arras Memorial to the Missing, Faubourg d'Amiens. The following day, 4th May, 116439 Driver William Purvis (21) 9/DAC, died of his wounds. He was born in Liverpool. Buried in plot IV.B.18 of Duisans British Cemetery, Etrun.]

Friday, 4th May
"Evening – 7:30: very quiet all day today. The first thing of importance is taking place at the present time. About half an hour ago a huge fire broke out at an ammunition dump in Arras – it is still burning fiercely and exploding with huge reports. It is chiefly small arms stuff [thousands of rounds of S.A.A.] and is crackling away like a huge rifle or machine-gun firing, backed by an occasional shell. Huge columns of smoke reach right up to the sky; the cause of the fire is unknown as yet but was possibly a German shell or bomb. The heat today has been terrific. Last night our camp and dumps were again raided by German 'planes; they bombed all around us at intervals from ten o'clock until daylight this morning.

"Late evening – 11:30: Since writing the

last few lines earlier in the evening, we have had great excitement. About 8:30 the gas alarm was sounded and horses and men from the direction of Arras came dashing by."

Saturday, 5th May
Gas!
(Thundery rain)
"Continued from last night: The crashes from the dump were terrible to hear; apparently gas shells and all sorts were there and the clouds rose and covered the sky – they are all coming in our direction. We stood for an hour with our gas helmets on then the wind suddenly changed and the smoke and gas went away towards the trenches. Gradually the fire slowed down, so horses and men were collected and taken back to camp as soon as it was safe, which was about dawn. All night long the ammunition went on exploding but the worst of it was over at midnight. We then turned in for some sleep but before we had been in ten minutes, the order came, 'all lights out, another German air-raid'. The air was alive with machines but our 'planes were up as soon as the enemy appeared, chasing them away with no damage done. We had it fairly quiet for the remainder of the night – while the bright moon lasts we shall have the night visitors without any doubt."

Sunday, 6th May
"Nothing much doing except artillery battles during the past two days. On Saturday evening there was a small thunderstorm and a little rain. Today the 'Boss' [probably Lieutenant Ozanne] has been taken to hospital with a touch of dysentery. The cause of the fire at Arras on Friday night has been put down to a boxing competition amongst some infantry in a billet adjoining the dump – a fire started in the billet and caught the dump. The damage is estimated at £20,000 [present value would be well in excess of £1.25 million] – it was a dump belonging to the XIII Army Corps."

Monday, 7th May
(Becoming stormy)
"It has been very quiet on our front today but on our right, away to the south, the guns have been going since yesterday morning. Still further south, by Soissons, the French have made a big advance, taking some fortified positions and 5,000 prisoners. The weather looks very stormy and rainy tonight."

Tuesday, 8th May
(Wet)
"Today has been a wet one but it cleared before nightfall – the showers have done us good and conditions are looking brighter. Last night, about ten, the Germans put over about thirty shells around our camp. Tonight towards six they put over about thirty more and now our guns are going very heavily – it sounds like a counter-attack."

Thursday, 10th May
(Hot and clear)

"The past two days have been very hot and fairly quiet. The only incident worth recording is the passage of two tanks through our camp. We saw what they can do in the way of crossing bad country. So far nothing else out of the ordinary has happened."

Saturday, 12th May
Attacking the 'Comical Works'

"Last evening at 7:30 our infantry once more attacked the Chemical Works [though known to Tommy as the 'Comical Works', it was a tough nut to crack] at Roeux and the Greenland Hill; they obtained a footing at the top of it and held it. This morning at 6:30, under cover of a heavy bombardment, they went forward again and captured the ridge beyond it and up to now they are holding everything safely. We took just on 1,000 prisoners in obtaining every objective and we are holding fast."

Sunday, 13th May
Greenland Hill taken

"The news of the capture of the Greenland Hill is now confirmed and the details are splendid. The cause of the failure to hold the positions when taken before was due to the fact that the Germans had a huge cave on a ridge behind the Greenland Hill. We got intelligence of this from some other source and made our plans accordingly, with the result that we captured the whole lot plus 700 prisoners in the cave. We have advanced two miles beyond the Greenland Hill and the guns are again

moving up. Tonight the guns are going at a terrific rate – evidently a strong counter-attack is going on against us. The weather is still very hot."

Monday, 14th May
Anzin

(Hot then thunderstorms)
"Last night was rather a noisy one. A heavy bombardment went on just on our right and while it was in progress a heavy thunderstorm broke over us, the din was terrific for an hour or so and a lot of rain fell. Today has been quiet and hot until about three this afternoon when another heavy thunder shower broke over us and cooled us down a bit."

Wednesday, 16th May
Anzin

"Not much doing, except in the artillery line. This morning, for about an hour, the guns were going at a very heavy pace but they became quieter before dinner time. We have since found out that the Germans have once again retaken the Roeux Chemical Works and a bit of the ground with it. This morning we once again recaptured it and again tonight our guns broke out suddenly and kept going at a terrific pace for an hour. It was a counter-attack by the enemy but so far we have not heard the result."

Friday, 18th May
Arras Fades

"Things during the past day or two have been rather quiet. Guns and divisions

are being taken away in the direction of Armentières. There is not much doubt that this battle is now at an end and that big things are pending elsewhere. The weather is fine but unsettled."

CONTEXT

Friday, 18th May

'Two drivers killed and one wounded transporting ammunition to Battery position.'

[9/DAC War Diary]

[The two 9/DAC drivers to be killed in action on 18th May were:

35382 Driver John Sunlay of Cleveland
33670 Driver Walter Swainston of Kingston-upon-Hull

Both were killed in action and both men are buried in Anzin-St. Aubin British Cemetery on the north-western edge of Arras, Swainston in plot II.C.8 and Sunlay in plot II.C.9.]

DIARY

Tuesday, 22nd May 1917
Roeux sector
"Nothing much doing except an occasional artillery battle – a few guns here and there were wire-cutting but there was little more on our front. On our right, towards Bullecourt, a bombardment ended last

night that had been going on for about two days but the result has not yet been told to us. There was heavy rain last night and for the greater part of today."

Thursday, 24th May
Bullecourt
(Fine)
"The heavy bombardment away towards Bullecourt turns out to have been heavy attacks by us all along the famous Hindenburg Line. Most of it is now in our hands and quiet reigns along it at present. Yesterday morning at daylight we were raided by a German 'plane that dropped several bombs around us without doing any damage. Last night they [the Germans] shelled Arras with some very heavy guns, doing considerable damage to the buildings. Today has been quieter and the weather fine."

CONTEXT

The second half of the month of May saw an increase in the activity of the enemy's aeroplanes. In his 'Ninth Divisional History', John Ewing commented:

'At this time the activity and boldness of the German aeroplanes was very marked...now a regular practice... after dusk the enemy...flew low over our hinterland, dropped light bombs and fired machine-guns on our infantry and transport lines...a fresh and deadly terror had been added to modern warfare.'

DIARY

Saturday, 26th May
Anzin
(Hot)
"Last night, about ten, a squadron of German 'planes attacked our camp and dropped bombs all around us, wounding seven men and killing one. This morning at dawn they came over again and bombed us for about an hour, dropping about thirty all around but the damage is not yet known. The weather is very hot, though there is not much doing on our front."

CONTEXT

The soldier killed in the bombing on the night of 26th-27th May was 89289 Gunner John Bihet of Y9 Trench Mortar Battery, 9th 'Scottish' Division who died of wounds, aged 22 years. He was born in St. Martin, Jersey, the son of Pierre François Desiré (b.3rd November 1857, later a quarryman) and Marie Anne Desirée (née Picot, b.16th February 1865) Bihet (French nationals from Normandy who eloped to Jersey as their families opposed their marriage; moved to Alderney, leaving most of adult children in Jersey and thence to Guernsey at Grange, La Carrière, Vale.) John Bihet is buried in plot III.G.18 of Aubigny Communal Cemetery Extension, ten miles north-west of Arras on the St. Pol road.

Headstone of Gunner John Bihet in Aubigny Communal Cemetery Extension.

Also serving with 9th Divisional Ammunition Column were two of John Bihet's brothers, 32-year-old 89291 Driver Arthur Joseph Bihet and 21-year-old 89290 Driver Constant Henri Bihet. The three brothers' RFA numbers were consecutive and all three men had landed in France with 9th Divisional Ammunition Column on 12th May 1915.

[A more complete version of the remarkable Bihet family story appears in Appendix 4].

DIARY

Wednesday, 30th May
Anzin
(Thunderstorms)
"Not much doing on our line now. There

are frequent thunderstorms and showers of rain but very little else of note. The big push at Armentières is expected to start soon so we shall be going again sometime."

CONTEXT

Thursday, 31st May
[9/DAC War Diary]

> 'One driver killed and two wounded (one has since died) transporting ammunition.'

[The driver killed in action on 31st May was 59060 Sergeant William Henry Archer, (30) of 'A' Battery, 52nd Brigade, RFA. He is buried in plot III.B.200 of Bailleul Communal Cemetery Extension, Nord. The soldier who succumbed to his wounds on 1st June was 75083 Driver William John Punt of the Reserve Divisional Ammunition Column. He was born in Essex. He is buried in plot II.B.30 of Barlin Communal Cemetery Extension.]

DIARY

Friday, 1st June
'Air Raid Alley'
"The new month was ushered in for us in a very exciting way, to the tune of bursting bombs and flying pieces of shrapnel. We were simply covered with the shrapnel from our own anti-aircraft guns blazing at German aeroplanes overhead. From soon after midnight until nearly midday we had it at intervals but now calm reigns once

again on our front and still we live. The weather is still fine. Nothing much doing apart from occasional bursts of artillery fire which does not last long."

Sunday, 3rd June
Anzin
(Fine)
"Last night was another night of bombs and shrapnel. From ten until after midnight they kept it up; searchlights were on, guns were firing and bombs were dropping. I am getting a bit fed up with it night after night. The weather is still fine."

Tuesday, 5th June
A Near Miss
"Still more bombs! The past two nights have been perfect nightmares – it's not bad once in a while but night after night makes us a bit jumpy. We could not see the raider at all although it was bright moonlight. On Sunday night they were right on top of us. The camp next to us lost ten officers out of fifteen – one bomb dropped near the mess as they stood outside the door, killing four on the spot and severely wounding eight others. It made a terrific hole, large enough in which to put a ten-roomed house completely out of sight. The anti-aircraft guns opened up on them right over our heads and falling shrapnel whizzed around us like rain – for about a quarter of an hour it was hell on earth. The miracle was that none of our men was touched, though seven other men were killed in addition to the officers. Last night they came again and none of our guns took any notice of them, why we do not know.

They flew about over us just as they liked and bombed all around. During the last three raids there has been a Zeppelin and a fleet of 'planes – none of us saw the 'Zepp' but we could tell from the heavy roll of the engines and it has been seen by others. It is another lovely, hot day and without a doubt we shall get them again tonight – what a life!

"Evening – 10:30 p.m: news of the raid has come through again. It is now official that there were eight Zeppelins all around Arras as well as a fleet of 'planes. They killed nearly one hundred horses and over eighty men in and around Arras; we are expecting them again now.

"Evening – 11:30 p.m.: Sure enough they came. I had just got a few words down when – Bang! – Five bombs dropped just over the

hill near the camp. All lights were out in a moment. We have now got quiet again and we are hoping for a free night for a change."

CONTEXT

Records suggest that it was a Northumberland Fusiliers' officers' mess, as part of 102nd 'Tyneside Scottish' and 103rd 'Tyneside Irish' Brigades in 34th Division that was hit in the raid on 5th June. Northumberland Fusiliers' Scots and Irish Brigades were well used to tragic losses, having suffered heavily on 1st July 1916 near La Boisselle. 'Soldiers Died in the Great War...' indicates that in excess of 200 men of the Tyneside Scots and Irish Brigades were killed on 5th June 1917. The list of officers included:

2/Lt (TP) **Ernest Harrington Hawes,** (26), 20/Northumberland Fusiliers '1st Tyneside Scots', commemorated on bays 2 &3 of the Arras Memorial to the Missing [son of the late Major-General W.H. Hawes].
Captain (TP[13]) **Gerald Ogilvie Laing,** (30), 20/Northumberland Fusiliers '1st Tyneside Scots', commemorated on bays 2 &3 of the Arras Memorial to the Missing.
2/Lt (TP) **George Baillie,** (25), 21/Northumberland Fusiliers '2nd Tyneside Scots', commemorated on bays 2 &3 of the Arras Memorial to the Missing.
2/Lt **Hywel James Elias,** (20), 21/Northumberland Fusiliers '2nd Tyneside Scots', buried in plot II.P.41 Arras Road Cemetery, Roclincourt.
2/Lt (TP) **Stanley George Hardy Purnell,** 21/Northumberland Fusiliers '2nd Tyneside Scots', commemorated on bays 2 &3 of the Arras Memorial to the Missing.
2/Lt (TP) **Hugh MacDonald,** (24), 22/Northumberland Fusiliers '3rd Tyneside Scots', commemorated on bays 2 &3 of the Arras Memorial to the Missing.
2/Lt (TP) **William Kingsbury Simson,** (24), 22/Northumberland Fusiliers '3rd Tyneside Scots', buried in plot IV.H.21 of Faubourg d'Amiens Cemetery, Arras.
2/Lt (TP) **Oliver Howard Sprenger,** (24), 26/Northumberland Fusiliers '3rd Tyneside Irish', commemorated on bays 2 &3 of the Arras Memorial to the Missing.
Lt (TP), A/**Captain George Stewart,** 26/Northumberland Fusiliers '3rd Tyneside Irish', commemorated on bays 2 &3 of the Arras Memorial to the Missing.

1st to 27th June
Anzin

'Column remained encamped at Anzin [...in a north-western suburb of Arras]. Artillery in action. Normal supply of ammunition taken up to Batteries. Column GS wagons engaged in clearing old Battery positions of ammunition and empty cartridge cases.'

[9/DAC War Diary]

DIARY

Wednesday, 6th June
Anzin

"Last night we were visited at intervals by the bomb-dropper until daylight but they were half a mile or more away. Last evening, just on eight o'clock, our guns along our own front opened out at a terrific pace. Our infantry went over during the night and took three lines of trenches and all other objectives. Now a heavy counter-attack is in progress and our guns are now going at full speed. It is nearly time for our air raids again, for it is just after ten o'clock. About six this evening we had a thunderstorm and very heavy rain."

Friday, 8th June
Battle of Messines Ridge, near Ypres
(7th-14th June)
(Warm, thundery)
"Last night on our front the Germans made a big attack on our advanced positions at Greenland Hill but without success. They

fired a great number of 17-inch shells at the heavy guns at our camp – it was a very noisy night but it ended in a victory for us once again. Yesterday, after several days' heavy bombardment, our infantry went over along the Ypres and Armentières line; not very much news is through but over 4,000 prisoners have been brought in and all our objectives taken. The weather is fine but very thundery. This morning, one of our 'planes brought down a German just near our camp – he was loaded with bombs, for our benefit no doubt – he came down with a crash and his load of bombs went off, blowing him, his 'plane and all to eternity. A very heavy artillery shoot is in progress on our own front at present [8:30 p.m.] and it sounds like a counter-attack by the Huns."

CONTEXT

[The Messines Ridge mines detonation killed more people than any other non-nuclear man-made explosion in history. Up to 10,000 Germans are thought to have perished.]

DIARY

Sunday, 10th June
Anzin
"Not much news yet about the advance at Ypres except that everything is going well. The prisoners are now given as close on 10,000. Our own front is quiet during the hours of daylight but at night heavy artillery duels go on all through."

Tuesday, 12th June

(Warm, thundery)

"The morning started off very excitingly with three air fights over our camp, one German being brought down and the pilot and observer badly knocked about, while the machine was smashed up. After that everything went very quiet until dark, then the usual night attacks by the Germans started again but they were hammered by our artillery. The weather is still fine but very thundery."

Monday, 18th June

(Hot)

"The past week has been fairly lively, especially in artillery work. We have pushed ahead in two places, taking a good number of prisoners – all along the line we are continually worrying them. The weather is very hot."

Thursday, 21st June

(Cool and rainy)

"Things have been quiet during the past two days. Our little push on Infantry Hill got a slight check but it was a hot time for the enemy and we eventually got all we wanted. A lot of rain has fallen during the past two days and nights. Today is rather cold for June."

Sunday, 24th June

Achicourt-Beaurains

"Not much doing still but a lot of guns are coming back and getting into position to the south of Arras. On Wednesday we shift our camp there and for a time we shall be just outside of Achicourt. A big push is evidently coming off near there very shortly."

Wednesday, 27th June

Agny

"Today we have shifted to the right of Arras [described as if facing the front-line trenches from Arras, thus the move was slightly southwards], to a little village called Agny. It was originally our front line before the German retreat from the Somme to the Hindenburg Line. Our headquarters are in an old château; the whole village is rather badly knocked about and all the inhabitants are gone but are now expected back again. Nothing much doing except air-raids but a big move is anticipated for many guns are coming up this way again [to support the artillery at Ypres??], although a great many troops from this way are off to Ypres and we expect to follow soon."

CONTEXT

Wednesday, 27th June

[9/DAC War Diary]

'HQ established at Agny and the sections between Achicourt and Beaurains. Large ammunition dump at cross-roads at sheet 51.B M.4.C.1.9.'

1st to 31st July

Agny, Achicourt & Beaurains

Column HQ remained at Agny for the whole of July while the two Echelons remained encamped between Achicourt and Beaurains. Column wagons continued the task of clearing old Battery positions of ammunition and empty cartridge cases.

DIARY

Sunday, 1st July
Towards Lens
(3rd June-26th August, 1917)
(Persistent rain)
"One year ago today was the charge on the Somme and on our front we have celebrated it with a big scrap. We are on the right flank of the battle for Lens. It has been going on around the Lens district for nearly a week and yesterday the battle front extended to us – our guns have been going like blazes ever since. Last night a few shells dropped near us but we stuck tight, guns still going heavily. The weather is bad. For the past three days there has been a lot of rain – that's bad for our sports that we are having on Wednesday."
[The reference to the effects of weather on sports rather than on battles seems somewhat out of place!]

[Jack's Service Record shows that at this time Jack qualified for and retained, 'Class 1 Proficiency Pay.']

Saturday, 7th July
Agny, Achicourt & Beaurains
"Nothing much doing during the last week except occasional artillery duels. Early this morning we were raided by 'planes that dropped bombs all around us and fired on the streets of Arras with machine-guns. There is every sign of an early move which we think will be a train journey."

Tuesday, 10th July
In blissful ignorance…
(Wet and thundery)
"There has been nothing much happening except raids and artillery work during the past week. A number of shells have been dropped on Arras today, one French soldier being killed quite close to me at the barracks. The weather is thundery and rather wet."

CONTEXT

On the Somme, Jack Hickman was for obvious reasons quite unaware of the fate that had befallen his brother-in-law, G/24004, Private John 'Jack' Palmer.

On 10th July 1917, Jack Palmer became the second of Jack Hickman's brothers-in-law to die on the Western Front: he was killed near Arras.

When John 'Jack' Palmer was killed, he was serving on a sector of the Arras front with 2nd Battalion, the Queen's (Royal West Surrey) Regiment, part of 91st Brigade, 7th Division. Ada's younger brother was born in 1894 or 1895 in Plumstead, Kent and had learned his trade as a decorator through the traditional route of apprenticeship. He enlisted in the army probably in 1916 in Woolwich and almost certainly at the same time as his older brother Roy Palmer, both men joining the 1/6th Battalion of the Royal Sussex Regiment for basic training – their regimental numbers in the Royal Sussex were consecutive, being 2322 and 2323. When John reached his unit, the battalion was involved in the murderous battles on the Somme; John probably fought at Guillemont in September 1916, in Operations on the Ancre and towards the Hindenburg Line during February and March of 1917. After the pursuit of the Germans to the Hindenburg Line, 2/Queens held a front line in the Croisilles sector that incorporated several captured German concreted machine-gun posts, known as 'pill-boxes' on account of their shape. After the Bullecourt offensive of May and June, the Germans in the sector had lapsed into 'passivity', so British high command ordered an active

22 year-old Private Jack Palmer of 2/Queen's (Royal West Surrey), is buried in Croisilles British Cemetery, not far from where he fell.

Croisilles British Cemetery stands on a sunlit slope, just off the St. Leger Road.

policy that incorporated bombardment, vigorous patrolling, regular raiding and harassment by sniping. John Palmer was killed in action on 10th July 1917 but the 2/Queens Battalion War Diary gives mere hints as to what might have occurred:

> 'St. Leger camp – training in bayonet and grenades, musketry range, work on billets; one coy with RE for night work on 7/7/17.'

The middle of the Palmer brothers, Roy, survived the war only to die as a consequence of war wounds soon after the conflict ended.

So Jack Palmer's death in action may have been the result of a training accident or the consequence of enemy action against a working party. In the margin for 'remarks', is noted:

'...From hospital – 1; to hospital – 4, wounded 2.'

Having been killed in action on 10th July, the twenty-two-year-old was buried in plot I.B.2 of Croisilles British Cemetery (9 miles to the south-east of Arras).

John's older brother, Roy Palmer, who was born in Plumstead in 1892 or 1893 and who enlisted in the Royal Sussex Regiment with John in December 1915 in Woolwich, was badly wounded on the Western Front with 7th Battalion and died soon after the war ended. Thus did William and Polly Palmer lose all three of their sons to the Great War.

DIARY

Friday, 13th July
Agny, Achicourt & Beaurains
"It has again been quiet on our front. Today we had news of a big push by the Germans near Ostend [on the Belgian coast at Nieupoort on 10th/11th July, at the northern end of the line that 1st and 32nd Divisions were about to take over from the French] – they broke through on a front of over a thousand yards to a depth of six hundred yards. Details are not to hand yet but we hear that we have lost many prisoners.

"However, not much alarm is felt as we are quite confident of putting them back with a bump."

CONTEXT

This intense German bombardment near the Belgian coast lasted all day and employed some shells that contained Yellow Cross, a new gas that came to be known and dreaded as 'mustard gas', an agent that clung to and blistered the skin horribly. The Germans also employed flamethrowers to clear British dugouts. British casualties and missing amounted to 126 officers and over 3,000 other ranks, largely from 1/Northamptonshire and 2/King's Royal Rifle Corps of 2nd Brigade, 1st Division. It proved impossible to reinforce north of the River Yser as all bridges had been destroyed by the earlier shelling and the few survivors (55 from 2/King's Royal Rifle Corps, 9 from 1/Northamptonshire and four out of fifty men from 2nd Australian Tunnelling Company) from two entire battalions had to swim across the river.

In the event, commonsense advice from local commanders prevailed and a counter-attack planned for 11th-12th July was postponed by General Rawlinson until sufficient artillery was available and the main Flanders offensive had begun.

DIARY

Sunday, 22nd July
Agny, Achicourt & Beaurains
"During the past three days there has not been much action on our front except for artillery duels. On Tuesday night, the 12th

'Eastern' Division at Monchy-le-Preux made a slight push and took about five hundred prisoners. Today has been very bright and the 'Huns' have been very busy with aeroplanes and long-range guns. All the morning the Huns shelled our camp area with a big 15-inch gun but not much damage was done except to the ground."

Sunday, 29th July
(Very hot; thunderstorms)
"Little doing except a minor scrap at Monchy-le-Preux and on Infantry Hill, with the occasional artillery duels, chiefly at night-time. The weather is terribly hot and there were terrific thunderstorms on Friday last and early this morning.

The push in the north of France and in Belgium is expected any day now."

Wednesday, 1st August
Start: 3rd Ypres, 'Passchendaele'
(31st July-10th November, 1917)
"At last we have made a start in Belgium [on 31st July]. The long expected attack is underway – so far only rumours of the real thing are to hand, namely that we have advanced on a twenty-mile front, capturing all our objectives and 1,000 yards beyond. So far we do not know what the first objectives were but no doubt it was the first three lines of trenches – we are eagerly awaiting news."

THE PLAN AND OBJECTIVES FOR 3RD YPRES (31ST JULY TO 10TH NOVEMBER)

The opening of the offensive was set for 31st July on a fifteen-mile front from the River Lys to the Yser floods. Second Army under General Plumer was to feint to threaten Lille and so occupy vital German divisions, while Fifth Army under General Gough, allied to the French First Army under General Anthoine, were to overrun the Gheluvelt Plateau and the Pilckem Ridge and thus advance on Bruges, while a subsequent assault in early August would roll up the coastal strip so recently lost to the Germans' surprise attack. This grand scheme had been at the back of General Haig's mind for at least the previous eighteen months of the conflict on the

Western Front.

DIARY

Thursday, 2nd August
Agny
"Tomorrow we move from the camp down to the old Somme battlefield. We are going near to Bapaume for a start but what the programme is after that is unknown."

CONTEXT

Friday, 3rd August to end of August
The Column moved by route march to Four Winds Farm near Lechelle, from where Column HQ and the various

units moved on to Equancourt between 8th and 10th August.

'Column remained at Equancourt for the whole of the month [in fact until 3rd September]. Horse standings were built and water supply laid on to supply troughs erected in camp. Column engaged on fatigues during
the month. One man wounded by shell fire whilst on fatigues at Metz.'

[9/DAC War Diary]

9/DAC's subsequent move would return them to the Somme battlefields and, after that, the dreaded Ypres Salient beckoned.

---

1 Other Allied leaders present at Chantilly were General Porro (Italy), General Wielemans (Belgium), General Palitzine (Russia), Colonel Rudeanu (Rumania), General Rachitch (Serbia) and Lieutenant-Colonel Nogai (Japan).

2 Nivelle had made his name in the latter stages of the struggle for Verdun, where his plan to re-capture Fort Douaumont met with remarkable success in December 1916. He openly suggested that a similar plan, on a much larger scale, might achieve a final breakthrough on the Western Front. He convinced his French masters and beguiled the new British Prime Minister, David Lloyd-George, who was no supporter of Haig's 'attritional' approach.

3 The arrival of cavalry in numbers seemed to suggest an attempt at breakthrough and subsequent exploitation behind German lines.

4 This refers to the German Retreat to the Hindenburg Line. Many saw this as a great victory rather than as what it really represented – a shortening and rationalisation of the German line. Fewer troops would be required to defend the German front line.

5 The 'Hindenburg Line' was the Allied name for what the German forces referred to as '*die Siegfried Stellung*'.

6 A trench line that was built on a reverse slope made observation by attacking forces nearly impossible.

7 The most notorious instance of a 'scorched earth retreat' had been carried out on Tsar Alexander I's orders during Napoléon Bonaparte's advance into Russia and the subsequent retreat from Moscow in 1812.

8 Bapaume is north-east of Albert – the two towns are linked by an arrow-straight, Roman road.

9 Cuffley is in Hertfordshire, not far from Potters Bar.

10 As the epithet 'Bloody April' suggests, the Allies suffered hard in the skies over Arras during this offensive.

11 Quoted from Robert Hardman's excellent article in the Daily Mail on 15th March 2008, 'City under the Slaughter.'

12 One of the caverns in this sector, 'La Carrière Wellington', is now open to the public after eighteen years' hard endeavour, thanks largely to M. Alain Jacques, head of the Arras Archaeology Department and M. Jean-Marie Prestaux, Director of Tourism in Arras.

13 TP indicates 'temporary' or 'acting' rank, yet to be confirmed.

CHAPTER TEN
THIRD YPRES, AUGUST–OCTOBER 1917

 ## TOWARDS PASSCHENDAELE RIDGE

HOOGE & WESTHOEK

DIARY

Saturday, 4th August   **Ytres**
(Wet and cold)   *(near Bapaume, on the Somme)*
"Yesterday we moved from the Arras sector and came down to the Somme area. We are now just outside the village of Ytres, about four or five miles [south-east] from Bapaume. Things here are very quiet but there are signs of a push later on. The weather has for some days been very wet and cold, especially on Friday [3rd August]."

Monday, 6th August
(Hot then thunderstorms)
"It's August Bank Holiday and we're still somewhere in France! [This was the third anniversary of the outbreak of war between Britain and Germany.] The weather changed yesterday to a very hot afternoon and kept it up today until about six this evening, then a heavy thunderstorm broke over us and once more we are in the mud."

Thursday, 9th August
Equancourt
(Thunderstorms)
"After three days of fine and warm weather we were again visited by a terrific thunderstorm. It was a pretty severe one and the rain and hail was very heavy;

the lightning was strong and struck our telephone wires and putting all our communications out of action. Today mud and water lie everywhere and the weather is still looking very bad."

CONTEXT

On 8th and 9th August the various elements of 9/DAC moved to Equancourt where the unit remained for the rest of the month.

'Horse standings were built and water supply laid on to supply troughs erected in camp. Column engaged on fatigues during the month.'

[9/DAC War Diary]

DIARY

Monday, 20th August
Equancourt
(Warm and dry)
"*After a lot of bad weather, thunderstorms and rain for about a fortnight, we have come at last to real August weather. Not much doing on our front except occasional raids in which we take a few prisoners but at Ypres we are still carrying on with the good work. Rumour has it that our division is on the move shortly for that particular district but nothing official is known about it.*"

Friday, 24th August
"*Still quiet on our own front but on others our Allies are keeping the home fires burning. Our attacks at Ypres and Lens are still going forward; at Verdun the French have made a big advance on an eleven-mile front taking many guns and 7,000 prisoners; on the Italian front another big offensive has resulted in over 13,000 prisoners being taken. Things are looking more like Blighty every day!*"

Saturday, 25th August
"*The news that comes in from the other fronts is still good. The Italians now have over 16,000 prisoners and the French 7,640 men and hundreds of officers. We now expect a lull for a little while. Today it is rumoured strongly that our division is shortly moving to Ypres – it has been rumoured before but this time it is about true I think.*"

CONTEXT

Monday, 27th August
Although the unit was officially out of the direct firing line, care had to be taken even when on a working party, as the DAC War Diary shows,

> '*One man wounded by shell fire whilst on fatigues at Metz.*'

[9/DAC War Diary]

DIARY

Sunday, 28th August
9th Infantry to Ypres
"*The news from all sides is still of the very best, the Italians and French especially, as over 30,000 prisoners have been taken between the two of them and attacks are still going on. The Austrians are in full retreat and the French last night made another advance, details of which are not yet to hand but the biggest of all is expected in Belgium very shortly – our division hopes to play a big part in it. Our infantry left for that way today and we expect to follow any day now.*"

Monday, 3rd September
9th Artillery to Bihucourt, the Somme
"*Today we have moved back out of action and have camped at Bihucourt, near Achiet-le-Grand. We expect to entrain for Belgium any day now, so I think we shall soon be in the thick of it again. A lot of*

troops are all around us and it looks as if something big is coming here shortly."

Friday, 7th September 1917
To Steenvoorde, west of Ypres
(72°F, overcast)
"Today we left Bihucourt at 5 a.m. and travelled to Bapaume where we entrained and left at nine o'clock. After ten hours in the train we detrained at Poperinghe [eight miles to the west of Ypres] and we are now camped near the village of Steenvoorde [a further nine miles to the west of Poperinghe]. The weather is much finer and very warm. We expect to go into the line soon."

Tuesday, 11th September
Opposite Westhoek Ridge
(71°F, clear)
"Yesterday we moved up into action opposite the Westhoek Ridge [north of the Menin Road in the Hooge Château/ Bellewaerde Lake sector] which, we understand, we are to take if possible. Great things depend on us taking it – the enemy will have to fall back some considerable distance and both Lens and Lille will be ours, while Belgium will be more or less cleared from the coastline. The place around here has not altered much since we were here in 1915. We are lying close to Ypres and things are rather warm. Last night we were raided by 'planes and shelled at intervals during the night. Today has been fairly quiet for shells although about ten minutes ago one

dropped just over our camp about one hundred yards away but so far no more have followed."*

Wednesday, 12th September
Death from the sky at Hooge
(62°F, overcast)
"Today has been a rough and exciting one. We have been shelled at intervals and just after dinner nine aeroplanes raided our camp. They dropped many bombs and killed three men in our lot and wounded thirteen. We are having to dig in for safety – things are exciting!"

CONTEXT

Wednesday, 12th September
The 9/Divisional Column War Diary differs from Jack's figures.

'At 1:45p.m. (12th September) five large bombs were dropped in No.2 Section lines by E.A. (Enemy Aircraft). Four men were killed and ten wounded. Thirty-six animals killed and about thirty wounded, many having to be evacuated.'

[9/DAC War Diary]

In addition to the four men from the 9/ DAC killed on this day, four gunners from the divisional field gun batteries (3 from C/51 and one from A/50) were also killed. The DAC men were:

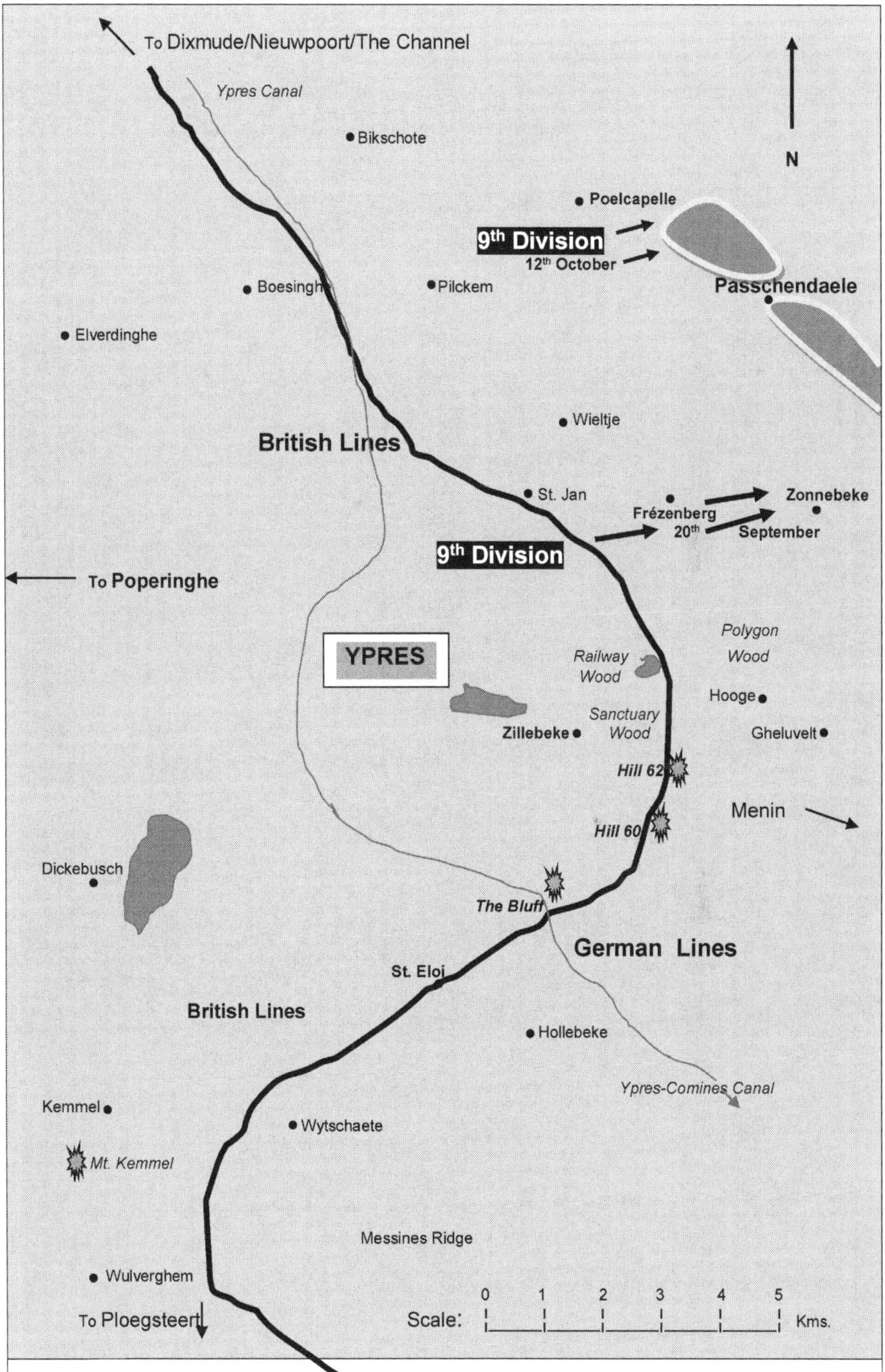

To Dixmude/Nieuwpoort/The Channel

Ypres Canal

N

● Bikschote

● Poelcapelle

9th Division
12th October

Passchendaele

● Boesinghe

● Pilckem

● Elverdinghe

● Wieltje

British Lines

● St. Jan

Frézenberg
20th   September

Zonnebeke

9th Division

To **Poperinghe**

YPRES

Railway Wood

Polygon Wood

Hooge ●

Sanctuary Wood

Zillebeke ●

Gheluvelt ●

Hill 62

Hill 60

Menin

The Bluff

German Lines

St. Eloi

British Lines

Dickebusch ●

● Hollebeke

Ypres-Comines Canal

Kemmel ●

● Wytschaete

Mt. Kemmel

Messines Ridge

● Wulverghem

To **Ploegsteert**

Scale: 0 1 2 3 4 5 Kms.

Map 5: 9th 'Scottish' Division at Third Ypres, September-October 1917

61007 **Battery Quarter Master Sergeant Thomas Walton Grant**, RFA (27), 9th Divisional Ammunition Column. From Kent. Killed in action on 12th September 1917. Buried in plot XII.H.3 of Vlamertinghe New Military Cemetery.

6731 **Driver William F. Hill**, RFA, 9th Divisional Ammunition Column. From Fife. Died of wounds on 12th September 1917. Buried in plot IV.D.13 of Mendinghem Military Cemetery.

BQMS Grant and Driver Ware of 9/DAC lie buried side by side in Mendinghem Military Cemetery, north-west of Poperinghe.

105175 **Driver David Thomas**, RFA, 9th Divisional Ammunition Column. From South Wales. Killed in action on 12th September 1917. Buried in plot XI.H.16 of Vlamertinghe New Military Cemetery.

132400 **Driver Frederick Ware**, RFA, 9th Divisional Ammunition Column. From Eastbourne. Killed in action on 12th September 1917. Buried in plot XII.H.4 of Vlamertinghe New Military Cemetery.

The men from the 9th Division artillery brigades were:

95909 **Acting Bombardier Reginald George**, 'C' Battery, 51st Artillery Brigade, RFA (25), 9th Division. From Yorkshire. Died of wounds on 12th September 1917. Buried in plot I.D.16 of Ypres Reservoir Cemetery.

34859 **Acting Bombardier Albert Edward Horsley**, 'C' Battery, 51st Artillery Brigade, RFA (21), 9th Division. From Yorkshire. Died of wounds on 12th September 1917. Buried in plot VII.A.7 of Dozinghem Military Cemetery.

Bombardier George and Gunner Thompson were laid to rest in Ypres Reservoir Cemetery.

L/11232 **Gunner Ernest Albert Marsh**, 'C' Battery, 51st Artillery Brigade, RFA (31), 9th Division. From Derbyshire. Died of wounds on 12th September 1917. Buried in plot XI.H.9 of Vlamertinghe New Military Cemetery.

99757 **Gunner Thomas Henry Thompson**, 'A' Battery, 50th Artillery Brigade, RFA, 9th Division. From Middlesbrough. Died of wounds on 12th September 1917. Buried in plot I.A.12 of Ypres Reservoir Cemetery.

DIARY

Friday, 14th September
Artillery at Work
(66°F, overcast)
"*Things are still lively. Artillery work is going on day and night – some very heavy guns close to us are pasting the German trenches without a rest. The big attack must be very soon as our infantry are going in tonight in readiness.*"

CONTEXT

Saturday, 15th September 1917
Bad family news from the front
(67°F, overcast)
There is no entry in Jack's diary for 15th September but he was soon to discover that what had already proven an ill-fated month for 9th Division's artillery units, was to become much more personally painful. His brother, Frank Hickman, his senior by ten years and like Jack a driver in the RFA, had become a casualty in the Salient. On his arrival in France in mid-June 1917, Frank had been posted to No. 1 Section, 42nd Divisional Ammunition Column but in mid-August was posted within the divisional artillery to the guns of 'C' Battery, 210th Brigade RFA. By September, 42nd 'East Lancashire' Division was, like 9th 'Scottish' Division, serving in the Ypres Salient, just a mile or so to the north of Frank's younger brother Jack. Neither man was then aware of the coincidence. On 15th September, a warm (67°F), overcast day, Frank's division was in the east of the Potijze sector where, with artillery support, 1/4th Battalion, East Lancashire Regiment of 126th Infantry Brigade was successfully attacking Sans Souci, an objective to the south of the Ypres-Roulers railway where it skirted Frézenberg village; 9th Division was also present on the Westhoek Ridge but closer to Bellewaerde Lake and the Menin Road. In an attempt to prevent 42nd Division from exploiting their local success, German artillery fired a number of gas shells; perhaps Frank was slow to don his gas-mask but whatever the cause Jack's elder brother quickly fell victim to the poison gas. He was moved down the line the same day to Needinghem (near Proven, just to the north of Poperinghe) where he was assessed and initially treated in No.12 Casualty Clearing Station. From there, Frank was transported to No. XI General Hospital at Camiers (that was possibly under American direction) and on 20th September he was, "...invalided to England aboard the 'Carisbrooke Castle.'" (The 'Carisbrooke Castle'[1] was built in 1898 but on the outbreak of war had been 'mothballed' as surplus to operating requirements; however, in September 1914 she was requisitioned from the Union Castle Line[2] for conversion to one of the many hospital ships that would be provided by that respected company.) On being disembarked on the south coast of England, Frank was transported by hospital train to South

Wales where he was duly admitted to 3rd Western General Hospital, Cardiff. He thus commenced seven weeks of medical treatment.

Despite being gassed, Frank was better off than one of his compatriots from the divisional artillery – 25-year-old 701094 Gunner Henry Arthur Fitzhugh of 'B' Battery, 210th Brigade RFA, 42nd Division was born in Blackburn, Lancashire and was killed in action on the day Frank was wounded (15th September). He is buried in plot XIX.B.9A of Lijssenthoek Military Cemetery, near Poperinghe.

As for 9/DAC, the War Diary records that on Saturday, 15th September the men moved their camp nearer to Poperinghe.

DIARY

Sunday, 16th September
A timely departure
(73°F, overcast)

"This morning 'Fritz' carried out another raid on the camp which we left yesterday afternoon – owing to the loss of horses we had had to move a little further back. All night on Friday they shelled us, from dark until daybreak. We were just packed up to leave yesterday when over came the shells again – one of them covered some of our chaps with mud and slime but no other damage was caused. This morning the anti-aircraft guns drew our attention and we saw a fleet of about twenty 'planes, two of which were monsters[3], the biggest I have ever seen. They bombed our old

camp mercilessly but we had already flown! The Germans have dropped a few gas shells near us tonight but apart from that our day has been relatively quiet. All along the line the batteries have been bombarding ever since early this morning and the big show will soon be starting off. Under present arrangements, the infantry go over on Tuesday morning but this is always liable to alteration. Troops are up here in their thousands and when the big show starts it will be hell upon earth."

"Evening: The start of the bombardment commenced this morning at three. All day our own batteries have been firing two rounds per gun; tomorrow at dawn our infantry go over the top. At the present time – 9:30 p.m. – the flashes and noise of the guns keep one's nerves tight. Our aeroplanes are overhead with their little bright lights shining and 'Fritz' is sweeping the skies with his searchlights – evidently he has the wind up. This is the start of what will develop into a very big affair [it would become known as the Battle of the Menin Road] if we can only get this ridge and hold onto it. The [Westhoek] ridge is the key to the big attack from here to the coast in which our Navy will take part and it falls to our division to take and hold the ridge. It has been taken twelve times before but could not be held. On our left we are being supported by Australian troops and on our right is the 55th ['West Lancashire'] Division. If we are successful on the ridge, ten divisions will take part in the next attack in a few

days' time between here and the coast but all depends on the ridge being captured. Everybody is on thorns tonight, from the C.O. to the drivers. What will tomorrow bring forth?"

CONTEXT

Tuesday, 18th September
(65°F, clear)
In what was the ultimate irony, on 18th September,

> *"...the 9th Division, from the Third Army, took over the right sector of the V Corps, astride the Ypres-Roulers railway..."*

(Edmonds, Official History of the Great War, *Military Operations in France and Belgium, 1917, volume II*)

Thus Jack was operating in the very sector in which Frank Hickman had been gassed three days previously. At the time, each man was utterly unaware of the presence of his brother.

Apart from the personal aspect, 9/ DAC lost,

> *'...three men wounded whilst carrying ammunition up to Batteries. Four horses killed.'*

DIARY

Thursday, 20th September
Battle of the Menin Road
(20th-25th September)
(66°F, overcast)

"Morning – 10:30 a.m.: The attack came off last night and the first reports are just through – at midnight the infantry went over the top and carried all objectives. The ridge is now in our hands, having taken a good many prisoners, though no details as yet. A good number of our wounded have come down by rail but again we are awaiting details. Now it is very quiet except for light guns; a counter-attack is expected."

"Evening: later news indicates that the push has been a great success, every objective being taken on time and the number of prisoners is estimated at 2,000. It was apparently all done fairly easily considering the struggles that have taken place for possession of the Westhoek Ridge – twelve times the top had been reached before and then lost again and now the 'old Ninth' has scored the success. If only we can hold it, it will mean big things."

Friday, 21st September
Bombed and strafed
(62°F, part cloud)
"Further rumours continue to flow through. Last night our troops made another advance, capturing Zonnebeke and a good number of prisoners. It is difficult to get much official news as yet but everything seems to have gone well. We had an exciting night in our camp – we were shelled from about midnight until daylight and then a German aeroplane made a raid on us, dropping four bombs and turning his machine guns on the

camt, though nobody was hurt. We are expecting more news from the line."

CONTEXT

21st September was a notable day for Jack's older brother, Frank Hickman. Frank had been evacuated to the UK, suffering from gas-shell poisoning and, on 21st September, was admitted to 3rd Western General Hospital in Cardiff, where he was treated until 7th November 1917.

DIARY

Saturday, 22nd September
A near miss
(63°F, clear)
"Heavy artillery work is the chief item on our particular front at present with slight progress being made by the infantry but not much in the way of a big effort as yet. The ridge and the other points taken are still held. Our camp had a visit from German 'planes last night about nine o'clock [p.m.] – it was a wonderful sight to see the searchlights on them. They dropped three bombs close to the tent in which I was lying, covering me with dirt and nearly choking us with the smell of gunpowder but no real damage was done. This morning, just after twelve, nine large 'planes raided us again, bombing the railway line and the big ammunition dump close to us. A big fire was started but soon put out again and, as far as we know, no other damage was done."

Monday, 24th September
Pre-battle barrage
(74°F, half cloud)
"Our own particular front is fairly quiet but on our left, towards the coast, a terrific artillery bombardment went on from Saturday evening until daylight. This morning, about 4:30, we heard several loud explosions that sounded like mines detonating but we don't quite know what they were. Just after that the bombardment ceased, so it looks like an infantry attack."

"Later: More news has come through concerning the heavy bombardment of the past three days. The Navy is joining in at Ostend and big things should take place within the next day or two."

Wednesday, 26th September
Battle of Polygon Wood
(26th September to 3rd October)
(68°F, mist)
"Early this morning our troops attacked again, capturing the whole of the village of Zonnebeke and establishing themselves at the foot of the last and most important [Passchendaele] ridge which commands the Menin Plain for some considerable miles. Many prisoners were taken and the infantry are pushing slowly on to the attack. The success is a good one and the next day or so should tell a good story for us. The weather looks full of rain but so far it has been fine."

Between 24th and 26th of the month:

'...one man [is] missing believed killed and three wounded whilst taking up ammunition.'

[9/DAC War Diary]

Saturday, 29th September
Towards Passchendaele
(65°F, clear)
"Continual artillery duels are the chief item on our particular front. Our infantry are pushing slowly through past Zonnebeke to the foot of the Passchendaele Ridge which is the final objective of the offensive at the present. To capture and hold the final ridge will mean great things happening; the final great attack will come off in a few days."

[On this day the War Diary mentions better news for one of the Column's number:

'...No.89266 Sgt. Allen S. awarded the Military Medal for gallantry under heavy shell fire.' [89266 Sergeant Samuel Allen had arrived in France in May 1915 with the 1st Contingent of the Guernsey Artillery in their new role as 9/DAC.]

Sunday, 30th September
All-night air raid
(67°F, clear)
"The hours of darkness were a nightmare, from about 7:30 p.m. until daylight this morning it was one long air-raid. Hundreds of bombs were dropped all

'For Bravery in the Field'. The Military Medal.

around us and though we just escaped it, the other camps all around caught it very bad. It was a most nerve-trying experience and one I don't want to go through again but as the moon will be just as bright tonight we shall no doubt get it all over again. The artillery work all night and this morning has been most terrific and now at midday the guns are going *at a most tremendous pace. Tomorrow the infantry go over for the assault on the Passchendaele Ridge so now we nervously await the result."*

Thursday, 4th October
Battle of Broodseinde
(4th October)

(60°F, overcast, 4.6mm. rain)

"The attack for the Passchendaele Ridge has not yet come off but a smaller attack was launched this morning and all objectives were taken with 1,650 prisoners. The weather is once again our usual 'offensive weather'[4] – yesterday broke up our lovely sunshine and turned to wind and rain, while today is the same but worse. News all round is quite good on our own front and on the Italian Front but bigger things will come off before the month is gone."

Saturday, 6th October
To the foot of the Ridge

(47°F, part cloud, 2.1mm. rain)

"The attack of Thursday is still being pushed home. The total 'bag' of Thursday's prisoners reached 3,000 and yesterday the infantry pushed on still further, taking another 2,000. They have now reached the foot of the ridge, and established themselves there. In about two days we are going into action again, to take part in the final smash. The weather is still very bad and the ground is getting in a very bad state."

Sunday, 7th October
Mud and more mud

(53°F, cloud, 10.4mm. rain)

"Another day of terrible cold and wet, making transport very difficult indeed. News from the line is still good; the infantry are still pushing slowly forward to secure the positions already taken. This afternoon a division of cavalry has come up and camped near us ready for the attack after we have taken the Passchendaele Ridge. Tomorrow we move up and take over the line near Langemarck for the big attack. We are still in the dark as to the exact day but believe it is to be Tuesday, yet the terrible weather may make a lot of difference."

Wednesday, 10th October
More air raids

(48°F, part cloud, rain showers, 2.5mm. rain)

"Yesterday we moved up near Ypres for the attack which we believe will come off early tomorrow. Not much news can be obtained except rumours but all we hear is good. The infantry keep pushing on and taking everything as they go. At times the fighting is hard; at other times it is all over without a fight. The next attempt is to be a bigger scale altogether, according to all rumours. We are massing men and guns, while the cavalry are up for the first time on this front. We are all getting impatient waiting for the blow that has been postponed so many times but everybody is confident of a big success very soon. Weather conditions are awful. Rain and mud make the going terrible. Last night we were raided from midnight until nearly dawn by 'Johnny'[5] and his

'planes; he bombed all around us but once again we were lucky enough to escape, although he nearly shook us out of bed with the concussion."

CONTEXT

Thursday, 11th to Saturday, 20th October

This ten day period was one of 9/DAC's worst for casualties, both human and animal. The War Diary notes that during that time, the Column lost two drivers killed, one sergeant and five drivers wounded, and eight of the hard-worked mules killed. The Column's officers did not escape the carnage as 2nd Lieutenant Watson and 2nd Lieutenant Fahy were wounded in action while on attachment to 9th Division's 51st Brigade RFA. [One of the two drivers killed in action during this period was 59127 Driver William James Percy Richards, (23), 9/DAC, killed in action on 16th October 1917. He is buried in plot XI. F. 7 of Vlamertinghe New Military Cemetery. He came from Pershore in Worcestershire. During the same period, at least seven other drivers of 9th Division's artillery brigades were killed – Drivers 96403 Alfred Allen, 825962 Isaac Herbert Stagg, 110511 T.H. Gilham, 175887 William Thomas Mackie, 104483 William Denny all of 50th Brigade RFA and Drivers 98726 George William Cutler, 43398 J.E. Dunn of 51st Brigade RFA.]

Friday, 12th October
1st Battle of Passchendaele

(12th October)
(55°F, 7.9mm. rain)

9th Division was part of Fifth Army's XVIII Corps for the first of the two battles that ultimately gave the alternative name to that of '3rd Ypres'. On a warm (55°F), wet day, just to the south of Poelkapelle, 8/Black Watch of 26th Brigade[6] made a successful start by taking Adler Farm but the Argylls lost their barrage and, despite follow-up by 27th Brigade[7],

> *'...the advance came to a halt 100 yards from the start line.'*

[Edmonds, Official History of the Great War, *'Military Operations in France and Belgium, 1917, volume II'.*]

Even the brave men of 9th 'Scottish' Division would be grateful that they were not later committed to the two-week struggle through the morass of 2nd Passchendaele (26th October to 10th November). Instead, the division would move north to the coast where it would face a very different and less familiar ordeal.

The deterioration in the weather was clearly reducing the battlefield below Passchendaele Ridge to a swamp of liquid mud overlying impermeable, wet clay where no roads were practicable and GSW transport was clearly impossible. Moving guns required superhuman effort; moving infantry was often possible only along slippery duckboard walkways from which men and mules might slide and drown. Early in the 3rd Ypres offensive the increasing destructive power of the guns had destroyed the drainage system between Ypres and the Passchendaele Ridge; as the rainfall intensified, so the former farmland took on the characteristics of an impassable swamp. Ironically, as artillery-based 'bite and hold' operations demonstrated their success, so the distance between usable roads and railways and the devastated battlefield increased. This 'Devastated Zone' posed a major problem for the DACs and their efforts to replenish ammunition supplies. Failing all else, limited ammunition could be transported by brigade mule-trains in which each beast bore an eight-pocket canvas carrier replete with (usually) 18-pounder shells to the field artillery gun-line. However, despite the sterling work of the mules, they could not come even close to sating the voracious appetite of the guns.

DIARY

Saturday, 13th October
Punch and counter-punch
(52˚F, part cloud, 10.7mm. rain)
"Yesterday morning our infantry went over in the first stage of the big attack. The weather is awful and the attack was received with very heavy artillery opposition from the enemy. Our own casualties were very heavy but all objectives were gained. Later in the day the enemy counter-attacked and very

heavy fighting took place. At some places we held on but at others we lost some positions. Today we had another attack but so far news has not come through; it is not very good so far as we know at the present time."

Friday, 19th October
Raid after raid
(48˚F, part cloud, 2.9mm. rain)
"The past week has been rather quiet except for artillery work. The great feature of the week has been great bombing raids by 'Fritz' with his Gotha bombers. He has had one or two attempts each night and a few by day but has not done a lot of damage except to a few horses. In a few days our division is moving out from this front and going further north, nearer the coast. The weather has been better for a few days, with just a few showers, mostly at night."

Tuesday, 23rd October
Ghyvelde, near Dunkirk
(50˚F, showers, 4mm. rain)
"On Sunday we left Ypres and travelled by road through Poperinghe and Watou to Wormhout [north of Cassel] where we stayed for the night. Yesterday we moved on again and finally reached Ghyvelde [south of Bray-Dunes] on the coast just above [east of] Dunkirk. It is a very sandy coastline with huge sand dunes and flat country inland. In about two days' time we move down to the outskirts of Dunkirk where we will stay for a short rest. The weather today was very rainy."

CONTEXT

Jack's comment of, "*...leaving Ypres on Sunday (21st) ...*", must refer to his Divisional Ammunition Column, the Sappers and the ASC[8] that would all have had to precede most of the 'Ninth' in order to establish camps and dumps before the main body of troops arrived.

Wednesday, 24th October
Ghyvelde
(48˚F, part cloud, 7.7mm. rain)
63rd 'Royal Naval' Division completed the relief of 9th 'Scottish' Division's infantry that then followed its Ammunition Column and Supply Train towards Dunkirk for a hard-earned 'rest'.

DIARY

Friday, 26th October
Malo-les-Bains
(48˚F, overcast, 7.8mm. rain)
"*Today we have moved back to the Royal Artillery at Malo-les-Bains, a port of Dunkirk, where we expect to remain for about a fortnight before we go into action again. The best news of the week is a fine success by the French on the Aisne front along the Chemin-des-Dames road – an advance of two miles on a six-mile front, taking over 5,000 prisoners and seventy guns of all sorts. The weather is fine and clear with a bright moon – everybody in the town has taken shelter as the air-raid warning has just gone. Several English*

torpedo-boats [There were three types – Motor Launches, pennant 'ML+ number'; Coastal Motor Boats, pennant 'CMB + number' and from 1917 there were 'Kil' Class Patrol Gunboats, capable of 13 knots, that were twice the size of the MLs and CMBs] are lying off the coast so we shall see some foam when 'Fritz' gets here with his 'planes. So far there is no sign of them."

Saturday, 27th October
Raids again
(49˚F, part cloud)
"*More news has come through today from the French front. The prisoners are now in excess of 11,000 along with 120 guns and the advance is still in progress. Last night the expected air-raid arrived about midnight – they dropped many bombs around us, most of them duds, and not much damage was done in our particular spot. A few smashed windows and a few dead horses being the only casualties. At the present moment the hooters are blowing for another air-raid so I expect we shall get a 'welcome' shortly. I stood on the beach tonight and heard the 'planes going in the direction of England, so I expect London will get another 'doing up' tonight.*"

CONTEXT

In fact, that night German 'planes reached the mouths of the Rivers Crouch, Blackwater and Thames but deteriorating weather forced them to drop their bomb loads on Essex where no casualties or damage occurred.

[Morris, 'German Air Raids on Britain, 1914-1918'.]

DIARY

Monday, 29th October
Sint-Idesbald near Nieuwpoort
(47°F, part cloud)

"Today we had a sudden order to go into action at once. Why the sudden change, we do not know as we were told yesterday morning that we were at Malo [-les-Bains] for three weeks' rest. We believe it to be owing to the setback which the Italians have received and we are sending some troops there. We are now settled in a place called [Sint-] Idesbald, near Nieuwpoort and Coxyde. Before we left Malo the Huns paid us a visit each night with their 'planes – last night they dropped four bombs all around our billet but no damage was done except to windows, though other units suffered the loss of a good many horses. The weather is fine and clear – we shall no doubt get a visit from 'Fritz' tonight."

CONTEXT

1st to 20th November
9/DAC War Diary commented:

'...unit remained in the Coxyde area and was engaged in clearing the area of ammunition and empty shell cases.'

DIARY

Thursday, 1st November
Sint-Idesbald

(51°F, overcast, 0.2mm. rain)

"Last night 'Fritz' had a great time. He started about ten o'clock and kept it up until about midnight – he gave Dunkirk a bad time but our searchlights picked them up and gave them 'jip' with anti-aircraft fire and our 'planes had a lively time with them. One German flew down so low we thought he was coming down on top of our camp – we ducked down, expecting machine-gun bullets but they did not come and our camp escaped Scot-free. At the present time, 6 p.m., a terrific bombardment is going on [all] along our front; it is rather strange as this is supposed to be the line where nothing is doing but it may be an attempt to put the wind up us."

Monday, 5th November
Coxyde shelled
(49°F, overcast and foggy)

"The past four days have been fairly quiet except for heavy shelling of Coxyde at intervals. Each evening we have had a visit from 'Fritz' and his 'planes. He has dropped a good load of bombs and badly damaged our dump but that is about all the benefit he has got out of it."

Sunday, 11th November
Coxyde again
(Wind and rain)

"The last day or two have been much the same as the past week – fairly heavy shelling of Coxyde and district. Our column had a nasty time on Thursday and Friday nights – they were shelled out of *their billets for over twelve hours. Friday dinner time, twenty Gothas came over our camp and hovered around for a long time but did not drop any bombs. However, that night, as soon as it was dark, they came over us and dropped about one hundred bombs all around us but did no damage at all. Last night was very windy so we were not bothered by the attacks. The weather is very unsettled, rough and rainy."*

Thursday, 15th November
Visitors – King Albert and Ferdinand Foch

"The last week has been one of very heavy artillery work on both sides. Every fine night has seen air-raids, especially on Dunkirk. Last night 'Fritz' shelled Dunkirk with a long-range gun from the sea. Yesterday the King [Albert] of the Belgians inspected the artillery on the sands and the French General [Ferdinand] Foch came to inspect our billets. They are taking over from us in a day or two. The French guns have arrived today."

King Albert Memorial, Brugge (Bruges).

---

1 HMHS 'Carisbrooke Castle' had beds for approximately 440 patients.
2 The Union Castle Line was formed from the merger in March 1900 of the Castle Packet Company and the Union Line; the new company dominated the passage of mail, passengers and general cargo on the UK to South Africa route.
3 The 'monsters' were most likely examples of the Gotha G.IV bomber. This identification was confirmed a month later by Jack's diary entry of 19th October, *"The great feature of the week has been great bombing raids by 'Fritz' with his Gotha bombers."*
4 It seemed that whenever a British offensive commenced, so did the rain or snow. In the

Ypres Salient, rain meant mud and mud was the curse of artilleryman and infantryman alike.
5 'Johnny' was another nickname for the Germans.
6 26 Brigade initially attacked with two battalions, 8/Black Watch and 10/Argyll & Sutherland Highlanders, with 7/Seaforth Highlanders and 5/Cameron Highlanders in support.
7 27 Brigade used 6/King's Own Scottish Borderers as principal battalion, supported by 11/Royal Scots & 12/Royal Scots.
8 Army Service Corps, whose task was to ensure the flow of appropriate supplies for their divisions. 104th, 105th, 106th and 107th Companies, ASC, (collectively known as the 'Divisional Train') were attached to 9th Division.

CHAPTER ELEVEN
SOMME AGAIN BUT CHRISTMAS LEAVE 1917

A BRIEF REST THEN...

CAMBRAI EPISODE

CONTEXT

Friday, 24th November

According to his Army Service Record, on this date Jack was,

> *"...posted to Headquarters, 9/Divisional Ammunition Column."*

However, 9/DAC HQ was on the move south. The division's task would be to bolster the right of the line against German counter-attack.

Cambrai Memorial to the Missing, at Louverval.

DIARY

Wednesday, 29th November
Near Hesdin

"After a week on the road we have at last landed at the end of our journey – we are at a little village near the town of Hesdin, miles from the lines. We expect to stay here for three weeks. After that we do not know but rumours lead us to believe it will be Italy for us. While we were on the road, we had the news of the great success around Cambrai – everything seems to be going well again for us on all fronts. The weather is not very good – one very heavy fall of snow last week tells us that winter is here."

Monday, 3rd December
Cambrai – The German Counter-Attack
(30th November-3rd December)
(Cold and frosty)

"Our rest did not last long. After three days we suddenly got orders to be ready to move. Following another day on the road, we entrained at a place called Wavrans-sur-Ternoise [immediately north-west of Saint-Pol-sur-Ternoise] and after ten hours in the train we stepped out at Péronne [on the Somme] and are, at present, in a small village called Haut Allaines [just north of Péronne]. A very long bombardment is going on and has not stopped since we arrived yesterday. We find that the reason for us being fetched up in such a hurry is due to the Germans breaking the line a few nights

ago. So the 'Old Ninth' has once again to save the situation. The weather is very cold and frosty."

Tuesday, 4th December
Haut Allaines, near Péronne
(Cold, clear, frosty)

"The battle around Cambrai is still raging. The artillery bombardment during the last few days has been as bad as any I have ever heard and it does not seem to abate at all. On the right, where the Germans got through our line last week, things are fairly quiet but preparations are going on fast to drive 'Fritz' well back. It falls to our division to get on with it – we go into action on the sixth, so we shall soon know what is going to happen. The Cambrai battle seems to be pretty rough for us. The weather is still cold with hard frosts each night."

Friday, 7th December
In Action

"Yesterday we moved up into action; our Royal Artillery is at present at Liéramont [north-east of Péronne]. Very heavy duels continue between our artillery and 'Fritz' but there has been nothing exciting so far. There are a lot of troops around this locality and we expect a big move soon."

Wednesday, 12th December
Bussu

9/DAC War Diary recorded that,

> *'No.1 Section of the Column marched to Metz-en-Couture to assist 50th Brigade, RFA, in salvage work.'*

Sunday, 16th December

(Cold, some snow)

"Little except very heavy artillery work on our front during the past week. One attempt by the Huns to break through our line was soon broken up with very heavy German losses. The weather is very cold with a slight fall of snow during the day."

[Three days later Jack left for England and a well-deserved leave.]

CONTEXT

On Leave

The second page of Jack's Active Service Record (1918-1919) reads,

'...19/12/17 to 3/1/18; In the Field; Leave to England with ration allowance; granted by the OC 9/DAC.'

This confirms that Jack was granted home leave for Christmas and the New Year, thus missing 9th Division's action on 30th December. In some respects Jack had been very fortunate with his allocations of leave; he had been granted a week's leave in November 1915 to wed his sweetheart, Ada Palmer. Then, towards the end of January 1917, Jack had been allowed home for a ten-day furlough – the first time he had seen Ada since their wedding. His third period of leave, that covered Christmas and the New Year, was his longest to date, amounting to fifteen days. Other lads in other units who survived as long as Jack

might well have received but a single period of leave – it was really a matter of luck.

While Jack was at home, most of the Column spent the days either side of Christmas 1917 on fatigues, either at Bussu or at Nurlu.

Monday, 31st December
Nurlu

9/DAC's HQ section, 1 and 2 Sections joined the Small Arms Section at Nurlu where they saw in the New Year – no doubt in appropriate style, despite the circumstances. They could not have known it but they were about enter the first hours of the final year of the war.

CHAPTER TWELVE
'DIE KAISERSCHLACHT'

THE SOMME – OPERATION 'MICHAEL'

JANUARY TO MARCH 1918

CONTEXT

The Column spent the entire month of January in the region around Péronne, near Sorel and Nurlu. Sections Nos.1 & 2 worked on building huts and horse standings, though the most telling comment in the DAC War Diary was, '...*Three Lewis Guns* [light machine-guns] *loaned to unit for defence against Enemy Aircraft.*' The need for these weapons is demonstrated by the first three entries in Jack's personal diary for January 1918.

DIARY

Sunday, 6th January
Sorel village, near Péronne
(Very hard frost)
"After Christmas and the New Year at home on leave, I am back again at the old camp. We are now at the ruins of Sorel [to the north-east of Péronne], once a pretty little village. The frost is still very severe and it is very dangerous on the roads. On arriving at Péronne in the early hours of this morning, we were met with a warm reception – 'Old Fritz' came over and bombed the station and the town, knocking down the ceiling in the old house in which we were sheltering. Then on my arrival at camp, 'Old Fritz' dropped a dirty big 5.9in shell about a hundred yards into the field. So, he welcomed me back in a

nice, friendly way! He is still massing men and guns behind his line on our front but the hard weather is all against anything big coming off."

"Increased German bombing and heavy artillery attacks on Allied ammunition and supply dumps, transport parks and road and rail communications, suggested that rumour of an intended German spring offensive was soon to become reality. Such destructive preparation was surely aimed to 'squeeze' Allied fighting troops on the Somme into a relatively shallow front and thus make a breakthrough more deadly."

Tuesday, 8th January
(Overnight ice then snow)
"Yesterday our weather turned to rain and a thaw set in, turning the roads into

a terrible mess. Then last night it froze hard and this morning the roads were in a bad state again. About midday the wind rose and a terrific blizzard began and lasted about an hour. It was awful while it lasted and the drifts are very deep. Tonight it is clear, starlit and freezing hard. This morning 'Fritz' bombed our camp about daylight and gave us a lively time but did no damage to us. I expect he will have another go tonight or early in the morning."

Monday, 14th January
Frequent dogfights
(Overcast, some rain)
"The past week has been very quiet. It has been dull and cold, with a little rain at intervals; nights have been frosty and days foggy, except for Sunday which was very sunny and bright. It was, however, one constant air-fight from daylight to dark – aeroplanes were up all day on both sides. We saw some very exciting fights; one of our fighters brought down two Gothas[1] in a few minutes and all day long 'Fritz' was making trips over our lines but got a very hot time of it and was always back again in double-quick time. About four in the afternoon, two of 'Fritz's' 'planes tackled an observation balloon over our camp, firing hundreds of rounds but with no luck. [The Germans particularly targeted observation balloons as they wanted to conceal their build-up of troops and matériel for the spring offensive.] Our anti-aircraft guns opened and fetched one down, then without any warning the balloon suddenly caught fire and burnt out. Nobody knows what the cause was as the 'planes had been gone quite two minutes. On Wednesday last, 'Fritz' tried to get through our line but was cut up before he got to our front line. The artillery fire for about an hour was terrific. Since then nothing much has happened. Today I was up at the guns and found extensive preparations going on at great pace for a big affair. Our troops are making a new line about four miles behind our present one in the event of 'Fritz' getting through the front line[2]." [What Jack described in this entry is the new system of 'defence in depth' that Third and Fifth Armies were adopting.]

CONTEXT

'Defence in depth'
As a result of Russia having surrendered to Germany during 1917, increasing numbers of enemy divisions were available to be deployed to the Western Front. Ludendorff viewed this window of opportunity for a decisive strike to be short-lived as the USA was already training and sending well-equipped 'Doughboys'[3] to France. He believed that America's potential to change the course of the war to be almost limitless; Ludendorff was handed an extra advantage by the Commander of the American troops in Europe, General 'Black Jack' Pershing, who refused to allow his divisions to be used piecemeal in the struggle, insisting that when

sufficient Americans were in France, the 'United States Army' would swing the balance of the conflict in the Allies' favour. A second advantage was furnished by the British Prime Minister David Lloyd-George, who obstructed Field-Marshal Sir Douglas Haig's repeated requests for fresh troop replacements on the Western Front. Lloyd-George was of the opinion that Haig's methods were unnecessarily wasteful of the troops under his command; the Prime Minister was not in a position to replace Haig but neither would he accede to demands for limitless quantities of British troops to be

sent to the Western Front. Deprived of essential reinforcements, Field-Marshal Haig took the decision in February of 1918 to reduce the number of battalions per brigade from four to three – in effect, three divisions were expected to do the work previously assigned to four. So, with the British expecting some form of last-ditch offensive by the German Army in the west, their resources were reduced as the enemy's increased.

T9 shows the 9th Division Infantry Brigades, as they were constituted before and after the 1918 reorganisation:

T9: 9th Division – Infantry Brigade reorganisation, February 1918

BEFORE

26th Brigade	8/Black Watch	7/Seaforth H.	5/Cam. H.	10/A. & S.H.
27th Brigade	11/Royal Scots	12/Royal Scots	6/KOSB	9/Scot. Rifles
S. Afr. Bde	1/S. Afr. Inf.	2/S. Afr. Inf.	3/S. Afr. Inf.	4/S. Afr. Inf.

AFTER

26th Brigade	8/Black Watch	7/Seaforth H.	5/Cameron H.
27th Brigade	11/Royal Scots	12/Royal Scots	6/KOSB
S. Afr. Brigade	1/S. Afr. Infantry	2/S. Afr. Infantry	4/S. Afr. Infantry

With experienced units increasingly exhausted and the prognosis grim, British High Command instituted a new defensive system – 'Defence in Depth', also referred to as 'Elastic Defence'. The long-established complex of trenches was in part replaced by a system of three principal zones, similar to the pattern adopted by the German defenders at 3rd Ypres. The 'front line'

became the Forward Zone in which each sector (often in the form of selected strongpoints) was held at just Company strength – unsurprisingly, this was regarded by the ordinary 'Tommy' as the suicide zone. The most strongly-held area was the Battle Zone, about two miles back from the Forward Zone – this was where the enemy was intended to be stalled and then pushed back. However, should the Battle Zone be penetrated, then a Rear Zone, comprising strongly-wired trench lines another couple of miles further to the rear, should serve as a reserve line to enable an orderly withdrawal by the forward units. Unfortunately, reality did not match up to the theory as neither Third nor Fifth Army had had sufficient time or resources to complete an effective Rear Zone. In the Official History of 'Military Operations in France & Flanders', volume 1 of 1918, Brigadier-General Edmonds demonstrates that when Operation 'Michael' commenced on 21st March, about one third of British troops were deployed in the Forward Zone, rather more than the planned system anticipated. The function of the elite German 'Sturmtruppen' was to by-pass the strongpoints of the Forward Zone and to infiltrate the Battle Zone, leaving the main assault troops to clear the front areas. Thick mist on the morning of Thursday, 21st March enabled many of the 'Sturmtruppen' to pass the British strongpoints in the murk without even being engaged.

DIARY

Tuesday, 22nd January
Nurlu
"Nothing much doing on our front – everything has been very quiet for about a week. Great preparations are going on apace for a coming scrap – the sooner the better! The weather is rather wet."

Friday, 1st February
At rest in Etinehem, south of Albert
"Today we have moved out from Nurlu and are now in a village called Etinehem [south of Albert], near where we were when we started the Somme offensive in July 1916. Things are a bit different now. Instead of being in the danger zone, it is now thirty miles from the front line. We are out for a month's rest. It is the third time that we have come out for a month but on each other occasion it has been three days – we hope for better luck this time."

CONTEXT

Until 4th February, 9/DAC remained at Nurlu on fatigues, erecting huts and horse standings. On 5th February however, the unit moved to huts in a new 'rest' encampment at Bray-sur-Somme, where a busy training regime was imposed. The beasts were unfortunate enough to remain in the open.

DIARY

Friday, 1st March
Haut Allaines
"After a month of it in a decent rest camp we are back again in the mud. We moved today into a camp near Haut Allaines where we first came off the train that first week in December. Everything seems to point to a big attack by 'Johnny'[4] very shortly so we are here in case of it coming off – it is expected now any day. The weather is cold and frosty."

Sunday, 3rd March
St. Radegonde near Péronne

"Heavy falls of snow and on Friday night and yesterday have nipped in the bud any chance of 'Fritz' making his offensive. Today a bit of a thaw has set in and there are rumours of us moving from here again. There are also rumours of Japan and China having joined hands against Germany and marching to meet them in Russia."

[The Rumour-Mill worked overtime when acute danger was at hand.]

Sunday, 10th March

"The big push has not yet come off by 'Johnny', owing no doubt to the bad weather at the expected time but for several days now the weather has been lovely and we once more have reason to think that he is about to make his attempt. We await his attack in readiness for anything he might do."

Tuesday, 12th March

"Today the division has moved up from the reserve lines to the front position and here we are in lovely weather waiting for any move that 'Fritz' likes to put forward. The weather could not be better for a good scrap and there is no doubt that it will soon come off."

CONTEXT

Wednesday, 13th March
Moislains

9/DAC War Diary records:

'Column marched up to Moislains and encamped. Up to and including the 21st inst. [this would be the first day of the 'Kaiserschlacht'], the column was engaged on Corps fatigues and supplying ammunition to Battery positions, also dumping a certain amount of ammunition at reserve Battery positions ready for any emergency.'

This suggests that the high command foresaw the possibility, even probability of the British being forced to retreat. Whether this simply reflects simple facts and figures (the German army had transferred many divisions from the Eastern Front to the Western Front in the wake of Russia's surrender in 1917) or whether it reveals that British preparations for their new 'defence in depth' stratagem were not yet complete, is uncertain.

DIARY

Thursday, 14th March

"Last night the artillery battle on our front was one of the most intense of any since the war started. 'Old Fritz' caught our positions for about half an hour at a terrible rate, then our heavies opened and he closed down. We gave him perfect hell then things quietened down except for occasional bursts at different points."

Tuesday, 19th March

"The past week has been one of lovely

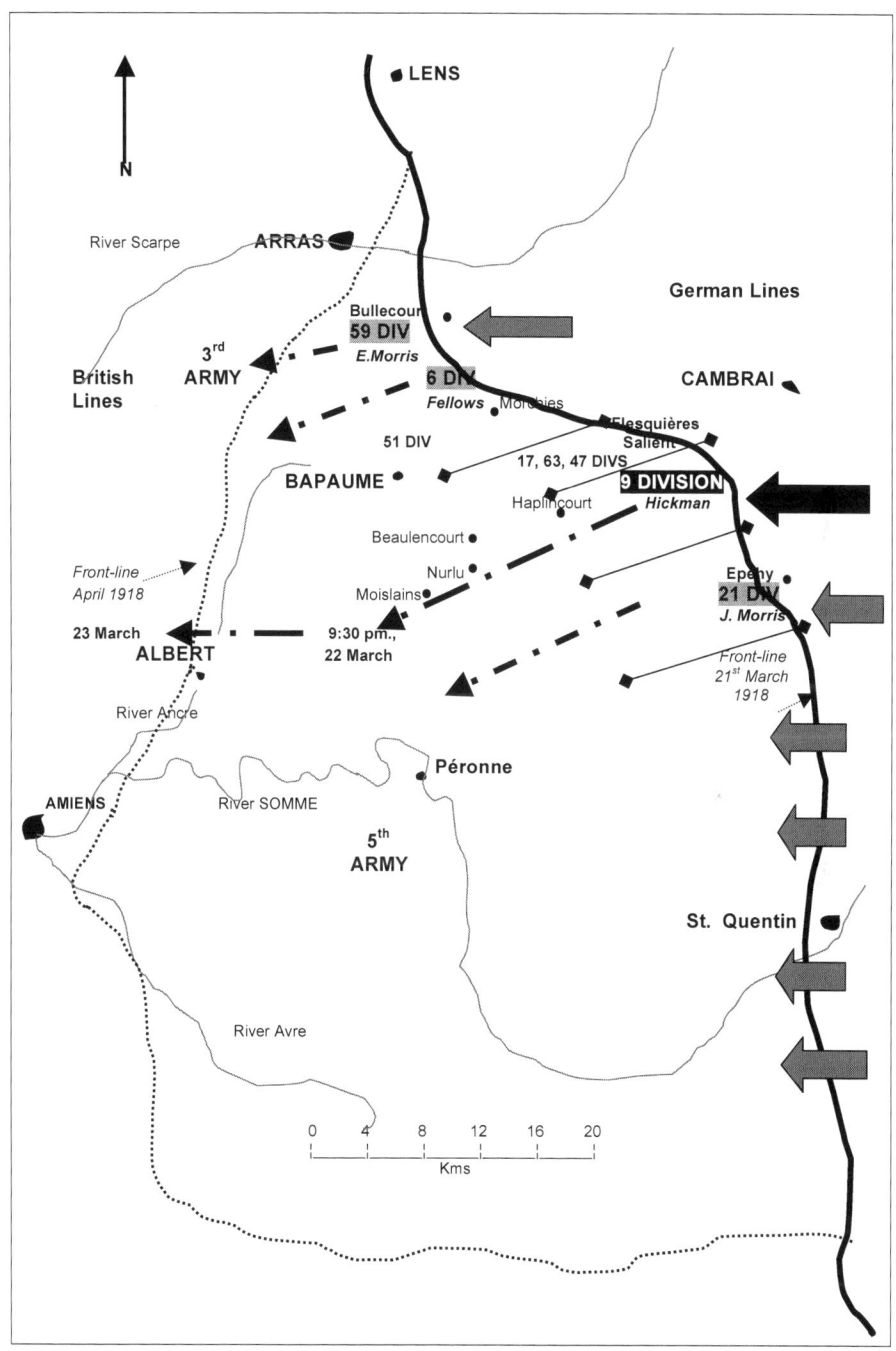

*Map 6: 'die Kaiserschlacht', Operation 'Michael', Bullecourt to Epehy sector –
9th 'Scottish' Division 21st-24th March 1918*

weather, of heavy bombardments at intervals and of expected attacks that have not come off but today the weather has changed and it is now raining heavily with a promise of more to come. It will no doubt top any thought of big attacks for a day or two."

CONTEXT

When the impending storm broke, at 4:40 a.m. on 21st March, an intense German barrage opened on a fifty-mile 'Somme' front that stretched from near Vimy Ridge in the north to the River Oise in the south. To a depth of almost a mile it battered mercilessly the entire length of the British Third and Fifth Armies – the boundary between the two armies coincided with the divisional boundary between 47th '2nd London' Division of Third Army and 9th 'Scottish' Division of Fifth Army. Orchestrated by *Oberstleutnant*[5] Georg Bruchmüller, the German artillery 'genius', a deadly cocktail of high explosive, shrapnel, mustard gas[6] and lachrymatory gas engulfed trenches and battalion headquarters alike for five seemingly endless, mind-numbing hours then, as synchronised watches reached 9:40 a.m., tense, front-line troops at their battle stations were shaken to see wave upon wave of dull, grey shapes emerging from the fog that blanketed No Man's Land. Operation 'Michael' (21st March to 5th April), the first phase of Ludendorff's great spring offensive known as *'die Kaiserschlacht'* ('The Emperor's Battle')

was under way and would eventually drive back the British almost forty miles to the outskirts of the city of Amiens.

Although the Flesquières Salient was not directly attacked in the infantry assault, it had been drenched with mustard-gas shells to prevent the main divisions there (17th, 63rd and 47th) sending reinforcements to their compatriots on their southern flank (9th and 21st Divisions). The latter two units were thus left to look to their own salvation in the face of attack by ten German divisions. Jack Hickman has left his own impressions of the German artillery tempest and was witness to the Scots' stubborn resistance to the German stormtroopers[7].

DIARY

Thursday, 21st March
'die Kaiserschlacht', **Operation 'Michael'**
Battle of St. Quentin (21st-23rd March)
[9th 'Scottish' Division was part of General Gough's Fifth Army, VII Corps, where three British divisions, 9th 'Scottish', 16th 'Irish' and 21st, faced almost ten German divisions.]

"At last the long-expected offensive by 'Fritz' has started. This morning, about 4:30 a.m., we were roused from sleep by the crash of bursting shells. They then began to shell our village [Haut Allaines] and our guns at once replied; from 4:30 a.m. to about 4 p.m. the artillery duel was awful. It was the worst I have ever heard

and he shelled our village all day and is still at it now at 5:30 p.m. Over two hundred shells of all sorts have been pumped at us alone and though loss of life is only about two, the material damage must be great. At present there is a lull in the front line but we can get no news except that our division repulsed the infantry attack made on them."

CONTEXT

Thursday, 21st March – 21st Division, to the right of 9th 'Scottish' Division

On the right flank of 9th 'Scottish', 21st Division was likewise immersed in the struggle for survival. Near Epehy, a young Midlander, Corporal Joel Morris, was manning the divisional gun-line with 'D' Battery of 95th Brigade, Royal Field Artillery and the day was not going well, as 95th Brigade war diary relates:

"21st March, The preliminary enemy bombardment of Epehy began at 4:30 a.m. and by 5:30 a.m. all men were wearing masks to combat the use of gas shells. Thick fog made the situation worse; 5:00 a.m., the slow barrage began and F.O.O.[8] reports showed a steady German advance. When the weather cleared about 11:00 a.m., it became apparent that the enemy had made a general attack at about 9:00 a.m. and had reached the trench lines.

1:30 p.m., the following message came from 94th Brigade, 'the enemy now holds Ronnsoy and Malassise Farm (two miles to the south of Epehy)'.

By 2:00 p.m., we were firing as required on the enemy.

2:30 a.m., repeated requests for artillery support to the right were frustrated by limited gun availability.

3:00 p.m., a message arrived that the officer and detachment on forward anti-tank duty in Epehy had fired all their ammunition, destroyed the guns and retired.

4:30 p.m., A/95[9] and D/95 were ordered to withdraw to the Yellow Line to rejoin B/95 and C/95. This was done and we were in action again at 6:00 p.m. The enemy broke through at Vaucelette Farm (one mile north of Epehy) and a barrage failed to help.

8:00 p.m., brigade retired to the Brown Line at Saulcourt (two miles south-west of Epehy) where we were in action again at dawn. D/95 was forced to leave one howitzer behind as it was damaged by shellfire."

Joel Morris of D/95 (Heavy[10]), evidently somewhat less 'lucky' than Jack Hickman would later be, was hit when one of his battery's 4.5 inch howitzers was damaged by enemy artillery – Joel was never seen alive again[11].

Thursday, 7th to Wednesday, 20th March – 6th Division, north of the Flesquières Salient

To the north of 9th 'Scottish', just the far side of the gas-soaked Flesquières

Salient and in the front line near the village of Morchies, 1/West Yorkshire (18th Brigade, 6th Division) experienced the same artillery onslaught as the Scots. Private Albert Fellows had been with the Yorkshiremen since January 1917 and had seen action at Hill 70 near Lens, had come safely through all three major engagements of the Battle of Cambrai (20th November to 7th December) after which his battalion had remained in the Lagnicourt sector, due west of Cambrai, through into late March of 1918. There, tours of duty in the front line proved to be relatively quiet but very tense affairs as a major German offensive had been expected for several weeks. In the event, there had not even been much 'daily hate'[12], as is confirmed by the 1/West Yorkshire battalion war diary:

"7th-12th March, in camp at Beugnatre. One company 'stood to' daily to occupy Morchies-Vaulx line on alarm."
"13th March, the battalion moved up to alarm post north of Morchies and was in position at 5:30 a.m. Returned to camp about 9:15 a.m. Relieved 2/ Durham Light Infantry in front line."
"14th March, very quiet day and night. Casualties nil."
"15th March, very quiet day and night. Casualties nil. "
"16th-18th March as per 15th. "
"19th March, still in trenches. Quiet. Casualties nil. "
"20th March, as per 19th."

This, however, was unlikely to last.

Thursday, 21st March – 6th Division, near Morchies, north of the Salient
The first few hours of Operation *'Michael'* north of the Flesquières Salient closely mirrored the experiences of 9th 'Scottish' to the south of the Salient. 1/West Yorkshire battalion war diary reported:

"21st March, an enormous enemy attack broke at 5:00 a.m. with intense barrage on all trenches, routes of approach and battery positions; much gas shelling; length of front of attack 50 miles from near Arras to St. Quentin[13]. Front line Companies, 'B' and 'D', suffered tremendous casualties from the barrage. Splendid stand made by whole of 6th Division along reserve line after both flanks had been pressed back and until evening when a (1½ mile) withdrawal was ordered to Vaulx-Morchies Line (the Corps Defence Line). Withdrawal carried out successfully. Reinforced by 11/Essex in reserve line. Enemy used enormous number of troops and the German artillery was assisted by Austrian batteries. Enemy reported holding Lagnicourt."

Thursday, 21st March
59th '2nd North Midland' Division south of Bullecourt, on the left flank of 6th Division
Feeling very exposed in the front line trench near Bullecourt and trying to

find what little shelter was available, Private Eddie Morris of 2/6th Sherwood Foresters listened to and felt the scream and crash of the massive German barrage that was the undoubted prelude to a major assault. If fear allowed, Eddie probably thought back over the past few months' many encounters with the enemy – the German Retreat to the Hindenburg Line, Passchendaele and Cambrai – those he had come through without too many scratches. Now, with the few of his mates that were left in the 2/6th Sherwood Foresters[14] (178th Brigade, 59th '2nd North Midland' Division), under the crescendo of the shelling, he wondered if he might be lucky yet again. Later, after the event, the adjutant wrote starkly in the battalion war diary:

"21st March 1918. Very heavy enemy barrage on front line from 5 a.m. to 9:30 a.m. when the enemy attacked. The battalion suffered very heavy casualties."

Subsequently, the battalion commander, added a more detailed, narrative appendix from which the following is taken:

"At a position just south of Bullecourt. Defence in depth. On night of 20th-21st, patrols were vigilant but saw nothing unusual in No Man's Land. At 5:00 a.m. began a great bombardment for four hours. The initial attack at 9 a.m. was stopped.

A renewed attack left our flanks 'in the air'[15] and we were isolated. At 10:30 a.m. we were outflanked and enfiladed[16] from the south by trench mortars and machine guns, causing heavy losses. The battalion fought until the ammunition was spent and most men had become casualties."

Surely a victim of the thunderous barrage, Eddie Morris was posted among those 'missing in action'. His body was never recovered, thus he is commemorated on Bay 7 of the Arras Memorial to the Missing.

Friday, 22nd March – 1/West Yorkshire (6th Division) withdrawn to Fauvreuil

"...fairly quiet night. Enemy continued attack at 5:00 a.m. At night, battalion was relieved by a battalion of 41st Division and withdrew to bivouacs near Fauvreuil. Casualties – killed, 1 officer and 8 other ranks; wounded, 3 officers and 18 other ranks; wounded and missing, 2 officers and 9 other ranks; missing in action, 17 officers and 531 other ranks.

Total casualties, 589."

[Extract from 1/West Yorkshire battalion war diary].

Bearing in mind that the battalion was already short-handed, sustaining 589 casualties meant, in effect, that the 1/West Yorkshire had been destroyed.

Twenty-nine year-old Albert Fellows, a miner from Staffordshire, was among those posted as, 'missing in action'. His body was never found, thus Albert is commemorated on Bay 4 of the Arras Memorial to the Missing.

DIARY

[As 9/DAC retreated, the Column ensured that it left caches of artillery shells for the Batteries and small arms ammunition for the infantry battalions. Retreat or no retreat, the Column still had its job to do.]

Friday, 22nd March
9/DAC – Nurlu to Moislains
"Early this morning we had to leave our camp and retreat to the village of Moislains, about a mile and a half back. The guns and infantry fell back at the same time and now, 9:30 p.m., our front line is in the camp that we left this morning at Nurlu. On both sides of our division the enemy got through the line, leaving us exposed in a sharp salient, so we had no option but to fall back. We could have held our line had it not been for the flanks giving way."

Saturday, 23rd March
9/DAC Towards Albert
"We once more had to pack up and retire. After a fairly quiet night we started off; at the present time, 9:15 a.m., we are camped for a few hours in amongst the old Somme battlefields [at Montauban, the

site of one of the few notable successes on 1st July 1916]. Just behind us our guns are going at a terrific pace and the machine-gun fire beats anything I have ever heard. It is a lovely day and much may happen in the next twelve hours. This is the third day with no sleep and not even our boots off."

Taking off his boots would no longer be Jack's problem after what was to befall him on the morrow.

---

1 The German 'Gotha' bomber was a large, three-seater biplane, nearly 40 feet long with a wingspan of over 70 feet. It was driven by two 260 horse-power Mercedes engines and the Gotha was capable of delivering up to 125 Kgs (275 lbs) of bombs. The aircraft had a service ceiling of up to 18,000 feet and a range of 600 miles.

2 This was part of the new concept of 'defence in depth' that, it was hoped, would stall any major enemy offensive.

3 'Doughboy' was the American equivalent of the British 'Tommy' and French 'Poilu'.

4 This was one of several nicknames that British Tommies reserved for the enemy soldiers.

5 The rank of 'Oberstleutnant' is the equivalent of Lieutenant-Colonel.

6 Mustard gas, whose terrible effects were long-lasting, was used only against the Flesquières Salient, an area that the Germans did not immediately intend to assault head-on.

7 Stormtroops were specially selected from existing units for their fitness and battle-hardiness; well-armed with sub-machine guns and stick grenades, stormtroops were trained for close-quarter fighting. Their task was to infiltrate between strong-points rather than assault head-on. Support troops, armed with flamethrowers, mortars and machine-guns were intended to 'mop up' after the stormtroops and consolidate the line.

8 Forward Observation Officer. His normal task was to observe the fall of shell and recommend adjustments in range but in this case he was reporting on the enemy advance.

9 'A/95' refers to 'A' Battery, 95th Brigade of the Royal Field Artillery.

10 By 1918, the Heavy battery of an RFA Brigade comprised six 4.5 inch howitzers.

11 Neither were Joel Morris's remains found, thus his name is recorded on panel 7 (Royal Field Artillery) of the Pozières Memorial to the Missing, adjacent to the Albert to Bapaume road.

12 'Routine' shelling, mortaring and sniping was known as the 'daily hate.'

13 This knowledge of the length of front could have been gleaned only after the event.

14 131 men (the second highest of all battalions) of 2/6th Sherwood Foresters were killed on 21st March.

15 This means that there were no supporting defenders either to the left or right of the Sherwood Foresters

16 This indicates that enemy fire was coming in from the flank (side) as well as the front.

CHAPTER THIRTEEN
WOUNDED

 <u>DOWN THE LINE TO 'BLIGHTY'</u>

DODGING DEATH

CONTEXT

Sunday, 24th March   9/DAC War Diary

'*Column marched to Grovetown and encamped. Position taken up was within a few yards of the position occupied by the Column during the First Battle of the Somme, 1st July 1916.*'

DIARY

Sunday, 24th March
The March Retreat – wounded

"*In Saturday's list of doings I prophesied that a lot may happen in the next twelve hours and I was right – it did. About one o'clock some of our guns[1] dropped into action close to us and when 'Fritz' let fly back at them I got one! Our horses were tied to old tree stumps and the shells dropped amongst them. As soon as they started I got my two horses untied and they were mad with terror; I was just getting the upper hand of them when another shell dropped about ten yards behind me. I felt myself go off my feet with the concussion and at the same time my horses gave a great spring and I flew through the air and landed in a big shell-hole. My left heel stuck in the ground and I heard a sharp crack and I found my left leg out of* action. I lay still for a few minutes while several more shells burst around, then I spent about an hour crawling from shell-hole to shell-hole and still under heavy fire. How the pieces missed me I don't know. An officer who tried to get to me was hit in the shoulder. After about an hour and a half of this I managed to get back with the help of a chum and I was carried for about a mile on a stretcher and was then picked up by an ambulance car that was passing. I was taken to the 38th Casualty Clearing Station[2] [just south-east of Abbeville at Pont Rémy, on the edge of the Maricourt Plateau, beside the Somme River].*"

CONTEXT

Many wounded men passed down the line from the location of their injury to the point of their final treatment. This was the same as for Jack Hickman.

C7: Evacuation chain for wounded – battlefield to UK convalescence

- **The Regimental Aid Post (RAP)** was the first line of support available in the trenches themselves and was run by the battalion Medical Officer, his orderlies and stretcher-bearers who were usually a mixture of RAMC and battalion. Survival for the wounded in No Man's Land was complicated by enemy artillery and machine-gun fire; the basic first-aid a soldier carried was a 'first field dressing'[3] and, from 1917, a small ampoule of iodine. A full water-bottle increased his survival chances. Any 'walking wounded' would head for an appropriate 'collecting station', while the more seriously hurt depended on help from a mate[4] or from the brave, unarmed stretcher-bearers.[5] At the RAP, the often-swamped battalion M.O. and his orderlies quickly assessed the wounded, cleaned wounds and tried to staunch bleeding. The last moments of the mortally wounded would be made as comfortable as possible. Every wounded man was tagged with a first diagnosis and a note of any drugs administered and was then moved 'down the line' according to urgency, usually by stretcher-bearer through overcrowded communications trenches. In battle conditions, communications trenches were supposedly designated 'up or 'down' in order to ease congestion, but in practice this had limited effect.

- **The Advanced Dressing Station (ADS)** was further back from the front line and was manned by divisional Field Ambulance personnel of the RAMC. There, a wounded man would usually receive an anti-tetanus inoculation, a clean dressing and a hot drink (and maybe a 'gasper' or cigarette!). In a major battle, the ADS, like the RAP, might soon be swamped by casualties.

- There was often one **Casualty Clearing Station (CCS)**, per division, though likely to be more in a major offensive – these were largely staffed by the RAMC. If a wounded man in an ADS needed further treatment, he would be moved further 'down the line' to a C.C.S. This was often a tented or hutted encampment located behind the lines; effectively, it was a field hospital with several doctors and surgeons who could use the better facilities and who could operate on some of the more urgent cases.

- More serious cases requiring specialised care or treatment would be moved by ambulance train, road, river or canal transport to a **Base** or **General Hospital** nearer the coast. A base hospital could provide the best standard of specialist treatment short of returning to the UK.

- The next decision was whether a man could be adequately treated in a Base Hospital or needed to be evacuated across the Channel to a **War Hospital in the UK**. The most grievously wounded were evacuated by Hospital Ship as soon as they were judged likely to survive the crossing. On arrival in the United Kingdom, most wounded men were moved on, usually by rail, to an appropriate hospital, though rarely close to home.

⬇

- After treatment and (hopefully) recovery, if an army medical board declared a man fit for service, he was sent for a period of **convalescence** at a **Command Depot**, whether home or abroad, prior to his return to duty. If a man was adjudged fit for front line duty, he would eventually reach his old unit or would be transferred whilst en route; a man might be judged fit for 'garrison duty' only, that was less demanding than front line service, though it might see him serve in places such as India, where the hazards of trench fighting were replaced by those of sickness.

'The medical treatment in these [Command Depots]… was of graduated exercises, including massage and therapeutic gymnastics, the ultimate object being to harden individuals sufficiently to enable them to join their reserve battalions within six months in a condition fit for drafting overseas.'

[Macpherson, Sir W.G., 'Medical Services, General History, volume I'].

If declared unfit for further military service, a man was discharged according to King's Regulations.

Reading between the lines of Driver Jack Hickman's written account of his own wounding, it becomes clear that he was not in No Man's Land[6] (as were so many infantrymen who had sustained wounds

on the Western Front) but was the victim of German artillery counter-battery fire near the British gun-line. During the Somme retreat of March-April 1918, British artillery batteries would retire to a fair distance from the German advance, then unhitch the guns in order to lay down harassing fire on the advancing German infantry. In turn, the advancing German artillery would be called into action by their infantry – hence the destructive counter-battery rounds that wounded Jack and killed his horses.

Note: There are certain discernible discrepancies between Jack's written account and the 'family legend' account as passed down orally through the generations by Jack and his descendants. This is a regular occurrence with oral history – tales vary with the teller, with the attention span of the listener, and with the passage of time from the original incident. As the listener later passes on the story, so the tale's detail and emphasis subtly shift – it's not deliberate, it's merely human nature! Below is offered a comparison of the two accounts.

The family legend – the oral account

Jack was riding or driving six horses during a German attack. He heard a voice in his head telling him to let go the reins to the lead horse that were wound round his arms. The voice in his head repeated the instruction. Jack loosed the reins, releasing the horses, which were blown to pieces; Jack was blown clear

by the explosion of the shell, though he sustained wounds to face and leg in the process.

THE WRITTEN ACCOUNT IN JACK'S DIARY, IN THE LIGHT OF OTHER RESEARCH

Sunday, 24th March

"About one o'clock some of our guns..." [most likely 18-pounders – see endnote 1 of this chapter] *"...dropped into action close to us and when 'Fritz' let fly back at them I got one [a wound]! Our horses were tied to old tree stumps and the shells dropped amongst them. As soon as they started I got my two horses..."* [most

Jack Hickman's Service Record for 1918-1919, showing his wounding and repatriation to England.

likely riding mounts[7] for Jack and his officer as there is no mention of GS[8] or ammunition wagons] *"…untied and they were mad with terror; I was just getting the upper hand of them when another shell dropped about ten yards behind me. I felt myself go off my feet with the concussion and at the same time my horses gave a great spring and I flew through the air and landed in a big shell-hole."* [Clearly, Jack had not been riding the horses; most likely, he was waiting for his officer]. *"My left heel stuck in the ground and I heard a sharp crack…,"* [a sound that could have been that of either ligaments or bone] *"…and I found my left leg out of action. I lay still for a few minutes while several more shells burst around, then I spent about an hour crawling from shell-hole to shell-hole and still under heavy fire. How the pieces [shell-case shrapnel] missed me I don't know. An officer who tried to get to me was hit in the shoulder…"* [This may have been Jack's officer, Lieutenant Ozanne, or an officer from the gun batteries]. *"After about an hour and a half of this I managed to get back with the help of a chum and I was carried for about a mile on a stretcher and was then picked up by an ambulance car that was passing. I was taken to the 38th Casualty Clearing Station."* [The diary reference to *"…flying through the air"*, is compatible with the *"…voice in his head telling him to let go the reins,"* in that whether riding or dismounted and calming his horses, Jack would likely have held the reins wound round his arm to give greater control of the terrified animals. The combination of holding tightly to the reins and a nearby explosion would have caused the horses to rear suddenly, throwing Jack off balance and leading to his injuries.]

According to Jack's service record (shown on page 283) he had suffered, *"…Gunshot wounds to face and left ankle…in the field…and was admitted to 38 C.C.S. on 24.3.18."* Rather than, *'… gunshot wounds'*, it is more likely that Jack was wounded by flying shrapnel from an exploding shell.

DIARY

Sunday, 24th March, continued…
38th C.C.S., Pont Rémy
(…on the Somme River, south-east of Abbeville)
"On Sunday morning, at daybreak, the doctors and attendants came round and got up anybody who could walk at all – even cases who were not supposed to sit up had to walk if they could. We were told it was our only chance to get away as the Germans were advancing and looked like taking the lot [that is, taking the whole of the British line in the Amiens sector, reaching the sea and effectively splitting the British from their French allies]. Two chaps picked me up and carried me out to a motor that was passing by and finally got me to the railway station and put me with others on an [ambulance] train. From about nine o'clock on Sunday until daylight on Tuesday (26th March) we were

on the rail until we finally reached the 22nd General Hospital at Cammiers (sic) at the army base." [Camiers/Dammes-Camiers, three miles north of Etaples – operated from mid-June 1915 to early January 1919].

Tuesday, 26th March
22nd General Hospital (Camiers, near Etaples)
"We are now fixed up well and are comfortable. We were told this morning that we are for Blighty tomorrow [Wednesday, 27th], so we are all smiling and waiting for tomorrow!"

[Sadly, Jack and his wounded mates would have to wait a few more days for their evacuation across the Channel, so it was fortunate that they felt well cared for. The doctors and nurses at 22nd General, a Canadian hospital staffed by Canadians and Americans, certainly left a profound and lasting impression on Jack Hickman and at the foot of the page that bears his diary entry for 24th March are written details of the ward sister, one of the, *"… very fine people"*, who cared so well for the young soldier:

'- - - - *Sister, Edith M. S- - - , 22 General Hospital, France'*, and *'St. John- - - , N.B. (New Brunswick), Canada.']*

[St. John, New Brunswick lies on the northern coast of the Bay of Fundy, on

An ambulance train with double-doors to facilitate loading stretcher cases.

Canada's eastern seaboard. In 1918 there were several hospitals at which Sister Edith might have worked in civilian life – Saint John T.B. Hospital, East Saint John, New Brunswick; Saint John Old General Public Hospital, Waterloo Street, Saint John, New Brunswick.]

Over the page is written in ink:

'Kathleen R. Harris, 22 General Hospital, 246 Summit Ave., Summit (City), (Union County) N.J. (New Jersey), U.S.A.'

[Summit is located ten miles west of Newark and Jersey City. There were three hospitals in Summit City in which Kathleen Harris might have worked in more peaceful times, the most likely one being Overlook Hospital, which was founded in 1906. Jack probably intended to write to the nurses after the war had ended – whether or not he actually did write will never be known.]

CONTEXT

Wednesday, 27th March
9/DAC War Diary
Despite the German onslaught, the men of the Column maintained a good spirit and continued to carry out their vital job after Jack's evacuation.

'During the whole of the retirement the Column supplied the Battery Wagon Lines with ammunition

and when possible dumped any ammunition available at any known future Battery positions. Officers, men, animals, wagons etc., were posted and handed over to Batteries to replace casualties and deficiencies.'

DIARY

Easter Sunday, 31st March
Base Hospital, Camiers
"I am still in the base hospital [22nd General Hospital]. I have been expecting to cross over to Blighty for three days but it has not yet come off. Things here are very comfortable – it is a Canadian Hospital run by Canadian and American staff; all the [medical] staff are very fine people [see details above of individuals]. The weather today has been lovely but the previous few days have been very showery. A large stream of wounded men still keeps coming in, with a few going out. Everybody tells of terrific fighting everywhere."

CONTEXT

Wednesday, 3rd April
Across the Channel to 'Blighty'
During the early hours of Wednesday morning a former Channel ferry, A.T. *'Ville de Liège'*, nosed out from the haven of Calais port and into the sea swell. Aboard were the seriously wounded Jack Hickman and more than one hundred similarly injured or sick soldiers. The vessel was not a fully-equipped hospital ship but a ferry that had been converted

A.T. 'Ville de Liège' in which a wounded Jack Hickman crossed the Channel on 3rd April 1918.

into an ambulance transport that saw service in that vital role from March 1917. *'Ville de Liège'* was one of four[9] major Channel ferries/Mail Steamers owned by Belgian steamship companies or the Belgian government that were converted into ambulance transports. A.T. *'Ville de Liège'* was in service as an ambulance transport from 16th March 1917 until 28th March 1919 offering accommodation for seven sick officers and 166 other ranks. The sick and wounded were tended by thirty RAMC and St. John Ambulance orderlies under three officers and one warrant officer. The escorted[10] transport, with its wearied and bloodied cargo, eased out into the Channel and headed towards the white smudge on the horizon – for Dover and *'Blighty'.* Jack's front line service was over – for the moment.

DIARY

Thursday, 4th April – Fusehill War Hospital, Carlisle, Cumberland

"At last I am back in Blighty! We left France yesterday morning about three a.m. and came via Calais to Dover [by Ambulance Transport ship, 'Ville de Liège']. We left the latter place [Dover] about three p.m. and came up [by train] through Chatham, Clapham, Kensington and Rugby, finally reaching Carlisle about three o'clock this morning, where I am now installed in what was once a workhouse[11], now a Voluntary Aid Detachment [V.A.D.] ward."

CONTEXT

Thursday, 4th April to Friday, 21st June – Fusehill War Hospital, Carlisle

Fusehill War Hospital, previously the Carlisle Workhouse.

The hospital in Fusehill Street to which a travel-weary Jack was admitted in the early hours of the morning, had begun life in 1863 as the Carlisle Union Workhouse. Designed by Lockwood & Mawson, it accommodated 478 inmates and had cost the princely sum of £11,195.15s. The First World War saw the first use of the buildings as a military hospital. As a whole,

Fusehill War Hospital was established in the buildings and grounds of the Poor Law Hospital and two Carlisle schools – Brook Street School and Newtown School, whose children were, *"...drafted to other schools."* Following a Red Cross meeting at Workington in April 1916, to discuss the need for a, *"...large military hospital for 500..."* in the area, a letter was sent by the Carlisle Board of Guardians[12] proposing the, *"...use of Fusehill Workhouse as a military hospital."*

The *'Carlisle Journal'* announced that, *"...Carlisle is to become an important centre for the treatment of wounded soldiers..."* So many wounded soldiers were returning to Blighty for treatment that, *"...Fusehill was to become a base hospital in place of (Fazakerley) Liverpool"*, which had reached its capacity. The transformation of the workhouse and

two schools required extensive work and also meant that new homes had to be found for the workhouse inmates – the children in the workhouse at Harraby Hill (formerly St. Cuthbert's Workhouse) were moved into Shap and the adults at Fusehill were duly transferred to Harraby Hill. The new Fusehill War Hospital opened on 16th October 1917 and the first batch of 170 wounded arrived soon after its inauguration; the hospital was run, *"...under a strict code of military rules"*, and was administered by the Local Government Board (LGB). Fusehill accepted new cases until June 1919, during which time it treated 9,809 military patients with a maximum number of 861 beds occupied (...which actually far exceeded the hospital's official capacity of 650). The beds were located on three sites, as follows:-

Carlisle Fusehill War Hospital	400 beds (Other Ranks)
Brook Street School Section	170 beds (Other Ranks)
Newtown School Section	80 beds (Other Ranks)

This capacity was increased by a further 30 beds in November 1918 when the former munitions-workers' hostel at Eden Bridge was opened for the reception of wounded. So on 1st November 1918, when a new matron was appointed to oversee Fusehill Hospital, there were 680 beds and 80 nurses in her charge. Jack arrived six months prior to the Eden Bridge development, at a time when the hospital was working at near capacity to establish its reputation; the

Nurses accompany wounded soldiers wearing hospital 'blues' in the snow at Fusehill.

trepidation apparent in Jack's diary entry referring to, "*...once a workhouse...*", was to prove unfounded in his own case and he personally recorded no criticism of Fusehill Hospital.

The cessation of hostilities in November 1918 did not presage an end to the admission of military sick and wounded – in fact, hospital recreational facilities were even extended in December when a new entertainment hut was opened. Inevitably, with the passage of time numbers dropped noticeably as the hospital gradually lost its reason for existence. Finally, in June 1919 the hospital and its annexes closed completely[13] when any remaining soldiers undergoing treatment were transferred south. Today, the most obvious link with the Great War is the adjacent Carlisle (Dalston Road) War Cemetery that contains 134 CWGC[14] headstones of men who sadly died in Fusehill War Hospital.

DIARY

Friday, 21st June
Discharged from Hospital – On Leave
"*I was discharged from hospital today and proceeded on ten days' leave. I am still a bit groggy on my feet but I get about with the aid of a stick. My stay at Carlisle was a very pleasant one and the people of the town were very good to the 'boys in blue'[15].*"

[Jack's service record indicates that he was discharged on 21st June 1918, having spent seventy-nine days at Fusehill; his injury was noted as,

"*...Simple fracture.....face and left fibula (sustained in action).*"]

Monday, 1st July
Royal Artillery Command Depot
(Ripon, Yorkshire)
"*Today I left home for Ripon [south] in Yorkshire which is the Command Depot[16] for the Artillery [also for the Royal Air Force]. I arrived late in the afternoon and was not much impressed by my first sight of it but the countryside around looks very nice.*" [Jack's time at Ripon was undoubtedly intended as part convalescence and in part to test and increase his physical fitness with a view to returning him to the front line – an experienced artilleryman was a valuable commodity. Technically, he was serving with No.7 Battery.]

Saturday, 10th August
Charlton Park Training Depot
"*[After forty days] I left Ripon quite fit and I am now at Charlton Park Training Depot [Woolwich]. I shall soon be on my way to France now I expect but it won't be quite so 'hot' as when I left it, according to the good news lately.*" [Jack's information was clearly out of date; two days previously, 8th August, had seen the Allies, mainly British and Australian troops, turn the German tide in front of the vital Lower Somme city of Amiens. Although the Allies were essentially on the

front foot thereafter, Jack was quite wrong to employ the phrase, '...not quite so hot,' – the British Empire and its troops would suffer in excess of 375,000 more casualties between Amiens at the start of August and the November 11th Armistice.]

CONTEXT

Sunday, 11th August

This was the official date of Jack's posting to, '...*5C Reserve Brigade, Charlton Park*', (just to the south of the Woolwich Arsenal).

Wednesday, 18th September
Abbey Wood, Lessness Park

[Source - Service Record] Posted to, '...*61st Reserve Battery, RFA*', at Abbey Wood, Lessness Park, Bexley Heath (three miles east of Woolwich).

Wednesday, 25th September
Return to France

One week later, Jack Hickman received his posting to the British Expeditionary Force, France and was soon on his way to a Channel port.

1   Most likely 18-pounders of the 9th Divisional Field Artillery batteries (probably A/50, B/50, C/50, A/51, B/51, C/51; D/50 and D/51 were howitzers, less easy to bring rapidly into action during a retreat or advance.

2   38th C.C.S. had very recently returned from duty in Italy on the Southern Front and had set up at Pont Rémy just two days prior to Jack Hickman's wounding.

3   The '*first field dressing*' in 1918 contained, "Two dressings in waterproof covers, each consisting of a gauze pad stitched to a bandage, and a safety pin." (The quoted description appeared on the packaging of the dressing – the two dressings were for the 'entry' and 'exit' wounds).

4   Soldiers were instructed to not stop to help wounded comrades during an attack; this did not preclude gallant men leaving the relative safety of their trench to rescue wounded mates, as the incident of Jack Hickman's wounding demonstrates.

5   The most highly-decorated 'other rank' of the Great War was a stretcher-bearer, Lance-Corporal Bill Coltman VC, DCM and bar, MM and bar.

6   Once the German Spring Offensive broke through Allied lines, 'normal' No Man's Land on the Somme effectively ceased to exist – trench warfare gave way to open, mobile warfare as the retreat continued towards Amiens, forty miles distant.

7   All units had a proportion of riding horses. (Army classifications R1 – cavalry, & R2 - yeomanry). Yeomanry was the Territorial Force cavalry.

8   'GS' stood for 'General Service' wagon that was usually hauled by a team of six Light Draught horses (Army classification LD2).

9   The other three Belgian-owned ferries were 'Pieter de Connick', 'Jan Breydel' and 'Stad Antwerpen' – each served between two and four years as a cross-Channel ambulance transport. 'Pieter de Connick' was considerably larger than the other three Belgian-owned ferries.

10 A Royal Navy escort was essential as the threat from German U-Boats in the Channel was still valid.

11 'War Hospitals' were usually based upon asylums, poor law infirmaries, fever hospitals and school premises. At the time of the Great War, many such institutions were recently-

built and offered, "...*not only extensive grounds and gardens as well as recreation halls for entertainment but were also going concerns with ample stores and kitchens, water, steam, light and electricity supply – in fact, all that was required by a large hospital.*" ['History of the Great War, Medical Services', volume I.]

12 The Board of Guardians was responsible for administering the Poor Law.

13 Fusehill, however, became the City General Hospital under the 1948 National Health Act; the former workhouse infirmary became the City Maternity Hospital.

14 The Commonwealth War Graves Commission was established after the Great War.

15 'Boys in Blue' refers to the 'hospital blues' uniform (with red tie) that was worn by wounded and recuperating soldiers – it gave them a mark of respect in the eyes of the public and avoided '*why aren't you in the army?*' misunderstandings.

16 "*The medical treatment in these...Command Depots ...was of graduated exercises, including massage and therapeutic gymnastics, the ultimate object being to harden individuals sufficiently to enable them to join their reserve battalions within six months in a condition fit for drafting overseas.*" (Macpherson, Sir W.G., 'Medical Services, General History, volume I').

CHAPTER FOURTEEN
JACK IN HOSPITAL

THE 'NINTH' AT THE FRONT

APRIL TO OCTOBER 1918

CONTEXT

On 3rd April 1918, Jack Hickman crossed the Channel in a secure bunk aboard A.T. *'Ville de Liège'*, on the next leg of his journey to a war hospital in the UK.

Between 24th March and 3rd April Jack's mates in 9th 'Scottish', like the rest of Fifth Army, had been brutally forced to retreat towards the lines around Albert. There the infantry of the 'Ninth' was relieved by 4th Australian Division late on 27th March, though the division's artillery remained in action with the Aussies until 31st and was then itself relieved. British high command needed to hold the enemy's forward surge in front of Amiens, while the capture of that city was the prime objective in the German plan to drive a wedge between the French and British elements of the Allied forces on the Somme. The initial forty-mile thrust towards Amiens rattled the confidence of those on the receiving end, but somehow the line, though creaking, held and the rapid German advance began to lose its vital momentum.

Jack Hickman was one of 9th Division's 1,912 wounded; 330 had been killed and 2,865 were recorded as 'missing in action'.

In total, the Somme retreat had cost the Scots 5,107 casualties. Replacements were desperately needed.

Ludendorff's attempt to settle the issue before the American troops could swing the balance of strength towards the Allied side then turned north to try to smash through the British-held front on the River Lys, just to the south of the Ypres Salient. This second element of *'die Kaiserschlacht'*[1] was codenamed Operation *'Georgette'*. On 9th April, four days after the early impetus of Operation *'Michael'* had slightly eased on the Somme front, the whirlwind crashed into a twenty-five mile Flanders sector from La Bassée to Ypres. The initial aim of the Lys plan was to capture what remained of the town of Armentières, then surge westwards on to the transport hub of Hazebrouck; the obvious intention was to isolate the British troops at Ypres and thus force their withdrawal across the Channel. However, speed was of the essence as the arrival of American battalions on the Western Front[2] was building a formidable Allied force.

That the divisional artillery of 9th 'Scottish' had been well led for the two years since February 1916 was clearly confirmed when, on 28th March 1918, Major-General H.H. Tudor (the division's C.R.A.[3]) was appointed to command 9th Division. Tudor's reputation had always been sound but during the Somme retreat he was outstanding. His replacement as C.R.A. was Brigadier-General H.R. Wainwright DSO who served in the role until the Armistice.

On 2nd and 3rd April the bulk of the division had moved north by rail, DHQ being established at Scherpenberg and, as soon as 4th April, the 26th 'Highland' Brigade with 27th 'Lowland' Brigade were relieving part of 1st Australian Division in the 3,000 yard sector from the remains of Hollebeke village, across the Ypres-Comines Canal to Bulgar Wood. The division had moved north with the Army Commander's words of praise ringing in their ears,

'...*Great gallantry has been shown by the troops engaged in the fighting in this area [The Somme] and to the south of it. The Nineteenth ['Western'] and Ninth ['Scottish'] Divisions have distinguished themselves by the valour of their defence.'*

[Sir Douglas Haig, Press Communiqué, 25th March 1918.]

Within a few days 9th 'Scottish' Division's excellent, staunch reputation was to be put to another stringent test. The division was part of Second Army's IX Corps for the fighting of 10th-11th April, to be known as the Second Battle of Messines. The situation was soon critical, as shown by Sir Douglas Haig's remarkable Special Order of 11th April (see page 294).

The desperate nature of the coming German offensive was to be felt by all the divisions along the front line astride the River Lys. Near Wytschaete, just to the south of Ypres, nineteen year-old Private John Burgess's unit, 2nd Battalion, the Lincolnshire Regiment (62nd Brigade, 21st Division, Second Army, IX Corps), lay directly in the path of the German advance. John, prior to his enlistment on 16th February 1916, had worked on his father's farm at Newlands, Pelsall, South Staffordshire. He had not been sent to France until 12th March 1918 and thus had been at the front just one month when he stood on the fire-step in mid-April facing the grey-clad German swarms. However, during the course of that single month John Burgess had had to withstand the first four desperate days of Operation 'Michael' on the Somme (21st–25th March) before the Lincolns were moved north towards Messines and Bailleul on the southern edge of the Ypres Salient where they fought between 10th and 15th April. 2/Lincolnshire had arrived at Kemmel on 3rd April and next day relieved the Australians in the line near Wytschaete, remaining there

---

Special Order of the Day by Field-Marshal Sir Douglas Haig, K.T., G.C.B.

To all ranks of the British army in France and Flanders

"Three weeks ago to-day the enemy began his terrific attacks against us on a fifty-mile front. His objects are to separate us from the French, to take the Channel ports, and destroy the British army. In spite of throwing already 106 Divisions into the battle, and enduring the most reckless sacrifice of human life, he has as yet made little progress towards his goal. We owe this to the determined fighting and self-sacrifice of our troops. Words fail me to express the admiration which I feel for the splendid resistance offered by all ranks of our army under the most trying circumstances. Many amongst us now are tired. To those I would say that victory will belong to the side which holds out the longest. The French army is moving rapidly and in great force to our support. There is no other course open to us but to fight it out. Every position must be held to the last man; there must be no retirement. With our backs to the wall, and believing in the justice of our cause, each one of us must fight on to the end. The safety of our homes and the freedom of mankind alike depend upon the conduct of each one of us at this critical moment."

General Headquarters

D. Haig

F. M.

Commander-in-Chief
British Armies in France   Thursday, 11th April 1918

---

until 7th. The battalion then spent two days cleaning, refitting and reorganising before moving into a gap in the line in front of Wytschaete late on 10th April until their eventual relief on 15th when they marched to camp at Rossignol Wood (Nightingale Wood). Although out of the line on 16th, 2nd Battalion was stood to all day while their sister battalion, 1/Lincolnshire, experienced one of their grimmest days of the entire war as the *'History of the Lincolnshire Regiment 1914-1918'*[4] describes,

"...During the day of 16th April (from 4:30 a.m.) the enemy had attacked in thick fog after an hour-long barrage. The Germans broke through and inflicted huge casualties on 1/Lincolns. The heroic actions of 1/Lincolns enabled a defensive flank to be secured and 2/Lincolns, who had been standing to all day, were pushed forward to....take part in the

counter attack that evening…at 7:30 p.m.…..'The attack was most gallantly carried out under very heavy machine gun fire from the front and the right flank and pushed to a trench within fifty to one hundred yards of the first objective, which was made good. This attack was carried out by the battalion after a week's heavy fighting, no sleep the previous night and only partially reorganised after the recent Somme fighting. It was carried out with the greatest dash and vigour and only the Colonel's [5] fine leadership and the fine spirit of all ranks in the face of every difficulty…..enabled the attack to gain the ground it did. The battalion consolidated the ground won.' 17th April, the battalion remained in the front line until relieved by No. 2 Composite Battalion, 39th Division."

Young John Burgess was reported by the *'Walsall Observer'* newspaper as 'missing in action' but he had actually been killed on 17th April as 2nd Lincolnshire awaited their relief. A victim of Operation *'Georgette'*, he is buried in the beautiful Wytschaete Military Cemetery, just to the west of that village.

Throughout the remainder of the month of April, 9th 'Scottish' Division was almost continuously in action on the Lys, desperately grappling with an enemy that was throwing all its resources into securing a vital breakthrough. 9th Division was part of Second Army's XXII Corps for four consecutive battles that, though named separately, blended almost into one continual struggle – from 13th-15th April was the Battle of Bailleul; from 17th-19th April, the First Battle of Kemmel Ridge; from 25th-26th April, the Second Battle of Kemmel Ridge and on 29th April, the Battle of the Scherpenberg, though only the exhausted 9th Division's severely depleted South African Brigade[6] was involved, under 49th Division command. Whereas 26th and 27th Brigades were receiving good numbers of reinforcements, the South Africans enjoyed no such luxury. Even so, the replacements were but callow youths who, though fit, had seen no previous action at the front. To make matters more complex, 9th 'Scottish' was ordered to take over further sectors of the front from hard-pressed 19th 'Western' Division on their right – which the Scots duly accomplished on 10th April. The following day saw some ground ceded but 12th to 15th saw a lull in the infantry attacks on 9th Division – the artillery bombardment was, however, merciless and expensive of life. By 15th April 9th Division, strengthened by a number of attached reinforcements, was responsible for 9,000 yards of front line, though on 16th April Wytschaete was lost to the enemy and a valiant counter-attack was ultimately unsuccessful. From 17th to 24th April there were no infantry assaults but artillery fire was relentless. Covering the divisional front during this period were 50th and 51st Brigades, RFA; keeping them supplied throughout with shells was 9/DAC. According to the War Diary, during this terrible fortnight 9/DAC occupied camps at Westoutre, Poperinghe and Hoograaf,

'...*From the 9th Inst., Nos. 1 & 2 Sections were continuously engaged in assisting Batteries transporting ammunition to Gun Lines and Wagon Lines, the SAA Section being engaged on work for the Infantry.*'

In the Divisional History, John Ewing described in glowing terms the actions of 9th 'Scottish':

'*The stone-wall defence of the Highlanders (of 26th Brigade) had put a final stop to the enemy's northern onrush, which had rolled up the front and immediate supports of three brigades and threatened our hold on Ypres.*'

'*The shattered fragments of the Ninth, with the exception of the South African Brigade and the artillery, were relieved by the Forty-ninth Division at 11 a.m. on the 26th.*'

On 29th April, 6/Royal Scots Fusiliers resisted a vicious bombardment from Mount Kemmel then braved the infantry assault that followed. John Ewing recognises the significance of the defence on the Lys,

'*That date (29th April) marks the failure of the German designs in Flanders...*'

whose intention, according to Sir Douglas Haig, was to,

'...*separate us from the French, to take the Channel Ports and destroy the British Army.*'

9th 'Scottish' Division had thus played no small part in frustrating Ludendorff's plans on the Lys. The final comment on 9th Division's contribution should, of course, be reserved for Field Marshal Sir Douglas Haig,

'*Please convey to General Tudor and to all ranks of the Ninth Division my deepest appreciation of the great gallantry displayed by them during many days of severe fighting north of the Lys......they have shown the same high qualities which distinguished them throughout the Battle south of Arras and have most worthily upheld the traditions of the British Army.*'

For the division, the price of such 'glory' had been high – 3,879 officers and men killed, wounded or missing. On balance, the badly wounded Jack Hickman must be counted as one of the luckier members of the division.

Jack's enforced absence from his unit during June spared him experiencing an outbreak of one of the more virulent sicknesses that affected soldiers of the Great War. Trench fever, as it became known, was especially common on the Western Front as the disease was transmitted by infected body lice, a problem from which every soldier, irrespective of rank, constantly suffered. The disease, not well understood until the final year of the war, was frequently diagnosed as influenza as there were several symptoms common to both and at various times it was known as 'shin fever', 'five-day fever' and even confused with typhoid. In 1918 it was established that the disease was a result of the bite and the excretions of body lice, an unavoidable consequence of large numbers of men living in close proximity in the unsanitary conditions of the trenches. The incubation period for the disease was (and still is) about a fortnight, though the eventual onset of symptoms was strikingly sudden.

'In a typical instance the man was suddenly affected with faintness or vertigo, frontal headache and pain in the back, which so violently descended to the legs that the condition came to be known as "shin fever". By the time the patient arrived at the ambulance his temperature was 102 degrees and the tongue furred; there was nausea and constipation. The man was in much greater misery than the symptoms would appear to warrant, for the pulse was not above 80; there was no cough; the lungs were free...'

[Sir Andrew Macphail, *'Official History of the Canadian Forces in the Great War 1914-19: The Medical Services'*, 1925.]

A bout of trench fever generally lasted five or so days (hence one of its nicknames) and was of the relapsing type, with symptoms rising and falling. Full recovery took upwards of a month, though men were often returned to their units more 'promptly' than this! Sadly, the debilitating disease might recur as a first experience of it did not confer any immunity. Fatalities directly attributable to trench fever were almost unknown although where high fever persisted, a man became increasingly vulnerable to heart failure.

So, for a unit that had been used as a reliable spearhead, the outbreak in June of 1918 of trench fever with its debilitating side effects, spread concern throughout the entire division. Many men, both officers and other ranks, were hospitalised then returned to duty within two to three weeks, fortunately at a juncture when 9th 'Scottish' was out of the line.

There was also a welcome distraction in June when a number of American officers and N.C.O.s were temporarily attached to 9th 'Scottish' for instruction in the ways of trench warfare – the 'Ninth' was certainly highly experienced! John Ewing described the 'Doughboys' most favourably,

'...they were agreeable companions and enthusiastic workers and willingly joined in enterprises carried out by the units to which they were attached.'

[John Ewing: *'9th Divisional History'*]

For the Divisional Ammunition Column, 17th June witnessed a reduction in establishment of thirty-six drivers and seventy-two animals, leaving all ammunition wagons as four-horse teams. The new format was tested in battle just two days later, at Méteren.

That summer, 9th 'Scottish' Division was to be involved in just one more considerable action prior to the Allied armies commencing a long-awaited advance – the Capture of Méteren on 19th July as part of Second Army's XV Corps. The infantry's[7] capture of the village was meticulously prepared by the artillery.

'For a fortnight previous to the attack, heavies, field guns and trench mortars poured a never-ending stream of missiles into Méteren and completely flattened it.'

[John Ewing: *'9th Divisional History'*]

The work of the gunners more or less ensured that, *'...the operation....was a brilliant triumph.'* It was more than appropriate that the Ninth recaptured the village of Méteren; when the division had been there for the first time, on 17th May 1915, it had proved to be an experience that more than rattled the certainties of the Scots' youthful enthusiasm. Then, Jack Hickman had recorded his thoughts thus,

"We...travelled [due east through Hazebrouck] to the little village of Méteren [about two miles to the west of Bailleul], camping about a mile outside of the village at about 6 p.m. Here we had our first glimpse of the battlefields of Flanders. Just before we reached Méteren we saw several graves of British soldiers in cornfields by the roadsides – in the church at Méteren, the Germans had had two machine guns mounted and from there had mowed down the Warwicks."

Today, row upon row in the Méteren Military Cemetery, lie men of 1914 who were ambushed on 13th October by German defenders in the village who were nevertheless overwhelmed later that day; close by those *'Old Contemptibles'* are the graves of lads from 9th 'Scottish' Division who lost their lives in the successful quest to recapture Méteren[8] during June and July of 1918 [see Appendix 6 for more details]. The *'Warwicks'* referred to in Jack's diary entry was 1st Battalion, the Royal Warwickshire Regiment (1/RWR), part of 10th Brigade in Major-General Wilson's 4th Division; the division had been with the BEF on the Western Front since the Retreat from Mons in August 1914. 1/RWR comprised pre-war regulars topped up by reservists and the battalion knew how to fight but they buried many of their friends on the battlefield that day in October 1914 – German machine-guns ensured that. The *'roadside graves'* seen by the young volunteers in 1914 probably totalled about thirty-three as this is the number of 'Warwicks' whom a cemetery register later described as, 'buried near this spot'; another twenty-two men of 1/RWR were buried in the cemetery itself, reaching a final total of fifty-five Warwicks killed at Méteren on 13th October 1914. Not only were lads from 1/RWR killed that day – 10th Brigade also lost eighteen men from 2/Seaforth Highlanders and three from Royal Irish Fusiliers; 12th Brigade lost ten men from 1/King's Own (Royal Lancaster Regiment) and five from 2/Essex. One of the men from 1/King's Own, Lieutenant A.G.A. Morris (27), lies in an isolated but marked battlefield grave on the south-western outskirts of Méteren village.

Recapturing Méteren in July 1918 cost 9th 'Scottish' Division 171 men killed (on the day of the battle plus preparations and aftermath) – the small village had proven costly for both the Midlanders and the Scots.

It was outside Amiens on 8th August that the war finally turned in favour of the Allies as the German line was pushed back on what their commander, General Ludendorff, later described as the, 'Black Day of the German Army.' Though no-one knew it at the time, this success was to presage what subsequently came to be termed the 'Advance to Victory'. 9th Division's first substantial part in this incipient war of movement came in their orders from the XV Corps on 10th August when the Scots were tasked to capture the Hoegnacker Ridge that lay just over a mile beyond the recently-captured village of Méteren and afforded the enemy excellent observation posts. In the event, on the day of the assault, 18th August, meticulous preparation delivered an impressive success that was followed on 22nd by the start of the enemy's retreat from the Lys salient. As 'reward' for success, on 24th/25th August 9th 'Scottish' was withdrawn from the firing line for a well-deserved rest in the area of Wardrecques where the Small Arms Ammunition section of the DAC joined the infantry, leaving the rest of the Column in the Flêtre region. Interestingly, while at 'rest', the War Diary records that,

'...About ten wagons [were] working daily on harvesting work...'

So, it seems, that among the scars of battle, everyday life struggled to go on as it had ever done. However, between 1st and 12th September, the harvest of crops gave way to the harvest of war in that, between Flêtre and Caestre,

'...1 & 2 sections...were engaged in salving ammunition, camouflage etc. from vacated Battery positions.'

By now the Allied advance was getting under way and 9th 'Scottish', refreshed by three weeks out of the line, was transferred from the XV Corps to Lieutenant-General Jacobs' II Corps (though still part of General Plumer's Second Army). Somewhat less refreshed after its salvage exertions, 9/DAC moved camp to the east of Vlamertinghe and by

30th September the entire DAC was to the east of Ypres. The 9/DAC diary entry for the last date indicates that a new war of movement was not far off.

'...*Ammunition taken up to Zonnebeke area and east of it. Roads very congested with traffic and wagons [were] out from 14 to 18 hours at a time.*'

From 28th September to 2nd October, 9th Division played a part in the Battle of Ypres – 9/DAC was encamped near Potijze on the Zonnebeke road where the unit remained until 14th October. Zero hour on 28th September was at 5:25 a.m. and by 8 a.m. 28th and 26th Brigades had captured Bellewaerde and Frézenberg Ridges. For once, the artillery was soon required to advance in order to provide a creeping barrage for the infantry's final objective – Anzac Ridge. Success was the order of the day and by 11:30 a.m. the Scots had taken most of the main ridge from the Polygone de Zonnebeke to Broodseinde. At 12:30 p.m. Gheluvelt village and Broodseinde Ridge were clearly in Allied hands – taken by 26th 'Highland Brigade' of the 'Ninth', 29th Division and 8th Belgian Division. General Tudor of 9th Division sent forward the 27th 'Lowland Brigade' towards Becelaere village; though 11th and 12th Royal Scots met intense resistance from enemy gun batteries and machine-guns, at 4 p.m. Molenhoek Ridge, the high ground to the north of the village and Becelaere village itself

were under Allied control. This day's work marked a most impressive advance at relatively light cost. Now the problem remained of how to re-supply the guns and feed the men and beasts; hardly a single road was passable and the volume of ammunition, food and water had to be moved forward. It was at that point that it was decided that pack animals rather than wagons were the answer to a vital and difficult question.

By 11:25 a.m. on the following day, 29th September, the infantry had captured the Keiberg Spur, broken through the enemy's next line and taken Waterdamhoek. Hot on the heels of the 'foot-sloggers' was 50th Brigade RFA that soon was installed on the Keiberg Spur. General Tudor maintained the momentum of the attack and, despite more stubborn defence from the machine-guns of the '*Flanders I. Stellung*', Dadizeele had been captured by 4 p.m. – 9th Division's success, relative to the 36th 'Ulster' Division on the right and the Belgians on the left, both of whom had met stiff resistance, had left Tudor's men in a salient, rendered all the more worrying by the enemy's continued possession of Hill 41. This was confirmed the next day when almost no progress was made, except the capture then subsequent loss of Hill 41; however, 50th and 51st Brigades RFA moved forward to Slypskapelle and were brought into action. Now the weather took a hold and the rain that had bedevilled the advance intensified and ammunition supplies to the forward guns were restricted by impossibly difficult supply lines. The enemy took advantage of the brief lull to bring up reinforcements, attempting to frustrate 9th Division's efforts to attain their objective of Ledeghem – the battle ebbed and flowed about the village but the advance had temporarily lost impetus despite the raw courage of the divisional gunners. In respect of the latter, the bravery of Lieutenant Gorle of 50th Brigade RFA in advancing his guns under the noses of German machine-gunners[9], justifiably earned him a Victoria Cross.

The II Corps Commander, General Jacobs, praised 9th 'Scottish' in glowing terms,

'…The Ninth Division was specially selected to carry out the attack… you broke right through the enemy's line to a depth of 9¼ miles. In 1917 it took our army over three months to get only half that distance and at great cost. The Ninth Division has done it…in twenty-four hours. What further evidence is required of the magnificence of this exploit?' '…These last operations will be considered by history to have eclipsed all their (9th Division's) previous performances. In the last few days the conditions have been trying and you have had to beat off many counter-attacks. The weather has been bad and shelter has been very scanty. Yet…you have upheld the splendid traditions of the British Army and of the [Ninth] Division in particular.'

[Lieutenant-General C.W. Jacobs, *'Special Order'*, 3rd October 1918.]

As the Allies advanced, so minor salients based on Lille and Douai developed in the German front line, protruding invitingly towards the Allies. Rather than employ artillery to destroy these urban areas, it was decided to employ a strategy of encirclement, leading to a German evacuation to a safer line. Thus the next stage of the advance (to be known to history as the Battle of Courtrai) was planned for 14th October. 9th 'Scottish' Division was tasked by the II Corps command to take the Courtrai-Lendelede Railway line, then to secure the important crossings over the River Lys between the towns of Courtrai and Harlebeke – the required advance was of eight miles, a distance unimagined in the days of trench warfare. As the plan evolved and written orders were handed down, so the Scots suffered from the attentions of speculative German artillery shoots as well as from numerous aerial bombing raids – the worst enemy night 'visitation' cost the lives of seventy-six artillery horses in the transport lines. When the preparatory barrage opened at 5:32 a.m. on 14th October (incidentally the 952nd anniversary of the pivotal Battle of Hastings), the hurricane 'shoot' developed into a lifting barrage when the infantry advanced three minutes later. Ahead lay an enemy of unknown determination, the un-reconnoitred Wuldambeek stream, Rolleghem Capelle and dense fields of vicious barbed wire inter-laced with concrete pill-boxes housing machine-guns. Though the task was stiff, the Ninth's morale was sky-high and was typified by Private Tommy Ricketts of 1/Newfoundland Regiment who earned the Victoria Cross in 28th Brigade's action on 14th October. The citation reads,

"During the advance from Ledeghem the attack was temporarily held up by heavy hostile fire, and the platoon to which he belonged suffered severe casualties from the fire of a battery at point blank range. Private Ricketts at once volunteered to go forward with his Section Commander and a Lewis gun to attempt to outflank the battery. They advanced by short rushes while subject to severe fire from enemy machine guns. When 300 yards away, their ammunition gave out. The enemy, seeing an opportunity to get their field guns away, began to bring up their gun teams. Private Ricketts at once realized the situation. He doubled back 100 yards, procured some ammunition and dashed back to the Lewis gun, and by very accurate fire drove the enemy and their gun teams into a farm. His platoon then advanced without casualties, and captured four field guns, four machine guns and eight prisoners. A fifth field gun was subsequently intercepted by fire and captured. By his presence of mind in anticipating

the enemy intention and his utter disregard for personal safety, Private Ricketts secured the further supplies of ammunition which directly resulted in these important captures and undoubtedly saved many lives."

Pushing ever forward against unpredictable defence, units of 9th Division were crossing the River Lys by newly-constructed pontoon bridge before midday on 20th October; next day the spearhead paused to straighten the divisional line as the two 'wings' had experienced stubborn resistance. The final attack of this phase occurred on 25th October when brigades of the Ninth, 36th and 41st Divisions assaulted the Ooteghem-Ingoyghem Ridge; against a more determined defence the final significant ridge was eventually captured, though the Scots were harassed by artillery and machine-guns from the nearby Kleineberg. This final success was all the more remarkable as most battalions in Ninth Division could muster as few as 200 'effectives'. In the Divisional History, John Ewing stated,

'This was the last operation of the Division in the war. Since 28th September it had covered over twenty-six miles…and advanced from Ypres to the banks of the [River] Scheldt. And our losses suffered…amounted to only 188 officers and 3,604 other ranks….Throughout the advance the admirable co-operation of all

branches of the Division had been the principal factor in contributing to this glorious result…'

Among this helter-skelter of success, Driver Jack Hickman had returned to front line duty on 15th October with the Headquarters section of 9/DAC. Having suffered such a debilitating injury, Jack's Service Record comments quite simply,

'Posted to HQ 9th Divisional Artillery, from base.'

Jack's return was fortuitous in that over 26th-27th October, 9th Division was relieved by 31st Division and the Scots moved back to reorganise and recuperate in billets in the Lys valley near Harlebeke. On 5th November, the King of the Belgians inspected the division on a former German aerodrome near Harlebeke and Cuerne. The men would be in the same billets when hostilities ceased on 11th November.

The divisional artillery played a crucial and courageous advanced role during September and October but they in turn relied upon the effectiveness and courage of the Ammunition Column to keep the guns firing and the infantry moving relentlessly forward,

'During the whole of the period under review [October 1918] the Column engaged in ammunition duties. Forward dumps were established within easy reach of Battery wagon lines and vacated Battery positions

cleared forward to these dumps in addition to supplying batteries with ammunition or dumping it at convenient points. SAA worked for the infantry only and at each step of the advance established a forward echelon.'

[9/DAC War Diary]

---

1 *'die Kaiserschlacht'* means 'Kaiser's Battle"; it was also known as the Spring Offensive.

2 By the beginning of April there were already over 300,000 American troops in Europe, though their commander, General Pershing, did not want his divisions to fight 'piecemeal'.

3 Commander Royal Artillery.

4 Charles Rudyerd Simpson: '*A History of the Lincolnshire Regiment, 1914-1918'*, (1931).

5 The 2/Lincolnshire's newly-appointed C.O. was Lt.-Colonel Reginald Bastard, DSO.

6 The brigade had but 1,300 men fit to fight – little more than a single battalion.

7 2/Royal Scots Fusiliers and the South African composite battalion were the principal units.

8 Méteren had remained in Allied hands until 16th April 1918 when Operation 'Georgette' swept over some British positions.

9 On occasions his guns were firing over 'open sights' under heavy enemy fire.

CHAPTER FIFTEEN
BACK WITH THE 'NINTH'

ADVANCE & ARMISTICE

BACK TO 9/DAC HQ

CONTEXT

Tuesday 24th September   Crossed Channel to Boulogne

'Posted overseas to BEF France.'

[Jack Hickman's Army Service Record]

DIARY

Wednesday, 25th September
Rest Camp, Boulogne
"*I am once more back in France. We landed at Boulogne today and are now in Lieutenant Martyn's rest camp.*" [The actual name was, 'St. Martin's Rest Camp', which was situated on the hills overlooking the town of Boulogne.]

Sunday, 29th September to Tuesday, 8th October – 1st Convalescent Depot (Harfleur, Normandy)
"*After four days at Boulogne I came today to Harfleur, which is our base [depot]. I am expecting to go up the line any day from now.*"

[Jack was posted to the 1st Convalescent Depot, Harfleur, near Le Havre.]

Tuesday, 15th October
According to records, 15th October was the date Jack was officially,

"*...posted from RFA base to HQ 9/ DAC*".

[Jack Hickman's Army Service Record]

Tuesday, 15th October – Back with 9/DAC near Courtrai, Belgium
"*I have today arrived back at my old unit after a week's travelling from the base. I arrived just in time for some excitement. Our division attacked this morning towards Courtrai [Kortrijk] and they are going strong; many prisoners are coming down and all speak in a very dejected manner of the battle. The success seems too good to be true. This afternoon we moved after the infantry and had a few warm moments on the way. The battlefield*"

over which the infantry went this morning is just as they left it – the dead are still just as they fell and are not a cheerful sight to look upon. We are camped for the night in a German rest camp."

Friday, 18th October   Stokerijhoek
"Today we moved forward again after another attack and once more passed the battlefield with its heaps of dead men, horses, and smashed guns and transport. We are camped for the present in the village of Stokerijhoek – the villages since we left the old Passchendaele battlefield are practically intact while the farmhouses and villages are inhabited by the local Belgians. Many more are coming back into the safer places. Refugees from Courtrai and Harlebeke, which we took this morning, are coming down in their thousands and it is not a very good sight to see some of the poor devils with all that remains of their homes."

Friday, 25th October   Harlebeke
"Today we have moved into Harlebeke and have taken up billets for a rest. 'Fritz' is still going back and can reach us here only with long-range guns, so we hope to get a fortnight's quiet. After that, we don't know what will happen."

CONTEXT

"During these fateful days the Ninth was reorganising near Harlebeke. After a short spell of rest the troops recovered their wonted vigour and

the drawn, haggard look disappeared from the faces of officers and men."

[John Ewing: 'The History of the Ninth (Scottish) Division, 1914-1919']

Saturday, 26th and Sunday, 27th October – Heule
9th Division was relieved by 31st Division and the Ninth moved back to reorganise in billets in the Lys valley near Harlebeke. 9/DAC was encamped in billets in the village of Heule when hostilities ceased on 11th November.

DIARY

Friday, 1st November
"Early this morning we attacked again and everything is going well. Official news is through that both Austria-Hungary [3rd November] and Turkey [30th October] are out of it, leaving 'Fritz' on his own so we expect great things to happen in the near future." [Bulgaria, another of Germany's allies, had already surrendered on 29th October. Thus, by 4th November, Germany was effectively isolated.]

CONTEXT

Tuesday, 5th November
(Heavy rain)

"King of the Belgians inspected the division on a former German aero-drome near Harlebeke and Cuerne."

[Major E.F. Becke]

"On 5th November the whole division was inspected by H.M. King Albert of the Belgians. After the ceremony, H.M. Queen Elisabeth requested General Tudor to cut from his sleeve the divisional sign (a silver thistle on a blue ground that is shown at the head of each chapter); he did so, and she pinned it on her dress. Ever after, the G.O.C. wore only one (divisional) badge."

[John Ewing: 'The History of the Ninth (Scottish) Division.']

DIARY

Wednesday, 6th November
Harlebeke
(Heavy rain)
"We are still at rest in the village of Harlebeke. The news is good, what little we get, but we don't get much and we can't get any papers. The weather is awful, rain all day yesterday and today. Yesterday we were inspected by the King [Albert] and Queen [Elisabeth] of Belgium, from eight in the morning 'till one in the afternoon, soaking wet! I have a cold as a result – hang King Albert! It's pouring in torrents now [10 p.m.]."

Thursday, 7th November
Harlebeke
"The news is still good. The terms of the Armistice have been sent to Germany and they have been given seventy-two hours to decide one way or the other.

The time limit expires at eleven o'clock on Monday morning, the 11th November.

Roll on Monday! In the meantime a very big push is in preparation and if our terms are refused a big blow will be struck at once."

Sunday, 10th November
Armistice announced!
"At last the great news has come! Tonight, at ten minutes to eight, it came to us that Germany was finished and never shall I forget the scenes that followed afterwards. The Jocks' bands were out and we paraded the streets [of Harlebeke] and 'played' holy smoke. It seems impossible to believe that the greatest war in the world's history is now at a close – but it is so!"

CONTEXT

Monday, 11th November
Armistice enacted at 11 a.m.[1]

"...billets in the Lys valley near Harlebeke. In same billets when hostilities ceased on 11th November."

[Major E.F. Becke]

"The event (the Armistice announcement) occasioned the wildest rejoicings and all units in the division celebrated it by a special divine service on the 11th."

[John Ewing: 'The History of the Ninth (Scottish) Division]

OUTLINE OF THE 11ᵀᴴ NOVEMBER ARMISTICE WITH GERMANY

The Armistice simply represented a ceasefire agreement – it was far from a peace treaty or settlement. Its terms reflected the Allies' cautious understanding that the conflict might yet re-ignite. The Armistice was, however, the first necessary step towards peace. In brief, the following major demands were placed before the German delegation in a railway carriage in a siding near Compiègne in the Forest of Rethondes, north-east of Paris[2]:

- German forces were to pull back behind pre-war frontiers.
- The Allies would occupy the Rhineland, with control of several major bridgeheads[3] (notably Köln, Bonn, Koblenz and Mainz) to ensure German compliance. [This clause directly affected Jack Hickman].
- The German army would hand over 5,000 artillery pieces, 25,000 machine-guns, 3,000 *Minenwerfer*[4] and 1,700 military aircraft.
- The German navy would surrender all 150 of its submarines along with 74 of its powerful surface fleet (subsequently scuttled at Scapa Flow).
- All prisoners of war were to be released by Germany.

Failure on the part of Germany to comply with the terms would result in the immediate resumption of hostilities.

The German delegation of four comprising two civilian politicians (Matthias Erzberger and Count Alfred von Obersdorff), one navy representative (Captain Ernst Vanselow) and one army representative (Major-General Detlev von Winterfeldt[5]) duly signed this harsh document.[6] The intractable Maréchal Ferdinand Foch and Admiral Sir Rosslyn Wemyss signed on behalf of the Allies.

As a consequence of the clause in the Armistice terms referring to the Allied occupation of the Rhineland, the British army had to decide how many and which divisions, composed of which soldiers, to commit to the Rhineland force. This was necessarily complicated by the need progressively to demobilize a high percentage of 'time-expired' and 'war-duration only' men. For the bureaucrats, the post-war problems were only just beginning; however, for Jack Hickman and his mates in the front line, army life was about to be extended.

When the war came to a close on 11th November 1918, 9th 'Scottish' Division had changed somewhat in its composition from the raw unit that had crossed the Channel in May 1915.

Table 10: Units of 9th 'Scottish' Division on 11th November 1918

26th Brigade	8/Black Watch	7/Seaforth H.	5/Cameron H.
27th Brigade	11/Royal Scots	12/Royal Scots	6/KOSB
28th Brigade	2/R.Scots Fus	9/Scottish Rifles	1/Newfoundland
Artillery Brigades	50th Brigade RFA	51st Brigade RFA	
Batteries	A,B,C; D (Hows)	A,B,C; D (Hows)	
Mortars [Brigade]	26/Trench M.B.	27/Trench M.B	28/Trench M.B.
[Divisional]	X.9	Y.9	
Ammunition Col.	9/DAC		
M/Gun Units	9/Bn MGC		
Pioneers	9/Seaforth H.		
R. Engineers	63rd Fld Company	64th Fld Company	90th Fld Company
Signal Service	9/Div. Signal Coy.		
Field Ambulances	27th Fld. Amb.	28th Field Amb.	2/1 E. Lancs F.A
Div. Train	9th Div. Train		
Mobile Vet. Sec.	21st Mobile Vet.	Section	
Div. Employ. Coy.	212th Coy.		

1 Nevertheless, in excess of 11,000 casualties of various nationalities were recorded on 11th November.

2 When France surrendered to Hitler in 1940, the German commanders forced the French to sign the formal documents of surrender in exactly the same carriage in the same location.

3 The main bridges in Köln were the Hohenzollern Bridge (rail and road), the South Bridge (rail and road), Hindenburg Suspension Bridge (tram) and the Mülheim pontoon bridge; the bridge in Bonn carried a tram line. In addition, there were thirteen ferries across the Rhine. All crossings had to be guarded by the British military authorities.

4 The Minenwerfer was the German army's standard heavy mortar, nicknamed by the British Tommies in the trenches as the 'Moaning Minnie', partly on account of the sound it made and partly because the average Tommy would 'adjust' any foreign name!

5 Ironically, he was the son of the von Winterfeldt who had dictated terms to the French at the Armistice of the Franco-Prussian War in 1870.

6 Adolf Hitler would later claim that German politicians had 'stabbed in the back' an undefeated German army; this ignored the fact that Ludendorff and Hindenburg had supported the call for an immediate armistice. However, the terms were nowhere near as harsh as those imposed by the Germans upon defeated foes, such as Austria (1866), France (1870) and most recently Russia (1917).

CHAPTER SIXTEEN
ARMY OF OCCUPATION

ACROSS THE RIVER RHINE

RHINELAND & DEMOBILISATION

CONTEXT

At 11 a.m. on 11th November 1918, the Armistice between Germany and the Allies was announced. When the guns fell silent, 9th 'Scottish' Division was still located in the area of Harlebeke, Belgium. Since the Armistice was merely a ceasefire, the Allies feared that Germany might recommence hostilities and so the decision was taken, and swiftly implemented, to send Allied troops into Germany with the specific objective of seizing the vital River Rhine bridgeheads.

This would, it was hoped, convince the temporary German leadership to keep the military peace; 'back home', the invasion of German territory would emphasise the Allies' victory and perhaps soften some of the more difficult consequences of four and a half years of savage fighting. So the following day, 12th November, 9th 'Scottish' was among many divisional Headquarters in France and Belgium that were informed of the commencement of the advance to the Rhine, a move to begin on 14th. By 23rd-24th November, Divisional Headquarters occupied Mont St. Jean but it was not until 4th December that the division actually entered Germany, eventually crossing the River Rhine at Mulheim on 13th December. 9th 'Scottish' Division settled into quarters and took responsibility for

the left divisional sector of the vital Köln (Cologne) bridgehead. Soon into 1919, the process of demobilisation began and both educational and recreational training commenced for the men whose civilian lives had, for the 'lucky' ones, been kept on hold for four years. On 14th February, 9th 'Scottish' was warned that a new 'Lowland' Division would be formed from the 9th 'Scottish' Division and that existing constituent battalions would be replaced by battalions from other divisions, largely employing young soldiers that had not seen much action, if any at all. By 22nd February the moves had commenced and on 16th March the division was formally renamed the 'Lowland' Division and attached to the II Corps (one of five British Corps in occupied Germany). During the

Great War, the 'Ninth' had earned a remarkable reputation for reliability and effectiveness; the loss of 52,055 men killed, wounded or missing clearly testifies to this immense reputation.

So passed into history the Great War service of 9th 'Scottish' Division.

DEMOBILISATION:

As soon as the Armistice had been announced, implemented and duly celebrated, hot on the heels of natural relief at having 'made it through', the thoughts of most 'duration only'[1] men would inevitably have turned to home and the long-dreamed-of return to family and friends. The 'Short Service Attestation' form [Army Form B.2505, updated to AF B.2512] signed by new recruits indicated that a man consented to sign on,

"For the duration of the war, at the end of which you will be discharged with all convenient speed. You will be required to serve for one day with the Colours (Regular Army) and the remainder of the period with the Army Reserve, in accordance with the provisions of the Royal Warrant dated 20th October 1915, until such time as you may be called up by Order of the Army Council. [In certain cases]…you may be retained after the termination of hostilities until your services can be spared, but such retention shall in no case exceed six months."

['Short Service Attestation'. Jack Hickman

signed Army Form B.2505, the wording of which was slightly updated in Army Form B.2512 later in 1915.]

Given the scale of the Great War, there was inevitably no precedent in British history for the process of demobilizing such huge numbers of servicemen and women. Moreover, no-one could have predicted when the war would come to an end, so any preparations would, necessarily, be untested in practice. First estimates of the probable length of the conflict were merely hopeful conjecture and the phrase, *"…over by Christmas"*, was little more than jingoistic, wishful thinking.[2] No such industrialised war had ever been fought between nations on anything like such a scale, so the British government first formally considered the intricate question of demobilization in Cabinet discussions as early as January 1915, just five months into the conflict. As the war progressed, so various committees[3] considered in greater detail the probable demobilization process – by November 1918, in excess of five million men and women needed to be efficiently discharged to civilian life.

Many a weary soldier's understandable view was,

'…first volunteered, first demobbed', that is, '…first in, first out'.

However, this took no consideration of the rehabilitation of the economy of a nation that had been fully adapted to a war footing in the world's first 'Total War'. Inevitably, there was friction and unrest, tantamount to mutiny, when 'old hands' perceived iniquities in the practicalities of the demobilisation process. While their continued reluctant service elicited sympathy, it was a situation preferable to that of the 750,000 British servicemen who would never go home and also to that of men whose severe physical or psychological wounds[4] rendered them unable to work in a harsh, post-war world.

In the event, most Regular soldiers remained to serve out their time with the Colours as there were continued demands upon the post-war British army. Territorial Force men resumed their part-time soldiering, with time-expired TF men entitled to immediate demobilisation.[5] 'Duration men' waited impatiently for demobilisation. The most immediate commitments of the post-Armistice army included, to man an effective Army of Occupation of the Rhine, to re-garrison the outposts of Empire (particularly those far-flung areas that had remained essentially peaceful during the Great War) and to provide several fully-equipped divisions to support the anti-Bolshevik 'White Army' in Russia. The Bolshevik or Communist 'Red' Revolution of October 1917 confirmed Germany's success over Russia as the latter was in no condition to continue the war but the murder of Tsar Nicholas II and his entire family had turned most of

the Great Powers against the new regime. In the summer of 1918, Britain, France, the United States, Japan and at least ten other countries committed themselves to the cause of the 'White', anti-Bolshevik, cause. The industrialised nations wanted to forestall possible Communist agitation in their own homelands, while the British particularly wanted to 'repatriate' valuable military stores they had sent to aid Russia while their erstwhile ally was still fighting the Germans. The latter goes some way to explaining the presence of 40,000 or so British troops in the northern ports of Murmansk and Archangel where the war matériel was stock-piled.

The daunting process of selecting, prioritising and demobilizing those eligible to return to 'Civvie Street' was set out in, '...*Army Demobilization Instructions, France*', issued at General Head Quarters, France in January 1919 and which consisted of 180 printed foolscap pages. It explained the intended process thus,

'Every Command at home and abroad rendered a return showing the composition of its forces by 'Industrial Groups' (trades and industries were grouped by the Army); the return also showed how many men were desirous of repatriation into each of the nineteen Dispersal Areas into which the United Kingdom had been divided. The number of men selected to go home for demobilisation was fixed periodically at a rate that

depended on the transport available and the receptive capacity of the labour market and, of course, according to a 'priority' order of Industrial Groups that necessarily varied. The allotment per category was eventually communicated to unit commanders, by whom the actual selection was made.'

'As an example of the process, the I Corps was directed to find 800 men for Dispersal Area VA, Dispersal Station Ripon, at a the rate of 24 per day, with priority for the trades as previously notified. The chosen men were sent to an Area Concentration Camp, such as those opened at Düren and Köln (Cologne) on 19th December 1918; they were then forwarded to an Embarkation Camp adjacent to

the coast and thence to their chosen Dispersal Station in England…A scheme for re-mobilization, in case of necessity, was always kept in hand.'[6]

A number of other factors had to be taken into consideration, salient amongst which was to effect the transition from an economy geared to full-scale warfare to a peacetime economy. This raised the obvious politico-economic questions of how best to get the country back on its feet and how to channel ex-servicemen back into employment. To achieve this, men were largely discharged in 'industry groupings', and since Britain's pre-war economy had been highly reliant upon primary industries, agricultural workers and miners were afforded a high degree of priority.

CHART 8: WARTIME ARMY TO DEMOBILIZED SOLDIER: THE PROCEDURE

Area Concentration Camp – the soldier was first sent to a camp local to his unit's sector – for Jack Hickman this would have been the camp in Köln or at nearby Düren.

By motor transport to the camp
By rail to the Channel coast

Embarkation or **Transit Camp**, such as an Infantry Base Depot (IBD), close to the French or Belgian coast – one such was the Mardyke Demobilization Camp near the port of Dunkirk – prior to being warned for a homeward sailing.

By troop transport across Channel
By road/rail to Dispersal Camps.

A Dispersal Camp, of which there were variously between 17 and 28 ranged throughout the United Kingdom, was a hutted or tented camp or barracks. Examples were Harrowby DC, Grantham (Lincolnshire); Ripon DC (Yorkshire); Prees Heath DC (Shropshire); Park Hall Camp, Oswestry DC (ceased to work on 16th March 1919); Sandling DC, Folkestone (Kent); Clipstone Camp, (Nottinghamshire); Shorncliffe Camp (Kent); Fovant DC, Salisbury (Wiltshire); Chisledon, south of Swindon (Wiltshire). Sling Camp, Bulford (Wiltshire) was used by the New Zealanders as a Dispersal Camp prior to embarkation for home. Jack Hickman underwent the final demobilization procedure at, *'No.1 Dispersal Unit, Fovant, 18th February 1919'.*

 By road or rail to home town.

The two Wiltshire dispersal centres were at Fovant, near Salisbury, and at Chisledon, south of Swindon. They were selected on account of their good locations; both had a railway line connecting with main lines – Fovant was convenient for trains to the south and west of England (Devon, Cornwall, Hampshire, Somerset and Wiltshire) and for ferries to the Channel Islands and to the Isle of Wight; Chisledon was linked to the junctions at Swindon for the north and west of England.

Men with scarce industrial skills (including miners) were released early; those who had volunteered early in the war were given priority treatment, leaving the conscripts – particularly the trained 18 year olds of 1918[7] – until last. Even so, most of the war service men were back in civilian life by the end of 1919.

PROCESSES AND PAPERWORK AT DISPERSAL CAMPS

☐ The *'Statement as to Disability'* (Army Form Z.22) outlined a man's possible claim for *'...disability due to Military Service'*. Consequently, each man was subjected to a medical examination to record any war-related injuries or debilities. In March 1915 Jack's attestation medical examination in Guernsey had classed him as 'A1'; since then, he had suffered severe wounds on the Somme in March 1918, rejoining the BEF in France only on 25th September, a mere seven weeks prior to the Armistice. Nevertheless, on Jack's *'Protection Certificate'* he was again placed in the medical category 'A1' and thus Jack saw no reason to claim debility consideration, confirming, *'...I do not claim to be suffering from a disability due to my military service,'* which is duly signed by Jack and counter-signed by the examining officer of the 2/1 East Lancs Field Ambulance (originally 66th 'East Lancashire' Division) on 11th February 1919 – the location is barely legible. [From 26th September 1918, 2/1 East Lancs Field Ambulance was attached to 9th 'Scottish' Division and this may well explain Jack's medical examination declaration.]

☐ Just as each new recruit had been supplied with a number of items of kit and equipment on enlistment, so an inventory of equipment was taken on his demobilisation and, as always with the army, deficiencies had to be paid for.

☐ Any foreign currency that a man still held as a consequence of overseas service could be exchanged for sterling.

☐ Each man's final pay and war gratuity was calculated, eventually paid over and signed for.

EACH SOLDIER WAS ISSUED WITH SEVERAL FORMS TO RETAIN

☐ The *'Protection Certificate & Certificate of Identity'* (Army Form Z.11) confirmed the soldier's identity. It authorised an advance of £2 against all monies due to him and provided for more pay in instalments whilst on 28 days' final leave; these were paid by money orders or postal drafts in three instalments that could be cashed at a Post Office on production of the *'Protection Certificate'*. Jack's signature on his *'Protection Certificate'* confirms that he received his £2 advance on due monies.

☐ Army Form B.108E was a *'Character Certificate'*, vital for his next employment, as employers could afford to be very choosy in a 'flooded' market. It also certified the length of a man's army service (Army Form Z.18).

☐ Army Form Z.21 was possibly the most important form as it made official his immediate future on leaving the army. There were four categories of release:

    i)   Discharge (final release from army).

    ii)   Transfer to one of the classes of Army Reserve.

    iii) Disembodiment (a Territorial Force man released from full-time active service).

    iv) Demobilization – the date a man left the army but usually with conditions such as reserve service.

☐ Much to his credit, Jack maintained a clean conduct sheet throughout the war (according to Army Form B.120/33 in his *Army Service Record*).

☐ It also gave some medal entitlement and where to rejoin if recalled to the Colours. As long as the Military Service Act was enforced, all men were liable for service under the Act who were not remaining with the Colours in the regular army; or who had not been permanently discharged; or who was not on a Special Reserve or Territorial Force Reserve engagement, was discharged into Class 'Z' Army Reserve and liable to recall in the event of a grave national emergency. Jack Hickman was advised on his, *'Protection Certificate'* that his, *'...Place of rejoining in case of emergency...'* was Larkhill on Salisbury Plain.

☐ In addition, a soldier could keep his helmet, boots and uniform but not wear it with any insignia/badges after 28 days; the army greatcoat might be kept or exchanged for £1 (as per Army Form Z.50).

☐ The man was also given a ration book. He could take his *'Demobilisation Ration Book'* to the nearest Food Office and exchange it for an Emergency Ration Card, which he could later exchange for a civilian Ration Book.

☐ An *'Out-of-work Donation Policy'* insured him against unavoidable unemployment of up to 26 weeks in the twelve months following his demobilisation (Jack's policy number was *'A10/077692'*).

☐ A *'...railway travel warrant'* for travel home and civilian clothing (Army Form Z.44) were provided for each man – he could choose to have _either_ a clothing allowance voucher of 52 shillings and sixpence _or_ be provided with a suit of plain clothes. If a man chose the latter, he would hand in his Army Form Z.44.

☐ A man's final leave began the day after he was 'dispersed'. He left to go home, still in uniform and with his steel helmet and greatcoat. While on final leave he was still technically a soldier although could now go about in plain clothes. Legally he could not wear his uniform after 28 days from dispersal.

TYPES OF ARMY RESERVE CREATED DURING THE WAR

Class 'W' Reserve and its Territorial Force equivalent **Class 'W' (T)** were introduced in June 1916 by Army Order 203/16. They were,

> *'...for all those soldiers whose services are deemed to be more valuable to the country in civil rather than military employment'.*

Men in these classes were to receive nothing from army funds and were not to wear uniform. They were liable at any time to be recalled to the Colours, though from the time a man was transferred to Class 'W' until being recalled to the Colours, he was not subject to military discipline. This effectively dealt with soldiers who were more valuable to the war effort via their civilian trades or professions and was especially applied to miners.

Class 'T' Reserve was introduced in October 1916 by Army Order 355. There was no Territorial equivalent. Class 'T' consisted of men in about thirty specific skilled trades (almost all were industry and munitions-related) who would otherwise have been transferred to Class 'W'. Terms and conditions were as for Class 'W'.

Class 'P' Reserve and Class 'P' (T) were introduced by the same Army Order 355/16.

These classes consisted of men:

- '...whose services are deemed to be temporarily of more value to the country in civil life rather than in the Army'.
- '...and who were '...not lower than medical grade C iii'.
- '...and as a result of having served in the Army or TF would, if discharged, be eligible for a pension on the grounds of disability or length of service.
- 'Men in Classes 'P' and 'P' (T) were, for the purposes of pay, allowances, gratuity and pension, treated as if they been discharged on the date of their transfer to Class 'P' or 'P' (T); that is, they did receive money from the Army. Other terms and conditions were as for Class 'W'.

Authorisation was given in early December 1918 for all classes of the 'P' and 'W' Reserves (with the exception of conscientious objectors) to be discharged immediately, irrespective of their original terms of engagement.

Class 'Z' Reserve was authorised by an Army Order of 3rd December 1918. There were fears that Germany would not accept the terms of any peace treaty, and therefore the British Government decided it would be wise to be able quickly to recall trained men in the eventuality of the resumption of hostilities. Soldiers who were being demobilised, particularly those who had agreed to serve *"...for the duration"*, were at first posted to Class 'Z'. They returned to civilian life but with an obligation to return if called upon. The 'Z' Reserve was finally abolished on 31st March 1920.

> *"The only immediate obligation on men passed to Class 'Z' Army Reserve is that they have to notify change of address to their record offices. This in any case is necessary in order that they may receive their medals in due course. Soldiers in Class 'Z' will be liable, at any time before the end of the War, to be recalled to the Colours in case of urgent military necessity only."*
> [W.S. Churchill, 3rd March 1919, House of Commons debate, *'Hansard'*, volume 113]

In Jack's case, he was transferred to Class 'Z' Army Reserve on 18th February 1919 at Woolwich Dockyard, with an instruction to report to Larkhill Barracks, a Royal Artillery training depot on Salisbury Plain, if so instructed. Brother Frank's *'Protection Certificate & Certificate of Identity'* indicates that it was the Dispersal Section of the Casualty Clearing Station at Eastleigh (he was, '...sick and wounded') from which he was similarly transferred to Class 'Z' Army Reserve on 6th March 1919, also at Woolwich

Dockyard; as a signaller, he was to report to Woolwich in time of emergency. Frank also was a carpenter by trade and was responsible for the running of a golf course near Margate; he too was married.

> *"The agricultural group has been opened for demobilisation for a considerable time, and, together with the coal-mining group, receives priority over all other industrial classes for dispersal, including pivotal men. Except in the case of men registered by the War Office as pivotal or for special release before the 1st of February, 1919, demobilisation is of course subject to any liability for retention under Army Order 55 of 1919. Up to the 15th instant the number of agriculturists demobilised is 2,471 officers, 165,904 other ranks."*
> [W.S. Churchill – 18th March 1919, House of Commons debate, 'Hansard']

> *"It is provided by Army Council Instruction 69 of the 30th January, 1919, which must be read in conjunction with Army Order 55 of 1919, that a large percentage of each dispersal draft will be composed of coal miners (Group 3) and agriculturists (Group 1), preference being given to coal miners so long as any are available. This procedure is subject of course to the officer or man in question being eligible for demobilisation under Army Order 55. One hundred and ninety-five thousand miners have already been demobilised, and as far as I am aware the number remaining in the Army is very small."*
> [W.S. Churchill, 5th March 1919, House of Commons debate, 'Hansard', volume 113]

Not all discharge groups were entirely composed of these men however; some priority was also given to men who had pre-war employment waiting for them, the so-called, '*...slip men*', those who had been employed before August 4th, 1914 and whose employers had been invited to complete a form saying that his job was still open to him – the term, '*...slip men*' referred to the completed slip that employers returned to the army. Women serving in the QMACC, WRNS, WRAF and other organisations under the control of the War Office, were represented by the Women's War Workers Resettlement Committee.

Jack Hickman was a volunteer, described as a '*...Carpenter*' on his 1915 Attestation Form (Army Form B.2505, '*Short Service*' or '*Duration of War*') – all workers in wood and timber were classed as essential to the post-war recovery effort. It seems that he also had a job to which to return and thus qualified as a '*...slip man*'. He was also a married man, as from November 1915. Effectively, he qualified in all respects.

Not all 9th Division soldiers were demobilized as promptly as the Hickman brothers. Ian Turner's grandfather left testimony to the bitterness and ill-feeling that was caused by the initial demobilization decisions:

> *"In the case of my grandfather's division, (the celebrated...) '9th Scottish'..., once demobilisation started when the division was established on occupation duty at Cologne, there was at first a lot of discontent amongst the men. It seemed that fresh intakes, who had not seen action, were being demobbed before the older hands who had been through the fighting. Eventually a fairer system was devised, taking into account the duration of a man's service and, I think, his marital status."*

[Ian Turner is a member of the *'Great War Forum'* and kindly gave permission for the above extract to be used.]

WAR-DISABILITY PENSIONS

Depending on the severity of an injury or wound incurred on military service (and a claimant was continually put before medical boards that had the power to adjust or even cancel payments) pensions were paid to incapacitated officers, men and nurses. By March 1920, in excess of one million such awards had been made, though many were for limited duration. Spouses of severely disabled men were awarded a supplementary allowance. Almost two million dependants (mainly widows and children of the war dead) received a small pension.

THE ADVANCE INTO GERMANY

CONTEXT

Once the Armistice had been announced,

"...camp gossip chiefly revolved around which British divisions would be accorded the honour of marching through Germany to the bridgehead that was to be formed across the Rhine. There was great jubilation when it became known that the Ninth had been chosen as the left division of the Army of Occupation. It was the only division of the New Armies to take part in the triumphal march."

[John Ewing: *'The History of the Ninth 'Scottish' Division.'*]

Jack thus enjoyed a front-row seat on the march into the Rhineland and recorded his observations until 21st December 1918. On 12th November, the division was informed that the advance to the Rhine would begin two days later. By 23rd-24th November, Divisional Headquarters occupied Mont St. Jean. The division entered Germany on 4th

December and nine days later (on 13th) crossed the River Rhine at Mulheim. Settled in quarters and responsible for the left divisional sector of the Cologne bridgehead, demobilisation began, initially with educational and recreational training.

DIARY

Tuesday, 12th November
Armistice and brief hiatus at
Harlebeke

"Everything is now very quiet. On Sunday next, 17th November, we start our march to the Rhine and from there to a line inside the German frontier where we shall no doubt stay until the peace is signed."

CONTEXT

Thursday, 14th November
Joining the Army of Occupation
9/DAC War Diary indicates that the Column commenced its march to the Rhine at Köln on 14th November rather than the 15th indicated by Jack. Since leaving Potijze just outside the pivotal town of Ypres on 29th September, 9th Division had moved steadily due east until it reached Harlebeke in the eastern suburbs of Courtrai on 27th October, where the Column remained for what proved to be the final fortnight of the war. The first leg of the march to the Rhine was quite short, reaching the hamlet of Vichte on the road towards Renaix. The entire journey of approximately 190 miles was

accomplished in thirty-two days, only half of which were spent on the road.

DIARY

Friday, 15th November
Renaix

"Today we started our march towards Germany, two days before the expected time. We left Harlebeke this morning at seven o'clock and arrived here in the town of Renaix about five [p.m.]. We stay here for two days."

Sunday, 17th November
Renaix

"The town is a very fine place. This morning a thanksgiving service was held and all the local people turned out as well as our Divisional Staff Officers. After the service they marched round to the Town Hall, played along by our Pipe Band and our Staff was presented with two large bouquets of flowers and was given a warm welcome by the local people. The town is smothered with flags and everything is like the old peacetime days long-since forgotten. Tomorrow we start on the second stage of our journey and expect to be in Brussels on Tuesday night."

Monday, 18th November
'The Column marched from Renaix town to Nederbrokel.'
[9/DAC war diary]

Tuesday, 19th November
Nederbrokel

"Our journey is not as quick as expected. We left Renaix yesterday and travelled to a small town about ten miles further on, Nederbrokel [north-east of Renaix, today called simply Brokel], where we will stay for about two days. Some snow fell yesterday and then turned to rain. It is fine today but not so cold."

Wednesday, 20th November
Grammont
"Today we left the village of Nederbrokel and are staying the night in the big town of Grammont," [south-east of Nederbrokel].

Thursday, 21st November
Halle
"Today we left Grammont and are staying for a couple of days in the town of Hal or Halle" [east of Grammont and south-south-west of Bruxelles/Brussels[8]].

"Our entry into the town was a grand affair. We were the first English (sic) to enter and the people were out in force. The place was decorated with flags and the people covered us with streamers of coloured flags and gave us a great reception."

CONTEXT

Friday, 22nd November
On this day, King Albert made his formal return to his capital city (Bruxelles/Brussels).

"Every place gave evidence of the universal respect and affection of the people for their heroic monarch and there were tremendous rejoicings (… on the king's return)."

The British army contributed to the parade in the form of a 'composite' battalion, comprising Englishmen from 29th Division, Highlanders from 9th 'Scottish' Division, Irishmen from 29th Division and Newfoundlanders, also from 9th 'Scottish' Division – it was commanded by a New Zealander, Brigadier-General Freyburg, V.C., D.S.O. and headed by the massed pipe bands of the 26th Infantry Brigade and 9/Seaforth Highlanders (both units of 9th 'Scottish'). The infantrymen marched eight abreast with bayonets fixed.

[John Ewing: *'The History of the Ninth 'Scottish' Division'.*]

DIARY

Saturday, 23rd November
Brussels
"Yesterday was a day of days. Early in the morning about twenty of us set out in a motor lorry to Brussels to see the state entrance of the Belgian King Albert and his Army for the first time since the war started."

"Officers and men were also given the opportunity of visiting the city, and so overwhelming was the welcome of the citizens that they had the greatest difficulty in tearing themselves away from the attractions of Brussels."

Members of 9th 'Scottish' Division at Charleroi, Belgium in 1919.

[John Ewing: 'The History of the Ninth 'Scottish' Division'.]

"...It was a great show and the people went mad at the sight of an English (sic) 'Tommy'. We were given the best of everything. I got a place in a window with some Belgian ladies in a top room where I could see everything splendidly. We had a great time in the evening – crowds followed us down the street shouting, 'Tipperary', so we gave them a rendition of 'Tipperary' until they all went mad. It was the most exciting day of my life. From nine in the morning 'till nine at night we were followed by huge crowds and were given a fine time. Today we left Halle and tonight we are standing on the famous battlefield of Waterloo [immediately south of Bruxelles/Brussels], near the monuments erected to that battle."

Sunday, 24th November
Waterloo and Gistoux
"Today we left Waterloo [eastwards] and are now in the village of Gistoux – it is only a small place but they did all they could to give us a great welcome. The local band played us into the village and in the evening a dance was given in our honour. All the boys went and had a great time."

Tuesday, 26th November
Gistoux

"We are still at Gistoux but we move early tomorrow towards Liège. Last evening the village gave us another dance and all the boys enjoyed themselves."

Wednesday, 27th November
Burdinne

"Today we moved [east-south-eastwards] from Gistoux to Burdinne where we had quite a good reception from the local people. The village band turned out to welcome us and played outside our billet."

Thursday, 28th November
Ampsin

"Today we moved to Ampsin [west of Amay] on the River Meuse – it is a rotten day with nobody about. I think they must be half German."

Friday, 29th November
Flémalle Grande

"Today we moved to the decent-sized town of Flémalle Grande, still on the River Meuse. We had a great reception everywhere for the whole of the eight miles as we passed through village after village."

Sunday, 1st December
Verviers

"Today we moved to the large town of Verviers, about eight or nine miles from the frontier with Germany. It is a fine place and we had a fine reception on arrival."

Tuesday, 3rd December

"Still at Verviers. Yesterday a fete was held in our honour; it started at one o'clock

and they kept it up until midnight. We all had a great time dancing and listening to bands playing and everybody off their heads with excitement."

CONTEXT

Disturbances in Köln were reported by repatriated French prisoners,

"On 3rd and 4th December crowds had looted shops and on the afternoon of the latter day had been fired on by order of the German commandant."

9th Division passed through Eupen and Rötgen on the way to Düren.

[Brigadier-General Sir James Edmonds – Official History, 'The Occupation of the Rhineland, 1918-1929.'

Wednesday, 4th December
Belgian-German Frontier

9th 'Scottish' Division crossed the frontier, most units to the appropriate tune of *"A' the Blue Bonnets are over the Border."*

Thursday, 5th December

"On the 5th (December)...the heads of the 29th and 9th Divisions reached Kesternich and Vassenack (respectively). The marches were only ten to twelve miles air-line in length; but on twisting, hilly roads through dense woods were tiresome and painful. A great many (enemy)

ammunition dumps were reported and occasionally one exploded. The troops were therefore warned to keep away from them as it was impossible to examine every shell and pick out those which had demolition fuzes, only distinguishable from gun fuzes by a tiny mark.

"....at 1 a.m. a message was received at Düren [then the Headquarters of the 1st Cavalry Division] from the German General Staff in Köln, again asking that the British troops might be hastened to help the civil authorities, as the German troops were due to leave the city that day."

[Edmonds, 'The Occupation of the Rhineland, 1918-1929.']

DIARY

Friday, 6th December
Across the Rhine into Germany
[Kornelimünster]
"Today we left Verviers and are now on German soil at a small place called Kornelimünster [north-east of Verviers and south-east of Aachen]. After crossing the frontier everything was very quiet. Not a sign of anybody was to be seen in the houses – everybody kept indoors except those who had work to do outside. Those we have seen seem quite friendly and are inclined to help us but we have learned from experience not to trust a live German. Tomorrow we expect to move on again a bit further."

CONTEXT

The decision was taken by 1st Cavalry Division to send British troops into Köln with the intention of occupying and protecting the major bridges in the area and also to help the civil authorities in the event of further disturbances.

"Meanwhile, General Plumer had ordered the 28th Brigade Group (1/ Royal Newfoundland Regiment; 9/ Cameronians; 2/Royal Scots Fusiliers; 63rd Field Company, Royal Engineers section; a Machine-Gun company; a Field Ambulance; a Royal Army Service Corps[9] company) of 9th 'Scottish' Division, then at Düren, to move by rail to the western suburbs of Köln and directed the GOC 9th Division, Major-General H.H. Tudor... to assume command at Köln."

[Edmonds, 'The Occupation of the Rhineland, 1918-1929.']

DIARY

Saturday, 7th December
Düren
"Today we moved from Kornelimünster and are now in the fair-sized town of Düren," [due east of Aachen and west-south-west of Köln]. *"We are now about twenty miles from Cologne [Köln] where we stay for the rest of our occupation of Germany. The most noticeable thing as*

we get further into Germany is how ill the people look, especially the women. They are treating us very well up to now but of course they have no other option open to them." [28th Brigade Group was sent by rail from Düren to Ehrenfeld, an outer western suburb of Köln.]

Sunday, 8th December
Frechen

"Today we moved forward one more stage on our journey and are now at a small village near Frechen [east-north-east of Düren and seven miles west of Köln], about twelve kilometres [west] from Cologne." [28th Brigade Group, along with 1st Cavalry Division, secured all the river crossings and placed guards on the Mülheim wireless station and on all public buildings.]

Monday, 9th December
Köln [Cologne]

[The vanguard of 9th 'Scottish' Division reached Köln. Köln City was made a special area and put out of bounds to troops except those on duty. On this order's cancellation on 20th December, all troops had to be out of the city by 9 p.m.]

"Today we moved to a suburb of Cologne, on the banks of the River Rhine, a place called Riehl," [a northern suburb, on the west bank of the Rhine]. "Cologne is a lovely place and the people seem quite sociable and decent to us. It is a very busy place and does not seem to have suffered so very much in any way."

CONTEXT

Tuesday, 10th to Thursday, 12th December

"...was spent in Köln cleaning muddy kit and polishing tarnished brasses."

[John Ewing: 'The History of the Ninth 'Scottish' Division'.]

DIARY

Friday, 13th December
Mülheim

"Today we crossed the Rhine [by either boat- or 'pontoon-'] bridge to another suburb of Cologne called Mülheim" [a north-eastern suburb, beside the river; this was a very short move, simply crossing the Rhine (boat) bridge, now called Mülheimer Brücke. During the occupation, a new suspension bridge was built across the Rhine at Mülheim and was opened in 1929].

"We move on our final stage on Sunday." [At the division's crossing of the Rhine, the salute was taken by a former commander of 9th 'Scottish' Division, Sir Charles Fergusson[10], who had been appointed British Military Governor.]

CONTEXT

This date, 13th December at 5 a.m., had been agreed under the terms of the Armistice for British troops to cross the Rhine.

"The inhabitants of Köln were friendly and anxious to make the troops comfortable; the authorities were pleased to see the troops, as they were in fear of further rioting."

[Edmonds, 'The Occupation of the Rhineland, 1918-1929.']

"The salute was taken by the British Military Governor (of Köln), Lieutenant-General Sir Charles Fergusson, but the ceremony [of crossing the Rhine] was spoiled by the torrents of rain that descended all day."

[John Ewing: 'The History of the Ninth 'Scottish' Division'.]

Saturday, 14th December
Veteran war-reporter Philip Gibbs[11], who had accompanied the troops on the Western Front for several years, filed the following report on the Allied Occupation of the Rhineland,

"This morning at 10 o'clock our cavalry passed through the streets of Cologne, crossed the Hohenzollern Bridge, and went beyond the Rhine to take possession of the bridgeheads.
"For some days not many British soldiers had been seen in the City of Cologne, the troops being camped in the outskirts, and it was only yesterday afternoon that the British Governor made his entry and established his headquarters in one of the hotels which had been taken over

for the purpose.

"Crowds of German people gathered to see the man who will control their way of life during the British occupation, and were kept back in a hollow square by their own police when the Governor's motor car drove in with an escort of lancers (light cavalry), while a band of Scottish pipers played a greeting.

"This morning the passing of the cavalry over the Rhine was an impressive sight for all the people of Cologne, and for the British was another historical episode on the long journey of this war, which has led at last to this river flowing now behind the British lines.

"To the German people the Rhine is the very river of their life, and down its tide come drifting all the ghost memories of their race, and its water is sacred to them as the fount from which their national legends, their old folk songs, and the sentiment that lies deep in their hearts have come forth in abundance.

"In military history the Rhine has been their last line of defence, the moat around the keep of German strength; so today when British troops rode across the bridge and passed beyond the Rhine to further outposts it was the supreme sign of victory for them and of German defeat."

[Philip Gibbs, 'Report from Cologne', December 1918.]

DIARY

Sunday, 15th December
Leichlingen

"Today, at last, we are at the end of our journey. We are now at a place called Leichlingen, about ten miles [north] from Cologne," [four miles due north of Leverkusen]. It is a small village and the people seem very decent to us."

CONTEXT

"By the 15th December the division had taken up its position on the perimeter of the bridgehead near Solingen, Wald and Haan, Divisional Headquarters being established at Ohligs."

[John Ewing: 'The History of the Ninth 'Scottish' Division'.]

"It was eminently desirable that the men should realise in some tangible form that they had won the war. Only first-rate billets were accepted; halls were taken over for concerts and reading-rooms, and cinematographs were run for the entertainment of the men. Groups of soldiers were given permission to visit Cologne…every unit was allotted tickets for the Opera House…and all soldiers were allowed to travel by tram or rail without payment."

[John Ewing: 'The History of the Ninth 'Scottish' Division'.]

DIARY

Saturday, 21st December
Benrath

(Cold with some rain and snow)
"Our stay in our snug little camp did not last long. Owing to some mistake we have had to move today into our proper area and we are now in a large farm near a village called Benrath," [downriver from Köln and Leverkusen, just south-east of Düsseldorf, on the east bank of the River Rhine].
[It is…] *"…a rotten place and the sooner we get out of it the better. The weather is very cold, with a little rain and a little snow."*

The diary ends abruptly here, though Jack Hickman's army service record (having survived the air raids of the Luftwaffe during the Second World War) offers an insight into the final three months of his unintended soldiering.

CONTEXT

"9th Division…had responsibility for the left divisional sector of the Cologne bridgehead."
[Major E.F. Becke, 'Order of Battle of Divisions'.]

"…demobilisation began in 1919; educational and recreational training were undertaken. On 14th February the division was warned

that a 'Lowland' Division would be formed from the 9th Division and the existing battalions would replaced by battalions from other divisions. On 22nd February the moves began; and on 16th March 1919, the history of 9th 'Scottish' Division came to an end when the division was renamed the 'Lowland' Division. During the Great War the 9th Division lost 52,055 killed, wounded or missing."

[John Ewing: *'The History of the Ninth 'Scottish' Division'.*]

There is no definitive evidence available to ascertain the exact date of Jack Hickman's departure from the Divisional Ammunition Column in Germany. The only indication appears to be the final entry on his Active Service Record that reads,

'...12/2/19, Proceeded to Fovant Dispersal Centre',

...though another entry indicates that Jack set sail for England aboard a troopship on 16th February 1919, the very day that 9th 'Scottish Division ceased to exist as a separate unit, becoming part of the 'Lowland' Division in the II Corps. However, Jack would have had to pass through an Area Concentration Camp close by his unit in Germany; from there, Jack would have travelled to an Embarkation or Transit Camp near to his Channel port of departure, such as Boulogne or Calais.

Thus it is more than possible that Jack left his unit around the end of January 1919 to commence the demobilisation process. A day after landing in England, 17th February, he reported to No.1 Dispersal Unit, at Fovant in Wiltshire. From there, on 18th February, he travelled by rail to Woolwich Dockyard where he was officially transferred to the Class 'Z' Army Reserve. Luckily for Jack, his marital home was in Raglan Road, Plumstead, just a few minutes' walk from Woolwich Barracks.

Back on 12th November 1918, acclaimed war reporter, Philip Gibbs, in *'... The War Dispatches'*, had observed,

"Last night for the first time since August in the first year of the war there was no light of gun-fire in the sky, no sudden stabs of flame through the darkness, no long spreading flow above the black trees, where for four years of nights human beings were smashed to death. The fires of hell had been put out. It was silent all along the front with the beautiful silence of the nights of peace."

[Philip Gibbs, *'The War Dispatches'.*]

A lyrical and most fitting epitaph to one of the most destructive wars in human history.

Table 11: British Army of the Rhine (BAOR)

Back in the occupied zone of Germany, the first British Army of the Rhine was inaugurated in March 1919. It was originally composed of five corps, composed of two divisions each, plus a cavalry division:

II Corps: Commanded by Lt.-Gen. Sir Claud Jacob and comprising:
The Light Division (formerly 2nd Division, Regular): Commanded by Major-General George Jeffreys.
The Southern Division (formerly 29th Division, Regular): Commanded by Major-General William Heneker
IV Corps: Commanded by Lt.-Gen. Sir Alexander Godley and comprising:
The Lowland Division (formerly 9th Division, New Army): Commanded by Major-General H.H. Tudor.
The Highland Division (formerly 62nd Division, TF): Commanded by Major-General D. Campbell.
VI Corps: Commanded by Lt.-Gen. Sir Aylmer Haldane and comprising:
The Northern Division (formerly 3rd Division, Regular): Commanded by Major-General A.A. Kennedy.
The London Division (formerly 41st Division, New Army): Commanded by Major-General Sir S. Lawford.
IX Corps: Commanded by Lt.-Gen. Sir Walter Braithwaite and comprising:
The Western Division (formerly 1st Division, Regular): Commanded by Major-General Sir P. Strickland.
The Midland Division (formerly 6th Division, Regular): Commanded by Major-General G.F. Boyd.
X Corps: Commanded by Lt.-Gen. Sir Thomas Morland and comprising:
The Lancashire Division (formerly 32nd Division, New Army): Commanded by Major-General Sir H. Jeudwine.
The Eastern Division (formerly 34th Division, New Army): Commanded by Major-General Sir L. Nicholson.
The Cavalry Division: Comprised three brigades and commanded by Major-General Sir W.E. Peyton.
Artillery: Commanded by Major-General C.R. Buckle – various RGA brigades over and above the divisional artillery. As far as ammunition supplies were concerned, 75,000 tons were retained – 15,000 tons in the Rhineland and 60,000 tons in French depots.
Engineers: Commanded by Major-General Sir R. Buckland – various units over and above the divisional engineers.
Royal Air Force: Two brigades (24 Squadrons) and a Balloon Wing commanded by Major-General Sir J. Salmond.
Tank Corps: Two brigades of tanks commanded by Brigadier-General E.B. Hankey.

In total, more than a quarter of a million British troops remained in occupied Germany.

JACK HICKMAN'S DEMOBILISATION

'Sir, reference your letter, 89238 was my correct number in the R.F.A. from the 20th of March 1915 until the 19th of March 1919, I served with the 9th Division the whole of that time; from the 1st October 1917 until I was demobilised I was on the R.A. Headquarters, 9th Division; my 28 days' leave expired on 19th March 1919. I did not claim any disability of any kind, I left the Army A.1. Hope this will give required explanation.

Yours truly, John Hickman.'

89238 Driver Jack Hickman's Medal Index Card

COMMEMORATIONS FOR JACK HICKMAN

Jack's Medal entitlement: [Medal Index Card]	1914-15 Star	(Roll RFA/9AIB. Page 6433) BWM/VM (Roll RFA/225B, page 25082)
Medal delivery: Victory Medal Army will was returned and acknowledged British War Medal This last one was despatched to Thanet Golf Club, Hengrove, Margate	1914-15 Star	(19th August 1920) (21st September 1921) (13th October 1921) (4th November 1922)

COMMEMORATIONS FOR 9ᵀᴴ 'SCOTTISH' DIVISION

After a shaky start to their front-line war at Loos in September 1915, 9th 'Scottish' Division, the senior of the 'K1' Kitchener 'New Army' divisions, built an impressive reputation for bravery and reliability. Consequently, the 'Old Ninth' fought in most of the major battles on the Western Front – Loos, the Somme, Arras, 3rd Ypres, Cambrai, *'die Kaiserschlacht'* and the Advance to Victory. In many respects for the 'Ninth', the Arras offensive was the longest and the most costly of life and it is fitting that the principal memorial to the exploits of the Scots is to be found on the former Arras battlefield, close to the Point-du-Jour Military Cemetery.

British and French troops at the 9th Division Memorial's inauguration and dedication.

The War Memorial to 9th 'Scottish' Division was unveiled and dedicated on 9th April 1922 – an appropriate date as it represented the fifth anniversary of the commencement of the Battles of Arras in the spring of 1917. Today, the memorial does not stand on its original site as a major dual carriageway has taken precedence. The associated danger involved in visiting the memorial led, in 2006, to the cairn being relocated, stone by Scottish stone, to the south side of

The original memorial site, with the 'unit' rocks fronting the cairn. Contrast the horse and motor – the old and new.

the main road and adjacent to the Point-du-Jour Military Cemetery. The striking memorial bears the understated but apposite inscription,

> *'Remember with honour the 9th Scottish Division who on the fields of France and Flanders 1915-1918 served well'.*

The memorial cairn, bearing the names of the battles in which the 'Ninth' was involved, stands on a broad square of grass that is edged by imposingly large, Scottish stones, each of which is inscribed with the name of each battalion or corps that was serving with the 'Ninth' at Arras. Above the inscription is each unit's distinctive badge.

The cairn of Scottish stone at the centre of the memorial square.

Two examples are shown below.

Above: 9/Divisional Ammunition Column, Royal Field Artillery
Below: 4th South African 'Scottish' Regiment

Not for nothing was the 'Ninth' was generally known as the division of the 'Jocks and Springboks'; add to that mixture a later Newfoundland battalion and a DAC largely comprising Guernseymen and a leavening of English and Irish lads – the end product had a polyglot accent but a massive fighting heart. Hence 9th 'Scottish' was often one of the first divisions on the order of battle.

---

1 Most men signed on for military service, '…for the duration of the war', only. Initially, few men knew the details of what was likely to happen at the end of hostilities, thus most were impatient to be demobilized and to return home as soon as possible.

2 Even at an early stage, Lord Kitchener was expecting the war to last at least three years.

3 The Army Demobilization Committee, set up by the Cabinet Ministers of the Reconstruction Committee, was chaired by Mr. E.S. Montagu M.P. The A.D.C. set the principal parameters by which demobilization was carried out.

4 In excess of 2 million British servicemen sustained wounds (some more than once) during the Great War.

5 This was confirmed by Winston Churchill in a House of Commons written answer on 13th March 1919 (Hansard, volume 113).

6 Every soldier, on demobilisation, was issued with Army Form AF Z.11 (for Other Ranks) or Army Form AF Z.3 (for Officers), 'Protection Certificate and Certificate of Identity', that designated a 'Place of re-joining in case of emergency'.

7 Many of these youngsters were sent to serve in the BAOR and some served in Russia prior to their demobilisation.

8 Today, Belgium is divided by language and history – the Flemish-speakers have much in common with their Dutch neighbours, while the Wallon-speakers have more in common with their French neighbours.

9 Immediately post-war the Army Service Corps was granted the prefix 'Royal', recognising the contribution of the supply chain to the victory.

10 Lieutenant-General Sir Charles Fergusson commanded 9th Division from 28th October 1914 to 31st December 1914.

11 Philip Gibbs was knighted in 1920 for his services to war reporting.

PART THREE

Inter-War Years
1919-1939

CHAPTER SEVENTEEN
CLUB PROFESSIONAL AND CLUB DESIGNER

A LIFE AT HENGROVE

JACK AND THE 'BAMFEE' PATIENT

Holding an exemplary disciplinary record in the RFA (Army Forms B.120), Jack underwent his final army medical in France on 11th February, thanks to the ministrations of 2/1 Lancashire Field Ambulance who passed him as category 'A1' and he finally left French soil on 16th February 1919 and landed in England the following day where he *'...proceeded to (No.1) Fovant Dispersal Unit'* on Salisbury Plain. Driver Jack Hickman became a civilian again on 18th February 1919 when he was officially discharged from his wartime army service at Fovant Dispersal Camp and was released to Class 'Z' of the Army Reserve, with orders to report to the R.F.A. Depot at Larkhill on Salisbury Plain if an emergency was declared in respect of the 1918 Armistice. It never was.

As far as has can be ascertained, Jack Hickman did not return to his job of assistant professional at the Royal Guernsey Golf Club at L'Ancresse, although the *'Golfer's Handbook'* indicates that Jack was connected with the RGGC until 1921 and Alan Jackson's *'British Professional Golfers, 1887-1930'* states that Jack was attached to Guernsey until 1922. However, it appears that from the day of his demobilisation Jack went to live in Woolwich, with his wife, Ada, and her family at 29, Raglan Road; his 1914-15 Star[1] was received at that address on 19th August 1920, as was his Victory Medal[2] on 24th September 1921. However, it seems that within two years he had taken up a life-changing post at the Thanet Golf

Consummate professional: Jack's easy stance at address.

Club in Hengrove near Margate, Kent – he was evidently living at Hengrove by 4th November 1923, as his British War Medal was sent to and received at that address. Jack remained at the Hengrove Golf Club until May 1940 when war again intervened in his life; at Hengrove Jack became a most respected professional and, as will be demonstrated, a golf innovator.

Jack the club-maker in his Hengrove workshop with an apprentice.

Prior to his becoming an assistant professional on Guernsey, Jack had trained as a carpenter, a craft that was to stand him in good stead for life after the war. According to the *'Golfer's Handbook'*, it was during 1923 that Jack joined the Thanet Golf Club in Hengrove, Kent, a club that had been established in 1897 as an eighteen-hole course one mile from Margate. Initially laid out by Ramsey Hunter of nearby Royal St George's, the parkland-style course covered about two hundred acres and a former farmhouse had been refurbished and converted into the clubhouse. 5,880 yards in length, the course was well-drained and gently undulating. For unknown reasons the course was temporarily reduced to fifteen holes at some time by 1906 but by 1914 it had been extended to its original eighteen. In something of an echo of Jack's former club at Rye, special golf club tickets were available from London to Margate at 15/- (equivalent to 75 pence!)

return, with electric trams running to within a short walk of the course.

Hengrove soon developed a reputation for being a course frequented by the good, the great and the celebrated. Before the Great War, Thanet numbered amongst its Vice-Presidents the 13th Earl of Westmoreland (an amateur cricketer who played for Northamptonshire as well as being a noted golfer and during the Great War he served as a Lieutenant-Colonel in a battalion of the Lancashire Fusiliers), Lord Avebury, a remarkable scientist, politician, author and banker, and Lord Harris, the 'spiky' Kent & England cricket captain; as a politician,

he served as under-secretary of state for India and as under-secretary of state for war. These early connections with politicians at Westminster were to continue during the inter-war years, a time when more entertainers and celebrities also enjoyed the game as an ideal relaxation.

The pre-war professional at Hengrove was A. Davey, who, between 1901 and 1914 attained the professional course record of 77. This card seems quite high but it should be remembered that in many respects the course was still 'settling' so the surfaces were yet less than perfect. It appears, according to

Jack outside his workshop with green-keeper Mr. Sellars and three of the regular Hengrove caddies.

the records, that Thanet maintained a professional throughout the war years 1914 to 1919, although it is quite likely that the club pro, G. Doughty, was unfit for war service. Unusually, Sunday play was permissible and there were ample rooms available at the club for overnight stays. The club membership had by then risen to 270.

The post-Great War Thanet Golf Club that Jack helped to fashion had suffered damage during the Great War, on account of the fact that most German Zeppelin and aircraft raids crossed the English coast over Kent[3]. However, it was not bomb damage that left its mark on the fairways. On 22nd August 1917, during the eighth daylight raid carried out by German *Gotha* heavy bombers, ten aircraft targeted the coastal towns of Margate and Ramsgate along with the Channel port of Dover. Ten *Gothas* reached their target area and, in the face of spirited fighter defence, unloaded in excess of forty bombs. Ramsgate, with seven fatalities, fared worst, while Dover suffered three deaths. On this occasion Margate was fortunate in that it sustained no bomb casualties, though it happened to be Thanet Golf Club's unlucky day as one of the *Gothas* crashed in flames on the Hengrove golf course, killing the crew of three. Two more of the raiding *Gothas* crashed into the sea, one off Margate, the other off the port of Dover. Fortunately, the damage to the course that would provide Jack Hickman's post-war living was largely superficial.

Just as the course had to overcome the scars of war, so did Jack, both physically from his serious wounding and mentally from what he had witnessed in the front line. To make his processes of recovery even more complex, less than a year after his demobilisation Jack's father, Henry Hickman, died at the age of seventy-seven in 1920. He was buried alongside his beloved wife Naomi in St. Mary's churchyard at East Guldeford, where the couple is commemorated with Henry's own father, Henry, who had been born during the Napoleonic Wars and who had died in 1877 at the age of seventy-one. Both Henrys had endured long, hard, working lives as 'lookers' on the Romney Marshes, among the last who pursued that way of life on that windswept pasture. On the lichen-covered headstone at St. Mary's is engraved the following:

In

Loving Memory

of

NAOMI

Beloved Wife of

HENRY HICKMAN

Also of

HENRY HICKMAN

'Peace, Perfect Peace'

By 1924 Jack Hickman had been appointed as the club professional at Hengrove and he would have worked in tandem with the head green-keeper, Mr. S. Sellars. This was a partnership that would endure for many years. 1928 shows the same combination of pro and green-keeper, while Jack had cracked the professional course record with a return of 69. A local directory published in 1936 commented,

> "...There are no entrance fees; subscriptions are gentlemen - five guineas; ladies four guineas; secretary, John A. Sisley; honorary secretary C. Waterer."

At Thanet Golf Club, Jack's carpentry skills and thoughtful approach to the game led him to experiment with, and finally perfect, a new type of golf club. He set his mind to a specific problem – how could he overcome the almost inevitable loss of shots when playing from a difficult or rough lie? The solution, reached in his workshop at Hengrove after much reflection, trial and error, was to adjust the weighting in the club-head and thus increase the club-head speed on contact.

In his application for a British patent, Jack stated that, '...the object of this invention is to construct the head of a golf club in such a manner that a ball can be readily struck and given an upward rise even when lying in indifferent places or rough grass.' To achieve this, he had to enable the club-head more effectively to cut through obstructive, tough grass and other difficulties; it was thus similar in some respects to the modern 'rescue' or 'hybrid' style of club. Jack proposed the insertion of,

> '...a series of weights in holes drilled in the club-head from the sole at a position near the striking face and below the horizontal centre plane of the head and between the vertical centre plane of the head and the striking face, the weights being enclosed by the sole plate. The striking face is provided with an inset of hard material.'

This method ensured that the centre of gravity of the club-head was considerably lowered, commensurately increasing the club-head speed at the point of contact with the ball. Jack's application proposed that,

> '...the weight can be applied in a variety of ways but I prefer to drill holes, of the desired diameter and depth, into the head from the sole.....and I fill these holes with lead, preferably in a molten state. I cover the filled weights with the sole plate, the weights being positioned directly behind the lower portion of the striking plate or surface and below the horizontal centre plane thereof and not at some distance away as is known.'

Here the word 'lower' was vitally important, as this effected the lowering

Jack outside his workshop, probably during the 1930s.

of the centre of gravity. Jack's application for this patent was made through the Chartered Patent Agents H. Gardner & Son of Fleet Street, London on 20th November 1925 and was duly accepted on 10th June 1926. He named his invention the *'Hickman Bamfee Club.'* The design was approved by the Professional Golfers Association of which he was a member and his place in golf history was assured. The patent[4] is presently held in the British Golf Museum, sited opposite the Royal and Ancient Clubhouse and the eighteenth green of the Old Course at St. Andrews. In recent years, original *'Hickman Bamfee'* clubs and a *'Bamfee'* long-hosel putter, have been sold at auctions though, sadly, their selling prices have not been recorded.

Through 1938, 1940 and briefly resuming in 1947 the Hickman – Sellars partnership continued. Club membership stood at 230 (not bad for two years after a world war!) and the eighteen-hole course had a Standard Scratch Score of 71. Jack Hickman had lowered the professional course record to 66 and was becoming something of a legend, often partnering political figures and the occasional entertainer who was performing in one of the nearby Kent towns.

However, despite sterling efforts to save the war-damaged course, Thanet (Hengrove) Golf Club had closed down by 1951. Jack Hickman had to move on as he needed to work. Jack had remained at Thanet throughout the inter-war years until the early months of the Second World War when the evacuation of 300,000 troops from the beaches of Dunkirk in May 1940 put the Margate area in imminent danger of subsequent invasion. The authorities deemed it necessary to evacuate civilians from the region, ensuring their safety and facilitating the defence of the coastal tract within striking range of the narrowest crossing-point of the Channel. For their part, Jack and his family were removed to Broxbourne in Hertfordshire, twenty miles north of Central London, from where he worked in the Royal Small Arms Factory (R.S.A.F.) at Enfield Lock, making guns for the ensuing five years of war. Bombed by the Luftwaffe on several occasions, it was hardly a 'place of safety' but the family survived the war.

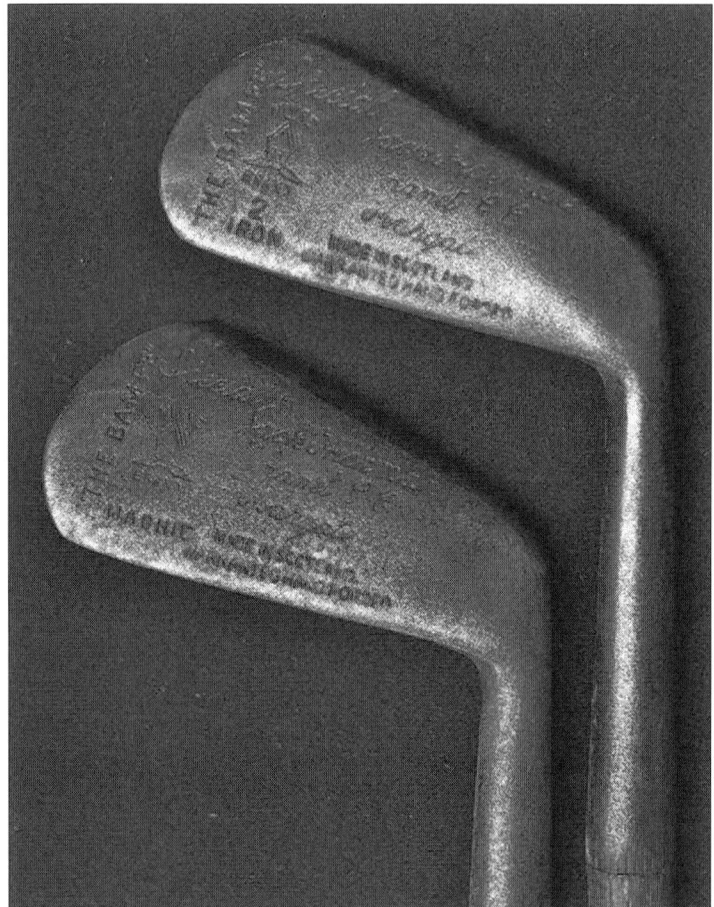

*From a 2012 catalogue at Mullock's auctioneers & valuers,
Shropshire, showing a 'Mashie' and an old 2 (modern 4-iron). In
the photo, 'The Bamfee' may be seen inscribed on the toe of each
club; less easy to read is the inscription, 'Jack Hickman, Thanet
G.C. Margate.' 'Made in Scotland, warranted hand-forged.'
'Special' and 'Mitre Brand' (shown above and below a Bishop's
Mitre trademark.*

1 The Medal Roll reference for Jack's 1914-15 Star
is Roll RFA/9AIB, page 6433.

2 The Medal Roll reference for Jack's Victory
Medal and British War Medal is Roll RFA/225B,
page 25082.

3 The range of the German bomber aircraft was
relatively short, so most took the shortest route
across the Channel. Consequently, aborted
raids often led to bomb-loads being randomly
dropped on the towns and villages of Kent.

4 The patent reference number is GB252993.

PART FOUR

'Doing His Bit Again'
1940-1945

CHAPTER EIGHTEEN
EVACUATION & MUNITIONS 1940-1945

TO BROXBOURNE AND SAFETY?

ROYAL SMALL ARMS FACTORY

Following the process of his army demobilisation, Jack returned to golf and took over as professional at the Hengrove Golf Club in Margate, working there until the Second World War. After the Dunkirk episode in 1940, the inhabitants of the Kent coastal region were obliged to leave as the authorities deemed it necessary to evacuate civilians from the region, ensuring their safety and facilitating the proper defence of the coastal tract. For his part, Jack removed his family to Broxbourne in Hertfordshire and worked for the ensuing five years of war at the R.S.A.F. Enfield Lock, a vital munitions factory making weapons.

Weaponry and explosives had formed a major source of employment in the Enfield and Waltham Abbey area for hundreds of years. Just a few miles south of the Waltham Abbey Royal Gunpowder Factory[1] (established in 1787, further up the Lee valley) the Royal Small Arms Factory was located east of the main town of Enfield, at Enfield Lock (though originally inside the parish of Waltham Abbey but later in part of Enfield parish when the river's course was diverted). The factory was sited on a formerly marshy island bordered to the east by the River Lee and to the west by the River Lee Navigation. Building was commenced near the end of the Napoleonic War on the instructions of the Board of Ordnance on land acquired in 1812; the Royal Small Arms Factory was completed by 1816[2]. The site had the advantages of water-power to drive the machinery and the River Lee Navigation for the easier transportation of raw materials and finished weapons. The factory was expanded again during the Great War and by 1918 was producing well in excess of one million Short Magazine Lee-Enfield Mark III rifles, again the mainstay of the British Army. Almost all the weapons in which the Royal Small Arms Factory had a hand in design or production carry either the word Enfield or the letters 'en' in their name:-

The Lee-Enfield Rifle carried by most British infantrymen

The Enfield Revolver

The Bren gun (from <u>Br</u>no and <u>En</u>field)

The Sten gun (from <u>S</u>hepherd, <u>T</u>urpin and <u>En</u>field)

Polsten Oerlikon (from two Polish designers and the name Sten)

For the second time, Jack Hickman had made a full contribution to the war effort.

---

1 The first Royal Ordnance factory, the Royal Arsenal, was built at Woolwich in about 1695. Waltham Abbey was the second R.O. factory and Enfield Lock was the third.

2 The R.S.A.F. was originally established for manufacturing and assembling the 'Brown Bess' muskets, the main firearm of the British Empire for countless years.

PART FIVE

A Time at Peace
1945-1975

CHAPTER NINETEEN
A TIME AT PEACE

WESTGATE PROFESSIONAL

... THE END OF THE ROUND

With the coming of peace in May 1945, the long-neglected Thanet Golf Course at Hengrove was considered so badly damaged that it was abandoned as not worth the cost of repair. Jack, who still had to earn a living at the age of fifty-four, became the professional at Westgate Golf Club (now the Westgate and Birchington Golf Club) in 1947[1], just west of Margate in Kent and a short walk from Hengrove. Installed at his new course, Jack taught the club-making craft to young apprentices who benefited from their tutor's undoubted skills as a golfer, carpenter and club designer – bonuses they added to their budding golf talents. Jack's brother, Frank, the first of the golfing Hickmans, was employed nearby as a professional at Ramsgate Golf Club.

Jack the family man.

'Elder statesman.'

Westgate and Birchington Clubhouse.

As for the Westgate course, prior to the construction of a golf course, the present fairways, greens and bunkers were not even a dream and the land was part of Westgate Farm. When the farmland was sold, it was expected to turn a good profit through building but economic circumstances saw good agricultural land lie untilled. Rather than leave the former farm to revert to a natural, overgrown state and possibly deter a potential purchaser, in the early 1890s its owners allowed Westgate-on-Sea Golf Association to lease it, with a view to setting out a small golf course.

Initially, the course comprised just six holes and the playing surface was understandably poor. Opened during the summer of 1893, the course was sufficiently popular to warrant extension by a further three holes by 1908 and, in the year before the outbreak of the Great War, the course was completely remodelled. Post-war, the Westgate G.C. boasted eighteen holes and by 1924 had its very own clubhouse, making it a popular venue and financing the laying of twenty tennis courts. On the golfing side of the club, there is a direct link to Jack Hickman as several of the club's trophies originated at the Hengrove G.C. where Jack had been the professional in the years leading up to the Second World War – the closure of Hengrove after the war was most certainly Westgate's gain. Not only did Jack become the professional at Westgate but many of the former Hengrove members followed in his footsteps to join him at the Westgate club.

The Westgate & Birchington Golf Club's official handbook for 1966 indicates on its front cover that Jack was one of two professionals employed at Westgate. The other was also a member of the Hickman family – James Morris Hickman was Jack's nephew whom Jack had taken under his wing to learn the intricacies of the game. James was evidently a very receptive pupil as he reached a very high standard, much to his mentor's delight and satisfaction.

Jack's daughter Maisie ran an excellent guest-house in Westgate-on-Sea; it was located in Adrian Square, an area of immaculate lawns and rose-beds that was surrounded by impressive houses. Jack worked until he was seventy-three and lived with each of his three children in turn – son Jack and wife Barbara lived in Cliftonville.

After a long and productive life, in which he twice served his country and reached the higher echelons of the golfing profession, Jack died aged eighty-four years in December 1975.

BOGEY TABLE					
Hole	Yards	Bogey	Hole	Yards	Bogey
1	325	4	10	450	5
2	319	4	11	147	3
3	177	3	12	364	4
4	373	4	13	211	4
5	139	3	14	115	3
6	311	4	15	182	3
7	450	5	16	327	4
8	228	4	17	195	3
9	322	4	18	291	4
Out	2644	35	In	2282	33
			Out	2644	35
			Total	4926	68

ANNUAL SUBSCRIPTION

	£	s.	d.
Entrance	10	10	0
Full Membership	13	13	0
Country	10	10	0
Lady (Full)	11	11	0
Lady (Country)	8	8	0
Green Fees		10	0
Saturdays and Sundays		12	0

Course yardage and bogey (par)

WESTGATE & BIRCHINGTON GOLF CLUB

WESTGATE-ON-SEA

Hon. Secretary: A. I. READ
Telephone: THANET 31115

Professionals: J. M. HICKMAN
JACK HICKMAN

OFFICIAL HANDBOOK

© TEMPLE PUBLICITY SERVICES LTD. 1966
224 Old Christchurch Road, Bournemouth, Hants; and London
Copyright

1966 W&BGC Official Handbook. &
Annual Subscriptions 1966.

---

1 According to the 'Golfer's Handbook', Jack Hickman was employed as professional at Westgate from 1947 to 1970.

About the Author

Ken Wayman was born in Hertfordshire and was, according to an early school report, a 'poor student of history'. However, he studied History and French at Bournemouth University and, in 1971, armed with a decent degree, moved to the Midlands and took up a post in 1972, teaching, contrary to earlier expectations, history at T.P. Riley School in Bloxwich. He taught there for the next twenty-six years. Over that time, Ken accompanied several groups of GCSE students on study-trips to visit the battlefields and cemeteries of the Great War in Flanders and Northern France – still among the most satisfying times of his career. Following early retirement in 1999, he was drawn into local research on the Great War and still regularly visits the old Western Front; he is a member of the Western Front Association and proudly supports the 'Help for Heroes' charity. His first book, 'The True and Faithful Men' (2004, ISBN: 0-9548875-0-6), traces the stories of the lads on the Pelsall war memorial; he managed to uncover sixty more lads with strong Pelsall connections and these names have now been added, thanks to local organisations, to supplementary panels at the foot of the memorial. His second book, 'Thank God I Am Trying to Do My Little Bit' (2008, ISBN: 0-9548875-1-4), traces the brief military career of a Walsall soldier, Private Jim Elwell, who served first in 1/5th Battalion, the South Staffordshire Regiment and then with 7th Battalion, the Suffolk Regiment. The story relies heavily upon Jim's original letters and cards from France. Ken's third book, 'Sorrow into Pride' (2013, ISBN: 978-1-908336-44-6), was written in conjunction with close friend Barry Crutchley, and tells the story of a 'missing' war memorial and the lads whose names are thereon carved. The memorial commemorates sixty-seven Old Boys of Elmore Green High School in Bloxwich, Walsall.

For many seasons Ken played cricket for Bloxwich C.C. and for three years, as a volunteer, compiled an annual Bird Report at RSPB Sandwell Valley. He lives in Pelsall and is married to a former Deputy Head-teacher, Sue, and has two grown-up children: Vicki, a Deputy Head-teacher and David, a Squadron Leader in the RAF. David is married to Carrie and they have a young son, George.

Other books by the same author:

'The True and Faithful Men – Pelsall Servicemen in the Great War' (2004)
'Thank God I Am Trying to Do My Little Bit – the war letters of Private Jim Elwell' (2008)

With Barry Crutchley:
'Sorrow into Pride – the story of a Staffordshire school's war memorial' (2013)

APPENDIX 1

CAMBER, JURY'S GAP AND BROOMHILL – MANPOWER CONTRIBUTION TO THE GREAT WAR

CAMBER GREAT WAR MEMORIAL

War memorials for both world wars are to be found in St. Thomas church, Lydd Road, Camber. The war memorial is fashioned from wood – the original Great War memorial on the church's altar rails was destroyed when the church was bombed during the Second World War.

DIED DURING THE GREAT WAR (5 MEN RECORDED)

James Henry NOAKES
> Born in late 1894 at Scotney Farm, Lydd, son of William and Mary Noakes. Enlisted in Dover.
> C/677, Corporal, 'D' Company, 7th (Service) Battalion, East Kent Regiment 'The Buffs', 55th Brigade, 18th 'Eastern' Division. Landed in France on 28th July 1915.
> Killed in action at Ypres on 10th October 1917, aged 22. Buried in plot XII.D.2 of Cement House Cemetery, Poelcapelle, Belgium.
> Commemorated on the Rye Harbour War Memorial & on the Camber War Memorial (St. Thomas church). Entitled to the 1914-15 Star, British War Medal & Victory Medal.

Henry Charles LEEDS-GEORGE
> Born in 1886. Son of Frederick and Sarah-Ann Leeds-George of Offens Farm, East Guldeford.
> 28127, Private, 'B' Company, 8th (Service) Battalion, East Surrey Regiment, 55th Brigade, 18th 'Eastern' Division. [Formerly 9240, Private, with 3rd Battalion, Royal Sussex Regiment.]
> Killed in action on the Somme during the Battle of the Ancre on 19th November 1916 aged 30. Commemorated on panels 6B & 6C of Thiepval Memorial to the Missing, France.
> Commemorated on the East Guldeford War Memorial. Entitled to the British War Medal & Victory Medal.

Robert MARSHALL
> Born in late 1894 at Broomhill Farm and enlisted in Rye; son of Samuel Arthur and

Emma Jane Marshall of 46, Grove Road, Ore, Hastings.

5/1851, Private, 1/5th 'Cinque Ports' (Territorial Force) Battalion, Royal Sussex Regiment, (from 21st February 1915) 2nd Brigade, 1st Division > (20th August 1915) Pioneer Battalion, 48th '1st South Midland' Division. Battalion arrived in France on 18th February 1915; fought at Aubers Ridge (9th May 1915). In August 1915 it became a pioneer battalion.

Died in base hospital of enteric fever on 10th October 1915, aged 20. Buried in plot III.D.5A of Etaples Military Cemetery, France.

Commemorated on the Rye Harbour War Memorial and on the Camber War Memorial (St. Thomas church). Entitled to the 1914-15 Star, British War Medal & Victory Medal.

Leonard MARTIN

No details except that his name appears on the Camber War Memorial (St. Thomas church).

Frederick SOUTHERDEN

Born in Broomhill, Jury's Gap in April 1884. Second son of Mr & Mrs. Frederick Southerden of Jury's Gap. Employed as a fisherman. Mother deceased by time of 1911 Census. Married to Alice; lived at Castle Hill Avenue, Folkestone, Kent.

130280 Driver, 'D' (Heavy) Battery, 63rd Brigade, Royal Field Artillery, 12th 'Eastern' Division.

Fought on the Somme in 1916 and at Arras in 1917.

Killed in action on 1st December 1917, aged 33, during the Battles of Cambrai; took part in the successful initial tank attack and in the capture of Bourlon Wood but died in the German Counter-Attacks, possibly as a result of his wounds. Buried in plot IV.L.16 of Péronne Communal Cemetery Extension, France.

Commemorated on the Rye Harbour War Memorial and on the Camber War Memorial (St. Thomas church). Entitled to the British War Medal & Victory Medal.

SERVED IN AND SURVIVED THE GREAT WAR (4 MEN IN ADDITION TO JACK HICKMAN TRACED)

Joseph Arthur MILLER

Born in 1893. Enlisted (aged 21 years and 8 months) in Newhaven on 10th November 1914; worked as an agricultural labourer. Married to Kate Brann and lived at 'the Bungalow' in Camber.

52333, Bombardier, 45th Siege Battery, Royal Garrison Artillery. Landed in France on 1st September 1915.

Entitled to the 1914-15 Star, British War Medal & Victory Medal. Demobilised to Army Reserve, Class 'Z', on 16th February 1919.

Charles SOUTHERDEN

Born in Broomhill, Jury's Gap c. February/March 1883. First son of Mr. & Mrs. Frederick Southerden of Jury's Gap. Employed as a fisherman. Mother deceased by time of 1911 Census. Brother of Frederick Southerden who was killed in action at Cambrai in 1917.

Single on attestation, aged 32 years, 9 months – 8th December 1915, Rye. Longshore fisherman. Embodied 27th March 1916 at Hilsea Barracks, Portsmouth.

130284 Gunner, 54th Battery, 39th Brigade, Royal Field Artillery, 1st Division.

Fought on the Somme in 1916, during the German Retreat to the Hindenburg Line and at the Battle of Messines in June 1917.

Served in France from 29th July 1916 to 9th August 1917; wounded (gunshot wound, right arm, 'severe') on active service on 23rd July 1917. Home until 24th October 1918, when discharged as 'physically unfit to serve'; Silver War Badge No.B32464, List RA/2537.

Entitled to the British War Medal & Victory Medal. Pension of 16/6d; applied for campaign medals in March 1921.

Harry SOUTHERDEN

Born in 1889 at Broomhill Farm, son of Samuel and Alice Elizabeth Southerden. Married to Elizabeth Isabella – one son.

86733, Lance-Bombardier, 142nd Heavy Battery, Royal Garrison Artillery. Attested on 9th December 1915 (aged 26 years and 11 months); mobilised to Royal Garrison Artillery on 27th May 1916. With the British Expeditionary Force in France and Flanders.

Entitled to the 1914-15 Star, British War Medal & Victory Medal.

William Daniel SOUTHERDEN

Born in Camber c.1877, son of Samuel and Alice Elizabeth Southerden.

Attested on 17th November 1915. Longshore fisherman. Adjudged fit for garrison duty only.

G/49331, Private, 25th Battalion, the Middlesex Regiment. Posted to Hong Kong on 9th September 1916; returned to England on 14th February 1919. Due to serve in Siberia but adjudged 'unfit for service' (general debility and deformed feet – medical at Netley Hospital).

Discharged on 9th May 1919. Silver War Badge No.205641, List E/1633/1.

APPENDIX 2

GUERNSEY'S 9TH 'SCOTTISH' DAC

OFFICERS, AWARDS & CASUALTIES

Officers

Lieutenant-Colonel	Hubert de Lancey Walters DSO	[Guernsey]
Captain	R.T. Perry MC, MiD	[Guernsey]
Captain	W.R. Powell	[Guernsey]
Lieutenant	W.W Le M. Goff (later Captain) Commanding 'A' Section	
Lieutenant	R.C. Sowells	[Guernsey]
Lieutenant	R.H.B. Lorraine	[Guernsey]
2nd Lt	R.M. Nicholls later 53rd Bde, RFA	[Guernsey]
2nd Lt	W.H. Ozanne MC, MiD	[Alderney]
2nd Lt	W.H. Bainbrigge	[Alderney]
2nd Lt	A. Delves	[not C.I.]
2nd Lt	Watson	
2nd Lt	Fahy	
2nd Lt	Joseph J. Eveson	[91216 Gunner, 2nd Draft; commissioned RFA]
2nd Lt	Wilfred Hansford Gallienne CBE	[89246 Driver, 1st Contingent; commissioned RFA February 1916]

Awards

Military Cross (MC)

Captain	R.T. Perry
2nd Lieutenant	W.H. Ozanne

Military Medal (MM)

89266 Corporal	S. Allen	(9/DAC)

89302 BSM	Percy Edward de Carteret	(C/53 RFA)
89304 Sergeant	Stanley Collins	(50 Bde RFA and 9/DAC)
89285 Gunner	William P. Herivel	(D/50 RFA)
90956 Sergeant	Alexander C. Ferguson	(D/311 RFA, 62nd Division)

Mentioned in Despatches (MiD)

Captain	R.T. Perry
2nd Lieutenant	W.H. Ozanne
89239 Fitter/Corporal	W.H. Herring (killed in action with 122 Battery, 52nd Brigade, RFA)

Meritorious Service Medal (MSM)

89220 Sergeant	George Le Page	(9/DAC)

Commander of the Order of the British Empire (CBE)
2nd Lieutenant Wilfred Hansford Gallienne (1931)

Known Casualties

The lists of casualties include men who were serving with 9/DAC, or were attached from or transferred from the unit; included are men from Guernsey and from mainland UK.

Killed

12498 Driver Charles Henry Ashworth	born, lived and enlisted in Liverpool; married; died of wounds, (40), with 9/Division HQ; Arras sector; 24th April 1917; IV.E.20 Duisans British Cemetery, Etrun.
89325 Gunner Clifford Philip Baker	born St. Martins, Guernsey; killed in action (23) with B/51 RFA; Somme; 14th November 1916; VII.L.41 Warlencourt British Cemetery.
89321 Gunner Alfred Bichard	killed in action (20) with D/51 RFA; Arras sector; 17th April 1917; C.16 Athies Communal Cemetery Extension.

89289 Gunner John <u>Bihet</u>

killed in action (22) with 50 Brigade RFA; Arras sector; 26th May 1917; III.G.18 Aubigny Communal Cemetery Extension.

89317 L/Bombardier Emile <u>Blaise</u>

died after the war on 17th April 1926. Thought to be buried in St. Sampson's, Guernsey[1].

204334 Gunner Benjamin <u>Bursey</u>

born Walsall; died from illness, with 9/DAC; the Somme; 18th February 1918; I.B1.26 Bray Military Cemetery.

168882 Driver Harold Edward <u>Buss</u>

born in Tonbridge, Kent; killed in action (22) with 9/DAC; Arras sector; 28th March 1917; II.L.3 Faubourg d'Amiens Cemetery, Arras.

89301 Sergeant Thomas <u>de la Mare</u>

born Les Messuners, Guernsey; killed in action (29) with C/53 RFA; Ypres Salient; 19th December 1915; I.B.58 Ypres Reservoir Cemetery.

90886 Gunner Cecil M. <u>de la Rue</u>

died of wounds 70 (H) Battery, 34 Bde RFA; Arras sector; 29th April 1917; burial site uncertain.

61007 BQMS Thomas Walton <u>Grant</u>

born in Kent; killed in action (27) with 9th DAC; Ypres Salient; 12th September 1917; XII.H.3 of Vlamertinghe New Military Cemetery.

91218 Gunner Stanley Slade <u>Green</u>

killed in action (24) with D/51 RFA; Arras sector; 22nd April 1917; I.G.12 St. Nicholas British Cemetery.

91352 Gunner A. <u>Hammond</u>

died of wounds with D/155 AFA; Dunkirk sector; 26th October 1917; B.21 Buffs Road Cemetery, Ypres.

89239 Fitter/Cpl W.H. <u>Herring</u>, MiD

born St. Peter Port; killed in action with 122 Battery, 52 Brigade, RFA; Arras sector; 28th August 1918; II.D.18 Monchy British Cemetery.

6731 Driver William F. Hill — born in Fife, Scotland; died of wounds with 9th DAC on 12th September 1917; Ypres Salient; IV.D.13 Mendinghem Military Cemetery.

89237 Gunner/Wheeler Arthur Jenkins — died (19), 5th 'C' Reserve Brigade, 11th July 1916; east of church, St. Peter Port, St. John, Churchyard, Guernsey.

89231 Gunner James Martin Keyho — born St. Peter Port; killed in action with C/51 RFA; the Somme; 20th November 1916; pier & face 1A & 8A of Thiepval Memorial to the Missing.

89223 A/Bombardier J.W. Le Noury — killed in action with A/232 RFA; towards Lens; 1st July 1917; I.B.9 Belgian Battery Corner Cemetery.

89222 Gnr William Thos. Le Noury — killed in action with 9/DAC RFA attached 77 Heavy Artillery Group; Ypres; 13th December 1917; IV.B.20 Ypres Reservoir Cemetery.

91734 Driver Wilfred Le Vasseur — died in UK, 17/DAC, 2nd November 1917; Screen Wall IIB, 125 Huddersfield (Edgerton) Cemetery.

89210 Gunner John Henry Luxon — killed in action (23) with 'V' TMB RFA 9/Division; Arras sector; 20th April 1917; Bay 1, Arras Memorial to the Missing.

89193 Bombardier Wilfred H. Nicolle — killed in action (20) with C/50 RFA; Arras sector; 20th April 1917; E.12 Athies Communal Cemetery Extension.

91389 Gnr Cecil Wm Jas Marquand — died of wounds (21) with C/23 RFA; Arras sector; 26th December 1916; XX.L.7A Etaples Military Cemetery.

89185 Gunner Henry Rupert Rabey — died of wounds (30) with 9/DAC;

109588 Gunner Sidney Wm Neighbour

59127 Driver William Jas P. Richards

89167 Gunner Bert Strappini

35382 Driver John Sunlay

33670 Driver Walter Swainston

105175 Driver David Thomas

91760 Gnr William James Tostevin

90948 Gnr Charles Thomas Wallbridge

the Somme; 9th November 1916;
I.Y.41 Bécourt Military Cemetery
Bécordel-Bécourt.

resident of Birmingham; killed in
action with 9/DAC; the Somme;
21st June 1916; A.28 Chipilly
Communal Cemetery Extension.

born in Pershore killed in action,
(23), with 9/DAC; Ypres Salient;
16th October 1917; XI.F.7
Vlamertinghe New Military
Cemetery.

killed in action (20) with D/175
RFA; south of Ypres Salient; 9th
June 1917; VIII.D.6 Cité Bonjean
Military Cemetery, Armentières.

born in Cleveland; killed in action
with 9/DAC; Arras sector; on 18th
May 1917; II.C.9 Anzin-St. Aubin
British Cemetery, Arras.

born in Kingston-upon-Hull; killed
in action with 9/DAC; Arras sector;
18th May 1917; II.C.8 Anzin-St.
Aubin British Cemetery, Arras.

born in South Wales; killed in
action with 9/DAC; Ypres Salient;
12th September 1917; XI.H.16
Vlamertinghe New Military
Cemetery.

died of wounds (20) with D/79
RFA; Arras sector; 3rd May 1917;
IV.M.41 Duisans British Cemetery,
Etrun.

resident of Guernsey; killed in
action (31) with D/47 RFA; Ypres
Salient; 15th August 1917; panels 5
& 9 Ypres (Menin Gate) Memorial
to the Missing.

132400 Driver Frederick Ware

born in Eastbourne; killed in action with 9/DAC; Ypres Salient; 12th September 1917; XII.H.4 of Vlamertinghe New Military Cemetery.

89156 Gnr Thomas Chas Waterman

resident of St. Peter Port, Guernsey; killed in action (33) with 9/DAC; the Somme; 21st June 1916; A.29 Chipilly Communal Cemetery Extension.

Wounded, injured or sick

2nd Lieutenant A. Delves

wounded bringing in captured enemy guns, Arras sector, April 1917.

2nd Lieutenant Watson
2nd Lieutenant Fahy

wounded with 51st Brigade RFA, Ypres Salient, 19th/20th October 1917.

89238 Driver Jack Hickman

wounded, the Somme, 24th March 1918.

89327 Gunner George Ash

hospitalised, Lillers, 26th August 1915.

89264 Driver J. Baron

hospitalised, Ypres, 24th October 1915.

89320 Gunner Clifford James Bichard

wounded with B/51 RFA, the Somme, 25th March 1918.

91717 Gunner Yves Boscher

wounded, Ypres, Dunkirk sector, 28th October 1917.

89310 Gunner Frederick A.J. Brown

wounded and sick, dates unspecified date.

89306 Sergeant Barrington Cherry

wounded with C/50 RFA, unknown 1915. [70952 BQMS Royal Garrison Artillery]

90954 Gunner G. John Corbin

wounded (right eye), 6th July 1917 [Silver War Badge]

89302 BSM Percy Edw. de Carteret MM

wounded with C/53 RFA, the Somme, 19th July 1916.

91676 Corporal Alfred L. Denbouy

hospitalised, 1917 (unspecified date).

91777 Gunner William Basil Despointes

wounded with 311 Brigade, RFA 62nd Division, Arras sector, 26th May 1917.

89299 Gunner Jack <u>Dorey</u> — wounded with C/50 RFA, Ypres Salient, 25th April 1918.

91789 Gunner George William H. <u>Dunn</u> — wounded with 92nd Bde, RFA, 20th Division, 3rd Ypres, 1st October 1917.

89296 Gunner Gerald <u>Duquemin</u> — hospitalised, Méteren, 22nd May 1915.

89252 Bombardier Charles <u>Falla</u> — slight wounds with 53 Bde RFA, 1917.

91764 Gunner Thomas Henry <u>Falla</u> — gassed with B/50 RFA, 3rd Ypres, 17th October 1917.

90956 Sgt. Alexander C. <u>Ferguson</u> — wounded with D/311, Arras sector, 28th July 1917.

89246 Dvr. Wilfred Hansford <u>Gallienne</u> — wounded, 1917, date unspecified.

89245 Wheeler Robert Thos. <u>Galpin</u> — wounded, Arras sector, 24th November 1916.

89??? Gunner G. <u>Gardner</u> — hospitalised, Loos, 28th September 1915.

89242 Acting-Bombardier Henry <u>Gill</u> — gassed, date unknown.

91290 Gunner Edgar George <u>Hamon</u> — wounded (burns) with D/107 24th Division, Arras sector, 5th August 1917.

89248 Gunner Clifford <u>Ferbrache</u> — wounded, Ypres Salient, 12th September 1917 but remained at duty.

91732 Gunner Arthur George <u>Huddle</u> — hospitalised, Ypres, 13th October 1917.

89236 Gunner Jack S. <u>Johnstone</u> — hospitalised with B/50 RFA, the Somme, 24th March 1918.

89234 Gunner Ted <u>Joughning</u> — hospitalised 3 times, Arras sector, 28/12/16 with C/51 RFA; 28/01/18 with C/51 RFA, the Somme; 08/06/18 with D/317, 63rd Naval Division near Méteren.

91712 Gunner Emile <u>La Joie</u> — hospitalised with 17/DAC, the Somme, 26th December 1917.

89227 Bdr William Henry <u>Lawrence</u> — wounded with 9/Heavy TMB, Arras sector, 7th April 1917.

89226 Gunner Cecil Le <u>Gallez</u> — wounded with RGA, Ypres Salient, 27th September 1918.

91656 Gunner Reginald Le <u>Huray</u> — hospitalised in Mesopotamia, 26th April 1917.

91674 Driver Phillip <u>Le Meur</u> — hospitalised with 84 AFA, Arras sector, 10th May 1917.

89221 Sergeant Ernest H. <u>Le Page</u> — hospitalised with RFA, 67 Division, Arras sector, 11th January 1917

89218 L/Bombardier Hilary <u>Le Page</u> — hospitalised with 9/DAC RFA, Lillers, 18th June 1915.

89282 Gunner J. <u>Le Roy</u> — hospitalised with 9/DAC, Loos sector, 12th September 1915.

89212 Gunner Archibald <u>Le Tullier</u> — hospitalised with 9/DAC, St. Omer, 14th May 1915.

89202 Driver H. <u>Mahy</u> — hospitalised with 9/DAC, Ploegsteert sector, 2nd February 1916.

89??? Gunner C.A. <u>Mallett</u> — hospitalised with 9/DAC, 1917.

91393 Driver Frederick William <u>May</u> — hospitalised with SAA section in Mesopotamia, 10th June 1918.

91457 A/Bdr Nicholas G. W. <u>Mugford</u> — hospitalised with 227Bde RFA, 45th Division in India, 20th July 1918.

89194 Gunner Thomas <u>Naftel</u> — wounded with C/50 RFA, Ypres Salient, 15th October 1917.

89277 Gunner J. <u>Ollivier</u> — hospitalised with 9/DAC, The Bluff, Ypres, 5th October 1915.

91807 Gunner Alfred <u>Pagnier</u> — wounded, 1917.

89168 Gunner James <u>Stagg</u> — wounded with 52nd Brigade RFA, 1917.

89167 Gunner Bert <u>Strappini</u> — resident of Guernsey; wounded with 9/DAC, the Somme, 21st June 1916. [Later killed in action on 9th June 1917]

89254 Gunner W.C. <u>Sebire</u> — wounded with 9/TMB, unknown date.

89??? Bombardier W.G. <u>Taylor</u> — hospitalised with 9/DAC, Lillers, 18th August 1915.

89175 Gunner W.H. <u>Walbridge</u> — hospitalised with 9/DAC, Ypres Salient, 29th November 1915.

90961 Gunner C.E. <u>Wright</u> — wounded, RFA, 1917.

---

1 Details of Emile Blaise are confusing, though some excellent research has been carried out by Liz Walton in her article, 'A Case of Mistaken Identity', that appears in Journal 17 (December 2007) of the Channel Islands Great War Study Group.

APPENDIX 3

THE HICKMAN FAMILY TREE (OUTLINE)

Name = Shepherd or 'Looker'
Name = to Australia/Tasmania

GGP = Great grandparents
GP = Grandparents
F/M = Father/Mother

GGP   William Hickman   1800   m.   Anne Bean GGP
(1781-??) Iden   (1780-1840)

                          1838
Mary   GP   Henry   m.   Martha Pope GP
1811   1806   1811
(Iden)   (EG)

Elizabeth   Hannah
1814   1817
(EG)   (EG)

(Iden)
William   James m Frances
1803   1809
Wm/Eliz/Thos   Geo/Eliz/Maria/Ben

m
Sarah = Eliz/Wm/Nellie

                          1868
F Henry   m.   Naomi M
1843-1920   Butchers
(Broomhill)   1845-1909
               (Rye)

Benjamin   Maryann   Sarah   James
1821   1830   1834   1836

William   m Naomi   John Bean   m Isabella   George
1834   1828   1840   1838
= John F/Ben James   = James H./Edward
1867   1871   1874   1877
= Chas Edward   = Elizabeth
1869   1872

                          1915
Henry William   'JACK'   m.   Ada Palmer W
1871   1891-1975   Roy/Wm.Chas/Jack
                (Broomhill)   Kate

Geo Ernest   Julia
1873   1876

Anna Maria
1869

Frank   Charles Joseph   Catherine
1882   1884   1888

Edmund
1879

Jack   Maisie   Ronald   Barbara
1919   1920   1921   1925

APPENDIX 4

THE BIHET FAMILY AT WAR

Like so many other Channel Islands families, the Bihet family must cherish their contribution to both the Great War and the Second World War. Between them, members of the family served in both the British and the French forces, as well as in the army, the navy and civilian services. Among the Bihet servicemen, two were killed during the Great War and at least two more were killed during the Second World War.

The family originated on the French mainland closest to the Channel Islands or 'Les Iles Normands' as they are known in France. Pierre François Desiré Bihet (who was born in Normandy on 3rd November 1857) and Marie Anne Desirée Picot (born in Normandy on 16th February 1865) were French nationals who eloped to Jersey as their families opposed their mixed-religion marriage. Having initially settled by 1891 on the east coast of Jersey at 'Les Viviers' near St. Martin, the couple moved to St. Anne on Alderney (by 1901), the smallest of the three principal islands, although most of their adult children remained on Jersey. According to the 1901 Channel Islands Census, the family lived at 'Doyle Place, Crabby' – fourteen residences, not differentiated by number or name. Today, 'Route Crabby' runs from the eastern end of 'Platte Saline' to the base of the eastern mole in the harbour though 'Doyle Place' does not appear on modern-day maps. The Bihet family lived in a dwelling comprising four occupied rooms, housing (in 1901) eleven persons:

Pierre	(43) stone quarryman	born: Normandy (French national)
Marie	(36)	born: Normandy (French national)
Ernest Peter	(16) stone quarryman	born: St. Helier, Jersey
Arthur Joseph	(14) stone quarryman	born: St. Martin, Jersey
Marie Louise	(11)	born: St. Martin, Jersey
Marcel George	(9)	born: St. Martin, Jersey
*John (Jean)	(6)	born: St. Martin, Jersey
Constant Henri	(5)	born: St. Martin, Jersey
Ada	(4)	born: Vale, Guernsey
Joseph	(2)	born: Alderney
Justine	(6 months)	born: Alderney

*John Bihet's name is mis-spelt on some records as 'James Bihet'.

Later, the couple moved from Alderney to Guernsey where they lived at Grange-au-Val, La Carrière, in the northern Parish of Vale. All the children, with the exception of Marcel and Justine, made their homes in Jersey.

When war came in August 1914, the young men of the extended family did more than 'their bit'. For Marcel Bihet, who was born on 9th May 1891, war was simply a hazard of his trade as he was a professional soldier who had volunteered for the Royal Field Artillery as a driver (No. 71086 then 1008623) in November 1912, serving in 119th Battery from 28th January 1913. Marcel travelled on H.M.T. '*Rohilla*' to India where he landed in December 1913; he was transferred to 90th Battery from 12th January 1914 and was stationed in Nowshera and Peshawar (now part of Pakistan) on the North-West Frontier, near the border with Afghanistan. He served in India until August 1917. At that point, with crisis looming large in Mesopotamia, Marcel was then sent to modern-day Iraq, where he served until 25th December 1918 – he was again transferred, to 336th Brigade from 14th May 1918. Unlike younger brother John, Marcel survived the war and eventually returned home to Guernsey in April 1919, where he married his wife Marie Josephine (née Allain) and lived at Woodlands Cottage, Le Bouet, St. Peter Port, and remaining a member of the RFA Reserve until November 1932. For his war service Marcel was awarded the 1914-15 Star (medal roll RFA/360B, page 51001), the British War Medal and the Victory Medal (medal roll RFA/233 A-B, page 8107). Although Marcel came through the conflict, for his wife Marie the war brought heartache. Her brother, Pierre Marie Allain who was born in Plouha, near Paimpol in Northern Brittany on 24th September 1879, joined the 355ème Régiment d›Infanterie (of France) that served with 127ème Division, 6ème Corps d'Armée during the First World War. He was killed in action on 4th April 1918 during '*die Kaiserschlacht*' offensives on the Somme in 'hand-to-hand' fixed-bayonet fighting in the village of Grivesnes (18 miles east of Amiens) during an attempt to retake the village from the advancing Germans. For his bravery, Pierre Allain was awarded the Médaille Militaire and the Croix de Guerre. He is commemorated on the St. Peter Port War Memorial, the St. Magloire War Memorial in St. Joseph's Church and on the French Consulate's Memorial in St. Thomas' Church, Jersey.

Three of the Bihet lads enlisted together in the Royal Field Artillery, their numbers being consecutive – 89289 Gunner John Bihet, 89290 Driver Constant Henri Bihet and 89291 Driver Arthur Joseph Bihet. Initially, they served in 9th 'Scottish' Division's Ammunition Column (9/DAC), landing in France on 13th May 1915 but John later transferred within the division to a newly-created mortar unit – Y9 Trench Mortar Battery, 9th 'Scottish' Division. It proved to be his undoing. On the night of 26th-27th May 1917 John Bihet died of wounds sustained during a night bombing raid on his camp. Just 22 years-old, John is buried in plot III.G.18 (towards the south-eastern corner) of Aubigny Communal Cemetery Extension, ten miles north-west of Arras on the St. Pol road. Gunner John Bihet was entitled to the 1914-15 Star (medal roll RFA/9ATB, page 6439) the British War Medal and the Victory Medal (both on medal roll RFA/226B, page 25096).

John Bihet's two (literal) brothers-in-arms, Arthur and Constant, both survived the Great War, serving in 9th Division Ammunition Column for much of the conflict and had previously served with the Guernsey & Alderney Artillery. All three of the brothers went to France with the 1st Alderney Contingent. On 6th August 1916 Arthur Bihet was posted to 'D' Battery, 52nd Brigade RFA, retaining the rank of driver, though on 10th January 1917, as a consequence of DAC reorganisation, he was posted to 'D' Battery, 50th Brigade RFA and assumed the rank of gunner.

The oldest of the Bihet brothers, Ernest, was born in St. Helier, Jersey on 30th January 1885; in his mid-teens he began work as a quarryman, like his father Pierre, yet five years later on 19th April 1906 he chose to volunteer to serve as a regular in the Royal Navy. According to records, Ernest was five feet six and an half inches tall, had medium brown hair, light hazel eyes and a fresh complexion. His service number was 310014 and he reached the rank of Leading Stoker, serving aboard HMS *'Empress of India'* and HMS *'Warrior'*. Ernest was invalided out of the Navy in April 1915.

Marie Louise Bihet, the third oldest of the Bihet children, was born in St. Martin, Jersey in 1890 or 1891. As an adult, she married Henry 'Harry' Thomas who had served pre-war with the RGA & E Alderney Contingent; as part of the wartime army he was posted to a Trench Mortar Battery in the rank of Bombardier. Harry was awarded the Military Medal for his brave actions on 15th November 1916.

The sisters of the Bihet lads made a considerable contribution to the war effort. Ada worked in the munitions industry making cordite while Justine and (Marie) Louise served as nurses, the former with the Red Cross and the latter with the Queen Alexandra Imperial Military Nursing Service. Two of these sisters had husbands who served in the wartime Army.

The next generation of the Bihet family also played a part in the Second World War. Constant Bihet's son, Ken, served in the Royal Navy and was killed aboard H.M.S. *'Hood'* when the ship was sunk by the German battleship *'Bismarck'* on 24th May 1941 in the Battle of the Denmark Strait, off the west coast of Iceland. Only three men of the *'Hood'*'s crew of over 1,400 men survived.

Bernard Joseph, was the son of Ernest Peter Bihet and of Katharine Matilda Bihet (née Harvey); he served in the Second World War as 14914991, Private, 7th Battalion, the Duke of Cornwall's Light Infantry. He died on Monday 21st May 1945, drowning in the River Ouse. He is buried in plot J.18 of Kempston Cemetery, Bedfordshire.

The following details have been gleaned from surviving army service records at the National Archives, Kew, London:

Arthur Joseph Bihet

Born in July 1886 in St. Martin, Jersey.

Son of Peter Francois Bihet and Mary Bihet.

Lived at Grange-au-Val, Vale, Guernsey.

28 years 8 months on 17th March 1915.

Quarryman.

Single.

1st Alderney Contingent.

Enlisted by Corporal Richings, 2nd RGLI.

Medical examination by Surgeon Major Livesey on 5th March 1915 at Fort Albert, Alderney. Category 'A1'.

Attested for the RFA in Guernsey on 17th March 1915.

Height: five feet three inches; *'scar of boils on back'*; 125 lbs; good physical development; perfect vision.

Joined at Bordon, Hampshire.

89291 Driver

9th Divisional Ammunition Column

9th 'Scottish' Division

Guernsey Artillery Contingent.

Embarked on 12th May 1915 from Southampton for the BEF; landed at Le Havre, France on 13th May 1915.

6th August 1916 posted to 'D' Battery, 52nd RFA Brigade with the rank of Driver.

10th January 1917 posted to 'D' Battery, 50th RFA Brigade with the rank of Gunner (a consequence of DAC reorganisation).

3rd September 1917 to 15th September 1917 granted leave to England with ration allowance (returned to Guernsey?).

1st July 1917 – granted Class 1 proficiency pay.

15th October 1918 to 29th October 1918 – granted leave to UK with 14 days' ration allowance.

25th April 1919 – to continental dispersal centre to prepare for release.

1st May 1919 – left France.

2nd May 1919 arrived at dispersal centre on Guernsey for demobilisation.

Transferred to Army Reserve Class 'Z' on demobilisation.

Entitled to the 1914-15 Star (medal roll RFA/9ATB, page 6439), the British War Medal and the Victory Medal (medal roll for both medals, RFA/226B, page 25096).

Constant Henri Bihet

[Papers endorsed, *'Alien Origin – parents French'*.]
Born: 1895 in St. Martin, Jersey.
Lived in Alderney.
Son of Peter Francois Bihet and Mary Bihet.
Joined at Bordon, Hampshire.
89291 Driver
9th Divisional Ammunition Column
9th 'Scottish' Division

Constant enlisted in the Royal Field Artillery as a driver at the age of 19, on 18th August 1914. Prior to that he was employed as an 'assistant cook', His service records describe him as being 5ft 4½in tall, with a chest *'girth fully expanded'* of 35½". He had a scar over his left eyebrow, and *'various scars of boils about lower chest'*. He weighed 132lbs. He married Laura Suzanne Grivel on Alderney in 1915, and lived with Mrs. Love at The Val on Alderney.

Constant landed at Le Havre, France on 13th May 1915. He served in France with the 9th Division Ammunition Column (same as his brother Arthur and initially as his brother John) as part of the *'Expeditionary Force France 1915, 1916, 1917, 1918'*. However, on 18th April 1917 he was posted to 'B' Battery, 51st Brigade, RFA and in November 1918 he was posted to the XIX Corps. Surprisingly, late in 1918 he was stated to be *'of Alien Origin'* due to his French parentage and this was investigated at the request of the RFA by the Alderney Police. The War Office declared, in October 1918 that, *'having been born in the Channel Islands he is a British Subject. His parents however are French Subjects and his documents should therefore be marked "alien origin" and he should be considered as coming under the provisions of A.C.I.578 of 1918'*. Of the five brothers who enlisted and fought in the Great War, he is the only one whose records indicate he was investigated in this manner.

Constant Bihet was despatched to the Dispersal Centre at Wimbledon on 10th January 1919 where he was assessed as medical category: 'A1'. He was demobilised on 5th February 1919 and transferred to class 'Z' of the Army Reserve. He returned to the Channel Islands later in February 1919 and subsequently lived on Alderney. He was entitled to the 1914-15 Star (medal roll RFA/9ATB, page 6439), the British War Medal and the Victory Medal (medal roll for both medals, RFA/226B, page 25096).

Medal Index Cards

Medal Rolls are in WO329 at the National Archives; consult, *'Key to Medal Rolls'* in WO329/1 to convert roll reference to a specific reference in WO329.

APPENDIX 5

SALIENT DATES IN JACK HICKMAN'S LIFE

1891

1st May   Born in Broomhill hamlet, Camber near Rye, Sussex.

1901

April   Living with his parents, Henry & Naomi, at 'The Lodge', Camber, Rye, Sussex. Attending Camber School.

c. 1905   Apprenticed as a carpenter and maker of golf-clubs in Sussex – the latter at Rye Golf Club.

1905-10   Member of Rye Athletic Club.

1910   Applied successfully for a position as assistant golf professional at Royal Guernsey G.C. Lodged with Mr. Charles & Mrs. Emily Shipton, 'Glencoe', 293, Les Landes, Vale, Guernsey.

1911-14   Served in the Royal Guernsey Militia – No.1957.

1915

Mar   Enlisted in Royal Field Artillery, 89238 Driver.

Mar   RG & A E 'en bloc' to 9th Scottish DAC, Bordon Barracks, UK.

Mar-May   RFA and divisional training around Bordon area.

May 13th   Landed Le Havre, France, to join the BEF.

Sep/Oct/Nov Loos and Ypres.

Nov 29th   UK on leave. Married Ada Palmer in Plumstead.

Dec 5th   Rejoined unit from leave.

1916

Jan 14th   Admitted to 29th Field Ambulance, France for denture repair.

Jan-Dec   Ploegsteert and the Somme.

1917

Jan 25th   UK leave '...with ration allowance'.

Feb 10th	Returned to unit near Larresset (west of Arras) after being delayed at Dover and Boulogne.
Feb-Dec	Hindenburg Line, Arras, Lens and Cambrai.
Christmas	UK leave; time with Ada and family.

1918

New Year	UK leave continued.
Jan 6th	Returned to his unit at Sorel near Péronne (on the Somme).
Mar 27th	Battle of St. Quentin – *wounded* – to 38th Casualty Clearing Station at Pont Rémy.
Mar 31st	To 22nd General Hospital at Camiers, near Etaples, then evacuated to UK aboard H.T. *'Ville de Liege'*.
Apr 4th	Arrived at Fusehill War Hospital, Carlisle, England.
June 21st	Discharged from Fusehill War Hospital, Carlisle; granted ten days' leave home leave after 118 days in hospital.
July 1st	To Artillery Command Depot, Ripon, Yorkshire – part convalescence, part medical check on progress.
Aug 10th	To Charlton Park Training Depot, Woolwich, officially posted to 5C Reserve Brigade, RFA.
Sept 18th	Posted to 61st Reserve Battery, RFA at Abby Wood, Lessness Park, Bexley Heath.
Sept 24th	Posted to BEF, France and crossed Channel to Boulogne.
Sept 29th	Posted to 1st Convalescent Depot, Harfleur, Normandy.
Oct 15th	Rejoined HQ, 9/DAC near Courtrai, Belgium.
Nov 5th	Unit inspected by King Albert of the Belgians.
Nov 11th	Armistice. Harlebeke, Belgium.

1919

Feb 18th	To Fovant Dispersal Camp No.1, Wiltshire to prepare for demobilisation.
Mar 19th	Demobbed to Class 'Z' Army Reserve.

1922

	Ended his association with Royal Guernsey G.C.

1923-40

	Employed by Thanet Golf Club, Hengrove, Margate – professional golfer and club-maker.

1925

Nov 20th	Applied for British patent for new golf club.

1926

June 10th   British patent granted for Jack's club innovation that he named, 'The *Hickman Bamfee Club*'. Now retained in the archive at the Royal & Ancient Golf Museum, St. Andrews, Scotland.

1940

May   Danger of invasion following 'Dunkirk' in May. Evacuated with family to Broxbourne, Hertfordshire.

1940-45

'Duration'   Worked in the Enfield Lock Royal Small Arms Factory (R.S.A.F.).

1945-6

Hengrove course was badly damaged during the war, so he sought employment as a golf professional at Westgate Golf Club, near Margate, Kent.

1968

Retired from the world of professional golf.

1975

December   Died aged 84 years.

APPENDIX 6

LOSSES AT MÉTEREN VILLAGE, 1914 & 1918

4TH DIVISION CASUALTIES AT MÉTEREN, 13-14TH OCTOBER 1914

33 men of 1/Royal Warwickshire Regiment were either re-buried or had the cemetery built around them – these men are recorded as *'buried near this spot'* [shown as 'bnts'].

22 other men of 1/RWR [10th Brigade] are buried in the cemetery.

18 men of 2/Seaforth Highlanders [10th Brigade] are buried in the cemetery.

9 men of 1/King's Own (Royal Lancaster Regiment) [12th Brigade] buried in the cemetery.

5 men of 2/Essex [12th Brigade] buried in the cemetery.

3 men of 1/Royal Irish Fusiliers [10th Brigade] buried in the cemetery.

1 Lieutenant of 1/King's Own (Royal Lancaster Regiment) [12th Brigade] – is buried in an isolated grave in Méteren.

91 Total

4TH DIVISION – MÉTEREN MILITARY CEMETERY, ACTIONS OF 13-14 OCTOBER 1915

10 Brigade	1/RWR	2/Seaforth H.	1/R. Irish Fus	**Total**
	55	18	3	76
12 Brigade	1/King's Own	2/Essex		
	10	5		15
				91

Pte T.W. Andrews 1101 (25) bnts 1/RWR	13/10
Pte G.E. Barnes 7273 bnts 1/RWR	13/10
Pte J. Alexander 9199 (34) 2/Seaforth Highlanders	13/10
L/Cpl A. Bates 412 bnts 1/RWR	13/10
Pte E.F. Bayliss 9991 (28) bnts 1/RWR	13/10
Pte W.H. Berry 6501 bnts 1/RWR	13/10
Pte S. Billington 2035 bnts 1/RWR	13/10
Pte Joseph Blackmoor 2356 (22) bnts 1/RWR	13/10

Pte H. Brassington 2118 bnts 1/RWR	13/10
Cpl C. Brooks 815 1/RWR	13/10
Pte A. Brown 9955 1/RWR	13/10
Pte A. Burrows 9762 (35) bnts 1/RWR	13/10
Pte W. Cairns 2148 1/RWR	13/10
L/Cpl W. Calder 960 2/Seaforth Highlanders	13/10
Pte J. Calderbank 804 bnts 1/RWR	13/10
Pte W. Cholmes 9044 2/Seaforth Highlanders	13/10
Major Wm. Charles Christie MiD twice (41) 1/RWR	13/10
Pte John Cleaver 225 (30) 1/RWR	13/10
Pte T. Coldicott 2119 1/RWR	13/10
Pte J. Cooke 7916 (29) 1/King's Own	13/10
Pte T. Cooper 7791 bnts 1/RWR	13/10
Pte W. Cramp 157 (29) bnts 1/RWR	13/10
Pte H. Daft 717 bnts 1/RWR	13/10
L/Cpl Joseph Dunn 8996 (29) bnts 1/RWR	13/10
Sgt H.C. Easey 9361 (26) 1/RWR	13/10
Pte William Everitt 9549 (21) 2/Essex	13/10
L/Cpl M. Gordon 7632 2/Essex	13/10
Cpl A.E. Green 2133 1/RWR	13/10
Pte H. Hales 2105 (22) bnts1/RWR	13/10
Pte Frank Harris 9158 (31) bnts1/RWR	13/10
Pte S. Haskey 8971 bnts 1/RWR	13/10
Pte R. Hastie 8898 2/Seaforth Highlanders	13/10
Pte W.E. Hawthorne 2185 (20) Spec Memorial 1/KO	13/10
Pte W.O. Hoden 9066 (36) bnts 1/RWR	13/10
Pte W. Innes 9934 2/Seaforth Highlanders	13/10
Pte A. Irvine 9648 2/Seaforth Highlanders	13/10
Pte O. Jephcott 425 bnts 1/RWR	13/10
Pte T. Jordin 98668 2/Seaforth Highlanders	13/10
L/Cpl A. Knight 79 bnts 1/RWR	13/10
Pte K. Mackay 8883 2/Seaforth Highlanders	13/10
Pte S. Magson 2199 bnts 1/RWR	13/10
*Pte A. Morris 166 [Served as Rodgers] 1/RWR	13/10
Pte C.F. Moseley 9390 bnts 1/RWR	13/10
Sgt. J. Murray 10490 (26) 2/Seaforth Highlanders	13/10
Pte J. McGlennon 2085 1/KO	13/10
Pte E.H. Narborough 9196 bnts 1/RWR	13/10

Cpl D. Owen 1355 bnts 1/RWR	13/10
Pte B. Palfreyman 9868 bnts 1/RWR	13/10
L/Cpl Benjamin E. Palfreyman 7118 (31) bnts 1/RWR	13/10
Pte Charles Paton 8970 (28) 2/Seaforth Highlanders	13/10
Pte W. Payne 7458 2/Essex	13/10
L/Cpl E. Pickett 9820 2/Seaforth Highlanders	13/10
Pte T. Potter 9552 2/Seaforth Highlanders	13/10
Pte T. Piggott 8137 1/KO	13/10
Pte A.W.N. Price 2010 1/RWR	13/10
Cpl A.H. Proctor 9163 1KO	13/10
*Pte Fred Rodgers 166 [served as Morris] 1/RWR	13/10
L/Cpl John Ross 9482 (26) 2/Seaforth Highlanders	13/10
Pte W. Rowley 97 bnts 1/RWR	13/10
2/Lt Arthur Molesworth Samuels (25) 1/R. Irish Fus	13/10
Pte William Shaw 8772 (26) 2/Essex	13/10
Pte Isaac Shortman 681 (24) 2/Seaforth Highlanders	13/10
Pte H. Simmons 9058 bnts 1/RWR	13/10
Pte J. Smart 270 bnts 1/RWR	13/10
Pte John Smellie 9492 (29) 2/Seaforth Highlanders	13/10
Pte H. Smith 8735 2/Essex	13/10
Pte N. Smith 3/6769 (23) 2/Seaforth Highlanders	13/10
Pte A. Stewart 9372 (27) 2/Seaforth Highlanders	13/10
Pte D. Swanson 9514 2/Seaforth Highlanders	13/10
Pte J. Taylor 9951 bnts 1/RWR	13/10
Col. Sgt Philip Thornton 9484 (33) bnts 1/RWR	13/10
Pte E. Valentine 8829 1/KO	13/10
Pte C. Wall 9439 bnts 1/RWR	13/10
Pte H.J. Wall 9296 bnts 1/RWR	13/10
2/Lt Arved Waterhouse (23) 3/Bn attached 1/KO	13/10
Pte Alfred Edward Williams 3 (27) bnts 1/RWR	13/10
Pte Richard Alexander Wilson 10840 (19) 1KO	13/10
Pte J. Connor 4716 1/Royal Irish Fusiliers	14/10
Pte Victor William Fisher 10936 (20) 1/King's Own	14/10
Pte Samuel Shiveral 9115 (27) 1/R. Irish Fusiliers	14/10

Each entry above is set out in the following order:

* Also known as…; Rank; Initial(s); Surname; regimental number; (age if known); buried near this spot; unit; other information such as 'Special Memorial'; date killed.

Abbreviations used in the tables:

Ranks:

Pte = Private	Gnr = Gunner	L/Cpl = Lance-Corporal
Cpl = Corporal	L/Sgt = Lance-Sergeant	Sgt = Sergeant
Col Sgt = Colour Sergeant	CSM = Company Sergeant-Major	
2/Lt = 2nd Lieutenant	Lt = Lieutenant	

Units:

1/RWR	1st Battalion, Royal Warwickshire Regiment
2/Sea H	2nd Battalion, Seaforth Highlanders
1/KO	1st Battalion, King's Own (Liverpool) Regiment
2/Essex	2nd Battalion, Essex Regiment
1/R. Irish Fus	1st Battalion, Royal Irish Fusiliers
Coy	Company (standard military abbreviation)
M-i-D	Mentioned in Despatches in an officer's report

9TH 'SCOTTISH' DIVISION – CASUALTIES AT MÉTEREN, JUNE TO AUGUST 1918

50 men of 8/Black Watch [26th Brigade] are buried in the cemetery.

26 men of South African composite battalion [South African Brigade] are buried in the cemetery.

19 men of 2/Royal Scots Fusiliers [28th Brigade] are buried in the cemetery.

14 men of 11/Royal Scots [27th Brigade] are buried in the cemetery.

14 men of 5/Cameron Highlanders [26th Brigade] are buried in the cemetery.

13 men of 7&7/8 Seaforth Highlanders [26th Brigade] are buried in the cemetery.

11 men of 6/King's Own Scot. Borderers [27th Brigade] are buried in the cemetery.

7   men of Scottish Rifles [28th Brigade] are buried in the cemetery.

7   men of 9 Battalion MGC [9th Division] are buried in the cemetery.

5   men of 12/Royal Scots [27th Brigade] are buried in the cemetery.

2   men of 9/Seaforth Highlanders [Pioneers] are buried in the cemetery.

2   men of 26th Trench Mortar Battery are buried in the cemetery.

1   man of 50th Brigade, RFA is buried in the cemetery.

171   Total

9TH DIVISION – MÉTEREN MILITARY CEMETERY, ACTIONS OF SUMMER 1918

				Total
26 Brigade 'Highland'	8/Blk Watch 50	5/Cam. H. 14	7/Seaforth H. 13	77
27 Brigade 'Lowland'	11/R.Scots 14	12/R.Scots 5	6/KOSB 11	30
28/S. Afr Bde	S. African Bn 26	2/R. S. Fus 19	9/Scot Rifles 7	52
26 TMB				2
9 Bn MGC				7
50 Bde RFA				1
9/Div Pioneers			9/Seaforth H.	2
				171

Cpl J. Shaw S/8766 7/Sea H	30/05
L/Cpl E. Fernie 28753 6/KOSB	03/06
Pte J. Foster 27015 6/KOSB	03/06
Cpl D. Pearson 6845 (22) 6/KOSB	03/06
Pte J. Prinsloo 12708 2/S Afr Inf	04/06
Pte J. Tutlis 48699 12/RS attached 26/TMB	09/06
Pte T. Day 30313 9/Sco Rif	15/06
Pte J. Masterton S/18387 (20) 8/BW	15/06
Pte D.F. Failes 17626 2/RSF	16/06
Pte J. McEwan 53643 2/RSF	17/06
Pte L.A.F. Norrie 13260 1/S Afr Inf	17/06
Pte W.H. Collins 46248 (22) 11/RS	20/06
Pte C. Smithson 41803 11/RS	20/06
L/Sgt Samuel Mark 23816 (31) 2/RSF	21/06
Pte Henry Cunningham 41184 (28) 2/RSF	24/06
Pte Bert Evans 53375 (19) 12/RS	24/06
Pte Robert Williamson 51298 (19) 'D' Coy 12/RS	24/06
Pte Henry James Lavell 11292 (29) 4/S Afr Inf	24/06
Pte Percy Harry Samuel King 204307 (19) 7/Sea H	28/06
L/Cpl Donald J. Macdonald S/24579 (19) 7/Sea H	28/06
L/Cpl Colin Alex. Smith S/16972 (39) 'B' Coy 7/Sea H	28/06

Sgt Archibald Selkirk S/12392 (23) 7/Sea H	30/06
Pte Arthur Lewis Barnett 2015 (21) 'E' Coy 4/S Afr Inf	12/07
Pte J. Gillespie 16141 (33) 4/S Afr Inf	12/07
Pte A. Buchanan 11605 (27) 2/S Afr Inf	12/07
Pte R. Pepper 42960 12/RS	13/07
Cpl Alexander Anderson 7505 (32) 4/S Afr Inf	19/07
Pte Sidney Stephen Ball 16710 (21) 2/S. Afr Inf	19/07
Pte Ernest Lister Burnett 15648 (27) 4/S Afr Inf	19/07
Cpl Edward Sextus Davidson 8612 (29) 2/S. Afr Inf	19/07
2/Lt Francis Douglas (24) 4/S Afr Inf	19/07
Pte A.L. Fanning X/734 4/S Afr Inf	19/07
Pte A. Gordon 15811 4/S Afr Inf	19/07
Pte E.F. Gouws 6561 (28) 4/S Afr Inf	19/07
Sgt George John Alfred Hatfield 5773 (29) 4/S Afr Inf	19/07
Pte J.H. Henning 10121 4/S Afr Inf	19/07
Pte Wm. Slater Robinson King 10287 (22) 4/S Afr Inf	19/07
L/Cpl Osmond Payne 16742 2/S Afr Inf	19/07
Pte Norman Sidney Shaul 12389 4/S Afr	19/07
Pte J. Stevenson 7305 2/S Afr Inf	19/07
L/Cpl S.W. Young 16740 (25) 2/S Afr Inf	19/07
Pte Thomas Sutton Clark S/30986 (41) 5/Cam H	19/07
Pte W.N. Gillies MM S/40448 5/Cam H	19/07
L/Cpl E. Kane S/18999 5/Cam H	19/07
Pte W. McBain S/23599 5/Cam H	19/07
Pte D. McDonald S/40081 5/Cam H	19/07
Pte Wm. McPhail S/41571 (18) 5/Cam H	19/07
Pte A. Robertson S/31200 5/Cam H	19/07
Pte Wm. Blane Smith S/31230 (19) 5/Cam H	19/07
Sgt G. Tew 8550 5/Cam H	19/07
Pte David James Waddell S/41529 (18) 5/Cam H	19/07
Pte Gavin Ralston Craig 24203 (38) 11/RS	19/07
Pte William Brennan 132263 (18) 9/Bn MGC	19/07
Cpl N. Dunbar 117055 (20) 9/Coy MGC	19/07
Sgt Roderick J. Walder MM+Bar 55928 (20) 9/MGC	19/07
Pte S. Williams 133287 9/Coy MGC	19/07
Pte J. Anderson 32299 2/RSF	19/07
Sgt R.A. Baxter MM 10353 (25) 2/RSF	19/07
Sgt Thomas Francis Brien 10723 (21) 2/RSF	19/07

Pte J. Campbell 7149 2/RSF	19/07
Sgt David Wm. Carrick Lunn 14081 (30) 2/RSF	19/07
Pte J Milligan 53718 (18) 2/RSF	19/07
Pte F McNelis 41555 2/RSF	19/07
Pte P. Baillie S/23969 8/BW	19/07
Pte C. Borthwick S/43540 8/BW	19/07
Pte A.W. Botterill [aka Davies] S/12230 8/BW	19/07
2/Lt. Robert Laurie Brown (28) 8/BW	19/07
2/Lt James Burt (20) 3/BW attached 8/BW	19/07
Pte G. Carter S/17059 (20) 8/BW	19/07
Pte A. Cook 291899 (27) 8/BW	19/07
Pte Wm. Macfarlane Craig 24203 (38) 8/BW	19/07
Pte A.T. England 267593 (20) 'C' Coy 8/BW	19/07
Pte J. Ferguson S/40471 8/BW	19/07
Pte Thomas Mackie Fleming (19) S/41510 8/BW	19/07
Pte J Forbes 268884 8/BW	19/07
Pte Thomas Forbes 40866 (23) 8/BW	19/07
Pte J. Fraser 235055 8/BW	19/07
CSM John Galloway 5766 (40) 'A' Coy 8/BW	19/07
Pte T. Girvan S/42069 8/BW	19/07
Pte Peter Davidson Gordon 240039 (26) 8/BW	19/07
Pte A. Hay S/40818 8/BW	19/07
Pte A. Inglis S/12543 (22) 8/BW	19/07
Pte W.N. Johnston S/20758 (19) 8/BW	19/07
Pte A.M. Kiddie 267920 8/BW	19/07
Pte T.A. King S/15963 8/BW	19/07
Pte R. Macdonald S/41543 (21) 8/BW	19/07
Pte A. Maxwell S/11700 8/BW	19/07
Pte W. McGregor S/11188 (41) 8/BW	19/07
Pte Peter McIndeor 285033 (24) 'B' Coy 8/BW	19/07
Pte J. McIntyre 42076 8/BW	19/07
2/Lt J.W. Musgrove (21) 4/BW attached 8/BW	19/07
Lt Hugh Dobie McMillan (36) 8/BW	19/07
Sgt S. Nelson 846 8/BW	19/07
2/Lt Peter Peebles (28) 4/BW attached 8/BW	19/07
Pte G. Phillips S/9369 8/BW	19/07
Pte R. Quinn S/41474 (19) 8/BW	19/07
L/Cpl J. Rochford S/3510 8/BW	19/07

L/Cpl Thomas Seaton S/40698 (21) 8/BW	19/07
L/Cpl John Duncan Sim 292003 (28) 8/BW	19/07
Pte A. Spence 350252 (21) 8/BW	19/07
Pte Alfred James Stewart 268216 (30) 8/BW	19/07
Pte David Wm Taylor S/40255 (22) 8/BW	19/07
Pte Chas. Randall Thomson S/42046 (19) 8/BW	19/07
2/Lt John Archibald Tillie (19) 8/BW	19/07
Pte H. Todd S/42050 (19) 8/BW	19/07
Pte Wm. Gifford Johnson Tulloch S 41576 (19) 8/BW	19/07
Pte Bernard Tully S/42083 (18) 8/BW	19/07
Pte Samuel H. Turnbull 290443 (34) 'B' Coy 8/BW	19/07
Pte D. Wright S/23279 8/BW	19/07
Lt James Logie Young (24) 'B' Coy 8/BW	19/07
Pt Robert Black 43438 (23) 12/RS	20/07
Sgt John Wm Wall Murray MM 6067 (26) 2/S Afr Inf	20/07
Pte O.J.F. Du Toit 13275 2/S Afr Inf	20/07
Pte W. Haddow S/24164 (19) 9/Sea H	20/07
Pte B.G. Clow 48039 (30) 2/RSF	20/07
Cpl C.G. Harwood 452 (27) 'A' Coy 2/S Afr Inf	21/07
Pte J.H. Bedwell 127181 9/Bn MGC	21/07
Pte E. Birch 154674 9/Bn MGC	21/07
Pte G. Richardson 107374 (18) 9/Bn MGC	21/07
2/Lt T.D. Don (27) 5/BW attached 8/BW	21/07
Pte C. Harrison 35473 9/Sco Rif	22/07
Pte Samuel Rugg S/22967 (19) 8/BW	23/07
Pte A.J. Best 2003 4/S Afr Inf	23/07
Pte W. Blackwood S/2491 9/Sea H	23/07
Pte Harry Smith Hoskins 43328 (21) 9/Sco Rif	23/07
Pte Hugh McPhee S/31557 (19) 5/Cam H	23/07
Pte S/12072 T. Dewhurst (26) 7/Seaforth	24/07
Pte John Maclean S/ 24889 (18) 7/Sea H	24/07
Cpl Peter Fowler Glass 28034 (35) 9/Sco Rif	25/07
Cpl A. Waters 15307 11/RS	25/07
Pte C. Dunnigan 42641 11/RS	26/07
Sgt John Todd MM, 12655 (23) 'C' Coy 11/RS	26/07
Pte James Wm Smith 41672 (32) 'C' Coy 6/KOSB	26/07
Pte J. Warren 41633 6/KOSB	26/07
L/Cpl John R. Matheson S/12681 (24) 7/Sea H	30/07

L/Cpl Mervyn John Murphy 1023 (23) 7/Sea H	30/07
Pte Wm. Stewart Roger S/24043 (19) 7/8 Sea H	30/07
Pte R. Walker S/40916 7/Sea H	30/07
Pte W. Watt S/24094 (19) 7/Sea H	30/07
L/Cpl J. Brown 29010 2/RSF	30/07
Pte Alex Stuart Ireland 201724 (25) 2/RSF	30/07
Pte W. Rose 20946 2/RSF	30/07
Pte W.B. Sinclair 41416 2/RSF	30/07
Pte T. Roberts 302601 11/RS	31/07
Pte Harold Moir Weaver 38521 (25) 'C' Coy 11/RS	31/07
L/Sgt J. Hanby 51726 11/RS	05/08
Pte D. Clark S/22566 5/Cam H Special Memorial	07/08
Pte W. Docherty S/41515 5/Cam H Special Memorial	07/08
Pte W.A. Ferguson MM S/22518 5/Cam H	07/08
Pte Matthew King S/17001 5/Cam H + 26/TMB Sp M	07/08
Pte J. Keith 36990 (19) 9/Sco Rif	12/08
Pte T. Brown 42412 9/Sco Rif	18/08
Pte J.C. Whittle 42362 9/Sco Rif	18/08
Cpl J.M. Hanssen 3988 1/S Afr Inf	18/08
Pte J. Donnelly 51772 (20) 11/RS	18/08
Pte J. Haggart 41810 2/RSF	18/08
Pte W. Hunter 41835 2/RSF	18/08
L/Cpl T. McKie 51306 2/RSF Special Memorial	18/08
Pte H. Finnie (19) 42238 6/KOSB	18/08
Pte Henry Glass 32539 (19) 6/KOSB	18/08
Pte H. Hill 242112 (19) 6/KOSB	18/08
2/Lt E.I. Martin (25) 6/KOSB	18/08
Pte W. Plain 41284 (36) 6/KOSB	18/08
Pte Frank Young 242232 (18) 6/KOSB	18/08
Pte J.W. Cope 273085 (18) 11/RS	19/08
Pte Patrick John Henry 1181 (33) 11/RS	19/08
Pte Wm. F. Gordon 50627 (19) 11/RS	19/08
Pte A.L. Plenderleith 59560 11/RS	19/08
Pte A. Petrie 24492 12/RS	19/08
Pte S. Johnston 204965 7/Sea H	22/08
Gnr Harry Sawyer 786085 (21) 50 Bde RFA	10/09

<u>Note</u>: Among the dead were seven men who had earned Military Medals (MM); one

man, twenty year-old Sergeant Roderick Jesse Walder of 9/MGC had earned a bar to his MM – in effect he had won the medal twice.

Each entry above is set out in the following order:

Rank; Initial(s); Surname; regimental number; (age if known); unit; other information such as 'Special Memorial'; date killed.

Abbreviations used in the tables:

Ranks:

Pte = Private	Gnr = Gunner
L/Cpl = Lance-Corporal	Cpl = Corporal
L/Sgt = Lance-Sergeant	Sgt = Sergeant
CSM = Company Sergeant-Major	Lt = Lieutenant
2/Lt = 2nd Lieutenant	

Units:

6/KOSB	6th Battalion, King's Own Scottish Borderers
7/Sea H	7th Battalion, Seaforth Highlanders
9/Sea H	9th Battalion, Seaforth Highlanders
11/RS	11th Battalion, Royal Scots
12/RS	12th Battalion, Royal Scots
2/RSF	2nd Battalion, Royal Scots Fusiliers
9/Sco Rif	9th Battalion, Scottish Rifles (Cameronians)
8/BW	8th Battalion, Black Watch
5/Cam H	5th Battalion, Cameron Highlanders
1/S Afr Inf	1st Battalion, South African Infantry
2/S Afr Inf	2nd Battalion, South African Infantry
3/S Afr Inf	3rd Battalion, South African Infantry
4/S Afr Inf	4th Battalion, South African Infantry
9/Bn MGC	9th Battalion, Machine Gun Corps
9/Coy MGC	9th Company, Machine Gun Corps
50 Bde RFA	50th Brigade, Royal Field Artillery
26/TMB	26th Trench Mortar Battery
Coy	Company (standard military abbreviation)

APPENDIX 7

THE HICKMAN & PALMER FAMILY AT WAR

THE HICKMAN BROTHERS

89238 Driver Jack Hickman
Royal Field Artillery
HQ Company (from 1917)
9th 'Scottish' Division Ammunition Column (9/DAC)

Jack Hickman was born in May 1891 in Broomhill, near Rye, East Sussex, the youngest of Henry and Naomi Hickman's nine children (six boys and three girls). Jack was still single on the outbreak of war. He qualified as a carpenter, as had his older brother Frank, and similar to his brother Jack trained at Camber (Rye) Golf Club to be a professional golfer and club-maker. In 1910 Jack went to live on Guernsey at age nineteen approximately, as an assistant golf professional at the Royal Guernsey Golf Club on L'Ancresse Common in the north of the island. [See A.E. Rose, '*History of Royal Guernsey G.C.*'] On Guernsey Jack lodged with Mr. & Mrs. Shipton of 'Glencoe' in the Parish of Vale.

While on Guernsey Jack enlisted in the Artillery Company of the Royal Guernsey Militia where his regimental number was 1957. When war broke out in August 1914 many Guernseymen enlisted as individuals before the island's government decided to offer the War Office in Whitehall full companies of the island's infantry militia as well as the artillery and engineering units. The 'Gunners', including Jack Hickman, were sent as a single unit to 9th 'Scottish' Division to serve in the new role of Divisional Ammunition Column (9/DAC). Militiamen had to attest and enlist anew in the British Army and Jack's army papers fortunately survived the destruction of many records during the Second World War. His attestation on 20th March 1915 at the Town Arsenal in St. Peter Port was witnessed by Corporal R. Richings of the 2nd R.G. & A. Militia and counter-signed by 2nd Lieutenant E. Cowley, officer commanding the G. & A. Recruiting District. According to the records made at the time of Jack's army medical examination on 8th March 1915, he was 5ft 1½in tall, weighed 125 lbs., was of good physical development, had been vaccinated in infancy and, despite his youth, wore false teeth. Unsurprisingly, on enlistment Jack joined the Royal Field Artillery. He was just 23 years and 9 months of age.

Jack married Ada Mary Palmer in St. James's Church, Plumstead on 29th November

1915 during a week's leave that Jack had managed to obtain, possibly thanks to his sympathetic officer, Lieutenant Ozanne. Ada Palmer (always known to Jack as 'Flick') was born in Plumstead, Kent in 1894 and at the time of her wedding was a competent dressmaker living with her parents at 29, Raglan Road, Plumstead, SE18 (a quarter mile south-east of Woolwich Arsenal Railway Station). Ada's parents were William Palmer, a carpenter, who was born in Rye, Sussex in 1870 and Mary Ann Palmer (née Paine) who was born in Rye in 1870. Ada had three brothers – William Charles (Will), born in Whitstable, Kent in January 1892; Roy, born in Plumstead, Kent in 1892 or 1893; and Jack Palmer, born in Plumstead in 1895 or 1896. Ada also one sister, Catherine (Kate), who was born in Plumstead in 1900. Ada's mother, Mary Ann Paine, was the daughter of Edwin Paine, a carpenter, born in Iden, Sussex in 1849 and Joanna, who was born in Rye. Also living at the Raglan Road address in 1911 were Johanah (72 and a former dressmaker) and Edwin Paine (82 and a former carpenter). After the Great War Jack and Ada Hickman had four children, Jack (born in 1919), Maisie (born in 1920), Ronald (born in 1921) and Barbara (born in 1925).

Jack Hickman was seriously wounded during the early stages of the German Spring Offensive on the Somme in March 1918. He recovered sufficiently to return to the Western Front in October 1918 and crossed the River Rhine into Germany until his turn for demobilisation came around. Jack received three campaign medals, the 1914-15 Star [August 1920], the British War Medal [November 1923] and the Victory Medal [September 1921].

178336, Driver (later Signaller) Frank Hickman
Royal Field Artillery
42/DAC; 'C' Battery, 210th Brigade, 42nd '1st East Lancashire' Division; then
'C' Battery, 312th Brigade, 62nd '2nd West Riding' Division.

Frank Hickman was born in early 1882 in Camber, near Rye, East Sussex, the sixth of Henry and Naomi Hickman's nine children. He married his wife, Mary Elizabeth Alice (née Boultwood) in St. Lawrence Church, Thanet district on 29th October 1908. They had three children – Louise Naomi, born on 24th September 1910; Frank, born on 19th March 1914 and Mary, born on 24th September 1915 – all of whom were born in Ramsgate, Kent.

Frank initially worked as an agricultural labourer before qualifying through apprenticeship as a carpenter and subsequently as, '...a professional golfer and golf club-maker' at the St. Augustine's Links near Ramsgate (this appears on his army attestation form).

Frank attested his willingness to serve in the army on 8th December 1915 in

Ramsgate, Kent where he was resident with his family at 2, Strand Cottages, Cliff End, near Ramsgate, Kent. On attestation Frank was aged 33 years and 323 days. His army medical indicates that Frank was 5ft 5½in tall, weighed 135lbs, enjoyed excellent vision, was of 'good' physical development that was reflected in his categorisation as, '...A I'.

He was called up, first to Canterbury on 19th September 1916 and then on 13th October 1916 by Herne Bay sub-area Recruiting Office and was embodied as 178336, Driver (later Signaller), into Royal Field Artillery No. 4 Depot, on 16th October 1916 at Woolwich, where he soon qualified in '...signalling and telegraphy'.

15th June 1917 Frank was posted to the British Expeditionary Force in France where he joined No. 1 Section of 42nd '1st East Lancashire' Divisional Ammunition Column (DAC). The men of 42nd Division (an existing Territorial Force division) were drawn largely from, '...Manchester, Salford and the colliery and cotton towns of East Lancashire.' Prior to Frank's posting to '1st East Lancs', the division had been in the Mediterranean theatre, serving variously in the Suez Canal Defences and in the Gallipoli campaign in the Krithia sector. The unit was subsequently sent to the Western Front, reaching Pont Rémy in France on 15th March 1917.

From 42/DAC, on 17th August 1917 Frank was posted to the divisional guns of 'C' Battery, 210th Brigade that were then involved in the Ypres Salient. Between 6th and 10th September 42nd Division and 61st '2nd South Midland' Division were tasked to what were officially termed 'minor attacks', attempting to take strongpoints near Borry Farm and German gun-pits in Hill 35 (located between Wieltje and Passchendaele in the north-east of the Salient). Following the expensive failure of these operations (6th September cost in excess of 400 officers and men) General Haig subsequently ordered a suspension of minor attacks. Nevertheless, artillery 'duels' continued apace as the German artillery strove to inhibit the apparent British build-up of guns in the area of the Menin Road.

The frequent bouts of German high explosive, leavened with shrapnel and doses of poison gas were to prove Frank Hickman's undoing. His Army Record reveals that on 15th September 1917 he was admitted to No.12 Casualty Clearing Station at Needinghem near Ypres suffering from '...gas shell poisoning'. Frank was moved down the line to be admitted briefly to No.XI General Hospital near Camiers (possibly under American direction at that time) in France. On 20th September 1917 Frank was repatriated to the UK by hospital ship 'Carisbrooke Castle' and was sent to '3rd Western' General Hospital, Cardiff on 21st September. He was treated in South Wales until his discharge from Aberdare and Merthyr Red Cross Hospital on 7th November 1917.

On 19th November 1917 Frank was posted to the RFA Command Depot at Ripon in Yorkshire to complete his rehabilitation and medical assessment. Not until 20th April

1918 did Frank return to the BEF on the Western Front where he would remain beyond the Armistice. On 29th July 1918 he was posted to 'C' Battery of 312th Brigade. Frank suffered from a residual '...*ICT...damage to legs and right shoulder*'. ['*ICT*' was a general term used for suppurating skin diseases or *Pyodermia*]. The disability originated from 9th December 1918 when his unit was in Germany after the Armistice; admitted to 3rd Australian CCS on 24th December with numerous septic sores on both legs, right arm and right shoulder (a possible effect of earlier mustard gas poisoning); he was later transferred to 14th General Hospital, Wimereux. 21st January 1919 saw Frank's return to England as part of the demobilisation process; he was recorded as, '...*Signaller, C/312 Battery, 62nd '2nd West Riding' Division...*' and described as a, '...*carpenter*'. Prior to his demobilisation Frank was repatriated across the Channel to Southampton where he was temporarily sent to Eastleigh Casualty Clearing Station. This was not a CCS in the battlefield sense but was used to assess returning soldiers who had suffered battlefield injuries. Finally Frank was transferred to Class 'Z' of the Army Reserve.

He was entitled to the British War Medal and the Victory Medal (Medal Roll RFA/279B, page 35,791). Frank received his medals on 27th October 1921 at 2, Strand Cottages, Cliff End, near Ramsgate, his pre-war address.

Both the Hickman brothers survived the Great War. Unfortunately, no firm traces remain of the war service of Jack and Frank Hickman's other four brothers, George Ernest, Henry William, Edmund and Charles Joseph. Frank died in March 1957 at the age of 75 years.

THE PALMER BROTHERS

Parents: William Palmer married Mary Ann Paine in 1889 or 1890. William Palmer was born in Rye, Sussex in 1868 or 1869 and was a skilled carpenter; Mary was in born Rye, Sussex in 1869 or 1870. In 1901 they lived at 48, Purrett Road, Plumstead, Kent and in 1901 they lived at 29, Raglan Road, Woolwich, Kent.

The couple had five children: William 'Will' Charles (1892), Roy (1892 or 1893), John 'Jack' (1894 or 1895), Ada Mary (1893 or 1894) and Kate (1900). All three of the brothers died during, or as a direct result of, the Great War. Ada married Jack Hickman in November 1915 while he was still serving in the Great War.

S/19346, Rifleman William Charles Palmer
16th Battalion, the Rifle Brigade
117th Brigade, 39th Division

William Charles 'Will' Palmer was born in early 1892 in Whitstable, Kent. He was married to Alice and they lived at 26, Speranza Street, Plumstead, close to Will's parents. Like his father, Will was a skilled carpenter. He was 5ft 3in tall and Wesleyan by religion. He enlisted in the army in December 1915 in Woolwich and was embodied on 22nd May 1916. His army service record indicates that he served as S/19346, Rifleman, 16th Battalion, the Rifle Brigade, 117th Brigade, 39th Division. He landed at Le Havre in France on 27th August 1916 and joined his battalion on 7th September 1916. He had served just over three months before he was killed in action on 17th December 1916. As Will Palmer's body was never identified he is commemorated on panel 48 of the Menin Gate Memorial to the Missing in Ypres. He was entitled to the British War Medal and the Victory Medal (Medal Roll M/102B22, page 2886).

Apparently Roy and Jack Palmer enlisted together into the Royal Sussex Regiment as their regimental numbers were consecutive. However, they did not continue to serve in the same regiment as Jack was transferred to the Royal West Surrey Regiment.

G/17518, Private Roy Palmer
7th Battalion, the Royal Sussex Regiment
36th Brigade, 12th 'Eastern' Division

Roy Palmer was born in early 1893 in Plumstead, Kent. In 1911 he was an apprenticed plumber. Roy enlisted in the army in Woolwich, serving first in 1/6th Battalion of the Royal Sussex Regiment (as 2322, Private) and then as G/17518, Private, 7th Battalion of the same regiment. Roy served on the Western Front on the Somme, at Arras, at Cambrai and during the Kaiserschlacht. He was entitled to the British War Medal and the Victory Medal (Medal Roll E/2/101B8, page 1499). Roy was badly wounded during his army service and died soon after the end of the Great War.

G/24004, Private John 'Jack' Palmer
2nd Battalion, the 'Queens' (Royal West Surrey) Regiment
91st Brigade, 7th Division

John 'Jack' Palmer was born in 1895 or 1896 in Plumstead, Kent. In 1911 he was an apprenticed decorator. Jack enlisted in the army in Woolwich, serving first as 2323, 1/6th Battalion, the Royal Sussex Regiment then as G/24004, Private, 2nd Battalion, the 'Queens' (Royal West Surrey) Regiment in 91st Brigade, 7th Division. With this battalion Jack fought on the Somme in the following battles – 1st to 5th July 1916 in the Battle of Albert including the Capture of Mametz (1st July); 14th to 17th July 1916 in the Battle of Bazentin; 20th July 1916 in the Attack on High Wood; 21st July to 3rd September 1916 in the Battle of Delville Wood. 3rd to 7th September 1916 in the Battle of Guillemont. His battalion was back on the Somme after the turn of the year from 11th to 15th January 1917 and 21st February to 5th March 1917 in Operations on the Ancre. Between 14th March and 5th April 1917 they were in pursuit of the German Retreat to the Hindenburg Line. 2nd Queens then fought on the Arras front from 11th April to 16th June 1917 in the Flanking Operations around Bullecourt including from 3rd to 17th May 1917 in the Battle of Bullecourt and from 20th May to 16th June 1917 in the Actions on The Hindenburg Line. Jack Palmer remains in the Arras area as he was killed in action on 10th July 1917 at the age of age 22 years. He is buried in plot I.B.2 of Croisilles British Cemetery, 9 miles south-east of Arras. He was entitled to the British War Medal and the Victory Medal (Medal Roll E/1/101B12, page 2362).

GLOSSARY

TERMS, EXPRESSIONS AND NICKNAMES USED IN JACK

HICKMAN'S DIARIES & CONTEXT

NOTE ON 'OLD' UK MONEY

Until the early 1970's, one pound (£1-00p) consisted of 240 pennies; it could be divided into 20 shillings (each worth 12 pennies). Prices were shown in pounds (£), shillings (s) and pence (d). Today, one pound (£1-00p) consists of 100 pennies or pence – much simpler! So, one new penny is the same as 2.4 old pennies, except that inflation (we won't go there!) means that money was worth much more in 1914. For example, in 1899 the level of a family's 'poverty line' was judged to be £1 and 1 shilling per week.

GLOSSARY

Adjutant = senior administrative officer in a battalion; usually responsible for writing up the battalion war diary.

Armistice = a ceasefire; it is not a treaty but does stop the fighting. The Armistice was agreed and implemented from 11 a.m. on 11th November 1918. If it had been 'broken', the fighting would have re-commenced.

Army Reserve = following military service, most men who were demobilised were placed on the Army Reserve, in case of military emergency.

A.S.C. = Army Service Corps (insultingly nicknamed 'Ally Sloper's Cavalry' after a music-hall act). The ASC's role was to re-supply the troops in the field. Their job was often carried out under fire, was under-appreciated but vital. 'Royal' was added to the name (making the corps 'RASC') after the Great War ended. In modern times it has become the RLC – Royal Logistics Corps.

Artillery duel = a term used when the artillery of both sides attempted to neutralise each other. The infantrymen in their trenches were frequently caught in the hail of shells.

Attestation form = this was an army form used to 'enlist' a new recruit. It was signed by the recruit who then underwent a medical examination prior to acceptance by the army.

Aerial bombing = The Great War saw the first use of aerial bombing. Aircraft were initially used by both sides for observation purposes, while Germany used Zeppelins to bomb England. However, both sides came to use aircraft to bomb military targets at the 'front' and mixed military, industrial and civilian targets in their enemies' homelands.

Anti-typhoid inoculation = before being posted abroad most soldiers were inoculated against the dangerous disease typhoid that may be caught from contaminated food or water – not uncommon in the crowded trenches. Untreated, it could kill up to 40% of its victims. The inoculation itself caused many men to experience mild symptoms of this deadly 'flu-like disease.

Balloon, observation = tethered balloons were used for observing enemy troop movements and for observing the fall of artillery shells. Such balloons were, of course, very vulnerable to aerial attack. Observers in the balloon's basket were equipped with 'escape' parachutes.

B.A.O.R. – from March 1919, several divisions of the reorganised British Army occupied the German Rhineland, hence the name 'British Army of the Rhine'.

Barbed wire (also, the wire, wiring-party, re-wiring) = huge amounts of barbed wire, kept in place by metal stakes, were used in No Man's Land to protect the parapet of trenches. Damage to the 'wire' had to be repaired under the cover of darkness – it was a dangerous and unpopular duty.

Barrage (also artillery…, machine-gun…; creeping…, lifting…) = a barrage was another name for a bombardment. A 'creeping' barrage gradually extended the range of the artillery; a 'lifting' barrage moved forward in pre-arranged steps or lifts ahead of infantry, e.g. 100 yards forward every minute.

B.E.F. = British Expeditionary Force. This was the name for the British army that was sent to France and Belgium from August 1914; however, the name was retained throughout the war.

'Big push' = a major, set-piece attack such as at Arras in April 1917.

Bivouac or 'bivvy' = an improvised shelter, using whatever materials are available. In a wartime trench, soldiers often used a 'funk-hole' dug onto the trench wall and covered themselves with an oilskin cape and steel helmet as their only protection against the elements.

'Blighty' (also 'Blighty one') = Army slang originating on Indian service; possibly from an Urdu word meaning foreign or European. By association it came to mean 'home' or 'UK'. To 'cop a Blighty one' meant to suffer a wound serious enough to be invalided to UK but not serious enough to maim or kill.

'Boys in blue' (also **'hospital blues'**) = wounded or very sick men who were evacuated to hospital in the UK, wore a distinctive blue garb (with red tie) once they had improved sufficiently to leave their beds and get dressed.

Bridgehead, Rhine = this was an important river crossing such as at Köln (Cologne) in 1919, where the post-war Lowland Division garrisoned part of the Rhineland prior to the Peace Settlement.

Burst (also 'air burst', ground burst') = an artillery shell carried a fuze that could be set to detonate at various distances, thus it might explode on impact or, especially in the case of shrapnel shells, might be set to explode at several hundred feet above a trench or above attacking troops.

Casualty = a term covering any soldier who was put out of action, from 'walking wounded' to killed in action. Casualty 'figures' included those men who were ill, wounded, missing in action or killed. To a battalion, a casualty was, to put it bluntly, a man who could not carry out his military duty.

C.C.S. = Casualty Clearing Station where casualties were assessed, initially treated and sent 'down the line' for further treatment as necessary.

'Catch it', to/'Catch a packet', to... = to experience a heavy or especially accurate enemy bombardment.

Channel-crossing dangers = before air power, all troops, supplies, ammunition, artillery, transport, mail and the numerous wounded men had to risk the Channel crossing by ship. Inevitably, despite Royal navy escorts, atrocious weather, enemy mines and submarines took their toll of the transport vessels.

Chantilly Conference = Allied war leaders' held a conference in December 1915 at Chantilly near Paris to decide on military priorities for 1916. Another such conference was held in Chantilly during November 1916 to discuss Allied priorities for 1917.

'Civvy Street' = life outside the military.

Close-quarter fighting = hand-to-hand fighting, using any available weapons such as bayonets (difficult in a narrow trench), knives, sharpened entrenching tools, knuckle-dusters and coshes. In clearing an enemy trench, hand grenades (known as 'bombs') were especially effective.

Command Depot = this was a military convalescent camp, originally set up to free much-needed hospital beds. In early 1916 Command Depots were introduced to rehabilitate and re-train men between convalescent camp and the front line. Initially these Depots were in the UK but gradually similar Command Depots were established for wounded men treated and recuperating in France and Belgium.

CO/OC = Commanding Officer, was usually employed in respect of a battalion or similar unit. 'Officer Commanding', generally referred to the commander of a smaller unit, such as a Company.

Communication trench = a trench that linked fire-trench, reserve trench and support trench. The communication trench followed a zig-zag pattern to avoid enemy fire 'enfilading' the length of the trench. The communication trench was used for moving troops back and forth, re-supplying the front-line and evacuating casualties. During battle, movement along such trenches was supposedly in one direction only.

Cordite = a smokeless, explosive powder used as a propellant for shells and bullets. It has a distinctive smell.

Counter-attack = to carry out an attack in response to being attacked. German forces in particular were always expected to counter-attack.

CRA = Commander, Royal Artillery.

CRE = Commander, Royal Engineers.

D.A.C. = Divisional Ammunition Column, employed on re-supplying the guns with ammunition. It also re-supplied small arms ammunition (S.A.A.). Driver Jack Hickman belonged to 9th 'Scottish' D.A.C.

'Daily hate' = even when a sector was relatively quiet, both sides usually fired a few shells at each other. This was regular and was referred to as the 'daily hate'.

Defence in Depth = a system of defence, employed by the Germans at Passchendaele, to frustrate and absorb enemy attacks. It depended on the careful preparation of three 'zones' – the Forward Zone, the Battle Zone and the Rear Zone. Field-Marshal Sir Douglas Haig ordered the implementation of this system in the Somme sector prior to the German Spring Offensive of 1918. Please see Chapter 12 for a more detailed explanation of the system.

Demobilisation = the complex process of returning servicemen to civilian life.

Dispersal Area/Depot = a military centre (comprising barracks, huts or even tents for temporary accommodation) in the UK through which demobilising soldiers passed as part of their return to civilian life. There, a man was medically examined, surrendered his Army kit (and paid for losses!) and was issued with an Army employment certificate. Examples of such dispersal camps are Fovant and Chiseldon in Wiltshire, Clipstone in Nottinghamshire and Oswestry in Shropshire.

Diversionary attack = a minor attack to divert the enemy's attention from a main assault elsewhere. On the Somme on 1st July 1916, the attack on Gommecourt by 46th and 56th Divisions was intended to divert enemy resources from the major targets in the northern sector of the Somme front-line.

Divisional boundary (also corps… and army…) = official orders always specified the boundary between major units. This was done to avoid troops becoming intermingled during attacks.

Drumfire (also barrage fire) = known to the Germans as *'trommelfeuer'*, this referred to near-continuous, heavy shellfire. Prior to the start of the Somme offensive, this drumfire lasted for several days without respite.

Dump (also ammunition…, supply…) = a dump was an open-air supply store, whether weapons, ammunition, food, clothing or any other of the necessities of war. From the supply port, stores were moved usually by rail (standard then narrow gauge) to main dumps at the Corps or Divisional railhead; they were then moved on to brigade or battalion dumps by motorised or horse-drawn wagons. Each unit's stores were then collected by sections of each division's ASC units.

'Duration man' = soldier who enlisted for the 'duration of the war' only.

Eastern Front = the fighting front-line between Germany, Austria and the Russians in Eastern Europe.

Enfilading fire = firing down the length of an enemy trench, thus causing maximum casualties.

Entraining procedures = the process of moving say, a battalion from barracks to a railhead, boarding a military train and reversing the process at the destination. Practice decreased the time needed to put a unit into action.

Fire-bombs = also known as incendiary bombs. Initially dropped from Zeppelins, the bombs were wrapped in tarred rope to extend the burn after hitting the ground.

Fire-step (also reversing the…) = below the trench parapet was a fire-step cut into the earth of the trench, enabling infantry to fire over the top of the sandbags when under enemy attack.

Flank (also outflank) = military term referring to the vulnerable 'sides' of a unit. To outflank meant to partly surround and enemy.

F.O.P./F.O.O. = Forward Observation Post/ Forward Observation Officer – their function was to observe the fall of artillery shells on enemy targets and recommend adjustments to the artillery battery officers. Much of this role transferred to 'spotter' aircraft during the course of the war in the trenches.

Fritz, Old Fritz, "der Alte Fritz ist kaput." = soldiers spoke of 'Fritz' and 'Old Fritz' as a general term for their German enemies. They looked forward to the day when, "… der alte Fritz ist kaput" (when 'Old Fritz' is finished off.)

Front line (also the line, up the line, into the line) = front-line fighting trenches; came to mean 'in harm's way'.

Fuze settings = at the nose of an artillery shell was a carefully-milled, adjustable brass fuze. This determined in what position the explosive was detonated.

'Gallows humour' = the dark humour of the Tommies, very pessimistic in nature – making jokes at their own situation's expense.

GHQ, France = General Head Quarters in France, where the military 'top brass' planned the conduct of the war on the Western Front. For much of the war after 1915 General Haig's GHQ was at Montreuil, north-east of Etaples.

Ghurkas = renowned fighters of mainly Nepalese origin. 100,000 Ghurkas fought on the side of the British Empire in France, Belgium and in the Mediterranean theatre.

GS wagon = General Service Wagon – general purpose transport pulled by a team of horses. Used throughout the war but gradually superseded by lorries.

GSW = 'Gunshot wound'. Simple abbreviation employed in official Army records and communications.

'Go over the top', 'Go over the bags' = to climb over the sand-bagged parapet of a trench to cross No Man's Land to attack enemy lines.

Gotha bomber = the huge Gotha G.V was the first successful heavy bomber. With a wingspan of 77 feet, a crew of three, a bomb-lad in excess of 1,000lbs and defended by three machine-guns, the Gotha had a range of 500 miles. Consequently, from May 1917, Gotha raids on England were described as the 'First Blitz'.

Gun-lines = the gun-line was the 'front-line' for the artillery. The lighter the artillery piece battery, the further forward its gun-line. This depended on the range of the gun/howitzer and the time it took to withdraw the weapon from harm's way. Each gun/howitzer was dug in to its own gun-pit.

Gun-pit = a single position from which to fire an artillery piece; carefully sited, camouflaged and the guns dug-in, often reinforced by steel, timber and dozens of sandbags. Usually part of the 'gun-line'.

Hand grenade or 'bomb' = hand-held, small iron 'ball', filled with explosive and detonated several seconds after a securing pin has been removed from the top of the grenade. Commonly referred to as a 'bomb', hence a 'bomber' was really a grenadier. The alternative name of 'bombers' was coined when the Grenadier Guards objected to 'lesser' units being called grenadiers.

Hand-to-hand fighting = close-quarter fighting with bayonet or any makeshift weapon that came to hand when under attack.

Hard rations = emergency food supply to be consumed only when necessary. Derived from old name 'hard tack', a solid biscuit that was almost inedible unless soaked first. German troops used the term, 'iron rations'.

Headquarters (also H.Q.) = each army

unit on active service had its own HQ, from General Headquarters (Haig's was a Montreuil for much of the war), through Army, Corps, Division, Brigade and Battalion down to Company at the lowest level.

H.E. = high explosive that produces a powerful, violent effect such as gelignite and Tri-nitro tetrachloride (TNT).

Hindenburg Line/Siegfried Stellung (German name) = powerful, defensive line constructed by the Germans in 1916-17. It shortened and strengthened their front line from Arras to south of the Somme River.

Hospital = base or stationary hospitals were located far back from the frontline in France/Belgium. Unlike Casualty Clearing Stations, base and stationary hospitals rarely moved in reaction to changes to the front-line. Many of the wounded were transported to 'war hospitals' in the UK.

Howitzer = a short-barrelled, usually heavy, gun that fired a shell in a high trajectory. Derived from a German word for catapult.

'Hun', the Hun = another insulting term for Germans, deriving from the name of ancient barbaric Germanic tribes. This reflected animosity created by alleged German 'war crimes' early in the Great War.

'Jack Johnson' = black American heavyweight champion of the world from 1908 until 5th April 1915. Became slang name for German 15cm mortar and 21 cm howitzer shells that gave off a lot of black smoke on detonation.

'Jip' or 'Gyp' = pain or discomfort, as in "... giving me jip", or "...giving the enemy jip."

Jocks = a colloquial collective term for soldiers of Scots origin.

'Johnny' = yet another nickname for the Germans on the other side of No Man's Land.

'Kitcheners' = logical nickname given to lads who joined the 'New Army' that was raised by Lord Kitchener.

Light railway = a quickly-built, narrow gauge railway that linked standard gauge track to positions closer to the front.

Limber = two-wheeled 'cart' attached to a field-gun, pulled by a team of six horses; was used to enable the gun to go into (and out of) action. A GS wagon carried ammunition and all items necessary to keep the gun in action.

Line, breaking the... = the stuff generals dreamed of! Breaking through the enemy's lines of trenches and re-starting the war of movement.

Logistical problems = supply problems, such as ammunition, food, water, kit, medical supplies, tools, R.E. stores; often in the hands of the Army Service Corps (ASC).

Machine-guns (Lewis light m/gun, Vickers heavy m/gun) = on 30th November 1915 machine-gun changes were introduced – 4 Lewis Guns per battalion, while the Vickers Guns formed M/gun Companies and were allocated one per brigade – each company comprised 4 sections, 2 m/guns per section (one m/gun was valued at approximately 30 rifles).

Mesopotamia = modern Iraq.

Mills bomb = hand grenade that became standard issue in the British army.

Minenwerfer = a German-developed, short-range mine-launcher (literally mine-thrower). The 25cm muzzle-loading mortar was as effective as a mortar ten times its weight. The *'Moaning Minnie'* (nicknamed by the Tommies for the sound it made) was an important weapon in trench warfare.

Missing in action = when the roll-call was taken after a battle, any man not definitely accounted for as killed or wounded might well be posted as 'missing in action'. Such men might have been captured or killed in action. The effects of shelling often made identification of the dead impossible. These men are commemorated all along the battlefronts on Memorials to the Missing, such as the Menin Gate at Ypres and the Thiepval Memorial on the Somme.

Mortar = otherwise known as trench artillery, a mortar comprised a firing-tube attached to a base-plate containing a firing-pin. The standard British weapon was the Stokes mortar, while the German *'minenwerfer'* is described above. British mortar teams were unpopular with Tommy in the trenches as they attracted enemy fire in retaliation.

New Army = the 'civilian' army raised by Lord Kitchener became known as Kitchener's 'New Army', battalions of which were classified as 'Service' battalions available only for the duration of the war.

'Ninth', 'Old Ninth' = Abbreviated name of 9th 'Scottish' Division, that considered itself the cream of Lord Kitchener's New Army.

No Man's Land = the logical name for the area of land between the two frontlines as no-one could control it.

Offensive = a major, planned battle, attack, assault or a series of these. For example, the Arras Offensive, the Somme Offensive, the German Spring Offensive.

Offensive (objectives, tactical and strategic) = any kind of battle, attack or assault, usually on a large scale. Any offensive had both tactical (battlefield) and strategic (long-term) objectives

On home leave = being granted a brief, official break from military duty. A serviceman was provided with travel warrants, official passes (for absence from his unit) and a specific time and date for his return to duty. Failure to return on time was described as 'absent without leave', commonly known as going 'AWOL'.

'On thorns', to be... = to experience nervous anticipation, even 'wind up' before action.

'Our lot', 'our mob' = own troops, whether referring to 9th Division troops or the entire Allied side.

Patrol = patrols, comprising a few men and an officer, were often sent into No Man's Land at night in order to gain information on the enemy. It also gave the patrolling side the impression that they were 'dominating' No Man's Land.

Pioneer = from early in the war, each division was allocated a pioneer battalion (such as 9/Seaforth Highlanders of 9th 'Scottish' Division). Many such battalions were specially raised and contained men whose skills often complemented those of the Royal Engineers.

Poison Gas (also gas shells/gas cylinders/ Special Gas Companies) = both sides feared chemical warfare and the introduction of poison gases terrified many of the soldiers on both sides. Initially delivered by opening valves on gas cylinders, special gas shells made the delivery of gas easier for the attackers. The main gases employed were tear (lachrymatory) gas, chlorine gas, phosgene gas and most devastating, mustard gas that blistered skin and remained active for a long time.

Preliminary bombardment = most infantry attacks were preceded by a preliminary or preparatory artillery bombardment that was intended to destroy enemy positions, soldiers and communications. However, such a bombardment also announced an attack to the enemy. The preliminary bombardment on the Somme in July 1916 lasted for seven days, firing more than a million shells.

'Pots', big = a slang reference to 'heavy' shells.

QF gun = 'Quick-Firing' gun for example the British 18-Pounder QF Gun and the French 75mm QF Gun. Easily capable of firing fifteen rounds per minute, the French 'Soixante-Quinze' or '75' was generally considered to be the best field gun of the Great War.

Railhead = each main section of the front-line had a major railway centre to which were delivered, men, ammunition, supplies and weaponry. From the railhead, wagons and narrow-gauge railways delivered all of the above to Corps and Divisional dumps for onward movement.

RAMC = the Royal Army Medical Corps had the major responsibility for organising the transportation and treatment of wounded and sick men, from front-line to Military Hospitals back in the United Kingdom.

Retreat (also give ground, fall back) = a retreat usually seems to suggest defeat but a tactical withdrawal saved many an army unit to fight another day. Two of the best Great War examples were the Allied Retreat from Mons in August/September of 1914 and the German Retreat to the Hindenburg Line in 1917.

RFC/ RNAS/RAF = the single British air service, the Royal Air Force, was not created until 1st April 1918. Prior to that date, there existed two air services, one controlled by the Army (Royal Flying Corps or RFC) one controlled by the Royal Navy (Royal Naval Air Service or RNAS).

Rifles at the port = to carry a rifle at 45° to the vertical, held across the chest. It indicated that immediate opposition was not expected. The men who attacked on the Somme on 1st July were ordered to carry their rifles in this manner across No Man's Land – they were led to believe it would be a 'walkover' success.

Rifle grenade = a metal rod attached to a standard hand grenade. It was fired from a rifle using a blank cartridge. It increased the range of the grenade but quickly ruined the standard rifle in its normal role.

'Rough house' = a slang term for a fight, often used to refer to a 'pub brawl'.

Royal Marine Artillery (RMA) = Two RMA brigades served on the Western Front – the best-known of these was equipped with twelve heavy 15-inch breech-loading siege howitzers that fired a 1,400 lb shell.

S.A.A. = Small Arms Ammunition i.e. ammunition for hand-held weapons.

Salient = on a map a salient appeared as a bulge in the front-line, pressing into the enemy's line. A salient could be fired upon from three sides and was vulnerable to enemy weapons sited on adjacent high ground. The best-known salients were at Ypres in Flanders and at Flesquières to the south of Arras.

Salonika = in October 1915 an Anglo-French force landed at the Greek port of Salonika, with the intention of aiding Serbia against Bulgaria. The Allied presence remained there until the final year of the war.

Sapper = this was the lowest rank in the Royal Engineers. 'Sapper' became, by association, a nickname for any member of the RE.

Scotch infantry regiments = see 'Jocks' above.

Searchlight units = sections, sometimes companies, that logically were attached to anti-aircraft batteries

Service record, Pension record = every serviceman who served his country had a written service record. Those who were invalided from their service were granted a small pension, according to the severity of their injuries. During the Second World War, the records for men from the Great War were for the most part destroyed by incendiary bombs that hit the buildings housing the records. Only about 25% of the records survive in any shape or form.

Shell calibres = guns were rated according to the diameter (in inches or millimetres) or weight (in pounds) of the shells that they fired. The standard British field-gun in 1918 was the 18-pounder while the standard French field gun was the 75 mm (known as the 'Soixante-Quinze').

Shell types = many artillery pieces could fire a range of shells, according to the purpose of the firing. High explosive was used to destroy buildings, gun emplacements, transport systems and trenches; shrapnel shells were especially useful against enemy personnel while early in the war shrapnel was used to destroy barbed wire (rather unsuccessfully;) gas shells were more effective and accurate than the initial method of releasing the gas from iron cylinders.

Shrapnel – some shells were packed with small, iron balls; this shell could be fuzed to burst above troops causing numerous wounds. Shrapnel also refers to a shell's iron casing when it exploded into fragments, causing horrific 'rip' injuries to flesh.

Siege gun = these were heaviest and/or longest-ranged guns on the battlefield. The British used a small number of 15-inch naval guns mounted on railway wheels. The Germans used a huge, 42 cm. howitzer built by Krupps Armaments, and known as 'Dicke Bertha'. The Germans' legendary 'Paris gun', used against the French capital in the summer of 1918, had the longest barrel used in the Great War. It fired 210-pound shells a distance of eighty miles and reached a maximum height of 25 miles on its journey. Needless to say, its use against Paris was as a terror weapon.

Smoke candles = smoke candles were used to create an artificial fog to mask the advance of troops across No Man's Land. In the early use of poison gas, smoke candles were burned to intensify the natural 'fog' created by cylinder released gas.

'Silent Sue' = a trench-soldier's nickname for a huge fifteen-inch high velocity shell that exploded almost before it was heard – hence the name.

Sniper = this was a specialist marksman used by both sides in the war. A sniper needed to be an excellent shot, have good anticipation and be remarkably patient. Snipers were most effective where trenches were shallow or damaged. They were often given ironic nicknames by enemy troops (see also 'gallows humour'). Many snipers were experts in camouflage.

Southern Front = this was the battlefront between the Italian army and its Austrian and German enemies. In 1917, the Italians were under huge pressure so several British and French divisions were sent to the Southern Front.

Stand to (also 'stood to') = every available infantryman had to 'stand to' on the fire-step in his trench at dawn and again at dusk as these were considered the most likely times for the enemy to launch an attack. When the danger time was thought to be over, the men were 'stood down'. Whenever danger threatened at any time of day or night a man would be ordered to 'stand to'.

Stokes gun/trench mortar = this was a metal tube affixed to a base-plate; at the bottom of the barrel was a fixed firing-pin. A mortar shell, with fins for stability, was dropped down the barrel onto the pin, thus firing the shell in a high arc over No Man's Land. The firing-point or mortar-pit was easily traced by the enemy and so mortar teams quickly moved on, leaving the infantry to face the retaliation. Unsurprisingly, mortar teams were unpopular with the foot-soldiers.

Storm troopers = '*Sturmtruppen*' – German elite troops, specially-selected, highly-trained, lightly-equipped and capable of the rapid infiltration of enemy lines during an offensive. Most carried stick-grenades (known to the Tommy as a 'potato-masher') for close-quarter fighting and some were armed with the new 9mm sub-machine gun.

'*Time-expired man*' = a soldier whose period of enlistment has ended or is about to end.

'*Tommy Atkins*' (also shortened to '*Tommy*') = 'Thomas Atkins' or 'Tommy Atkins' was a name coined in the 19th Century possibly by the Duke of Wellington for the ordinary soldier when asked for a name to write onto a sample pay-book.

Training (also basic…) = basic infantry training lasted six months but was reduced as the demands of replacing casualties increased. Training continued once a man reached his battalion; as the war went on, so each attack was practised beforehand on the training ground.

Trench lines = the standard trench pattern on the British side was of three roughly parallel trench-lines – firing, support and reserve – each connected by zig-zagged communication trenches.

Trench mortar = see Stokes gun above.

Torpedo-boats = fast-moving coastal boats, armed with torpedoes, that could hit and run. German torpedo-boats caused problems off the Belgian coast.

Trench life = once trench lines had been established, both sides settled into recognisable patterns of trench life. This was dictated by weather, topography, enemy action, difficulty of adequate re-supply and the plans of the high command.

Trench raids = a trench raid might involve

any number of men up to company strength. The aim of such raids was to dominate No Man's Land and to raise morale; the objective might be to destroy a specific target, to cut enemy wire or to take prisoners for interrogation.

Troop transport = usually a troop-train or troopship, often requisitioned from civilian use.

Voluntary Aid Detachment (V.A.D.) = set up in 1909 (with the help of the Red Cross and the Order of St. John, the organisation provided voluntary nursing services. In excess of 38,000 VADs served in war hospitals or worked as ambulance drivers or cooks.

War correspondent = a journalist, e.g. Philip Gibbs, approved by the military authorities, who was allowed access to troops in forward positions or in rest.

War diary = during active operations, most units were required to keep a detailed record or diary of the unit's actions/ involvement. A unit's war diary recorded orders, changes in personnel, changes of location, details of enemy contacts, casualty lists; generally, only officers were mentioned by name, although early in the war Territorial battalions tended to mention casualties by name regardless of rank. Keeping the war diary up to date was the responsibility of the adjutant or another specified officer. Copies of the unit's daily diary was sent up to Brigade, Division or Corps H.Q. in order to give senior officers a wider view of the front-line.

War Hospital = in the U.K., war hospitals were distributed throughout the country; wounded men returned to the U.K. were often treated far from their homes.

'Whizz-bang' = a type of German shell. The name derived from the sound it made, giving men in a trench little warning of its arrival.

'Wind up', to have the… = a slang phrase to describe the acute feeling of fear prior to going into action or when under fire.

'Wipers' = Tommy's pronunciation of Ypres.

Wire cutting bombardment = originally, shrapnel shells were used in the attempt to cut enemy wire prior to an attack but early failures led to High Explosive shells replacing shrapnel for this task.

Workhouse, also Poor Law Union = several war hospitals occupied buildings that originally had a very different purpose. In the mid-19th Century across the UK, local authorities charged with the care of the poor in their areas (often by setting up Poor Law Unions), had replaced their old workhouses with newer buildings. Such buildings were appropriate to adaptation to much-needed war hospitals and this was so in the case of Jack Hickman's treatment once back in Blighty – the 650-bed Fusehill War Hospital in Carlisle occupied the former premises of the Fusehill Workhouse and of two hitherto school sites.

Ypres (Wallon-French) or Ieper (Flemish), battles of = Ypres/Ieper was an ancient 'wool' town in Belgian Flanders and became the symbol of Allied resistance in the northern section of the Western Front. Major battles were fought in the Ypres Salient in 1914, 1915, 1917 and 1918. 3rd Ypres was notorious and the name of the village of Passchendaele, a final objective of that offensive, became synonymous with mud and slaughter on a huge scale. Also see 'Wipers' above.

BIBLIOGRAPHY

DOCUMENTS, PUBLISHED MATERIAL & PRINCIPAL WEBSITES CONSULTED

A – ORIGINAL DOCUMENTS

Ballantyne, Maisie – holder of the diaries (and a transcription), cards, letters and a collection of photographs plus an oral history beyond measure.

Hickman, Jack – two original handwritten diaries, 11/5/15 to 26/11/15 and 9/11/16 to 21/12/18.

Patent for *'Bamfee'* club design.

9th Division, War Diaries – WO95/1733 to 1786 inclusive [National Archives, Kew, London]

9th Divisional Ammunition Column, War Diary – WO95/1753 [National Archives, Kew, London].

29th Field Ambulance, War Diary – WO95/1759/2 [National Archives, Kew, London]

National Archives, Kew, London –
'Soldiers' Medal Index Cards and Medal Rolls – Great War'.
'Soldiers' Service Records, Great War – The Burnt Records'.
'Soldiers' Pension Records – Great War'.

National Census of England – *1841, 1851, 1861, 1871, 1881, 1891, 1901,* and 1911.

B – BOOKS, BOOKLETS AND NEWSPAPERS

Anderson, Col. A.W., CMG (CRH 62nd Division, 1916-1919) – *'War Services of the 62nd West Riding Divisional Artillery'.* [1920, W. Heffer & Sons, Cambridge]

Bailey, Jonathan – *'British Artillery in the Great War'.* [1996, essay in *'British Fighting Methods in the Great War'*, (Griffiths, editor)]

Banks, Arthur – *'A Military Atlas of the First World War'.* [1975, Heinemann Ltd; 2001 Reprint, Pen & Sword Books Ltd.]

Barker, Ralph –
'The Royal Flying Corps in France, Mons to the Somme'. [1994, Constable & Co. Ltd]
'The Royal Flying Corps in France, April 1917 to Final Victory'. [1995, Constable & Co. Ltd]

Becke, Major E. F. – *'Order of Battle of Divisions, 1914-1918 (Parts 1, 2A, 2B, 3A, 3B, 4)'.* [First published 1935, 1936, 1937, 1938 and 1945 respectively, HMSO; Reprinted 1989, 1989, 1988 and two undated, Ray Westlake Military Books]

Beckett, Ian F.W. – *'The First World War – The Essential Guide to Sources in the National Archives'.* [2002, Public Record Office.]

Bilton, David – *'The Home Front in the Great War'.* [2003, Leo Cooper]

Bowyer, Chaz (Ed.) – *'Royal Flying Corps – Communiqués, 1917-1918'.* [1998, Grub Street]

Bridger, Geoff – *'The Great War Handbook'.* [2009, Pen & Sword]

Cherry, Niall – *'Most Unfavourable Ground – The Battle of Loos, 1915.'* [2005, Helion]

Cole, Christopher (Ed.) –
'Royal Flying Corps – Communiqués, 1915-1916'.
[1969, Wm. Kimber; 1990, Tom Donovan]
'Royal Air Force – Communiqués, 1918.'
[1969, Wm. Kimber; 1990, Tom Donovan]

Coombs, Rose E. B. (Revised by Karel Margry) – *'Before Endeavours Fade'.* [1976, Revised 2006, Battle of Britain International]

Crick, Nigel P. – *'The Lookers' Huts of Romney Marshes – A Photographic Exploration.'* [2010, Book Guild Ltd. ISBN 978-1-84624-426-1]

David, Saul [Edited] with **Weir, Michael** – *'Mud & Bodies – the War Diaries of Captain N.A.C. Weir,* (9th Division) *1914-1920.'* [2013, Frontline Books, London].

Eddison, Jill – *'Romney Marsh – Survival on a Frontier.'* [2000, (2001 reprint), Tempus Publishing Ltd. ISBN 0-7524-1486-0]

Edmonds, Brigadier-General Sir James – Official History, *'The Occupation of the Rhineland, 1918-1929.'* (1987, HMSO/Imperial War Museum).

Ewing, John, MC – *'The History of the Ninth (Scottish) Division, 1914-1919'.* [1921, John Murray, London; Modern undated reprint, Naval & Military Press]

Farndale, General Sir Martin, KCB – *'History of the Royal Regiment of Artillery – The Western Front 1914-18.'* [1986, the Royal Artillery Institution]

Forbes, Major-General A, CB, CMG – *'A History of the Army Ordnance Services.'* [Modern, undated reprint, Naval & Military Press]

Gavaghan, Michael – *'Loos, 1915'.* [1998, M. & L. Publications]

Gibbs, Philip –
'The Battles of the Somme'. [1917, Heinemann]
'The War Dispatches'. [1964, Times Press]

Gilbert, Martin – *'First World War Atlas.'* [1970, Weidenfeld & Nicolson]

Gliddon, Gerald – *'Battle of the Somme – a Topographical History'.* [1987, Gliddon Books]

Golfer's Handbook – Published annually; various copies held in the British Golf Museum, St. Andrews.

Griffiths, Paddy (editor) – *'British Fighting Methods in the Great War'*. [1996, Cass].

Gudmundsson, Bruce –
'The British Army on the Western Front, 1916'. [2007, Osprey]
'The British Expeditionary Force, 1914-15'. [2005, Osprey]

Hardman, Robert – *'City under the Slaughter.'* Excellent article on the Arras Tunnels and caverns published in the Daily Mail on Saturday, 15th March 2008.

Hay, Ian – (served in 10/A&SH, 27th Brigade, 9th 'Scottish' Division)
'The First Hundred Thousand'. [1915, William Blackwood]
'Carrying On – After the First Hundred Thousand'. [1917, William Blackwood]

Haythornthwaite, Peter J. – *'Source Book of the First World War'*. [1992; 1998 edition, Brockhampton Press].

Henshaw, Trevor – *'The Sky Their Battlefield'*. [1995, Grub Street].

H.M.S.O. –
'Official History of the Great War – Principal Events, 1914-1918'.
'Official History – Military Operations in France and Belgium, various volumes.' [HMSO original; reprint by IWM with Battery Press]
'Official History of the Ministry of Munitions', volumes 7, 8, 10 and 11. [HMSO original; reprint by IWM with Naval & Military Press]
'Statistics of the Military Effort of the British Empire during the Great War, 1914-1920'. [1922, HMSO; 1999 N & M reprint]
'War Establishments, Part I, 1913'.

Holding, Norman [4th edn. revised by **Iain Swinnerton**] – *'The Location of* British Army Records, 1914-1918'. [1984; 4th edition 1999, Federation of Family History Societies Ltd.]

Hurst, Sidney C. – *'The Silent Cities – A Guide to the War Cemeteries and Memorials to the Missing in France & Flanders'*. [1929, Methuen & Co.; Modern reprint, undated, Naval & Military Press Ltd.]

Hutchinson, Geoff. – *'The Royal Military Canal – A Brief History.'* [1995, ISBN 0-9519936-3-1]

IGN Maps – *'Institut Geographique National, Serie Verte (1 km to 1 cm)'*. Various sheets.

Jackson, Alan – *'British Professional Golfers, 1887-1930: A Register'*. [1994, Grant Books].

James, Brigadier E.A. –
'British Regiments, 1914-1918'. [1924, Gale & Polden Ltd; Modern reprint, Naval & Military Press Ltd.]
'A Record of the Battles and Engagements of the British Armies in France and Flanders,

1914-1918'. [First published in two volumes in 1969 & 1974; 1998 5th (single volume) edition, Naval & Military Press]

Jobson, Philip – *'Royal Artilllery - Glossary of Terms, Historical and Modern'.* [2008, The History Press]

MacPherson, Major-General Sir W.G., K.C.M.G., C.B., LL.D – *'Medical Services, General History, volume I.'*

McCarthy, Chris –
'The Somme, 1916 – the Day-by-Day Account'. [1993, Arms & Armour Press]
'Passchendaele, 1917 – the Day-by-Day Account'. [1995, Arms & Armour Press]

McGreal, Stephen – *'The War on Hospital Ships, 1914-1918'.* [2008, Pen & Sword Maritime]

Messenger, Charles – *'Call to Arms – The British Army 1914-1918.'* [2005, Weidenfeld & Nicolson]

Middlebrook, Martin –
'Your Country Needs You'. [2000, Leo Cooper]
'First Day on the Somme'. [1971, Allen Lane]
'The Somme Battlefields'. [1994, Penguin Edition]
'The Kaiser's Battle'. [1978, Allen Lane]

Ministry of Pensions – *'Location of Hospitals and Casualty Clearing Stations, British Expeditionary Force, 1914-1919'.* [1923; Modern reprint, undated, Imperial War Museum]

Mitchell, Major T.J. – *'Medical Services, Casualties and Statistics.'*

Mitchinson, K.W. – *'Pioneer Battalions in the Great War'.* [1997, Leo Cooper]

National Census of England – *1851, 1861, 1871, 1881, 1891, 1901.*

Nicholls, Jonathan – *'Cheerful Sacrifice – Battle of Arras, 1917'.* [1995, Leo Cooper]

O'Connor, Mike –
'Airfields & Airmen: Cambrai'. [2003, Pen & Sword Military]
'Airfields & Airmen: Arras'. [2004, Pen & Sword Military]
'Airfields & Airmen: Somme'. [2004, Pen & Sword Military]
'Airfields & Airmen: Ypres. [2004, Pen & Sword Military]
'Airfields & Airmen of the Channel Coast'. [2005, Pen & Sword Military]

Ordnance Survey Maps – *'Landranger Series, sheets 179, 189 (1:50,000; 2008 editions).'*

Parks, Major Edwin, RHA – *'Diex Aix – God Help Us (The Guernseymen Who Marched Away, 1914-1918)'* [1992, Guernsey Museums & Galleries]

Passingham, Ian – *'The German Offensives of 1918'.* [2008, Pen & Sword Military]

Perry, F.W. – *'Order of Battle of Divisions, 1914-1918 (Parts 5A & 5B)'.* [1992 & 1993, Ray Westlake Military Books.]

Randle, Dave – *'Romney Marsh, Past & Present – Britain in Old Photographs series.'* [2005, Sutton Publishing Ltd. ISBN 0-7509-2940-5]

Rawson, Andrew – *'Loos – Hohenzollern Redoubt'*, [2003 Pen & Sword Military]

Rinaldi, Richard A. – *'A Complete Order of Battle for the British Army in 1914'*. [2008, Ravi Rikhye]

Sandilands, Lt.-Col. H.R. – *'The 23rd Division, 1914-1919.'* [1925, Wm. Blackwood & Sons, Edinburgh; Modern undated reprint, Naval & Military Press].

Sheffield, Gary –
'The Somme'. [2003, Cassell].
'Forgotten Victory'. [2001, Headline Book Publishing].

Spencer, William – *'Army Service Records of the First World War'*.

Steel, Nigel & Hart, Peter – *'Passchendaele – The Sacrificial Ground'*. [2000, Cassell]

Strong, Paul & Marble, Sanders – *'Artillery in the Great War.'* [2011, Pen & Sword Military]

Sweetman, John – *'Cavalry of the Clouds'*. [2010, Spellmount]

Toland, John – *'No Man's Land - the Story of 1918'*. [1980, Eyre Methuen Ltd.]

Wade, Aubrey – *'The War of the Guns, Western Front 1917/1918.'* [April 1936, Batsford Ltd.]

Walton, Liz – *'A Case of Mistaken Identity'*. [Article: Channel Islands and the Great War - Journal 17, December 2007; www.greatwarci.net]

Webb, Dr. Eric – *'Military Medicine on the Western Front'* – [major article in "Stand To!" volume 65, Journal of the WFA].

Westlake, Ray –
'British Battalions on the Western Front, January to June 1915'.
'British Battalions on the Somme, 1916'.   [1994, Leo Cooper]
'Kitchener's Army'. [1989, Spellmount Ltd.]
'Order of Battle of Divisions – Index'. [2008, Naval & Military Press]

C – WEBSITES

www.cwgc.org Commonwealth War Graves Commission – *'Debt of Honour – Casualties & Cemeteries.'* Still the most reliable and the most comprehensive.

www.1914-1918.net The Long, Long Trail [Chris Baker] – *'Great War Forum.'* A wonderful forum that caters for experts and beginners. A polite, informative site. Highly recommended.

www.nationalarchives.gov.uk National Archives, Kew, London. Service records; battalion war diaries and much more to fascinate.

www.westernfrontassociation.com The Western Front Association is dedicated to the remembrance of the Great War in all its incarnations.

www.ww1cemeteries.com A site of remembrance and comprehensive guide to the military cemeteries and memorials around the world. An excellent, user-friendly site created by Terry Heard and Brent Whittam.

www.golfsmissinglinks.co.uk A site that tracks down and tells the story of golf courses that have fallen into disuse or been built over. A fascinating site.

www.greatwarci.net The Channel Islands and the Great War. The site is dedicated to improving understanding and knowledge of the impact of the Great War on the Channel Islands and their people. Highly recommended.

D – CD-ROMS, DVD-ROMS AND SUNDRY DATABASES

'Military Operations, France and Belgium, 1914-1918, Maps', (CD-Rom 2nd Edition, Naval & Military Press Ltd.)

'Nominal Roll of 9/DAC', [unpublished] (courtesy of Mark Bourgourd and the Great War Channel Islands Study Group.)

'Soldiers and Officers Died in the Great War', (CD-Rom version 2.5, Naval & Military Press.)

'The National Archives British Trench Map Atlas: The Western Front 1914-18', (2008, DVD-Rom, Naval & Military Press Ltd.)

'The Silver War Badge', (2013, CD-Rom, Naval & Military Press Ltd.)

'The First World War Campaign Medals', 2014, DVD-Rom, Naval & Military Press Ltd.)